TRUE**CANADIAN**

BATTLES
THAT FORGED OUR NATION
1759–1953

TRUE**CANADIAN**

BATTLES
THAT FORGED OUR NATION
1759–1953

Arthur
Bishop

Library and Archives Canada Cataloguing in Publication

Bishop, William Arthur, 1923-
    True Canadian Battles that forged our nation / Arthur Bishop.

Originally publ.: Toronto : McGraw-Hill Ryerson, 1996, under title: Canada's glory.
Includes bibliographical references and index.
ISBN 978-1-55267-549-6

    1. Battles--Canada--History. 2. Canada--History, Military. I. Title.

FC226.B57 2008   971   C2007-906843-X

This collection produced for Prospero Books.

Key Porter Books Limited
Six Adelaide Street East, Tenth Floor
Toronto, Ontario
Canada M5C 1H6

www.keyporter.com

Printed and bound in Canada

08 09 10 11 12 5 4 3 2 1

O Canada, Glorious and Free,
O Canada, We Stand on Guard for Thee.

CONTENTS

FOREWORD TO *CANADA'S GLORY*

It is my great honour to write the foreword for Arthur Bishop's book, *Canada's Glory*. I counted his father, Air Marshal Billy Bishop, as my close friend and have shared a friendship with Arthur for many years. Like Arthur, and Billy before him, I proudly went overseas to fight for Canada and flew with No. 1 Fighter Squadron R.C.A.F., the same squadron in which Arthur Bishop served. It is this shared history that prompted me to agree to take pen to paper and review his latest book.

Canada's Glory: Battles that Forged a Nation covers the earliest days when the French and English battled for control in the northern part of the Americas and continues through the two great World Wars and in Korea. In all cases, Canada has proven it has courage, it has character, and the result has been to add greatly to the stature and the self-confidence of all Canadians.

The First World War saw lengthy battles for position in the most intolerable conditions with heavy casualties. It demonstrated once and for all that our nation could proudly take its place alongside those of older nations who had proved that courage and sacrifice are virtues well worth their cost to a nation. In the Second World War conditions were more bearable for those serving on the allied side, although there were extensive casualties, and Canadians once again earned an enviable reputation for a willingness to serve bravely when called anywhere in the world.

Covering more than 30 major battles, *Canada's Glory* illustrates in fascinating detail how and why Canada developed through the fire and stress and cost and suffering of war. It is not only informative reading, but also extremely interesting. You are left with a better understanding of how Canada became a real nation and why it is a country worth fighting for.

I, for one, feel that Arthur Bishop has done a great service to his country by writing this book, just as he did by enlisting in the Air Force in the Second World War and as his father did in the First

World War before him. I have no hesitation in saying that it is a book that should be read by Canadians of all ages.

Hon. Hartland de M. Molson
September 1996

ACKNOWLEDGEMENTS

I begin by saluting my friend Don Loney for originating the idea of this book. Don and I have worked closely together for several years on a variety of subjects, chiefly the *Canadian Military Heritage* series and *Our Bravest and Our Best*, the story of Canada's Victoria Cross winners. Don suggested that all the research I acquired could be gainfully employed in telling the stories of the outstanding battles that forged our nation.

I would also like to thank Ron Edwards for a dogged and masterful job of copy editing this book on short notice. Working under pressure to meet the deadline, he honed my original manuscript to the nth degree. His efforts were a lesson in editing under fire.

Special thanks to my editor Erin Moore and her assistant Alistair Wentworth for their help with the photo and map research as well as to artist Paul Kelly for a skilful job of map charting. Thanks also to Steve Eby for designing a book jacket that sets just the right mood. In addition I would like to thank regimental historian and researcher John Grodzinski for his suggestions. Anne Melvin, the Royal Canadian Military Institute librarian was her usual helpful self in providing me with sources.

In the necessary studying for the writing of this book, I freely admit to having stood on the shoulders of the giants and sat at the feet of the masters as the bibliography will attest. Among those noted Canadian writers and historians from whose compendia I learned are: Terry Copp, Mary Beacock Fryer, George Nasmith, Patrick Wohler, John Swettenham, Eric Maguire, Denis and Shelagh Whitaker, Victor Suthren, Albert Marrin, Pierre Berton, Daniel Dancocks, George Kitching, Vincent Scott, Carmen Miller, Philip Warren, Charles Stacey, Herbert Wood, Denis Judd, Thomas Pakenham, Kenneth Macksey, and John Maclean.

Finally I should like to tender a special thanks to my agent and dear friend Frances Hanna without whom this volume would never have got off the ground. As usual she stood by my side all the way through and guided me over the rough spots.

Arthur Bishop
Toronto

INTRODUCTION

It took less than five minutes to forge the face, fate and future of Canada. At approximately 10 o'clock on the rainy morning of September 13, 1759, that cornerstone of our heritage cemented itself upon the Plains of Abraham west of Quebec City. At a range varying between 40 and 60 yards, Major General James Wolfe's scarlet coated riflemen delivered a devastating volley of gunshot that tore into the ranks of the Marquis de Montcalm's charging grey and white-uniformed infantry. As the British musket ball fire and artillery grapeshot scythed into their columns slicing them apart, the French line broke, its ranks fleeing in disarray towards the city, hotly pursued by the English.

That sharp, short encounter spelled doom for the century and a half old New France. The fall of Quebec (the official surrender came five days later) also marked a turning point in the establishment of British Imperial power even though the French army remained on North American soil for another year. The victory brought to a climax 150 years of discovery, conquest, settlement, and warring. To all intents it had begun on July 24, 1534 when Jacques Cartier, an explorer in the service of French King Francis 1, charged with looking for gold in the New World, raised the cross of France in a small kanata — the Huron-Iroquois designation for a village or settlement from which Canada derived its name — on the shores of Gaspe Bay bearing the arms of his nation.

Surrender of that colony to the British led to the shaping of a unique military tradition that is distinctively Canadian. Little more than two generations later, English- and French-speaking Canadians fought side by side and have ever since. In today's absurd political climate it is worth remembering that during the War of 1812, Upper and Lower Canada united in a common cause to defeat the mighty American invader.

The first British Empire call to the colours brought military fame to the struggling nation of five and a half million people. In February, 1900 at Paarderberg, action by the Canadian contingent was the key factor in winning the battle which became the turning point of the South African War.

Not all the Canadian battles that made military history were vic-tories, however. During that same Boer War, the Battle of Liliefontein was a retreat. But Canadians so distinguished themselves in this rearguard action that three of them were awarded the Victoria Cross for individual acts of valour under enemy fire.

In their first action against the enemy during the Great War of 1914-1918, the Germans introduced poison gas to the battlefield at Ypres in Belgium. On the morning of April 22, 1915, as the evil looking yellow green clouds of chlorine drifted towards the Allied trenches, the French troops fled, but the Canadians stood their ground. In that action the Canadian contingent had so distinguished itself that it became known as the "Salvation Army."

The name Vimy Ridge is not only synonymous with Canadian valour but stands as an example of battle tactics as well. Occupation of this elevation dominating the Artois Plain between Thelus and Avion was critical to controlling the battle on the Arras front. Its execution was a masterpiece of planning and organization. Prior to the assault, the four divisions of the Canadian Corps were trained over terrain simulating the actual battlefield. On Easter Sunday, April 9, 1917, the Canadians began their advance in driving snow and sleet. By mid-afternoon they had captured the ridge.

Vimy, which has often been called the most brilliant success of the Western Front, marked the coming of age of the Dominion as a military force to be reckoned with.

The Battle of Passchendaele which took place between October 30 and November 10, 1917 was described by Winston Churchill as a "forlorn expenditure of valour and life without equal in futility." Relentless machine-gun fire, bottomless waist-high mud, and contin-uous rain were equal enemies to the attackers. By the time the entire crossroads town was in Canadian hands, casualties had risen to a shocking 16,000 men, all for a ground gain of four and a half miles.

By the last year of the war, 1918, the Canadians had gained a reputation as storm troops. British prime minister Lloyd George wrote that "Whenever the Germans found the Canadians coming into the line they prepared for the worst." It was small wonder that they were chosen to spearhead the Allied attack that ended the war. In the period from August 4 to November 11, that became known as "Canada's 100 Days," the Canadian Corps advanced from the Amiens salient to Mons, scene of the war's first battle, a distance of 85 miles. Its four divisions had overcome 47 enemy divisions, a quarter of the entire German strength.

Historic Canadian battles of the Second World War ranged far and wide and ran the gamut from sacrifice to debacle, to rout, to success, to siege. Hong Kong was a deliberate political sacrifice in which, in December 1941, two untrained divisions were thrown to the wolves, as part of a British defence force up against an experienced, battle hardened Japanese army. They never stood a chance and the survivors were imprisoned under the most shocking inhumane conditions.

Dieppe was nearly as bad, though there were lessons learned — namely that it was suicidal to try and invade through a defended port. On the morning of August 19, 1942, six Canadian infantry battalions, a tank regiment, along with 1,000 British commandos and 50 American rangers, landed at the French coastal resort on a ten mile front. From the heights the Germans decimated them. Less than half the Canadians who set out returned to England. Casualties amounted to 3,367 — 907 killed, and 1,946 taken prisoner.

In Italy, five days before Christmas 1943, the First Canadian Division finally reached the port of Ortona perched high on a ledge on the Adriatic coast. Over the next week the Canadians were to see some of the bitterest fighting of the entire Italian Campaign. Steep, narrow streets filled with rubble meant neither artillery nor tanks could be used. It was an infantryman's struggle all the way, house-to-house, using anti-tank guns and explosives to blow gaping holes in the walls through which they could charge with guns blazing, "mouseholing" they called it. By the time the town fell, the division strength had been reduced by half.

The part played in the Battle of Normandy from D-Day, June 6 to August 20 was the largest, most coordinated operation ever undertaken by a Canadian army, beginning with the landings on the Normandy beaches to the capture of Caen and the closing of the Falaise Gap. By the end of D-Day, 14,000 Canadians had landed in France with losses a fraction of those suffered at Dieppe: 1,074, of whom 350 were killed. The next step was consolidation and preparation. On July 25 the Canadians occupied Caen, the same day the Americans broke out at St Lo. Then on August 17, Falaise fell to the Canadians and the Battle of Normandy was over.

In September, the Canadians fought their last major battle in Europe in an effort to free the port of Antwerp. The Allied supply line had been stretched to the limit, all the way back to Normandy. It had become critical to open up this Belgian port, the second largest in Europe, to shipping. But it was heavily defended by six German divisions that had escaped the Normandy breakout. It took the Canadians 85 days to capture it in the toughest fighting they had yet had to endure in Europe. Before it was over, it cost the Canadians 6,370 casualties, losses magnified in importance by the Conscription Crisis at home that sent out untrained reinforcements.

During the Korean War, which lasted from June 25, 1950 to July 27, 1953, the Canadian Army Special Force (25th Canadian Infantry Brigade) took part in one notable battle, Kapyong. Fought between April 23 and 25, 1951, it prevented the Chinese from occupying the southern capital of Seoul for a third time. At one stage, the Canadian unit was surrounded and its supplies cut off, but it managed to hold on until reinforcements arrived. For this action the regiment received the United States Presidential Citation.

This overview is only part, a very small part in fact, of the story of Canadian battles that made military history. The real story is about the Canadians who took part in them. If it is true that great men make great battles, then it is equally true that great battles make great men. And in this, Canada is no exception.

Arthur Bishop
Toronto

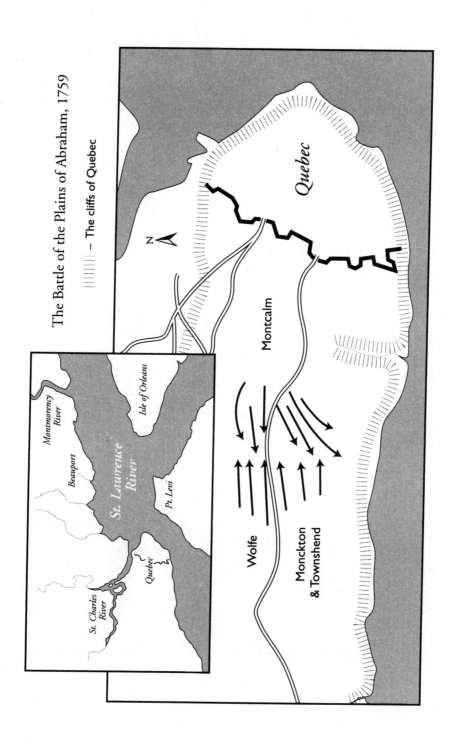

The Battle of the Plains of Abraham, 1759

||||||| – The cliffs of Quebec

N

Quebec

Montcalm

Wolfe

Monckton
& Townshend

Montmorency
River

Beauport

Isle of Orleans

St. Lawrence
River

Pt. Levi

St. Charles
River

Quebec

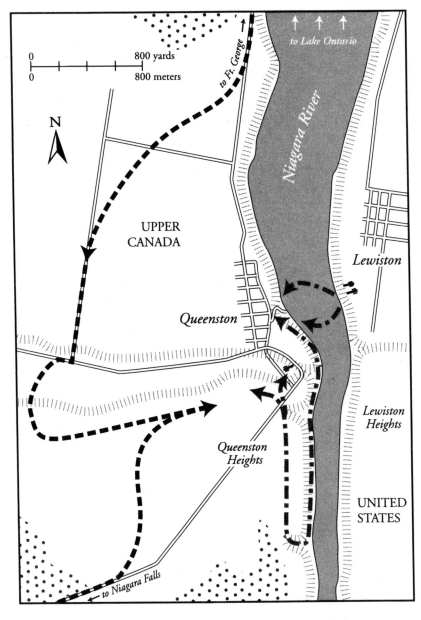

N

0 _____ 800 yards
0 _____ 800 meters

to Ft. George

to Lake Ontario

Niagara River

UPPER
CANADA

Lewiston

Queenston

Lewiston
Heights

Queenston
Heights

UNITED
STATES

to Niagara Falls

The Battle of Queenston Heights, 1812

⬌ Battery
▬ ▬ ▬ British
▬ ∙ ▬ American

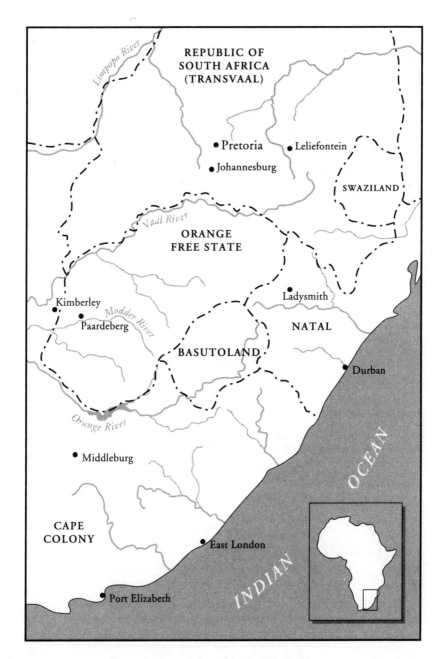

The South African War (Boer War), 1899-1902

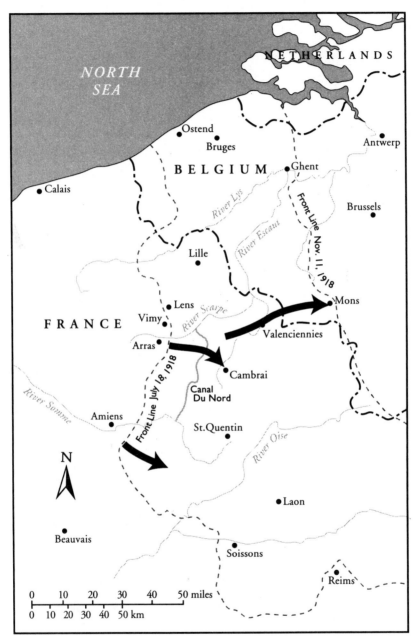

Operations – Canadian Army Corps, Aug.-Nov. 1918

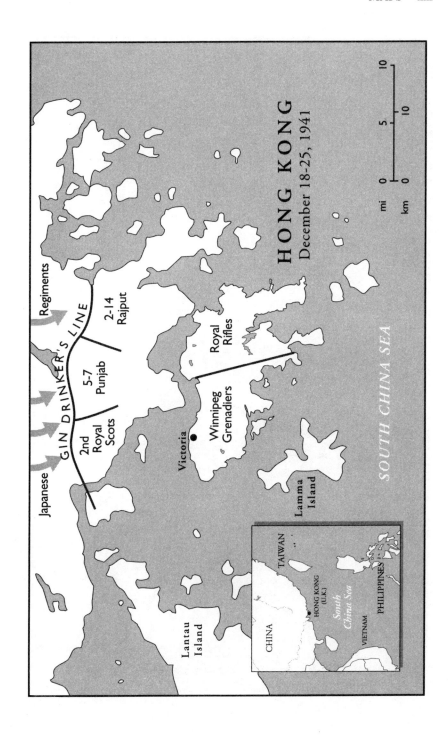

HONG KONG
December 18-25, 1941

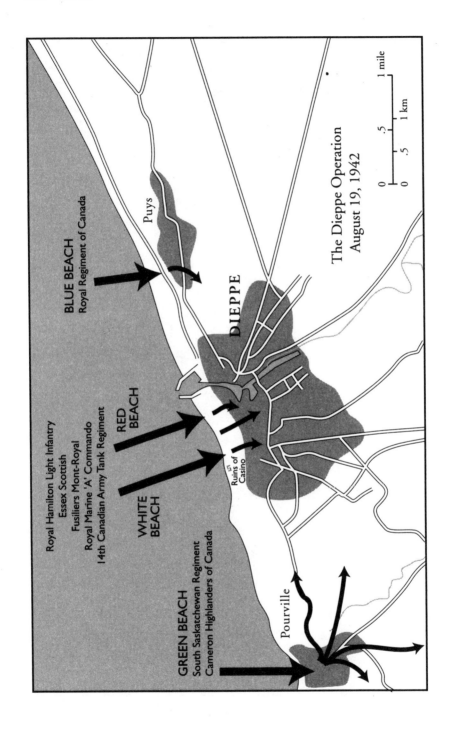

BLUE BEACH
Royal Regiment of Canada

Royal Hamilton Light Infantry
Essex Scottish
Fusiliers Mont-Royal
Royal Marine 'A' Commando
14th Canadian Army Tank Regiment

RED BEACH

WHITE BEACH

GREEN BEACH
South Saskatchewan Regiment
Cameron Highlanders of Canada

Puys

DIEPPE

Ruins of Casino

Pourville

The Dieppe Operation
August 19, 1942

0   .5   1 mile
0   .5   1 km

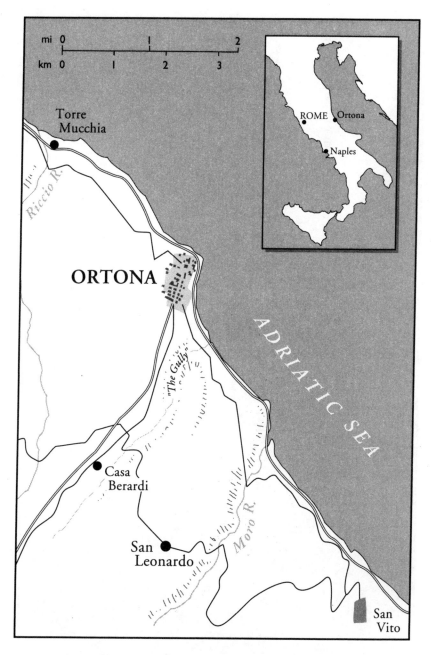

Ortona, Italy December 20, 1943

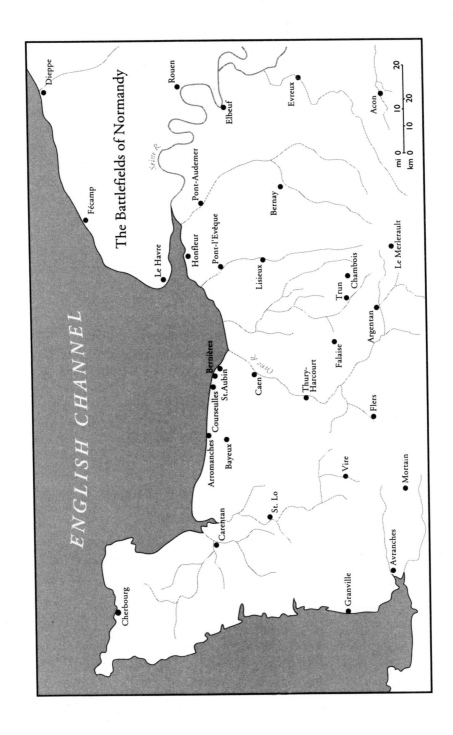

The Battlefields of Normandy

ENGLISH CHANNEL

Dieppe
Fécamp
Le Havre
Rouen
Elbeuf
Pont-Audemer
Honfleur
Pont-l'Evêque
Evreux
Acon
Bernay
Lisieux
Le Merlerault
Chambois
Trun
Argentan
Falaise
Flers
Bernières
Courseulles
St.Aubin
Caen
Thury-Harcourt
Arromanches
Bayeux
Vire
Mortain
St. Lo
Carentan
Avranches
Granville
Cherbourg

Seine R.
Orne R.

mi 20
km 20
10
10
0
0

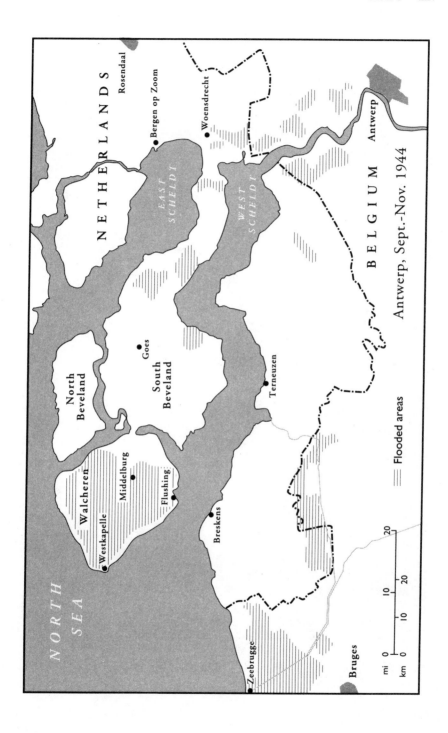

NORTH SEA

NETHERLANDS

Rosendaal

Bergen op Zoom

Woensdrecht

Antwerp

BELGIUM

EAST SCHELDT

WEST SCHELDT

North Beveland

South Beveland

Goes

Terneuzen

Walcheren

Middelburg

Westkapelle

Flushing

Breskens

Zeebrugge

Bruges

Antwerp, Sept.-Nov. 1944

Flooded areas

mi 0 10 20
km 0 10 20

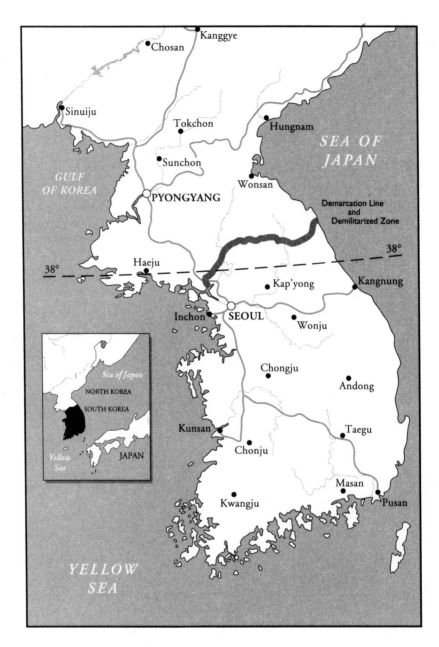

Korea – July 27, 1953

1

WARRING WITH THE INDIANS

From Jacques Cartier's charts, Samuel de Champlain knew that the gateway to North America was the St Lawrence River and the key to it lay in winning the friendship of the Algonkians. By the time Champlain first set foot in Canada on May 27, 1603, the Algonkian (Algonquin), Etchemins, Huron, and Montagnais tribes had joined in a common cause against the vaunted Iroquois who had banded together into a well-organized, aggressive confederacy in what is today northern New York State. In the interests of establishing a colony along with a thriving fur trade, Champlain allied himself with the Algonkians and their allies even at risk of war with their enemies to the south. This had two significant consequences. It led to the establishment of Quebec as a fortress against the Iroquois (it had been initially selected by Champlain as a warehouse for furs and other trade goods). It also caused the British and Dutch to side with the Iroquois.

On June 22, 1603, while exploring the St Lawrence, Champlain arrived at the narrow spot in the river that the Algonkians called *kebek*. Five years later he established Quebec as a warehouse, trading post, and a defense against Iroquois raids. It was from there that he had agreed to lead the Indians in a raid into Iroquois territory. In July 1609, Champlain and 11 Frenchmen armed with powerful arquebus matchlock muskets, and 60 Indians with their bows and arrows, set out by canoe through a lake south of the St Lawrence which Champlain named after himself — Lake Champlain.

1

At ten o'clock on the evening of July 29, the invaders had arrived at a cape that is today Ticonderoga, New York, where they met a war party of Iroquois paddling north. Taken by surprise, the Iroquois pulled into shore and formed a barricade while the invaders lay offshore.

Two of the Iroquois canoes paddled out for a parley to find out whether their enemies wanted to fight. They were told that was exactly what the invaders had in mind but that they should wait until daylight in order to distinguish one another. The Iroquois agreed.

When dawn broke Champlain's party went ashore and formed up in battle array. Outnumbering the Algonkians by more than three to one, the Iroquois ceremoniously marched out of their barricade to join battle. The ensuing fight is graphically described in Champlain's own words.

> They came slowly to meet us with a gravity and calm which I admired, and at their head were three chiefs. Our Indians likewise advanced in similar order, and told me that those who had three big plumes were the chiefs, and that I was to kill them.
>
> Our Indians began to run toward their enemies, who stood firm and had not yet noticed my white companions who went off in the woods. Our Indians began to call me with loud cries; they divided into two groups and I marched on until I was within some 30 yards of the enemy who, as soon as they caught sight of me halted and gazed at me. When I saw them making a move to draw their bows, I took aim with my arquebus and shot straight at one of the three chiefs. With this shot two fell to the ground and one of their companions was wounded. I had put four bullets in my arquebus. Our people began to shout so loudly that one could not have heard it thunder, and meanwhile the arrows flew thick on both sides. The Iroquois were much astonished that two men would have been killed so quickly. As I was reloading my arquebus, one of my companions fired a shot from within the woods, which astonished them again so much that they took to flight into the depths of the forest, whither I pursued them and laid low two more of them. Our Indians killed several and took ten to twelve prisoners.

Thus began the long bloody war in North America, pitting the French against the Iroquois and their British and Dutch Allies, one that set the course of history for two centuries. It was ironic that the one who, in a mere matter of minutes, had expanded tribal rivalry into a continental conflict which claimed thousands of lives and caused untold suffering, should have been Samuel de Champlain. This was the man of whom the noted American historian Samuel Eliot Morison wrote: "No other American colonial founder . . . had a more attractive character or such humanity with the natives."

Before that day was out, Champlain had been witness to Indian torture.

The Indians, toward evening, took one of the prisoners, to whom they made a harangue on the cruelties which he and his friends had practiced upon them, and that he should resign himself to receive as much. They ordered him to sing if he had the heart. He did so, but it was a very sad song to hear.

Meanwhile our Indians kindled a fire and, when it was well lighted, each took a brand and burned this poor wretch a little at a time. . . . Sometimes they would leave off, throwing water on his back. Then they tore out his nails and applied fire to the end of his fingers and to his private member. Afterward they scalped him and caused a certain kind of gum to drip very hot upon the crown of his head. They then pierced his arms near the wrists and with sticks pulled and tore out his sinews, and when they saw they could not get them out, they cut them off. The poor wretch uttered strange cries, and I felt pity seeing him treated in this way. Still he bore it so firmly one would scarcely have said he felt any pain.

For the next two years Champlain struggled to develop the French colony, spending the summers in Canada and the winters in France. In 1614 an institution was formed named the Compagnie de Champlain, which became the recognized power in New France. When Champlain returned to Canada in May, 1615, he learned that the Iroquois raiders were becoming increasingly bold as the Huron trade developed. These incursions were strictly commercial. Every Iroquois wanted a steel tomahawk and knife for himself, and an awl and needle for his wife. The best way to get them was to ambush a Huron canoe carrying them. The Iroquois also captured fur-bearing canoes which brought a handsome exchange price of European treasures from the Dutch. To the Hurons these raids had become intolerable. The time had come for them to strike at their enemies in their own home ground.

Champlain agreed to help organize the venture. By October he had assembled 500 Huron warriors and 12 Frenchmen armed with arquebuses. An advance party was sent to enlist the aid of the Hurons' allies, the Susquehannahs, in present-day Pennsylvania. The plan called for a joint assault on the Iroquois stronghold at what is today Syracuse, New York.

The war party reached enemy territory on the south side of Lake Ontario on October 5. Hiding their canoes near the water, it took them the next four days to cover 50 miles walking in single file. On October 9 they drew up a battle strategy; creep up on the enemy, hide in the woods, and attack at dawn.

Next day as the party neared the fortified village, Iroquois braves surprised a group of the Hurons. The others ran to their rescue. When Champlain and the other Frenchmen fired off their arquebuses, the Iroquois hastily retreated into their fortification. The element of surprise had been lost.

In making a reconnaissance of the fort, Champlain found it was protected by a lake on one side and streams along two others. Furthermore it was walled with stout palisades 30 feet high, as well as supporting galleries. It simply could not be stormed.

Champlain devised a tower of logs topped with a platform protected by heavy breastworks, from where three arquebusiers could fire down into the enemy garrison. It was a marvel of improvised engineering but effective as it was, the operation never materialized. The Hurons, ignoring Champlain's orders, ran out in the open, leaping and yelling, and tried to set fire to the palisades. However this was in the lee of the wind and the smoke simply blew back into their faces. Champlain shouted to his Indians to take cover but with all the noise they were making they failed to hear him. Meanwhile the Iroquois, taking advantage of the confusion, put out the fire.

The fight lasted some three hours, Champlain, two of the Huron chiefs, and a score of others were wounded. Champlain tried to rally his forces to no avail. The Indians refused to take part in any further action until they were joined by the Susquehannas. They would wait four days. If by then their allies had not arrived they would call the whole thing off. On the following day a strong wind arose in a direction ideal for setting a fire to the stockade but the Hurons refused to act. On October 16, not knowing the Susquehannas were en route only two days away, the beaten, disillusioned Hurons decided to withdraw. Champlain, by this time in excruciating pain from two arrow wounds, had to be carried from the battlefield.

However, defeat and his wounds did not deter Champlain from his objective of establishing a wealthy community at Quebec. In 1618 he outlined the commercial, industrial and agricultural opportunities for the French court. By 1629 his dreams were becoming realized when war broke out with Britain and Quebec, inadequately armed and supplied, fell to an English expedition led by David Kirke. Champlain sailed for France sadly disillusioned after watching the English flag being hoisted over his fortress.

Luckily, three years later, King Charles 1 of England, who was short of funds, allowed the French to buy back New France and Champlain returned to Canada. Although he found the settlement in woeful shape, he set about rebuilding and refashioning it once more into a thriving community.

In 1633 Cardinal Richelieu appointed Champlain governor of Quebec but in 1635 he suffered a paralytic stroke and died that December. Ironically, over a century later, the fortress that Champlain had so painstakingly built and cultivated would suffer a fate far beyond the worst fears of the man who was called the ''Father of Canada.'' It would fall into the hands of France's enemies forever.

2

THE FALL OF QUEBEC

Reference map "The Battle of the Plains of Abraham."

The climax to the British-French struggle for North America was an offshoot of the Seven Years' War of 1756 to 1763. The French had some early victories. In August 1756 the new French commander in New France, Field Marshall Marquis de Montcalm-Gagzen, Seigneur of Saint-Veran, captured the forts at the mouth of the Oswego River, and the following August he seized Fort William Henry.

Despite these early setbacks British Prime Minister William Pitt was determined to conquer Canada, placing it above all other military objectives against France, and he committed the necessary men and equipment. The first venture ended in disaster. Due to the poor judgement of the expedition's commander, Major General James Abercromby, an attack against Fort Carillon on July 8, 1758, failed.

But the worm quickly turned. On July 27 Major General Jeffrey Amherst, Brigadier James Wolfe, and Admiral Edward Boscawen captured Louisbourg, on present-day Cape Breton. Then on August 25, Fort Frontenac fell to Brigadier John Bradstreet and on November 23 Brigadier John Forbes forced the French to abandon Fort Duquesne, which he renamed Fort Pitt (modern-day Pittsburgh).

In 1759 the British captured Fort Niagara on July 25 and the following day the French withdrew from Carillon. On August 4 they retreated from Fort St Frederic but retained a fleet of ships on Lake Champlain to prevent Amherst from advancing on Montreal. But the principal British objective was Quebec City, the main bulwark of the

7

French defense, which was virtually impregnable. Pitt had given James Wolfe, by now a major general, the assignment of capturing it. Perched high on a cliff, the stronghold was isolated by the St Lawrence and St Charles Rivers. Only its landward quarter to the west, south of the fortress was vulnerable to attack.

The defenders were commanded by professionals subordinated to a rank amateur. Montcalm, the New France commander-in-chief, was a career soldier. His professional associates were Brigadier General Gaston-François the Chevalier de Levis who commanded Montreal, and Colonel Antoine de Bougainville, a scientist who, ironically, was a member of the Royal Society of Great Britain. The Governor General was native-born Pierre de Rigaud de Vaudreuil, Marquis de Vaudreuil who disapproved of imported French officers. Vaudreuil and Montcalm had been at loggerheads ever since the latter's arrival from France in 1756 at the beginning of the war. It did not help that the Court of Versailles decreed that Montcalm defer to Vaudreuil on military matters. Vaudreuil had no military experience whatsoever and after he had inspected the defences Montcalm wrote ''he was like a blind man given sight.'' The two were also at dagger points over strategy. Montcalm believed that in dealing with the British a strong defense was the best offense. Vaudreuil, in the manner of all amateurs, believed in boldness no matter what the situation.

The chain of command was eventually reversed by the Court of Versailles. This arose after Montcalm outlined his plans for the defense of New France and requested support in the form of reinforcements and supplies. Vaudreuil's insistence that Montcalm be recalled also played a part. On the advice of his ministers King Louis XV was compelled to make the military decision to favour Montcalm. In retrospect this decision was unwise, for there were two alternatives. Levis was the equal of Montcalm and he got along with Vaudreuil. It might even have been better both militarily and politically to recall both Montcalm and Vaudreuil. The snag was that Montcalm had distinguished himself at Fort Carillon and was a national hero. In an explicit despatch to Vaudreuil the king wrote:

His Majesty's intention is that M. le Marquis de Montcalm shall not only be consulted on all operations but also on all areas of administration relating to the defense and preservation of the colony; you will ask his advice, communicating to him the letters I write to you on all these subjects.

This naturally heightened the hostility between Montcalm and Vaudreuil. Moreover, New France got a lot less help than Montcalm had requested. Troop dispositions amounted to only 400 replacements, 40 gunners and a few engineers, although sufficient supplies of food and equipment reached the colony to continue to the war with the British.

The court was fully aware that the governor general and the commander of the troops were bitter enemies. It also knew that New France was riddled with corruption, with officials syphoning funds to line their own pockets. It did nothing about either. In effect, it had abandoned Canada to its fate.

French military strength at Quebec amounted to five battalions of French regular troops, 5,000 to 6,000 militiamen commanded by Vaudreuil, and 2,760 marines. Montcalm had fortified the vulnerable area known as the Beauport shore, between the St Charles and Montmorency Rivers. To the west Montcalm had stationed Bougainville with 2,000 men, among them Canadians, Indians and some cavalry, to keep open communications with Montreal and to protect his inland supply lines. The 20 ships that had arrived with supplies from France were sent up the St Lawrence to Batiscan, about 60 miles away, where they would be safe from attack.

By June 26, the British were anchored off the Ile d'Orleans southeast of the Beaufort shore. The force comprised 13,500 sailors of the Royal Navy, manning a fleet of 49 warships, 22 of which were ships of the line, each carrying 50 or more guns. In addition there were 119 transport vessels manned by 5,000 merchant seamen. Most of them carried flat-bottomed boats for amphibious operations, the forerunners of the modern landing craft. It was the most formidable force yet to set sail.

James Wolfe, who was in poor health suffering from tuberculosis, gravel (kidney and bladder inflammation), and rheumatism, had 8,500 regular troops, including six companies of American rangers, organized into three divisions under his command. All these men were highly trained professionals many of them battle-tested veterans. His subordinates were three seasoned brigadier generals, Robert Monckton, George Townshend and James Murray. The naval commanders of the expedition were just as impressive: Vice Admiral Charles Saunders and his subordinates rear admirals Charles Holmes and Philip Durrel.

Offshore from the Ile d'Orleans, Wolfe could see the formidable defences he faced. Four miles to the west was Quebec City perched high on the legendary rock, impregnable to assault from the water. Closer, to the north-west was the Beaufort shore. There, from the St Charles to the Montmorency he could see camps, batteries and redoubts which the French regular battalions had begun occupying three days earlier. The shoreline that Wolfe had hoped to take over had already been fortified by the French. Montcalm had anticipated him. Clearly, the situation called for a change of strategy.

Next day, however, Wolfe proceeded to land his army on the island. The French offered no resistance, withdrawing the detachments stationed there. But some sort of retaliation was called for and that night they despatched seven fire boats downstream towards the enemy fleet. It proved to be a fiasco. The closest British ships simply cut their moorings and ran for it, firing their guns to warn the rest of the fleet. Meanwhile rowboats were sent out to grapple the burning menaces and tow them out of harm's away.

Two days later, on the recommendation of Vice Admiral Saunders, Wolfe landed troops at Point Levis on the south shore directly opposite Quebec. He was afraid the French might occupy the site. That they had not done so earlier seems inexplicable. However such a move had finally come under consideration; Montcalm had urged Vaudreuil to send a detachment to oppose the British and, in fact, this very nearly took place. A British force under Brigadier General Monckton, landed on the point on June 29 where they were met by token resistance from a scouting party of Canadian militiamen and some Indians. A British soldier taken prisoner during the skirmishes reported that the attack was merely a feint. The real assault, he told his captors, would take place between the small parish of Beauport and the St Charles River. On the basis of this information the plan to cross the river was cancelled. This left the British in a position to bombard Quebec with their artillery.

As the building of a gun battery for this bombardment neared completion, Quebec's citizens became increasingly jittery. On July 11 they delivered a petition to Vaudreuil offering their services for an expedition to destroy the British force at Levis. The result was a ragtag, undisciplined detachment of 1,600 made up of merchants, several regular volunteers, a few Indians and even some school boys from the Jesuits' College, led by Jean-Daniel Dumas, a celebrated forest fighter. It was doomed before it began. For such a group to try and tackle a formidable, well-trained professional British force was ludicrous. This was no time or place for amateurs. On the night of July 12/13, as they neared the objective, they soon fell into disorder and panic. By morning the entire force was back on the north shore, the British barely aware of the failed expedition. (They only learned of it five days later from a deserter.) Just as Dumas led his men across the river at nine o'clock, the British began their bombardment with six 32-pound guns and five 13-inch mortars. Directed at the Upper Town, and particularly against those areas with the largest buildings and the most concentrated housing, the bombardment was intended to create panic, forcing the populace to leave the city — and that is exactly what it achieved.

People began flocking from their homes, taking refuge on the ramparts. At daylight when the gates to the city were opened, women and children fled across the fields. Nearly 300 bombs had been fired into the city from the time the battery opened fire until noon the following day. Considerable damage had resulted but incredibly, not a single person had been killed or wounded.

Wolfe continued to build up his battery on the point until he had 29 pieces of artillery pounding the city. Using carcasses — incendiary projectiles — the entire centre of the Upper Town was burned out on the night of July 22/23. The worst destruction of all took place on the night of August 8/9 in the Lower Town when 152 houses were reduced to ashes, the Church of Notre Dame de Victoires among them. There is no record of casualties though doubtless they were heavy. It is just as certain that there was some deterioration of morale though that in itself could not win the war. Wolfe wanted to cause as much disruption as possible. But he knew that ultimately he still had to beat his enemy in the field.

Shortly after midnight on July 9, Wolfe, with the grenadiers of his army, landed on the north shore of the St Lawrence three-quarters of a mile below Montmorency Falls. Later he was joined by Brigadier General Townshend and the following day, Brigadier General Murray arrived with a large part of his brigade. This placed the British force on the east side of the Montmorency River directly across from the Chevalier de Levis' militiamen. Between them the water was calm and shallow enough to cross, but in the face of French reinforcements it still represented a formidable obstacle.

The French decided not to take an offensive action against the invaders, limiting themselves to harassing attacks by their Indian allies. From his dominant position on the high ground at Montmorency, Wolfe controlled the field and now began assembling a heavy artillery battery before attempting a twin-pronged attack on the Beaufort sector. By July 10 he had 50 guns ashore, many of them 24-

pounders. At the same time, rafts and floating batteries were being assembled. The plan called for Monckton's brigade from Point Levis to land on the French right between the parish of Beauport and the St Charles River. Meanwhile, on the enemy's left Wolfe's great batteries would pave the way for an assault from the north-east across the Montmorency.

Whether this plan would have succeeded, we shall never know. To take place on July 31, Wolfe cancelled it 11 days earlier and with good reason. On the night of July 17/18, ships of the Royal Navy slipped up the St Lawrence past Quebec, leaving the shore to the south-west of the city open to amphibious assault. This was a far easier, straightforward means of conquering the city than the Beauport plan, which would have meant that after a French defeat, the British would still face the problem of crossing bridges — over the St Charles — always potential bottlenecks in any military operation.

Montcalm viewed this latest turn of events with some alarm. "If the enemy takes a course of going up the river," he wrote in his diary, "and is able to land at some points, he cuts off all communication with our food supplies and munitions of war." The British ships having anchored off the Anse des Meres, the closest they could get to the city, Dumas the forest fighter, who had led the aborted assault on Levis, was sent there with 600 men and some Indians, while Le Mercier, the French artillery commander, mounted two 18-pound guns and a mortar and began firing on the enemy ships. It was at this time that the Samos Battery, which was to play a part in the subsequent ascent to the Plains of Abraham, was built below Sillery.

At this point, after considerable reconnoitering, Wolfe was unable to make up his mind where to land his troops. He had cancelled four different plans. On July 26 he turned his attention once again to Montmorency. Meanwhile the French made another stab at destroying the British fleet with a mass of rafts and small craft chained together and set on fire. It was no more successful than the first boats. Rowboats again towed it aside saving the British ships from disaster. If the French commanded the heights, the British controlled the river.

Wolfe decided to deliver a sharp, decisive blow by attacking the upper redoubt in the French entrenchments running along the Montmorency. The assault was to be made by only four companies, with the grenadiers to be ready "in case of need." On July 3, a British battleship moved into the channel north of the Ile d'Orleans and began shelling the two easternmost French gun batteries. At 1:00 a.m. two armed transports were run ashore near the redoubt. It was then that

Wolfe, who was aboard one of the landing craft known as "cats," saw how badly he had miscalculated the French position. The redoubt was much closer to the French entrenchments than it had appeared from the British camp and would be impossible to put out of action with the British guns.

Wolfe faced a dilemma. From a strictly military viewpoint the soundest tactical move would have been to cancel the operation. But his army had been expecting a major battle after nothing but minor skirmishing since arriving at Quebec and morale would seriously suffer. Also, the defenders seemed disorganized. He decided to attack and issued orders to Townshend at Montmorency and Monckton at Point Levis to "prepare for Action." And so a limited plan for seizing an isolated position was converted into a potential major action.

At 12:30 p.m. the boats with the landing force put out, laying in the channel under fire from French shore guns while waiting to land. It was late in the afternoon by the time they went in and then they ran into a barrier of boulders just above the low water mark. An order was sent to stop Townshend who was on the move and the landing was temporarily suspended. Wolfe went in with a naval officer in one of the flat-bottomed boats to look for a suitable place to go ashore. It was 5:30 p.m. before he found one.

Under a darkening sky and lowering clouds, 13 companies of grenadiers and 200 men of the Royal Americans led the attack. It quickly turned into a fiasco. Possibly in their eagerness to do battle, instead of forming up and waiting for Monckton's and Townshend's brigades to support them, the troops made a wild, frenzied dash for the enemy. The French quickly decamped from the redoubt and the gun battery but as the British rushed the entrenchments they were enfiladed with withering fire from the heights. However, the French were almost out of ammunition when the clouds burst open in a violent summer storm which, if it failed to dampen spirits on either side, certainly dampened their gunpowder. There would be no more rifle fire. Furthermore the grass turned so slippery that the British were unable to rush up the slopes and capture the heights at bayonet point. With the danger that Townshend and Murray's brigades across the Montmorency ford might be cut off, Wolfe decided to withdraw. Most of Monckton's men and what was left of the grenadiers were taken off and the brigades from the Montmorency camp withdrew across the ford in good order. It had been a well-disciplined retreat — but a retreat, nevertheless.

During the battle the British lost 210 killed and 230 wounded, the French 60 killed and wounded. Montcalm wrote that it "is undoubtedly only a small prelude to something more important which we are now waiting for." He was right. Wolfe recorded in his diary next day: "This check must not discourage us, the loss is not great," and gave instructions to keep the troops busy in preparation for "another and I hope better attempt."

Nevertheless, Wolfe was bitter over the defeat. Despondent and angry, he issued a proclamation to the effect that, in future, all Canadians captured would be treated "as they deserved." This was in direct response to the practice of raiding parties of habitants and Indians, which murdered, mutilated, and scalped his sentries and work details. Further, he let his army loose upon the countryside, the soldiers laying waste to those parishes which as yet had not been severely damaged. Throughout the middle of August, the English troops burned, looted, and at least in one instance, scalped and massacred a number of prisoners — Canadians dressed as Indians. There were no Indians in Wolfe's army, but his American rangers were adept at scalping, though Wolfe limited the practice to captured Indians and those inhabitants dressed as Indians. Whenever the inhabitants retaliated, British response was swift and merciless, fire and sword making quick work of any pockets of resistance. As his men burned and pillaged the communities and farms, smoke blackening the sky for miles, Wolfe brooded in his tent. Montcalm watched the rape of the country, sullenly biding his time. He was not about to be provoked by terrorism into a battle in the open which he knew he would lose.

Meanwhile Murray was busy reconnoitering a possible landing spot on the north shore south of Quebec. On August 8 he made two attempts to land at Point-aux-Trembles. He was frustrated by rocks, then high water. Also, 140 of his men were killed or wounded when fired upon by Bougainville's force. Next day he landed his entire body of troops at St Antoine on the south shore. When the Canadians and Indians fired on his detachments he threatened to burn every house in the parish if it continued. The threat was taken seriously and all resistance stopped.

On August 18, having journeyed up the river by night, Murray made a successful landing at Deschambault on the north shore where the French regular battalions' spare equipment and baggage was stored. The British torched the equipment and the building. Though they were fired upon by some French foot dragoons and Indians, the resistance was half-hearted. They kept their distance, out of range of the superior firepower of the British musket, for which they had fast developed a healthy, growing respect.

This raid greatly alarmed Montcalm who feared a threat to his communications. Vaudreuil appears to have cared less possibly because he failed to appreciate the situation, or perhaps due to his animosity towards Montcalm — or both. When word of the landing reached him, Montcalm mounted and left with the grenadiers to join Bougainville's force. On learning that the British had withdrawn, he returned to Beauport. By this time, August 27, Murray had returned to Point Levis.

Meanwhile Wolfe had proposed a renewed attack on the Beauport lines in a variation of the abortive July 31 attempt. His brigadiers were hardly enthusiastic after the earlier failure and this did not improve Wolfe's relations with them which were tenuous at best. On August 29 they tabled an objection in writing and at the same time made a counter-proposal.

Having this day met, in consequence of General Wolfe's desire, to consult together for the public utility, and advantage, and to consider the best method of attacking the Enemy; We read his Majesty's private Instructions which the General was pleas'd to communicate to us, and consider'd some propositions of his with respect to our future Operations, and think it our duty to offer our Opinion as follows.

The natural Strength of the Enemys Situation between the river St Charles, and the Montmorrenci, now improved by all the art of their Engeneers makes the defeat of their army if attack'd there very doubtfull . . . allowing we could get footing on the Beauport side the Marquis de Montcalm will still have it in his power to dispute the passage of the River St Charles 'till the place is sufficiently supply'd with Provisions from the Ships and Magazines from which it appears they draw their Subsistance.

We therefore are of the Opinion that the most probable method of striking an effectual blow, is to bring the Troops to the South Shore, and to direct the Operations above the Town: *When we establish ourselves on the North Shore, the French General must fight us on our own Terms;* [Emphasis is the author's] We shall be betwixt him and his provisions, and be-

twixt him and their Army opposing General Amherst [at Ticon-
deroga] :

If he gives us battle and we defeat him, Quebec and probably
all Canada will be ours, which is an advantage far beyond any
we can expect by an attack on the Beauport Side . . . We can
not conclude without assuring the General, that whatever he
determines to do, he will find us most hearty, & Zealour (sic)
in the execution of his Orders.

It was signed: Robt. Monckton. Geo: Townshend Ja: Murray and
it was given Wolfe's full approval. It was a document that was shortly
to have historic consequences. The chief advantages of the plan were
that the British army would be concentrated at a single point instead
of being split up, and that by cutting the French lines of communication it would force them to come out and fight. Wolfe began evacuating his troops from Montmorency and by September 5 they were
assembled on the south shore opposite Cap Rouge ten miles west of
the Quebec city wall. Token detachments were stationed at the Ile
d'Orleans and at Point Levis.

After much reconnoitering, Wolfe chose Anse au Foulon (now
known as Wolfe's Cove), about two miles west of the city wall, as
the landing point. Through his telescope he had noticed a narrow trail
running diagonally upwards from the beach to the top of the 175-foot
cliff. (That path is now the steep road, Cote Gilmour, with a commemorative plaque at the top.) The pathway to Quebec! He could
also see a cluster of a dozen or so tents guarding the approach. To
the west was the Samos Gun Battery. Neither of these defenses could
be considered obstacles to a mass landing, particularly at night.

This period of reconnoitering, planning and waiting was a stressful
one for both sides. Time was running out for the British. They had to
achieve a victory before ice closed the river. And their ranks were
being thinned by dysentery that left a growing number of troops unfit
for duty. With supplies running low, the French faced wholesale
desertions from disenchanted Canadians, sometimes hundreds in a
single night.

Montcalm's commanders were deceived by the British evacuation
of Montmorency. They thought the British were getting ready to
withdraw, and this brought a false sense of relief. However Montcalm
remained alert to possible British surprise moves. He slept with his
boots on; in fact at one period he had not taken his uniform off for
ten days.

On September 13, in the last half hour before darkness, the first British landing craft drifted to a stop on the gravel, in the shadow of the cliffs of Anse au Foulon, a bit further east than had been intended. In the vanguard were Colonel William Howe, who commanded the light infantry battalion and Major William Delaune of the 67th Foot infantry. Delaune opted to march west across a streamlet trickling down the cliff to the river and take the path to the top of the precipice. Howe, aware that dawn would soon be breaking and that the ships would be targets for the French batteries, decided on a frontal assault. He and his men climbed to the top by grasping branches and bushes to pull themselves upwards. There they were confronted with an outpost commanded by Louis du Pont Duchambon de Vergor who had been censured in 1755 for surrendering Beausejour to the British. He had not improved; his men were all asleep except for a sentry who was deceived by a French-speaking Highlander into thinking that nothing was amiss. To his credit Vergor did manage to dispatch an orderly to warn the city before Howe's men overran the outpost and opened the door to the cliffs of Quebec for Wolfe's army.

Meanwhile Montcalm had fallen victim to a giant hoax. A force of 1,200 men had sailed for Beauport from Point Levis in a feint. Montcalm had been completely taken in by the shouting of the British troops and the gunfire. Convinced that the detachment off the shore at Anse au Foulon was a diversion, Montcalm mustered his troops and headed for the beach near Beauport, a full ten miles from where Wolfe was marshalling his forces.

When Vergor's courier reached Vaudreuil's headquarters in the city to break the news of the landing, the French staff refused to believe him. Everyone knew the cliffs were impossible to scale. But the sound of shots soon convinced them and word was passed along to both Montcalm and Bougainville. By then Wolfe had lined up his troops on the Plains — or Heights — of Abraham, named after the seventeenth century pilot Abraham Martin, a patchwork of meadow and cultivated field on the plateau, on which the city is situated, a mile away.

By the time all his regiments had landed and had gained the summit Wolfe formed them up in a line with their backs to the river, their left to Sillery and their right to the city. By 6:00 in the morning he had some 4,500 scarlet coats in place. And while this had been going on the navy had dragged two light brass six-pound guns up the Foulon path. All this had not been accomplished without casualties. French militiamen and Indians, taking advantage of the wooded areas around the plains, had been sniping at the British troops. And before they abandoned it, the Samos Battery gunners had hit two British ships. Bounded by the St Lawrence and St Charles Rivers, the heights narrowed to less than a mile wide. Wolfe stationed his battalions in ranks of three, the columns stretching from the crest overlooking the St Lawrence. With Monckton and Murray he commanded the front line. Townshend's battalions were formed up at right angles to the others towards the rear, guarding the exposed flank which faced the St Charles. One battalion lurked in the woods behind, while another was held in reserve.

That Wolfe had established himself so quickly and solidly on enemy ground was due to a mixture of boldness, luck, super strategy, and strong naval support. To land on a hostile shore facing cliffs as high as 400 feet was a gamble. Had he been forced to retreat, the Foulon path would have been suicide. Montcalm was completely sucked in by the Beauport feint. And Saunders had wielded his fleet brilliantly.

Once Montcalm realized the situation, he swung into action, albeit too impulsively and with inadequate support. He moved his five regiments into the city and onto the plains expecting Vaudreuil, who had sent a token force of militia when he received word from Vergor's messenger that the redcoats had landed, to follow with more of his men. Vaudreuil, however, preferred to keep his troops in reserve and, although he had 25 field guns, he would only release five. This was a question either of poor judgement or stubbornness or both. If Montcalm was beaten in the field, Quebec would fall, reserves or no reserves. Meanwhile Montcalm sent word to Bougainville at Cap Rouge to join him with all speed to attack the enemy's rear. But Bougainville did not receive the message until 8:00 a.m.

By that time Montcalm had already begun preparations to attack, convinced that Wolfe's troops were firmly entrenched. This was not so, the British had not dug in, and even if they had, Montcalm did not have to attack immediately. That he would have been forced to do so eventually was without question. Quebec had hardly any food left and Wolfe had cut the city's communications and supply lines forcing a fight. Even if it had been provisioned the city could not have held out long. But instead of preparing to attack at once, Montcalm should have played for time: to bring up more artillery (even though Vaudreuil was holding back, this could have been overcome) and to wait until Bougainville arrived, all the while harassing his enemy with Indian-style skirmishing (which is exactly what was employed preparatory to the attack). It can be argued, however, that even had Bougainville been present, given the difference in fighting quality, experience and training between the French and the British, the chances of a French victory were slim. But battles have often been won on the slenderest of margins.

Numerically, both armies were about equal, about 4,500 on either side. However, all the British were highly disciplined professional soldiers, most of them sent from Britain. The French army opposing them consisted of five regiments of regulars possibly amounting to 2,000 men. The rest were made up of half-trained colonial militiamen and Indians. Logistically the French had one edge, they outgunned the British by five field pieces to two. But it was their use that counted, not their numbers.

While marshalling his troops in attack array, Montcalm now employed his most effective tactics against the enemy, a series of Indian-style skirmishes. In the face of this, Wolfe ordered his men to lie on their arms, low in the grass to avoid being hit by French marksmen peppering them from behind tree trunks, grassy knolls and abandoned houses. Then at ten o'clock Montcalm gave the order to attack: a serious blunder. Had he waited until Bougainville arrived he might have worn down the opposition by continuing to inflict casualties on the British with the skirmishing harassment and improved his chances. Slender though those might have been, by giving the order to attack prematurely, he had thrown them away.The battle straddled the Grande Allee over ground which today is part of urban Quebec City. The British line lay close to the modern prison. Montcalm's line was on the high ground (his one real advantage) then known as the Buttes à Neveu where the nineteenth century Martello towers now stand. A mere quarter mile separated the two armies as the British sprang to their feet and the French began their advance. The actual battle took place between the current Cartier and de Salaberry streets.

It started to rain as the French advanced. Montcalm on horseback led his men forward, the ensigns unfurling their colourful silk banners. Drums rolled out the charge to the accompaniment of the deep-throated roar of the troops as they ran down the slope, the white uniforms of the regulars mingling with the grey of the militiamen. It was this very panorama — mixing half-trained militiamen with professional regular battalions that led to the utter chaos and confusion that followed.

The formation began to fall apart almost immediately. It had not gone 20 paces when the left flank was too far in the rear and the centre too far in front. After opening fire, the Canadians knelt down to reload, as was their custom, a practice that left gaping holes in the advancing line. All the while the scarlet line facing them remained impassive.

Wolfe had given strict orders that no shot was to be fired until the enemy was within 40 yards ''of the point of a bayonet.'' The grape-shot from the British field guns tore into the French formations but the muskets remained silent. Then as the French advanced to within the specified range, what took place was falsely described by Sir John Fortescue's *History of the British Army* as ''the most perfect volley ever fired on a battlefield.''

The line was too long to effectively coordinate such a storybook fusillade. In reality, except for the centre where such orchestration was possible, the individual platoons fired in succession. The result was letter-perfect. After firing, the British advanced to get clear of the blinding smoke, the line still perfectly intact. French skirmishers in the woods near the cliffs inflicted far more damage than did the French main force. The British delivered a second volley, so devastating that it left those of the enemy still standing ''a frantic mob, shouting, cursing, gesticulating.'' They now broke and fled pell-mell into the city hotly pursued by the British, particularly the 78th Highlanders led by James Murray. With blood-curdling shouts like those of their Scottish forefathers at Culloden, they threw away their muskets and charged with their broadswords needlessly exposing themselves to unnecessary casualties.

But their field commander lay dead on the battlefield behind them. Accounts vary as to how Wolfe met his death. One version is that he was shot by a British deserter. While this is not impossible, it is highly improbable. It is more likely that he was fatally wounded by enemy marksmen in the bushes at the edge of the hill above the St Lawrence.

Most historians agree that, at the head of his men in the British counter-attack against the fleeing French, he was first hit in the wrist which he bandaged with a handkerchief. Then in quick succession he was struck in the groin and in the chest. As he lay dying on the battlefield he gave one last order — to cut the French off. That done, his last words were: ''Now God be praised, I will die in peace.'' His second in command, Robert Monckton, now took his place, but not for long. He too became a casualty, though only wounded, and he passed the command along to George Townshend. It was this time-lapse, and the fact that Townshend was a much less decisive commander than Wolfe that, more than any other factor, resulted in less than total victory for the British.

Almost simultaneously, as Wolfe was struck down, Montcalm met the same fate, though he lived until the following morning. Wounded in the lower part of the stomach and thigh, three soldiers helped him ride back into the city. When a woman saw his profuse bleeding, she began to scream. Montcalm consoled her, assuring her, "It's nothing, it's nothing. Don't be troubled for me." Taken to a private home, he was told his wound was fatal; he would not live 12 hours — not long enough to see the surrender of the city. But he was fatalistic enough to realize the cause was lost. His last official act was to send a message to Townshend asking him to have mercy on the defenders and "be their protector as I have been their father." By the time Bougainville finally arrived on the scene, the fighting had virtually ended. Townshend moved two battalions and two guns to thwart him. But neither commander showed the faintest desire to mix it. Bougainville decided to march back to Montreal. Townshend said in a despatch that he did not want to be blamed for "risking [the] fruit of so decisive a day" by pursuing a fresh army through "woods and swamps."

The British pursuit had been anything but successful. Only two French guns were captured and not a single enemy colour taken. Vaudreuil at last appeared on the field and took charge. Some of his men positioned themselves in a wooded area on the northern flank sloping down towards the St Charles, which offered the cover they needed to make the first, and only, stand against the British.

Murray had led his Highlanders almost to the city walls, then made a circuit back to the battlefield through the woods where they encountered the Canadians and quickly became embroiled in a shoot-out at the edge of the Cote d'Abrahad overlooking the General Hospital. It was a contest in which the Highlanders decidedly came off second-best. Forced to retire and reform, the Scotsmen were only able to force the Canadians back up the hill after two other regiments came to their rescue.

By then Vaudreuil had ordered a retreat to the Beaufort camp leaving the defense of the city to the Quebec garrison. The brief rearguard action had helped make the French retirement possible across the bridges of the St Charles to the Beaufort camp.

Losses were proportionately high for both sides. The British suffered 685 casualties, 58 of them killed. On the French side, though there are no accurate figures available, the casualties were estimated at somewhere between 660 and 1,000. The significance of these statistics underlines the fact that Montcalm might have succeeded marginally had he employed his tactics and strategy more shrewdly and less tempestuously; most of the British losses occurred during the pre-battle skirmishing while French casualties were incurred during the brief battle itself.

But the British victory was far from complete. The French army had been defeated but not destroyed. Much time passed between the moment the dying Wolfe gave the order to cut off the French before Townshend took command from the wounded Monckton. Murray's efforts in pursuit of the enemy to the city walls would have been more profitably spent preventing the French from crossing the St Charles. In retrospect it appears likely that Bougainville's very presence stopped Townshend from pursuing the French force across the St Charles.

That evening at nine o'clock Vaudreuil moved his army of 3,000 from the Beaufort camp around the British on the north side of the St Charles making good an escape without enemy interference, and headed west to ford the river. The following day they reached Point-aux-Trembles on the St Lawrence. All artillery, ammunition and food supplies had been left behind for lack of transport. Before leaving, Vaudreuil had issued two instructions. One was to Levis asking him to join him as soon as possible. The second was to the Chevalier de Ramezay, in charge of the Quebec garrison, advising him not to hold on until the city was taken by assault: "... as soon as the food runs short [you] will hoist the white flag."

Meanwhile Levis had reached Vaudreuil's camp and persuaded him to let him march the army, along with Bougainville's troops, back to Quebec. His plan was "to do and risk everything in the world to prevent the taking of Quebec, and, if the worst comes to the worst, to move all the people out and destroy the city, so the enemy will not spend the winter there." But he did not arrive until September 18. By that time it was too late.

On the 15th de Ramezay summoned his staff for a council of war. Food was fast running out. The British had begun building batteries to breach the fortification on the weak side of town. They had already brought up 60 guns and 58 howitzers and mortars. More terrifying still, the British ships, with their heavy naval guns, had moved into position. In the face of this, the militia and sailors, making up the greater part of the garrison, began to desert. And de Ramezay also came under pressure from the inhabitants to surrender. Vaudreuil had sent a message urging him to hold on until Levis could relieve him.

But by the time he received the despatch on September 17, he had already hoisted the white flag and sent the mayor of the city to the British camp to negotiate a capitulation.

The British army entered Quebec the next day and raised the Union Jack. At this moment the French came in sight of the city. Their hopes dashed, they fell back. Vaudreuil retreated to Montreal, having entrusted Levis with the army at a newly erected fort at the mouth of the Jacques Cartier River which now became the new frontier of the French territory.

Over the winter the British consolidated their conquest. Townshend and the wounded Monckton returned to England leaving Murray as governor and military commander. The better part of the army stayed at Quebec. In October Charles Saunders stationed a couple of sloops offshore and sailed the fleet for Halifax. There he left a large detachment of the fleet under Lord Colville with orders to re-enter the St Lawrence as early in the spring as possible. He then returned to England.

Departure of the British fleet allowed a few French ships to slip past Quebec but it was in a lost cause. Levis beseeched the Court of Versailles to send a large back-up force of 10,000 troops, a necessary train of artillery, and stores of every kind to support it, in the spring of 1760. An army of this magnitude could easily recapture Quebec, he assured the court, which could withstand, at the most, a siege of ten days. Thus the colony could be quickly restored to its rightful place and the force could return to France. But King Louis wasn't buying. He and his advisers were even less enthusiastic than they had been over Montcalm's request for reinforcements a year earlier.

A crushing defeat at Quiberon Bay by the British fleet in November 1759 virtually wrote off any chance of relief for the colony. However, the court did send a token force of 400 — all recruits — along with a small quantity of food supplies. But this tiny flotilla never reached Quebec. It was cut off by the British, who had entered the St Lawrence earlier, and was forced to take refuge in Restigouche where, in July, it was destroyed.

Nevertheless Levis gave a commendable performance. Certain the British would attack from three directions, up the St Lawrence, down the river from Lake Ontario, and by way of Lake Champlain, he gathered his eight battalions — a total of 7,000 men — and decided on an early attack in the spring against Murray before the British could mobilize their forces to advance, and before Buttes a Neveu at Quebec could be fortified. The odds certainly favoured Levis, for he outnumbered Murray, whose army had been decimated that winter by scurvy that killed half his men.

Levis struck early, on April 24, 1760, even before the ice was out. He had hoped to cut off Murray's advance posts at Lorette and Ste Foy but, warned in time, the British general withdrew them. Then, on April 28 he boldly marched his army out of Quebec to meet the advancing French. It was a replay of the Battle of the Plains of Abraham with the sides reversed and a different outcome.

The British brought up 22 field guns and proceeded to dig in on the heights of Butte a Neveu from where they commanded the battlefield. As such Murray was in an ideal position to slaughter Levis's force when he decided to attack. But Murray, like Montcalm, was impatient to force a fast decision. Seeing that the enemy was putting up redoubts, he decided to take the offensive. At first the British light troops gained a momentary advantage over the French advance guard, but quickly lost that edge when Levis concentrated his main force against the British flanks.

After a bitter fight, the left flank caved in and the main British line broke. Murray was forced to retreat just as had Montcalm. The British fled into the refuge of Quebec leaving 20 of their 22 field guns behind. Casualties sustained in the brief battle were heavy. The British: 1,104 officers and men, 259 of whom were killed; the French: 833, including 193 killed. This engagement, commonly known as the Battle of Ste Foye, had been far bloodier than the earlier encounter between the armies of Wolfe and Montcalm. But unlike the French, Murray refused to surrender the fortress.

Levis now laid siege to Quebec. Had he been given the help he wanted from Versailles, the city would have fallen and New France would have been restored to French rule. But with his limited resources of firepower, he might be capable of winning open field battles, but he was totally unequipped to besiege a fortress city. Even with the captured British weapons he had few guns, the largest being a single 24-pounder, and those he did have were second-class. On May 11, the French batteries opened fire on what they knew to be a weak spot, the right face of the Glacier bastion, which they severely damaged. But that was their only success.

Murray had been able to restore and reorganize his defeated but well-disciplined, highly trained army into a defensive force fit to withstand a siege. British fire from the ramparts was more than the French could bring to bear. This sustained cannonade was so damaging to the French guns that, along with the fact that supply was running low, on May 12, Levis was compelled to limit his fire to 20 rounds per gun per day. No great threat that.

Levis had hoped, in vain, that the French ships that had sailed past Quebec the previous fall, might rescue the situation. But the first vessels to appear at Quebec in the spring were British not French. On May 16, only five days after the siege began, three British ships destroyed the French frigates. Game over. That night Levis fled with his army leaving all their field guns behind. That was the end of New France. British forces everywhere crushed the French and converged on Montreal. There, on September 9, the French capitulated, laying down their weapons in the Place d'Armes. Canada had passed into British hands. But she never lost her French heritage. Only a little over two generations later, English and French-speaking Canadians were fighting side by side in defense of their country.

✦ 3 ✦

THE DEFEAT OF DETROIT

Search! Impress! Seize!

It was that zealousness with which the British Navy, all powerful since its victory over the French fleet at Trafalgar in October 1805, carried out these "duties," that led to hostilities between Canada and the United States, known familiarly as the War of 1812.

At the ocean bed of it lay Britain's strategy of trying to starve out Napoleonic France now that her navy was no longer strong enough to resist. That meant blockading American ships supplying food and goods to Europe. In its eagerness, the Royal Navy employed overly harsh means to do so.

British deserters provided England with the excuse it needed to stop and search American ships at sea, often within sight of their own ports. That desertions were commonplace was due to the rigorously severe treatment — and punishment — meted out by the Royal Navy to its seamen. In comparison, crews on United States merchant vessels were treated more humanely. They enjoyed better food and pay (ten times that of the British) and, above all, limited punishment. American captains could not order more than 12 lashes even for the most serious offenses.

Royal Navy boarding parties arbitrarily selected deserters who, for their crimes, were summarily whipped or spreadeagled, often flogged through the fleet, strung from the yardarm or keelhauled. As a bonus the British impressed — kidnapped would be a more fitting description — the most able-bodied among American crews into Royal Navy service. Finally, the British often seized the cargo. Facing well-armed British warships, the American merchantmen were powerless to resist and were sometimes captured outright.

Frequently ships and cargo were sold off at the British naval base in Halifax, Nova Scotia. In addition, the Royal Navy went a step further. They would send marines ashore to seize food and supplies. Any attempt at refusal brought a sharp rebuke in the form of broadsides fired from vessels offshore.

In 1807 matters came to a head when HMS *Leopard* demanded to be allowed to board the American warship *Chesapeake* to search for deserters. When the captain angrily refused, the British war vessel opened fire with most of her 50 guns, sending volley after volley into the U.S. ship. The Americans were only able to return a single shot. With 21 dead and wounded, *Chesapeake* pulled down Old Glory in surrender and allowed the British to board, seize deserters, impress others of the crew and loot her cargo.

This treatment of a national ship of the United States government was regarded as an insult and produced a public outcry. The Americans demanded an apology but none was forthcoming. The British, still smarting from the loss of her Thirteen Colonies, regarded the Americans as a bunch of uncultivated yokels undeserving of any such courtesies. The result was the passing of the Embargo Act banning U.S. trade with the entire world. It halted the British raiding but now hundreds of American ships, unable to sail the high seas, sat idle, rotting in the seaports. Thousands of seafarers went without jobs. By 1809 the law was repealed and replaced with the Non-Intercourse Act allowing Americans to trade with all nations except Britain and France.

While it put the ships back in business, it also allowed the British to renew their policy of what was, in effect, pure piracy. By 1812 they had captured 400 American vessels within sight of the U.S. coast. By this time American impatience had been stretched to the limit. Enough was enough. In retaliation, since it was impossible to attack England directly, and the Americans were certainly no match for the Royal Navy on the high seas, the U.S. decided to invade Britain's colony, Canada. In truth it was more a design of conquest than retribution. A God-given opportunity to make North America a single nation and bring an end to British rule — America's "Manifest Destiny."

On the surface the odds seemed overwhelmingly stacked in the Americans' favour. How could a mere 300,000 Canadians possibly defend themselves against 8,000,000 Americans?

However, the essential difference was not in population statistics but in the make-up of the armies facing each another. Great Britain had 17,000 regular troops, tough, disciplined professionals, many of whom had fought against Napoleon, and knew their business. The entire United States regular force numbered only 7,000, most of them poorly trained.

Strategically the British held a solid edge. The presence of the British Navy assured control of the waterways — lakes Huron, Erie, Ontario, and the St Lawrence River. These water routes formed the key to communications and mobility. Overland, most roads were simply rutted routes chewed up by carts. Everything had to be moved by water — troops, weapons, and supplies. While a British canoe could carry messages from the St Lawrence to Lake Superior without fear of attack, American express riders had to struggle through jungle-like forests and swamps to get their messages through.

Both sides faced problems with civilian morale. In this respect they were both totally unprepared for war. The only thing united about the United States was its name. While Westerners and Southerners cheered the declaration, New Englanders, who would be the most affected, condemned it as "Madison's War" after President James Madison. A Massachusetts congressmen was kicked through the streets of Plymouth by angry townsfolk.

There was strong Canadian apathy towards the war. Canada's citizens were convinced they would be overwhelmed by the Americans and that it would be futile to resist. Furthermore, in Upper Canada, American settlers posed a potential threat: they might aid and abet an invasion and the invaders.

The United States Army's chief problem was not its poorly trained troops, though that was worrisome enough, but its command. Its seven generals had seen better days. All had served with distinction in the revolution but now in their sixties, they had not seen fighting in 30 years. Proud but lazy, they had failed to keep up with the modern ways of war and were much more adept at eating and drinking than fielding an army. Henry "Granny" Dearborn, the senior major general, was too fat to mount a horse and had to lead his troops from a buckboard.

Nevertheless, Dearborn drew up a master plan designed to deliver a series of knockout punches to end the war quickly. Four invasion forces would cross the border at about the same time. One would move from Fort Detroit across the river to capture Fort Amherstburg. Two others would set out from Sackett's Harbor and Fort Niagara in New York State. These would link up with a fourth, moving north from Lake Champlain. Together they would capture Montreal, Canada's chief city.

It made sense. By capturing the key points along the 1,000-mile border stretching from Montreal to Detroit, the Americans would seize control of the waterways. The initial assault, from Detroit, was under the command of General William Hull, hero of the revolution and now governor of Michigan. Several weeks before the declaration of war on June 18, 1812, he had gathered 2,000 regulars and militiamen from Ohio and began marching north. But his potential protagonist, Major General Isaac Brock, commander of the army in Upper Canada and administrator of the provincial government, had already seized the initiative.

The 27-year British Army veteran, who had distinguished himself in Holland and the Baltic, had for five years foreseen that war with the United States was inevitable. With limited forces at his disposal he recognized that from the outset, the British-Canadians had to win the loyalty of the Indians. He also knew that an early decisive action against the Americans was needed to secure that allegiance, as well as to win the confidence of the Canadians themselves.

It wouldn't take much to sway the Indians. In their greedy quest for land, American frontiersmen throughout Ohio, Kentucky, and Tennessee had burned down Indian villages and slaughtered natives who stood in their way. Tecumseh, leader of the Shawnees, who dreamed of uniting all the tribes, still seethed with rage over the massacre of his village at the junction of the Tippecanoe and Wabash rivers a year earlier. He had already decided to cast his lot with the British, though the Indians still wanted to see how serious the English were about making war. In the meantime, Tecumseh's followers had shadowed Hull's army through Michigan Territory to Fort Detroit.

At the same time Brock had planned to seize Mackinac Island in Lake Michigan at the entrance to Lake Huron. That invasion was carried out by a combined force of his regulars at the British outpost on St Joseph's Island on the western end of Huron, together with a group of Indians — Sioux, Chippewa, Winnebago, Menomemee, and Ottawa — led by a Scotsman, Robert Dickson, whose wife was an Indian.

On June 19, the day after war was declared, the island surrendered without a shot. The night before, Dickson had run into an old crony, Michael Dousman, a fur trader who knew the island. Next morning at 3:00 a.m. a flotilla of ten bateaux and 70 canoes, led by the gunboat *Caledonia*, landed the invaders. Dousman quietly woke the civilians who were herded into a distillery at the end of town, three of them having been taken hostage. The garrison slept on. When it awoke, it faced two six-pound guns on the forested bluff above the bastion. With the spectacle of Indians in warpaint before them and the spectre of scalpings and burnings at the post, they raised the white flag. The natives, particularly Tecumseh, were impressed by the quick, bloodless victory and immediately went over to the Canadian side.

On June 18, as William Hull neared Detroit, where he was to cross the river and capture Fort Amherstburg, he was unaware that war had been declared. At the foot of the Maumee Rapids he relieved his exhausted troops of their equipment and loaded it, along with 36 officers and men under his quartermaster general, William Beall onto the schooner *Cayuga*.

It was a mistake. Though Hull had received no official word that the United States was at war with the British, he should have known it was imminent. The schooner would have to pass right under the guns of Fort Amherstburg. Though that garrison had not been officially notified of hostilities either, they took no chances. As soon as *Cayuga* came within range, they commandeered her and placed the occupants and their cargo under detention.

Next day, bugles heralded the arrival of Hull's forces directly across the river and only a day's march from Detroit, and alarm spread throughout Fort Amherstburg. Lieutenant Colonel Thomas St George, the fort commander, was in a state of panic. He was a staff officer and the situation was completely beyond him. He wasn't even sure how many troops he had and the civilian population, made up mostly of French-Canadians, was decidedly hostile. Indians added to the confusion, coming and going as they pleased and consuming the supplies. He knew by now that war had been declared and here was the enemy almost on his doorstep.

However, by the time Hull's army reached Detroit, a thriving community of 800 residents protected by a fort armed with British guns captured during the revolution, St George had calculated that the Americans would land at the small village of Sandwich directly across the river. He stationed several militia units there. But it wasn't enough. They were untrained and unready, virtually useless.

When Hull made his move, on Sunday, July 12, the militiamen fled in fright. Occupying the tiny town, Hull immediately issued a proclamation that the Americans had landed not as conquerors but as liberators. That was stupid. Because there had been no opposition, he had badly misread the mood of Upper Canada. These were settlers, mostly farmers, not frontiersmen or revolutionaries. Hull's taking them for granted had helped turn the pioneers into patriots. The British occupation of Mackinac Island reinforced that loyalty. When Hull learned of it on July 28, it threw him into a complete panic. He had already stretched his supply line to the limit; it was constantly threatened by six British gunboats along the shores of Lake Erie, and Indians, under Tecumseh, prowling the forests to the west. Now with the mouth of Lake Huron cut off, he envisioned Indians, of whom the Americans were deathly afraid, massacring the residents of the Michigan Territory. When he heard that Brock was bringing reinforcements to Fort Amherstburg, he decided to withdraw to the relative safety of Fort Detroit.

Brock met Tecumseh for the first time when he arrived at Fort Amherstburg. The two regarded each other with mutual respect. "This is a man," said the Shawnee chief. The British general replied: "A more sagacious and gallant warrior does not, I believe, exist." Then the pair got down to business and mapped out a plan to conquer Hull's army and capture Fort Detroit.

Their strategy was replete with ruses. The tactics played on fear and terror. Brock had marshalled a force of 300 regulars, 400 Canadian militiamen, and 600 Indians. Though Hull's army outnumbered him 2,000 to 1,300, Brock dressed his militiamen in red coats to make the Americans believe they were up against a large force of regulars. On the night of August 15, Tecumseh led his warriors across the river and surrounded the fort, cutting off Hull's army. Painted in weird colour patterns and naked except for moccasins and loincloths, they were armed with muskets, tomahawks, spears, bows and arrows, scalping knives, and stone-headed war clubs — a fearsomely ferocious sight. As if that wasn't enough to frighten their foes, all night long the braves war-whooped and danced around bonfires letting out blood-curdling cries.

In the morning Brock led his main force across the river while Tecumseh's warriors still whooped and hollered their war cries to the booming of British cannon. The bombardment did little damage but it totally unnerved the fort commander. One cannon ball struck a lieutenant in the midriff, cutting him in two and tearing the legs off a second man. Another missile killed two others splattering their blood and brains on the walls and gowns of some women. At the sight of this, added to the specter of an Indian massacre, of women and children being scalped, Hull collapsed. There was only one solution. He despatched a courier with a white flag to negotiate a surrender with the British.

Many of his officers were appalled that he would give up the fort without firing a shot, and demanded his arrest. Brock was dumbfounded. Hull had asked for a three-day respite. Brock demanded total surrender within three hours. It was all over. Down came the Stars and Stripes, up went the Union Jack. The booty was a boon to a badly armed Upper Canada. The British netted 2,500 muskets, 39 heavy guns, 40 barrels of gunpowder, a 16-gun rig, several small craft, a baggage train of 100 pack animals, 300 cattle, and provisions and stores. Prize money, amounting to $200,000, was distributed among the troops.

The most significant outcome of the "bloodless" battle was the effect it had on the Indian tribes and the populace of Upper Canada, who hitherto had taken a defeatist attitude towards the war. Most of the Michigan Territory was now in British hands and many of the Indians, such as the Mohawks, who had been reluctant to take sides, now enthusiastically committed themselves to the British cause. In a single blow, Brock had demonstrated that the Americans, far from being invincible, could be beaten. It proved that any attempted invasion of Canada could be thwarted if the country was willing to fight. Strategically, the victory left the British in command of the Great Lakes, allowing Brock to concentrate on the main frontier at Niagara. In Canada, Isaac Brock was the man of the hour.

It was a different story for the vanquished. William Hull was in disgrace, even though by surrendering he had saved countless lives, military and civilian, adult and children, and prevented his fort from being burned to the ground. Court-martialed, he was found guilty of cowardice and sentenced to face a firing squad, but President Madison, taking into account the gallant part he had played in the revolution, pardoned him. His soldiers, who felt that he had betrayed them, cursed his name until the very day he died.

✤ 4 ✤

QUEENSTON HEIGHTS — A BATTLE
WON — A GENERAL LOST

Reference map "The Battle of Queenston Heights."

From his headquarters in Lewiston, New York, General Stephen Van Ransselaer, in command of American troops camped at Lewiston Heights on the Niagara River opposite the small village of Queenston, had no idea that William Hull's army at Detroit had been defeated. His assignment was to keep the British army opposite him occupied and off balance, leaving Hull to begin the invasion of Canada by capturing Fort Amherstburg. In the belief that Hull had already been victorious, he was being urged by his officers to attack immediately.

Attack? How? With what? The British had control of lakes Erie and Ontario and the Niagara River and Van Rensselaer had only 1,000 men to guard a 36-mile front. A third of them were sick. Ammunition amounted to only ten rounds per man. There were no big guns nor gunners, no engineers and almost no medical supplies. And, to make matters worse, the state militia was exercising their constitutional right of refusing to fight on foreign soil. As if that wasn't bad enough, his military leaders, and he, himself, had no battle experience.

Assault the British? Quite the reverse. It was an attack by *them* that Van Rensselaer feared more than anything else. However there was relief in sight. On April 16 a temporary truce was reached between the governor general of Canada, Sir George Prevost, who believed that hostilities could be brought to a halt, and the American supreme commander of the army, General Henry Dearborn, who wanted to play for time to reinforce the Niagara frontier.

When he learned of the arrangement on his arrival at Fort Erie on April 22, Isaac Brock was furious. With 400 regulars, 800 militia, and up to 500 Mohawks available, he was ready to roll up the New York frontier and bring the war to a swift end. But even after the truce ended on September 8, Brock was restrained from taking an offensive action by Prevost who hoped that by not annoying or provoking the Americans, things might sort themselves out and bring a finish to hostilities. That was only foolish, wishful thinking. After the humiliating defeat at Detroit, American honour had not only to be satisfied but avenged.

In the meantime, on August 27, Van Rensellaer's partially reinforced Lewiston camp had been shattered by the sight across the river — so narrow it could be crossed by a row boat in ten minutes — of the bedraggled remnants of Hull's defeated army straggling along the opposite shore, shoeless, ragged, the wounded crying and moaning in open carts, prodded along by their captors.

The effect on the camp was twofold. The militiamen were awed at the demonstration of British power. But the warlike among Van Rensellaer's officers thirsted for blood. In Albany, Dearborn, who had expected to seize all of Upper Canada and Montreal by this time, was devastated by the Detroit defeat. He was convinced that the British were about to attack along the Niagara River. Besides reinforcing Lewiston, he decided to maintain his strength at Fort Niagara opposite Fort George at the northern mouth of the river, and to reinforce the camp at Buffalo at the southern mouth of Lake Erie. He also sent troops to relieve Detroit. He knew that he had to get a foothold on the British side of the Niagara River before winter set in, to be able to launch a major campaign in the spring of 1813. He assured Van Rensselaer that he would be supported by General William Henry Harrison (a future president of the United States) who would invade Detroit with a force of 7,000, while he himself would menace Montreal from Lake Champlain.

Among the reinforcements for the Niagara River were 1,700 soldiers under the command of Brigadier General Alexander Smyth, a regular officer who disdained the militia and made no bones about the fact he had no intention of cooperating with his nominal commander, Van Rensselaer. He told him in no uncertain terms that the best place to cross the river was above the falls, not below them, and promptly took his troops to Buffalo, neatly splitting the American force.

This decision had further repercussions and was at least partially responsible for the defeat that was to come. By this time Van Rensselaer had 8,000 troops, half of them regulars, under his command; 4,200 of them were at Lewiston, the rest at Buffalo and Fort Niagara. There now no longer seemed any danger of a British attack and, prodded by Dearborn, the time had come to take the initiative.

Van Rensselaer planned a twin-pronged assault that called for Smyth's regulars to cross the river near Newark (now Niagara-on-the-Lake) and storm Fort George from the rear, while Van Rensselaer, would simultaneously lead his militias from Lewiston and carry the heights above Queenston. This would divide the British forces, cut their lines of communications, and drive their shipping out of the mouth of the Niagara River while securing a springboard for a spring campaign and erasing the disgrace of Detroit.

It was a sound scheme, the success of which depended on Smyth's cooperation, but, predictably, he wasn't buying. When Van Rensselaer called a council of war in early October, to discuss the proposed plans for attack Smyth showed his contempt for the militia general by refusing to attend or even explain his absence. This was, by any measurement, a flagrant breach of conduct, an intolerable act of insubordination that, in any other army, would have resulted in the severest disciplinary action. But the United States had not yet become a true military nation.

On the other side of the river, with orders from the governor general to avoid any offensive action, Brock busied himself with shoring up his defenses. A request for 1,000 troops was denied on the grounds that no more men could be spared for Upper Canada. Indefatigably, Brock made the most of the resources he had. He ordered detachments to be sent from Kingston and Amherstburg. Batteries were built and mounted with cannons taken from the Detroit fortifications. Two thousand captured muskets and other accoutrements of Hull's defeated army were distributed among the militia. Brock then established an early warning network of beacons and despatch riders by which an alarm could be instantaneously spread across the entire Niagara Peninsula day or night, at the slightest suspicious enemy movement.

It was difficult for either side to disguise their deployments and preparations from one another particularly Van Rensselaer's. His build-up was by far the most visible, as reinforcements arrived and white tents proliferated on the heights. Daily, large bodies of men could be seen drilling with numerous pieces of artillery. A flotilla of boats, bateaux capable of carrying 30 troops, lay moored in the river directly under the guns.

Though the Americans did not know it, Brock's available troops were so sparse and thinly spread out on a frontier 60 miles long, that they were barely and rarely visible. Van Rensselaer's intelligence had to rely on his staff officers to visit the British lines on one pretext or another under the white flag.

Both sides overestimated the other's strength. In reality the British had less than 1,000 regulars, 600 militia, and a reserve militia of 600 and Indians. These had to be spread between Fort George and Queenston, the places where Brock logically had anticipated an enemy attack. That indeed had been Van Rensselaer's original plan. However, after being snubbed by Smyth he had abandoned the idea of a twin-pronged assault and concentrated instead solely on a crossing from Lewiston, where he had 900 regular soldiers and 2,270 militia. But Brock was completely unaware of this decision.

Van Rensselaer had scheduled his attack for October 10 for two very good reasons. The day before, a small American command captured two British ships anchored off Fort Erie, escaping with one of the gunboats. That night Brock reached the scene and, having established that the incident was no more than a local skirmish, returned to Fort George where he was sure the main assault would take place. The Americans mistakenly believed he had left for Detroit. With his troops elated over the gunboat incident and under the impression that Brock was on his way southwest, Van Rensselaer rightly calculated that the time could not have been more propitious for him to begin his attack. To reinforce his army, he had detachments sent from Fort Niagara and Buffalo. But just before midnight, while 500 of his men assembled in readiness to board the boats, a fierce rain and windstorm struck the camp. In the darkness the pilot of the expedition deserted, and the rain continued to pelt down unabated for the next 28 hours. The attack had to be postponed indefinitely.

Meanwhile a force of 350 regulars in three boats under Lieutenant Colonel John Chrystie, made an appearance at Four Mile Creek, east of Fort Niagara on Lake Ontario. The sight of these boats led Brock to believe that the main attack would come there, and he did not bother reinforcing the detachment at Queenston. When the attack there finally did take place at 3:00 a.m. on October 13, he was still convinced it was merely a feint. Chrystie's appearance had been a clever deception. The night of the attack, he and the Fort Niagara regulars, marched overland to join the main force at Lewiston.

At this point in the Niagara Gorge, the river was only 200 yards wide and flowed at a leisurely four miles an hour. The cliffs rose perpendicularly to some 200 feet but, on the Canadian side, many places were so overgrown with shrubs, trees, and roots that there would be little problem scaling them from the river's edge to the summit. Halfway up the side of the Queenston Heights, the British had built a redan, a dugout, facing the river and armed with an 18-pound gun. About a mile downstream, Vrooman's Point was manned with a 24-pound gun, also aimed at the landing.

Offsetting this the Americans had built a battery called Fort Gray, commanded by Colonel John Lovett, on Lewiston Heights. Its two 18-pounders were aimed at the British redan, while a second battery at river level, comprised of two six-pound guns and two mortars, set to cover the landings by bombarding the town of Queenston which was defended by a mere 200 men.

At first everything seemed to go according to plan. A heavy rainfall drowned out all signs and sounds of activity. By three o'clock in the morning Van Rensselaer had amassed 4,000 men without alerting the British. Twelve boats, capable of carrying 30 men each, were in place to be piloted by experienced local fishermen.

A slight personal confrontation intervened over who should lead the crossing. That old argument between the militia and the regular force reared its head. Colonel Solomon Van Rensselaer, the general's cousin, had originally been chosen to head up the river crossing. But the arrival of John Chrystie created a minor crisis. He refused to take second place to the militiaman. After his problem with Smyth, the general didn't need any more of this kind of hassle. If he was no military expert, a fact that became increasingly obvious, he proved at least to be a master of compromise. It was finally agreed that Chrystie would lead with 300 regulars followed by Van Rensselaer, who would embark with 300 handpicked militiamen.

Ten of the boats in the first wave landed 300 men on the Canadian shore. Another three drifted downstream, one of them carrying John Chrystie who received a musket wound in the hand. As soon as the boat came under fire, the terror-stricken pilot turned about and rowed back to the American side.

In Chrystie's absence, Van Rensselaer took charge of the disembarking and began to form up his infantry and artillerymen, the latter equipped with matches and ramrods which they expected to use on captured British cannon. At first their landing and subsequent movements went unchallenged, but then a Canadian militiaman suddenly spotted them. However, instead of firing a warning shot as he had been instructed, he became so flustered that he raced off to the village and spread the alarm personally. It wasted time but, immediately upon being alerted, Captain James Dennis, with 46 of his grenadiers, dashed forward to the landing area. Their first volley tore into the invaders' ranks, dropping some of them in their tracks and wounding others, among them Van Rensselaer, who was hit six times. In panic the survivors fled in disorder for the cover of the high banks along the river, taking their wounded with them, and began returning the fire.

In the meantime the Lewiston batteries had trained their fire on the British redan but as soon as John Lovett saw the musket fire, he aimed his 18-pounders at the defenders who took flight back into Queenston. This brief encounter now developed into an artillery duel, with the gunners at the redan and on Vrooman's Point returning the cannon fire at random in the direction of Lewiston. The Americans suffered 57 casualties, killed and wounded, the British, one dead and four wounded.

Disabled by his wounds, Van Rensselaer had to be evacuated to Lewiston and with no sign of Chrystie, Captain John Wool took command. This very junior, inexperienced, but highly innovative officer very nearly won the Battle of Queenston Heights for the Americans with his initiative and daring. Wool and his party held on determinedly for two hours while reinforcements were being pushed over to them. However, under the blistering British fire, the local fisherman, hired to pilot the boats, deserted. This left the vessels in the hands of men inexperienced with river craft who lacked the skill to maneuver them. The result, at first, was chaos.

One in a wave of six troop boats was sunk by a cannon ball shot from the hill, while two others were swept off course by the current. One, carrying Lieutenant Colonel George Fenwick, straggled into a cove south of Queenston, where it was immediately attacked by the defenders. Fenwick took a pistol shot in the face which partially blinded him, and after a brief skirmish in which he was again wounded twice, his party was taken prisoner. The other boat drifted ashore within range of the Vrooman's Point battery where it, along with the occupants, was captured. By dawn, as the rain stopped and the sun began to simmer through the clouds, all the wounded had been evacuated. Wool's force had been doubled to some 500 men.

At three o'clock in the morning, when Brock was awakened in Fort George by the sound of booming artillery fire, he was convinced it was a duel between sentries, nothing more. However, he got out of bed, dressed, mounted his grey charger, Alfred, and rode through the gate just as a despatcher, Samuel Jarvis, galloped up with the news that the Americans had landed at Queenston. Still skeptical, still believing that the main thrust would come from Fort Niagara, he nevertheless decided to inspect his defenses. He ordered Captain William Holcroft, an artillery veteran, to follow him with two guns and a party of Indians. Then with his two aides, Captains John Macdonnell and Charles Clegg, he galloped through the mud and rain toward the village.

On the way, he gathered up the militia companies stationed at Field's and Brown's points, leaving only a token force before leading the rest into Queenston. His arrival drew loud cheers from the troops positioned there but Brock, with Clegg and Macdonnell, rode up hill to the redan where they dismounted. There, in the chill of the dawn, they got their first view of the battle.

Below, John Wool, whose wound in the buttocks was sore, but not serious enough to take him out of action, had been frustrated by the redan which had his men pinned down. If something wasn't done about it soon they would all be taken prisoners. He had learned that there was a narrow, rocky path that wound around the point all the way from the river bank to the summit. This route would be unobserved by the British and could place the Americans behind them. From there they could charge down the hill, capture the redan and turn the cannon on the British — a bold and brilliant maneuver for a militia tyro. Leaving 100 men at the landing to occupy the enemy's attention, Wool led the rest on the ascent with strict orders that anyone who attempted to turn back was to be shot. The climb went completely unopposed, not a single sentry was to be seen.

From their vantage point, Brock and his two aides gazed down on the spectacle before them. At Lewiston, battalion after battalion of troops were lined up waiting to embark. Others were already climbing into the boats, some vessels were halfway across the river and others were landing men at Queenston. The enemy's guns were throwing up round and grapeshot into the village where James Dennis's detachment was struggling to maintain its foothold. They were holding their position well. In over three hours the Americans failed to gain a single inch and 300 of them had been taken prisoner. A company of light infantry occupied a crest just above the redan and Brock sent them to reinforce Dennis's party. Sizing up the situation, he now knew that this was no feint and sent messages to Major General Roger Shaeffe at Fort George, to join in with his guns and bring the remainder of his garrison to Queenston. He also ordered Captain Richard Bullock at Chippawa to send all available reinforcements.

Seeing a shell fired from the 18-pounder beside him burst prematurely, Brock had just finished telling the gunner to use a shorter fuse, when there was a crackle of musket fire and shouting as Wool's infantry made a bayonet charge down the hill. Brock ordered the gunners to spike the gun by hammering a ramrod into the barrel and breaking it off before taking flight. There was no time for Brock and his aides to mount their horses so they led them hurriedly down the road to the village. The Americans were too preoccupied with manning the redan to give chase. As they raised Old Glory, a cheer went up from their comrades across the river.

Brock knew he would have to recapture the battery — the enemy would waste no time unspiking the gun — or lose the battle. Whoever commanded the heights controlled Upper Canada. Rallying 200 redcoats from Queenston, and leaving an artillery detachment there, he began organizing a counter-attack.

Brock ordered James Dennis to take 70 men forward to skirt the Americans on their right, who had taken advantage of the natural cover of trees and hollows. From behind a stone wall at the base of the rise, he watched as Wool, spotting the British advance, despatched 150 of his own men to circumvent it. But after trading a few shots of musket fire with the British, the exchange became confused and the Americans began to yield ground. This was the moment Brock had been waiting for. After assigning a troop under Captain John Williams to attack Wool's left, sword in hand he leapt his horse over the wall and charged up the hill. Many of the men lost their footing on the wet leaves littering the slope. Despite this and the fact that Wool enjoyed a supremacy of two-to-one, even after British reinforcements arrived, Wool's line began to fall back.

Riding uphill at full gallop, hell-bent for leather, Brock and his aide, John Macdonnell, boldly presented conspicuous, tempting targets for Wool's riflemen. Thud! A musket shot struck Brock's sword hand, badly bloodying it. He paid no attention and waved that same arm, urging his men forward.

Suddenly an American rifleman stepped out from behind a thicket. From less than 50 yards he took careful aim with his musket. This drew immediate fire from the redcoats but too late. The American's bullet had found its mark and struck Brock in the right breast near the heart. Mortally wounded he sagged to the ground. His dying words purportedly, and a bit theatrically, were: ''My fall must not be noticed or impede my brave companions from advancing to victory.'' Some of his men gathered about their prostrated leader, one of them taking a cannon shot that wounded him so severely he fell across Brock's body.

Macdonnell quickly took charge, spurring the British on. As if in revenge for their general's death, they swiftly overran the redan. The fury of their charge sent the Americans reeling back in disorder up the slope to the summit. In panic, one of the officers raised a white handkerchief on the tip of his sword as a flag of truce. Wool hastily knocked it aside. They then retreated toward the river where, on the brow of the hill, with reinforcements arriving from the landing, Wool intended to make his stand. He now had sufficient troops to lengthen his line and outflank the British at either end.

In the confusion, the British had also fallen into disarray. The toll of dead and wounded was horrifying. John Williams was so severely wounded in the head he fell to the ground, unable to move. Lieutenant Archibald McLean, Canada's future chief justice, was wounded so badly he had to be taken from the field. As Macdonnell tried to regroup his men, a bullet struck his horse. As the dying animal reared, another bullet killed its rider. All this helped Wool gain the initiative. But even with reinforcements, he did not press his advantage, or his luck. This enabled James Smith, who was wounded in the thigh, to make an orderly retreat to the far end of Queenston, which was still being defended by a detachment commanded by Lieutenant Alan Crowther. Wool sent 150 of his regulars to give chase, but it was an uninspired endeavour that, after an interchange of musket fire, ended with the Americans retreating in disorder. The British managed to carry the bodies of Brock and Macdonnell with them along with the wounded who could be helped. A dozen or so wounded men had to be left behind and were taken prisoner. Dennis and his men eventually withdrew to Durham's Farm on the river road a mile away, near Vrooman's Point.

The struggle had an inspiring and uplifting effect on the Americans still at Lewiston. The militiamen, who had hitherto exercised their constitutional right to refuse to fight on foreign soil, now showed an eagerness to join in the glory of a victory. There were still sufficient boats to carry the rest of the contingent across the river completely unopposed. Why they did not take proper advantage of that situation remains a mystery.

At seven o'clock that morning John Chrystie, though wounded, had arrived on the Canadian side to take charge of the assault on Queenston village which Alan Crowthers' artillerymen were stoutly and stubbornly defending. Chrystie returned to Lewiston twice to bring up artillery of their own. On hearing a report of the situation first-hand, General Stephen Van Rensselaer finally put his foot down and ordered the recalcitrant Alexander Smyth to send his brigade from Buffalo — or else! — and to despatch an engineer with it to lay out a fortified camp.

While awaiting these reinforcements, Van Rensselaer and Chrystie examined the position on the heights and gave orders to dig in. The gun in the redan had been captured but the American troops had been unable to unspike it. With the troops from Buffalo came Colonel Winfield Scott, future invader of Mexico, United States commander-in-chief, and unsuccessful presidential candidate. After placing his guns in position at Lewiston, he crossed the river to take charge of the regulars. At the same time Brigadier General William Wadsworth took command of the militias. By then there were between 1,200 and 1,600 Americans on the Canadian side.

At Durham House, where Dennis's remnants listened apprehensively to the cannonade a mile away, morale was suddenly given a sharp lift with the arrival from Fort George of several companies of militia, commanded by Captain Henry Derenzy, two field guns with William Holcroft in charge, and a party of Indians led by Captain John Norton and Lieutenant John Brant. A false report that Dennis's command had been ripped to shreds, sent the reinforcements to Queenston on the double. Holcroft immediately planted his guns on the high ground below the village aimed at the disembarking point.

By this time small parties of Americans had penetrated the upper part of the village. Though they looted houses, they made no practical attempt to occupy the town. After firing a few wayward shots, Holcroft realized he was well out of range. Led by Captain Archibald Hamilton, who knew the area like the back of his hand from boyhood, Holcroft dashed across the ravine into the village where he reached the William Hamilton House which Brock had made his Queenston headquarters. There he took up a position with a company of Derenzy's infantry in support.

Now Holcroft's fire soon became effective. After driving the Americans out of the village, though he was still out of range of the

Lewiston batteries, he trained his guns on the enemy batteries at the landing point, as well as on boats in the river. Three were sunk and the accuracy of his fire prevented all but a handful of Americans from crossing the river from that point on.

In the meantime Winfield Scott sent out scouting parties to the edge of the woods forward to the left. Derenzy in turn deployed his Indians to drive them back. Caught by surprise as they entered the woods, the Americans were completely routed with heavy losses. Scott then counter-attacked with a detachment of infantry and the Indians ran into the woods where they kept up an incessant volley of rifle fire accompanied with blood-curdling war whoops.

The swiftness of the attack and the very presence of the Indians, though only a handful, was enough to create panic among the Americans. At Lewiston, where a militia company was getting ready to embark, the troops refused to get in the boats. On the Canadian side, many deserted and tried to get back to their own shore. The appearance of tomahawk-wielding Indians, conjuring up appalling visions of scalping, had, and would continue to have, a demoralizing and terrifying impact on the Americans and would, in no small way, become one of the major factors in the outcome of the battle.

Derenzy had sent a message to Brock's successor as commander of the British Army in Upper Canada, Major General Roger Shaeffe, at Fort George outlining the situation, whereupon the latter arrived on the scene and ordered every man that could be spared from Fort George and Chippewa garrisons to march to Queenston without delay. By two o'clock the Fort George contingent had arrived and reinforcements from Chippewa were on their way.

By this time the British had 1,000 men at Queenston, including the 200 Indians, but were still outnumbered by the Americans. Leaving Holcroft's artillery and a detachment of infantry to defend the village, Shaeffe decided on an outflanking maneuver to scale the heights and join up with Richard Bullock's Chippewa army marching from the south. He led his army three miles inland around the heights where they were out of range and out of sight of the Lewiston batteries. He then sent the Indians ahead to clear the way of American infantrymen before scaling the hill to come up behind the captured redan and Van Rensselaer's hastily built fortifications. As soon as Bullock's force arrived, Shaeffe planned on a three-pronged attack that would force the Americans to the brow of the hill where they could be encircled. For the first time the British outnumbered the enemy with a force of

930 against 700. The American number was constantly and rapidly being depleted by desertion due to the threat of capture by the Indians.

In the face of the impending assault, being outnumbered and with ammunition running low, Van Rensselaer was certain that his force would be overcome unless it was reinforced. With no wish to become a prisoner of the British, he decided to return to Lewiston and try to raise a force from among the militia who had hitherto avoided the battle. His difficulties were just beginning. As soon as he boarded a boat to cross the river, it was deluged with deserters despite his threats and warnings, and was in danger of being swamped by the weight of the fleeing "skulkers."

Van Rensselaer's departure left Scott in charge with Chrystie and William Wadsworth as his deputies. Scott was now forced to abandon his unfinished fortifications and retreat to the edge of the cliff where he planned to make a stand until reinforcements arrived. A barricade of sorts was put up using fence rails, logs, and brush with a single field gun to defend against the two the British had hauled up the slope. In the meantime, a message from Van Rensselaer arrived stating that he had been unable to rally a single regiment or even a company to the cause. He assured Scott, however, that he was sending a supply of ammunition and that if evacuation became necessary he would do his best to see that there would be sufficient boats on hand and that the Lewiston batteries would cover the retreat. However, Holcroft's deadly artillery fire from Queenston village blasted anything that moved on the river and the boatmen refused to attempt any further crossings. This would leave Scott's force high and dry, and he was already in deep trouble.

The British attack got off to a blazing start with a company of regulars, 35 militia, and a party of Indians firing a single volley then charging through the musket smoke with fixed bayonets straight at the Americans' right flank. It quickly caved in and Shaeffe gave the order for a general advance. Giving the Indian war whoop, the entire line fired a volley, which forced the Americans to the very brink of the cliff.

With a quick pincer movement, the British squeezed the American troops into a pocket from both flanks and captured their sole cannon. It was all over. Chrystie and Wadsworth surrendered along with 300 of their officers and men. Scott and a number of others ran down the hill, some to the landing as well as to the river bank, in the hope of finding boats waiting. When they realized the situation was hopeless, some of the more desperate decided to swim for it. Most drowned in the attempt. The remainder sought refuge in rock crevices and other cover. Meanwhile the Indians, lining the cliff above and perched in trees, kept up a steady fire on the fugitives below, all the while shrilling their war whoops. Realizing that he now had no alternative, Scott raised the white flag in surrender.

It was then nearly 4:30 in the afternoon: the battle had lasted over 12 hours. At first, Scott's surrender had failed to curtail the Indians who continued their rain of fire on the Americans. Shaeffe was furious. He threw his sword and hat on the ground in a rage and cursed and swore until his allies were finally restrained. There, on the spot, 390 Americans were taken prisoner. Some stayed hidden for some days before being hunted down or giving themselves up. When all the stragglers had been taken, the tally in prisoners had reached 958, including a general, five lieutenant colonels, four majors, 19 captains, and 45 other officers. British losses, exclusive of the Indians who suffered five killed and nine wounded, amounted to 14 killed, 77 wounded, and 21 missing. American losses included three captains and three subalterns killed, two colonels, four captains, and four subalterns wounded. One company alone lost 30 men killed or wounded, and four of the five captains of that regiment were disabled by wounds. Among the prisoners were 120 wounded, 30 of whom died. That was regrettable but could not be helped; British medical facilities were taxed to the limit. The hospital at Niagara was filled and the courthouse and church had to be requisitioned to handle the overflow.

The American defeat at Queenston had been a total and absolute disaster; a major blow to the country's war effort. For Van Rensselaer it spelled disgrace. He had lost all his best officers, the flower of his troops, and the entire force had been irretrievably destroyed, rendering it incapable of resuming operations in the field. Ten days after the surrender, Van Rensselaer bitterly resigned his command in despair.

Shaeffe could probably be called the man of the hour. He had astutely appraised the situation and his strategy and tactics were first-class, assuring the success that resulted. Where he could be faulted — and was officially censured for it — was in his failure to follow through. The way was wide open to capture Fort Niagara, which had been all but abandoned by British shelling that afternoon, and go on and seize the upper half of New York State. It is certain that that is exactly what Brock, who was the martyr of the battle, would have done.

Brock's body was brought to Newark (Niagara-on-the-Lake) where it lay in state for three days. He was buried on Queenston Heights close to where he fell. Today a 126-foot monument, begun in 1824, stands on the site, which is visited by an estimated 100,000 people annually.

The British victory has been called the most important battle ever fought on Canadian soil. It did not win the war, which went on for another two years, but it was a serious blow to American morale from which they never recovered. It gave Canada its first sense of nationalism.

5

LES VOLTIGEURS EN VICTOIRE

The seeds of separation were sown early. Less than half a century had passed since the Peace of Paris formalized the transfer of New France to Great Britain in 1763 before there emerged the first real deterioration of relations between English and French Canadians. Not language, not citizens' rights, not racism and not religion really. But taxes — taxes with a capital "T"!

In 1810, when Charles d'Irumberry de Salaberry returned to Canada a hero, as aide-de-camp to Lieutenant General Francis Baron de Rottenburg, after serving with the British Army in Europe, the issue of taxation that had precipitated a rift between the two factions quickly became a political nightmare. The merchants and entrepreneurs, who were primarily English-speaking, dominated the Lower Canadian Executive Council. They argued that taxes should be based on land. The landowners, being chiefly French-speaking, held the majority in the Legislative Assembly. They demanded that taxation be based on imports. The short-sighted, ill-chosen British governor of Canada, Sir James Craig, failed to recognize the conflict as an economic one. Instead, he pig-headedly insisted on treating it as a racial issue. On the advice of English extremists, his answer to the problem was to dissolve the assembly on May 15, 1809 and call an election. When the new assembly shared the same views as its predecessor, Craig, in late February, 1810, dissolved it as well. At the same time he also dismissed a number of French Canadians from government and militia positions. When the newspaper *Le Canadien* censured these actions, Craig had the publisher and editors thrown in jail without trial. One of the victims of Craig's policy was de Salaberry's father, Louis, who lost his government position along with his pension.

Craig's bigotry and lack of understanding created a crisis that caused a sharp division between French and English. With the Americans on the verge of invading the country, the last thing needed was a domestic squabble. If Canada was to be properly defended, unity and solidarity, above all, were of paramount importance. In June 1811 the British government replaced Craig with Sir George Prevost, a British army general.

With war clouds on the horizon, the new governor's first concern was to court French-Canadian loyalty. To achieve that, he needed someone who could command the respect of French-speaking Canada. Though they harboured a strong dislike for one another (as a recruiting officer in England, de Salaberry had stepped on Prevost's toes by enticing men away from the latter's regiment for his own) he wisely accepted the recently returned French Canadian hero's proposal to form a special unit made up of Canadians to bolster his flagging garrison. It was a logical, as well as a judicious decision.

At age 34, de Salaberry had already carved out a distinguished and impressive military career. He had first seen action in the West Indies where he came to the attention of the Duke of Kent, whose protégé he became, and who had him transferred to his own regiment. De Salaberry was next assigned to recruiting duty in Halifax, Nova Scotia, before returning to the Caribbean. In 1804 he was posted to England where he again engaged in recruiting. Then, after a period of duty in Ireland, hc fought in the Walcheren Island-Flushing expedition in Holland. Of his skill as a soldier and conduct as an officer, one of his commanders once wrote:

> He is a young man of distinguished bravery and he will make an excellent officer because he has a dedication to honour engraved in his soul.

Here was a man whom the French-Canadians could look up to with confidence. On April 1, 1812, Prevost assigned de Salaberry as Lieutenant Colonel to form his special infantry corps, the Les Voltigeurs Canadiens (Rovers). Armed with light muskets and knives, they wore slate grey uniforms, hooded tunics with black cuffs and buttons, red sashes, short boots, and light bearskin caps. Made up of Canadian officers who had served with de Salaberry's British regiment, the rank and file were *habitants* loyal to Lower Canada. Under de Salaberry's demanding tutelage — he was known as a harsh, but fair, disciplinarian — the unit was drilled in the North American style of backwoods fighting. Ordinary infantry maneuvers were enhanced with emphasis on flexibility, mobility and, in particular, sharpshooting. By September, 1813, the Voltigeurs, 500 strong, had been turned into an elite, hardened, cohesive outfit raring for a fight. It was not to be denied them for long.

The threat to Montreal had begun on July 23. Kingston in Upper Canada had originally been the Americans' proposed main target, but its strong defences mitigated against it. As General John Armstrong, the American Secretary of War, put it in his report to President James Madison:

> At Montreal, however, we find the weaker place, the smallest force to encounter...you hold a position which completely severs the enemy's lines of operations and which, while it restrains all below, withers and perishes all above itself.

The campaign to capture Montreal involved two American armies. One under Major General James Wilkinson, consisting of 7,000 men, was to march on the city via the St Lawrence valley. The second, commanded by Major General Wade Hampton, planned to cut through the Champlain Valley and join up with Wilkinson's force just south of the city.

Together they represented the largest force the Americans had yet fielded during the war; its size — 13,000 men — was staggering in the face of the Lower Canadian defence of less than 1,000. If the invaders reached their objective, Montreal would be forced to capitulate and the war would be lost.

Prevost had summoned all available militia to join the garrison force. But this did little to strengthen the defences overall. While some areas, such as Coteau-du-Lac, at the Beauharnois Channel, were reinforced, other positions were weakened by the various redeployments. But de Salaberry hit on a ruse that prevented the enemy from knowing how fragile the defences really were, and at the same time hoodwinked the Americans into believing that a far larger force existed than was actually the case. By marching his troops from one salient point to another, like Chambly to Plattsburg, New York, for example, he not only achieved both objectives, but boosted civilian morale in the area by giving the populace a look at the defenders.

Wade Hampton made his move on September 9. Ten days later he had moved his entire army across Lake Champlain from Burlington, Vermont to Plattsburg, New York, where he established a supply base. This move caught Prevost off guard: he'd expected a thrust north. Convinced that Hampton would now move further west to join up with James Wilkinson, he left General Roger Shaeffe in charge of Montreal, and proceeded to Kingston where he was now sure the attack would come. But Hampton had advanced north instead, though it was a wasted effort. By late September the streams and small rivers had run dry and even the Lacolle River was low. This bothered de Salaberry; he was afraid that this gave the Americans greater freedom of movement now that the waterways no longer constituted natural defence barriers. To the contrary, Hampton worried about the lack of water supply. He got as far as Odelltown then decided to pull back. His army retired to Chazy. Then on September 23 they began a march to Four Corners on the upper reaches of the Chateauguay River inside New York State which they reached three days later. After establishing camp they began improving the road to the supply base at Plattsburg.

When de Salaberry learned of Hampton's move west, he took most of his force to the area around St Martine in the Chateauguay Valley. On the way he set up pickets to keep the lines of communication open and to prevent incursions by enemy patrols. On the north bank of the river he set up his headquarters in a newly built stone tavern from where he directed an operation of constant harassment.

Already frustrated from lack of food and other supplies due to delays in deliveries from Plattsburg, and the light summer uniforms they wore in the cold fall weather, the Voltigeurs, with the help of some Indians, added to the Americans' discomfort by carrying out sniping night raids. These frightened the American sentries so badly they built small blockhouses for refuge and refused to venture out in the dark. This intimidation came to a head when Prevost ordered de Salaberry to attack the enemy with 200 soldiers and a band of Indians. Considering the strength and nature of the American fortified camp, this was downright suicidal. In his personal correspondence to his wife, the former Marie-Anne de Rouville, de Salaberry suggested that Prevost seemed to be trying to get rid of him or, at the very least, having him discredited.

However, orders were orders, and on the afternoon of October 1, de Salaberry led what was supposed to be a surprise raid. But as they cautiously approached the fortification, one of the Indians prematurely opened fire on a sentry, which alerted the camp. Without wasting a minute, de Salaberry led one company of Voltigeurs and the Indians through the outer defences. However, the Americans quickly rallied and tried to outflank their attackers. This was not the Indians' style of fighting and they backed off. Twice de Salaberry brought them back, but finally, along with most of the Voltigeurs, they made off. That left de Salaberry and three others to fend for themselves against an American counter-attack. They managed to hold them off until dusk when they were able to slip back through the enemy lines and join the others, who had escaped earlier. That night the party camped in the woods, some four miles away. De Salaberry determined to renew the assault at first light, but the Indians refused to participate. Without them, he knew, the force would be too small for a second attempt. The group returned to their own camp down a cart track on the bank of the Chateauguay River, along which they blocked the road with felled trees as they went.

De Salaberry sensed that an American attack was imminent. He anticipated that Hampton would advance to the north through the Chateauguay Valley and he began shoring up his defences. In addition to blocking the road, he destroyed bridges, and set up advance posts at two points, La Fourche where the English River flows into the Chateauguay, and at a junction where the Outarde joins it. At a bend in the Chateauguay River was a ravine which ran at right angles to the main road, where some cleared land made an open field of fire. De Salaberry established a line of log fortifications on each side of the river, with the strongest line to the south. This site was protected by a large swamp wood to the south, where Indians and buglers — for noise to suggest a large force — would be placed. This was the setting from which de Salaberry would make his stand.

On October 16, Hampton received instructions from Secretary of War John Armstrong to "approach the mouth of the Chateauguay, or other point which shall better favour our junction, and hold the enemy in check." Five days later he began his march northward, without 1,500 of his militia who, exercising their constitutional rights, refused to "fight on foreign soil."

It took several days to clear the obstacles on the cart road set up by the Voltigeurs, before an advance party, led by Brigadier General George Izard, reached a clearing in the woods near the Outarde junction defended by an outpost of Canadians and Indians who eluded capture and were able to report the arrival of the Americans to their commanding officer, Major William Henry of the Beauharnois Sedentary Militia.

When word reached de Salaberry, he immediately sent a detachment upriver to the site he had chosen for his defence line. Next morning he arrived himself with more troops and two companies of his Voltigeurs. After occupying the ravine, they built an abatis, a log entanglement, in advance of their position. Meanwhile, the Americans had brought up their artillery after having spent two days clearing the road. By blocking it, de Salaberry had bought himself the time he needed to consolidate his defences. He also kept his men moving from one position to another to give the illusion of new units constantly joining him. Hampton reported to Armstrong that ''the enemy is hourly adding to his strength.''

Actually, confronted with Hampton's overwhelming army of 7,000, on the front line de Salaberry's force numbered between 400 and 500 Voltigeurs and about 150 Indians, but no artillery. Unknown to Hampton, in the rear, Colonel ''Red George'' Macdonell commanded the reserves of some 1,200 men he had brought up from Kingston.

Hampton's plan was to push his men through the swamp and bush on the south side of the Chateauguay River to the shallows at a bend in the river for an attack on the Canadians' left flank with the objective of driving in behind the Voltigeurs, while the main body engaged in a frontal assault. On the night of October 26, Colonel George Purdy set off with 1,500 infantrymen to carry out the flanking manoeuvre. Once they opened fire, it would be the signal for the main attack to begin. But by the next dawn, under overcast skies, they found themselves bogged down in the bush and swampland on the Chateauguay river bank, still a good distance from the Canadian abatis.

On the north side of the river, George Izard, who was to lead the frontal assault with a force of 5,000, anxiously awaited the sound of musketry from the opposite river bank. Hearing none, he sent an advance guard forward to reconnoitre. At approximately 10:00 a.m. the detachment came into view along the cart track and there was a sharp exchange of shots with Voltigeur and Fencible sentries. When Izard moved his main column forward the sentries retired to the abatis. Hampton's army was now only 35 miles short of its objective of Montreal. But he hesitated, still waiting for the signal from Purdy.

At 11:00, Purdy's advance guard finally reached the shallows where they fired on Captain Joseph-Bernard Brugiere's Chateauguay Chausseurs. Facing two infantry companies with only 40 men, Brugiere was soon forced to retire until reinforcements, two companies under Captain Charles Daly and Captain Georges de Tonnacour, arrived. Then with 90 men strong, they forced Purdy's companies to retreat.

Climbing a tree to survey the situation de Salaberry sized it up at a glance. The enemy was divided. Then and there he decided on two plans of action: to concentrate on the Americans' right flank, already in disarray, and to sound bugles from all four quarters on the field to create the impression that Hampton faced a considerably larger force than actually existed. This illusion was further exaggerated when Purdy's troops saw Macdonell's reserves for the first time. At this point an American officer on horseback rode forward and called upon the Canadians to surrender. Standing on a tree stump from which he would direct the battle, de Salaberry shot him dead. That shot was generally credited with being the first of the battle.

Izard's men now made a determined attack. It was swift and they were certain that they had been within reach of victory. Then the bugles sounded the charge from what seemed like every direction, and the Indians began their bloodcurdling war whoops and started sniping from behind the abatis, and from trees and in the woods. At the same time, the outnumbered Voltigeurs began delivering volley after volley into the American ranks. Hampton was now convinced that he not only faced a far superior force to his own but that they were on the verge of being decimated. A message from Purdy that he too was being besieged by superior numbers only served to reinforce that impression.

Actually Purdy had put up a brave fight, but his detachment was no match for the determined offense led by Brugiere and Daly. The Americans fled into the woods or surrendered. Finally Purdy decided to withdraw across the river to join Izard who had abandoned any further attack. After holding a council of war, Hampton decided to try and preserve the status quo and began a withdrawal the next morning.

It was far from orderly. De Salaberry's Voltigeurs and Indians, in pursuit, came upon discarded knapsacks, muskets, ammunition drums, provisions, shovels, and personal supplies, symbols of a disillusioned, defeated army in retreat. On October 29, the force reached Piper's Road where the army made camp. Harassed all night by the

Canadians and Indians, next morning they crossed the border back into the United States.

For Lower Canada, it had been an incredible victory. At odds of nearly 12 to one, de Salaberry had shown himself to be a brilliant tactician and strategist, and brave to boot. But his father had serious second thoughts about his son directing the fighting from a tree stump, which the younger de Salaberry called his "wooden horse." Following the battle, his father wrote him:

> I acknowledge that there couldn't be a firmer and steadier mount under fire but withstanding that I would advise and earnestly beg you to choose another horse. Perched on that you are only making a target of yourself. To face danger is worthy of a man of your character; but one need not look for opportunities to do it. You are I believe the first general to win battle while mounted on a stump. Believe me, change your mount!

Hampton's threat to Montreal had been defeated. But James Wilkinson's substantial army of 7,000 still remained in the field and was on its way down the St Lawrence to Montreal when, on November 11, it was attacked from the rear by an 800-man British force, which included three companies of Voltigeurs, commanded by Lieutenant Colonel Joseph Morrison at John Crysler's farm near Morrisburg. Morrison drove the Americans from the battlefield but failed to block their way to Montreal. However, next morning, when Wilkinson learned of Hampton's defeat, he decided to retire to winter quarters on the American side of the river.

Chateauguay was important for a number of reasons, not the least of them being that it prevented Hampton from joining up with Wilkinson. Had that happened, Montreal would have been easily captured and, when the St Lawrence froze over, all Canada in likelihood would have fallen to the American army of 14,000. Even more significant was the fact that the Union Jack was kept flying by a French-Canadian patriot and a few hundred of his comrades. Paradoxically, a recently conquered people had defended itself against the self-styled liberators. Charles de Salaberry's victory saved Canada from an early national death.

The war continued for another year and ended with the signing of the Treaty of Ghent on Christmas Eve, 1814. By its terms, all captured territories were returned to Britain — except one, Carleton Island, which in 1812 had a small caretaker garrison. A boatload of Americans rowed out from Millen's Bay, seized it, and declared the island a part of the State of New York, which it remains to this day.

Close to the site, an obelisk memorial commemorates the Battle of Chateauguay. But there is a legend surrounding that epic that has much more striking symbolic significance to Canadian history, though it is little known and seldom told. During the pre-battle training, de Salaberry had stressed the importance of camouflage to his Voltigeurs. To implement it he had branches cut from the maple trees in the Chateauguay Valley. He showed his men how to conceal themselves with sprigs of maple leaves stuck in the straps of their caps, their knapsacks and other accoutrements. It was more than just a lesson in disguise, however. While it no doubt saved many a life, it also represented the first appearance of a badge for which Canada became known throughout the world. At Chateauguay the maple leaf had been a symbol of victory. But it soon became recognized as ''our emblem dear'' by all Canadians.

✹ 6 ✹

BLOODY SUNDAY & MAJUBA DAY

Curs — who get a chance to bayonet human beings for 50 cents a day and the chance to get a piece of metal with a V.C. stamped on it.

Canadian labour press

Canadian now stands for bravery, dash and courage
Field Marshal Lord Roberts
British Commander-in-Chief, South African War

Reference map "The South African War."

Resplendent in their distinctive dark green serge uniforms with white cross belts and straps, and wearing white pith helmets on which a badge with a crown superimposed on a maple leaf and Canada marked below, clearly distinguished them from their imperial confrères. Before noon on the cool autumn day of October 30, 1899 the 1,009 men of the 2nd (Special Service) Battalion, Royal Canadian Regiment of Infantry, led by a pipe band, paraded proudly and smartly onto the Esplanade in Quebec City. There, standing rigidly at attention before a crowd of 50,000, many of them friends and relatives, they were inspected by the governor general of Canada, Lord Minto, who afterwards addressed them, as did Prime Minister Sir Wilfrid Laurier, the premier of the province, the mayor of the city, and a host of other civic dignitaries. It was mid-afternoon before the departure ceremonies ended and the First Canadian Contingent began its final march through the winding streets of the old town onto the Allan wharf to board the freighter-cum-troopship *Sardinian* bound for Cape Town. At 3:30 p.m., amidst the sounds of sirens, rockets, ships' whistles, and the cheering crowds, the Citadel's guns fired a 31-gun salute while two military bands struck up "God Save the Queen" to bid the troops farewell as the ship got under way. The wonder was that it set sail at all. Opposition to the venture had precipitated a national crisis.

When the Boer War, between the British and the two Afrikaner republics of South Africa and the Orange Free State, started on October 11, 1899, Canadian opinion was sharply divided over the question of sending troops to aid the British. Led by the Quebec nationalist leader, Henri Bourassa, French-Canadians, sensing growing British imperialism, sympathized with the Afrikaners. English-Canadians, with some notable exceptions, sided with the British. This was not entirely pro-English sentiment. In fact, the majority of Canadians, including politicians and the military, had very little, if any, understanding of what the war was all about or what had caused it.

The conflict between the British and the Dutch-speaking Afrikaners or Boers (farmers) in the Cape Colony had its roots extending back over a century. It was brought to a head in 1833 when the British Parliament abolished slavery which upset the Boers' economic structure, and sent them packing into the interior in search of better land, labour and freedom from British control. This resulted in the formation of the Orange Free State. For a while, the differences were social, ethnic, linguistic, legal, and cultural, but with the British discovery of diamonds in 1873 in the Transvaal, and gold a year later, the struggle turned into an economic one and war became inevitable.

These were hardly factors to appeal to a Canadian sense of patriotism or obligation to the mother country, however. But participation in the war was seen by English-speaking Canadians as an opportunity to demonstrate unity, strength, character, to shed the irksome colonial status and become a partner in imperial affairs. The country could also profit economically — manufacturing uniforms, equipment, and saddlery, for example. As the war propagandist Edward Biggar pointed out, "Canada has a strong commercial reason for seeing British ideals prevail in South Africa." Identity. Challenge. Purpose. All these views were strongly supported by the cosmopolitan daily press in Toronto, Montreal, Ottawa, Winnipeg, and elsewhere, and schools, churches, and volunteer organizations also exerted their influence for an early Canadian participation.

But the government sat on the fence. As early as July 1889, the Liberal government under Laurier, fearing a parliamentary defeat, refused to commit itself. The issue inevitably turned into a political football. The Montreal *Star* went so far as to write that Laurier was prevented from growing a beard only by a fear of ''betraying his sympathy for [Paul] Kruger (president of the Transvaal).'' Matters came to a head on October 13, two days after war broke out. During a stormy cabinet meeting a compromise was reached to avert a national crisis (in Montreal a riot between the French and English was narrowly averted). A public statement announced that the Canadian government would assist those wishing to serve the British in South Africa by recruiting, equipping, and transporting a ''certain number of volunteers by units of 125 men, with a few officers...the total force not to exceed 1,000 men.'' It was a step in the right direction but it did not go nearly far enough. Almost immediately, the cabinet reversed its decision to recruit small units for service in the British army, and instead decided on a Canadian contingent ''more worthy and representative'' of the country's size — five and a half million in population — and importance as Britain's senior dominion.

The regiment that evolved was one of 41 officers, 968 non-commissioned officers and men, and seven horses. It comprised two battalions, containing four companies each. Most of the volunteers were young, urban, low-paid clerks, grocers, bookkeepers, carpenters, machinists, painters, plumbers, blacksmiths, and electricians. Only a handful, among the permanent officers, had seen combat and this was marginal — in the North West Rebellion and during the Fenian Raids. Lieutenant Colonel William ''Plain Bill'' Otter, the officer commanding Military District 2, was placed in command. His orders were to shepherd the contingent to Cape Town where it would be placed under the jurisdiction of the British. He was free to return to Canada or seek an imperial appointment. But it had been firmly established that the men of the contingent were not British army recruits but on temporary service in the permanent Canadian militia. Any administrative difficulties between the British and Canadians that could not be settled in the field were to be referred to the Canadian government which would communicate with the British government.

Ironically Otter did everything he could to make his contingent conform to British standards. Ambitious and a stickler for detail and discipline, he saw the South African War as a means of furthering his career, in particular an imperial appointment and, who knows, in time, perhaps a knighthood. In the meantime he had no intention of giving up his command; he needed it as a stepping stone. His demeanour and behaviour in pursuit of this ambition did nothing to win him the respect and amity of his officers and men.

By the time *Sardinian* reached Cape Town the British Army had suffered a series of setbacks. During the first six weeks of the war, before British arms and men arrived in force, the Boers had run roughshod over their enemies culminating in what became known as "Black Week." Between December 10 and 15, the Boers routed the British at Stormberg, massacred them at Magersfontein, and defeated the troops of Britain's commander-in-chief in South Africa, General Sir Redvers Buller at Colenso. Shaken and disillusioned over his failure to relieve the fortress at Ladysmith, "Reverse" Buller, as he was labelled shortly afterwards, ordered its surrender. The fall of this prestigious symbol of British fortitude and resistance brought about his instant dismissal and he was replaced by Lord Roberts whose son had been killed at Colenso.

Meanwhile the Canadians were greeted and fêted royally at Cape Town before boarding a train to take them north the day after their arrival. On December 3, after an arduous, uncomfortable journey, they reached De Aar, a small village in a red-sand desert depression surrounded by flat-topped hills. They had no sooner made camp when a vicious sandstorm hit that confined them to their tents. On December 7, they were on the move again, this time to Orange River Station, known as the "Dust Bin of Creation," to relieve a Scottish battalion. That had not been Otter's intention; he wanted to take his regiment further north to join Lord Methun's forces on the Modder River. But after a heated discussion, Major Lawrence Buchan, his second in command, and two imperial officers, had talked him out of it. A lucky thing they had, for it spared the Canadians the massacre of Magersfontein.

On December 9, the contingent moved 20 miles north to Belmont but their hopes of seeing combat were soon dashed. Belmont proved to be merely a tertiary base as far as the battle was concerned. Otter was given command of the 1,800-man camp, but it was an on-again, off-again assignment. Time after time he was subordinated to a British commander. For the Canadians, this at least fulfilled their aspirations of tasting some action.

On the last day of 1899, led by Lieutenant Colonel Thomas Pilcher, a flying column set out from Belmont on a foray against Boers raiding positions and homes in the vicinity of Douglas 40 miles to the northwest. The detachment, which combined infantry, mounted infantry and artillery, included C Company of the First Canadian detachment under Major Buchan and Captains Robert Barker and Stephen Denison. Next day they found the enemy at Sunnyside Kopje (flat-topped hill) midway between Belmont and Douglas and immediately laid down a heavy artillery barrage. The Boers retreated to the summit and returned accurate rifle fire. In the end they pulled back in typical guerrilla fashion, spreading out and disappearing into the countryside, making it impossible to follow them. It had been a brief skirmish that accomplished little but it exhilarated the Canadians. They had been bloodied for the first time and were filled with confidence. But that was the only plus side to their tour of duty at Belmont.

From the beginning they had to fight boredom and illness. Most suffered from dysentery and the heat was appalling. But far more serious was an epidemic of typhoid that accounted for more deaths than did battle casualties for the entire war. The continual revolving of commanding officers created confusion over battle tactics. One CO favored mobility, the next concentration, another believed in holding patterns, and so it went. Punishment meted out by Otter for even the slightest infraction or violation of military regulations was harsh. The men, even the officers, regarded it as both galling and unfair and they resented it. It did not help either that the men had to supplement their meagre food rations at their own expense. Otter refused to allow a canteen to be built because he believed, quite wrongly, that it was against military rules. Belmont was a highly unhappy situation. But relief, of a sort, was not far away.

On February 8, 1900, the new commander-in-chief, Lord Roberts, together with his chief of staff, Lord Kitchener of Khartoum, visited the camp. After inspecting an honour guard, he announced that the Canadians were to become part of the 19th Brigade under General Horace Smith-Dorrien. A veteran of the Zulu War and two Egyptian campaigns, he was regarded as one of Britain's best field commanders in South Africa. He quickly became popular with the men of the Royal Canadian Regiment. Two days after Roberts' visit, Smith-Dorrien arrived at Belmont and ordered the Canadians to move to his brigade camp at Graspan, seven miles away, where they joined three British battalions: the Duke of Cornwall's Light Infantry, the King's Own Shropshire Light Infantry, and the Gordon Highlanders. From there they trudged to the front at Ramdam in intolerable heat of between 100° and 114°F. The first Canadian Contingent was about to become embroiled in its bloodiest battle of the war.

The military offensive for which they began to prepare formed part of a master plan to turn things around. Unlike Buller's strategy of fighting on three fronts to encircle the Boers, which only ended in a holding battle, Roberts and Kitchener wanted to drive their army deep into enemy territory. Now outnumbering the Boers by five to one, they were in an ideal tactical position to do just that.

By concentrating their force on the northern Cape front and striking at the Boer capitals of Bloemfontein and Pretoria, their objective was to drive a wedge into the heart of the republics forcing the enemy to withdraw to protect their cities and allow the British to relieve their fortresses of Ladysmith, Kimberly, and Mafeking, all under siege. In this way they hoped to draw the outnumbered Boers into a decisive knockout battle in which the British held all the numbers. By choosing the north-east front, however, they had to abandon the single-track rail line and march their men overland towards Bloemfontein. Roberts reckoned it was worth the price. Boer General Piet Cronje, his opponent, calculated that the British had made a strategic misjudgement. He intended to take advantage of it.

At Ramdam the 19th Brigade was joined by Major General Hector MacDonald's 3rd Highland Brigade to form the 9th Division under General Sir Henry Colville. With it were the 6th and 7th Infantry divisions, a cavalry division, an artillery corps and naval guns: all told a force of 37,000 men. Opposing Roberts' invading force, Cronje had only 12,000 men at his disposal, 1,600 of them mounted, a small but elite, determined band. Typically encumbered by growing numbers of women and children, he entrenched at the notorious Magersfontein between the railway line and the Modder River with the objective of blocking the road to Kimberly. Cronje was convinced that the British, so far from the railway line, posed no great threat and would not survive for long. He scoffed at the suggestion of his subalterns that he take a more aggressive stance.

Now Roberts made his move. At 4:00 a.m. on St Valentine's Day, the Canadians began marching to Waterval Drift, a watering hole on the Riet River 13 miles north-west of Ramdam. When they reached it they spent the next three hours hauling the 4.7-inch naval guns across the river.

Early next morning they were again on the move, this time to Wegdreal Drift, nine miles along the east bank of the Riet. Meanwhile Christiaan de Wet, one of Cronje's generals, attacked Roberts' supply depot left behind at Waterval Drift, capturing a third of the wagons, forcing Roberts to put his men on half-rations. In retaliation, on the morning of February 16, the Canadians captured the Boer supply base at Jacobsdal.

That evening the contingent joined with the British advance guard build-up at Klip Drift along the Modder River, only ten miles from Cronje's laager (encampment). Now that the cavalry, under Major General Sir John French, had freed Kimberly to the north the day before, Roberts had not only demonstrated his ability to survive and manoeuvre without the rail line, but his forces now threatened to cut Cronje's communications and supplies from the Transvaal and Orange Free State, and surround him. But the wily Boer general was far from being counted out.

After midnight on February 16, Cronje led a caravan of 400 wagons and 5,000 women and children, many of them barefoot, across the British front at Klip Drift. Forty-eight hours later he had reached Paarderberg Drift, 21 miles to the east. Now, positioned between the British and Bloemfontein, Cronje planned to halt their advance on the Orange Free State capital.

By next day both sides were girding for the inevitable fight. French's cavalry had moved down from the north-west and installed itself at Paardeberg where it was joined by the 6th Infantry Division. Only 14 hours after arriving at Klip Drift, the 19th Brigade continued on its way to Paardeberg. Early in the morning of February 18, a date to become known to Canadians as "Bloody Sunday," as they neared the drift they could hear the crackle of rifle fire. Kitchener, who took command when Roberts became ill and had to be left behind at Jacobsdal, was certain he had Cronje trapped and decided to storm the Boer defenses at daybreak, overcome any resistance in short order, then go on to capture Bloemfontein the same day. His senior officers argued that this would create unacceptable losses and urged caution, a sustained bombardment, and a wait for surrender. Cronje's laager, north of the Modder, and the Boers themselves, were more formidable than Kitchener had calculated. Surrounded by trenches and set among trees, the ox wagons and the women and children were sheltered on the dry river bed below. A strong defensive position, a donga (gully), lay two miles to the west. On the other side of the laager were more posts stretching for three miles to the east, capable of pouring out deadly low trajectory fire. But Kitchener, who made his headquarters directly south, asserted confidently: "It is now seven o'clock. We will be in the laager at half past ten, then I'll load up French and send him on to Bloemfontein." Brave words, that were to cost the Canadians dearly.

Kitchener's plan was to attack from the east and west on both sides of the river. He also ordered a frontal attack from the south. That assault got off to a bad start when accurate enemy rifle fire soon pinned down the infantry from the 6th Division and, as casualties mounted, the advance ground to a halt 300 yards from the river bank. In the east the troops were attacked from the rear by several hundred Boers who had arrived from Bloemfontein with two field guns. The British drove them off into the hills near Stinkfontein but it diverted the men from the pincer movement that Kitchener had envisaged.

In the west, the Highland Brigade on the south side of the river, the Royal Canadian Regiment and the Duke of Cornwall's Light Infantry on the north bank, began their attack at 8:00 a.m., but by 10:30 the northern troops had become bogged down in a stalemate. The Canadians had advanced to within 400 yards of the Boers' deadly fire. It was impossible to go any further. By noon the detachment had been reinforced by four companies but, due to the accuracy of the enemy's rifles, all unnecessary movements were halted. The men were forced to endure not only bullets from the Boer sharpshooters, but scorching sun, ants and flies, thirst and hunger. Then abruptly, late in the afternoon, an icy cold rainstorm brought them relief, but only temporarily. The sun soon returned.

Some men fell asleep from utter exhaustion. But there was no rest for the ammunition carriers and stretcher-bearers. Private John Kennedy spent all day driving his cart back and forth between the rear and the firing line. His mule was finally shot out from under him and Kennedy himself was badly wounded. Five stretcher-bearers were injured, three of them while carrying a company captain from the front line. The battalion's medical officer, Eugene Fiset, the "little French doctor," eventually rescued the captain, though the man died five days later.

At 4:00 p.m. Lieutenant Colonel William Aldworth's Duke of Cornwall's Light Infantry arrived to bolster the Canadian force and break the stalemate; in the brash young Britisher's own haughty words, "to finish the business and go in with the bayonet." Otter bitterly resented Aldworth's contemptuous comment that the Canadians' failure to achieve their objective had been due to lack of courage and poor leadership. Actually, the impatient, impulsive Kitchener had been frustrated by the stand-off, and when he found the Cornwalls guarding some baggage, went into a rage and ordered three of their companies across the Modder to marshal an advance with the Canadians.

At 5:15, the Canadians and the Cornwalls began their charge. It was sheer murder. The fate of John Tod, Philippine War veteran, was typical. As he rushed forward shouting, "Come on boys this beats Manila all hollow," the Boers shot him dead. The arrogant Aldworth and his adjutant were also cut down by the murderous enemy rifle fire as were many others. All for a niggardly ground gain of less than 200 yards, and a temporary one at that.

When the bugle sounded the recall, most men were powerless to move, either too badly wounded or afraid of risking exposure to Boer sharpshooters. They had no choice but to wait until nightfall and the protection of the dark to try and withdraw. Time hung heavy and horrific. "It was a night which I will never forget," Private William Campbell wrote later, "to hear the groans and cries of the wounded on the battlefield." Private Fred Living remembered the sight of "men stretched out and dying and covered with blood." Gruesome as it seemed, it was also a night of heroics.

Private Richard Thompson risked his neck to go to the aid of his friend John Bradshaw who had been wounded in the throat. Lying beside him for seven hours he kept the fingers of one hand pressed against Bradshaw's throat to stop him from bleeding to death until stretcher-bearers arrived. It saved his comrade's life.

Eugene Fiset and Charles Hancock, a former Halifax druggist, disregarded the bullets flying about them, to circulate among the wounded and treat them. Their diligence in ignoring the danger to which they exposed themselves was credited with being responsible for the remarkably low death rate from fever and wounds among the injured. Father Peter O'Leary, the tireless regimental Catholic chaplain, gave comfort to the dying, and provided first aid to the wounded.

As soon as the Boer firing began to fizzle out, Otter gave the order to retire to the main drift for food and rest. Simultaneously the enemy began moving back into their laager. For the stretcher-bearers and those who helped them, gruelling work lay ahead, stumbling through the darkness in search of bodies and struggling over the bumpy, rocky terrain to carry the wounded from the battlefield.

Not since the War of 1812 had Canadians sustained such frightful battle losses. Twenty-one men died, 63 were wounded, ten so seriously they had to be shipped to military hospitals in England. Three-quarters of the casualties took place during that last furious assault that climaxed the day's fighting. "Bloody Sunday" marked the bloodiest engagement for Canada of the entire South African War, accounting for half of the country's total losses of 39 killed and 123 wounded.

Roberts was horrified over the day's losses: total casualties amounted to 1,262, the highest of any day's fighting of the war. Now, fully recovered and back in command, he pulled Kitchener up on the carpet. There would be no more charges. Over his second in command's protests he vetoed a renewed assault. Patience. Let the enemy sweat it out. Surrender must inevitably follow. A matter of time. The ensuing days were spent consolidating the British encirclement of the laager and were limited to sporadic firefights. The Boers remained intransigent, determined to hang in there.

Smith-Dorrien, the brigade commander and a master of goodwill relations, made a point of boosting the Canadians' sagging morale over the debacle of "Bloody Sunday." He praised them for their stoicism, their bravery, and appointed them to a new, more strategic command position from which they might avenge their defeat. At the base of Gun Hill they faced the Boer laager from the north, 1,000 yards away. As it turned out Smith-Dorrien's intentions, good, sympathetic, tactical or otherwise, spelled a frustrating, deadly stand-off.

Entrenched on the rolling terrain in advance of their new position, on February 20, bordered by the Gordon Highlanders on their right and the Shropshire Light Infantry on their left, the Canadians endured 12 hours of the Boers' unremitting rifle fire and shelling from their Vickers-Maxim "pom-pom" gun, firing a round a second. Fortunately the gunners' aim was off, and most of the time they overshot. But still, it was nerve-racking and, combined with the searing heat of the sun, ants, flies and thirst, it was a thoroughly unpleasant, discomforting experience. But, at least when they retired to their new camp at day's end, there had been no more suicide charges. Bitterly, however, the Canadians named the day "Pom-Pom Tuesday."

Next day they covered a barrage by British naval guns shelling the laager. Three days later, in rainy weather, they joined the rest of Smith-Dorrien's brigade at Outpost Hill, a large flat-topped summit to the west. Christiaan de Wet's detachment had been sent out to occupy the many small kopjes in the area to facilitate a possible escape from the encampment. The Outpost Hill position had been chosen to deny him such access. But the rains flooded the post and the brigade was forced to move to a drier campsite downstream from the Boer laager on the banks of the filthy Modder River. And it was about to become even more putrid.

Cronje had asked Roberts for doctors and a truce to allow the Boers to bury their dead and rid themselves of the horse and mule carcasses killed by the British shelling. But the British commander wasn't playing; he adamantly refused. He didn't trust the Boers and suspected trickery. Over the next 24 hours the Boers dumped over 700 animal carcasses and nearly 100 decomposing bodies into the river. As the corpses collected, creating a jam, the Canadians were given the nauseating task of poling them downstream. The stench was frightful and it was in this contaminated water that they had to wash themselves and their clothes and from which, lacking any alternative, they drew their drinking and cooking water. The regiment was down to 750 men since leaving Quebec, and now its survivors were plagued with a new threat — rampant outbreak of typhoid fever.

On February 26, the Canadians relieved the Cornwalls in the trenches circling Cronje's laager. Seven of the regiment's companies occupied the north shore of the river with the other company entrenched on the south bank. On the north side they were within 600 yards of the Boer lines, close enough to launch a final assault. That afternoon they skirmished with the enemy, exchanging rifle shots, nothing conclusive, in preparation for their assignment the next morning. For Lord Roberts, the date held a special significance. Nineteen years earlier he had been sent to South Africa to quell the rebellion. On February 28, 1881, the Boers had humiliated the British at Majuba Hill and secured recognition of independence for themselves.

But that was not the true reason for choosing this date for the *coup de main* on the Boer stronghold, opportune and coincidental though that was at the time. Deserters from the laager reported growing dissention and deterioration of morale within their ranks. Food supplies could only last another four days at the most. Ammunition was running dangerously low. Entrenchments near the river had become flooded. Living conditions had reached a nadir. Cronje's officers advocated surrender and urged him to escape. He would hear of neither. Learning all this, Roberts hesitated; he saw no reason to risk further casualties by delivering a knockout blow. He preferred to wait it out. But his senior officers convinced him that the time had come to strike, to get it over with. That the Canadians were to take a prominent, and dominant, part in the coming victory was pure happenstance. They were in the right place at the right time; it was their turn to man the front line.

Otter received his orders from Smith-Dorrien at three o'clock on the afternoon before the assault. Beginning at 2:00 a.m., six Canadian companies supported by the Gordon Highlanders, the Shropshire Light Infantry, and the Royal Engineers, were to lead the charge in the darkness with fixed bayonets.

Right on the dot, the men left their trenches in two lines, six paces apart, the first one at the ready, the second carrying picks and shovels, ready to dig trenches when and where needed. Cautiously advancing, they moved ahead uninterrupted and undetected, until they reached a point within 100 yards of the Boers' emplacement. There they were met by a deadly fusillade of rifle fire. Most of the Canadians threw themselves to the ground. Behind them, the Royal Engineers began digging in.

Two of the companies drew the brunt of the volleys. Casualties were heavy, 12 men killed, 36 wounded, all within the space of 15 minutes. Private Martin Quinn was wounded nine different times. By this time the Canadians had begun to retaliate. Then a shout was heard: "Retire and pick up your wounded" — from where and by whom was never established. Suddenly the Canadians' line broke and four of the companies fled for the safety of their trenches where they remained for the duration of the battle. That left only two companies in the forward position.

At dawn a cry went out for help from a stretcher-bearer. Private Richard Thompson dropped his rifle and, braving enemy fire, dashed 300 yards forward from the trenches but he was too late. By the time he reached him, the wounded man was dead, killed by another bullet. His commanding officer, Captain Maynard Rogers, along with Otter, recommended Thompson for the Victoria Cross but the commendation was turned down. Instead he received a Queen's Scarf knitted by Queen Victoria, which was awarded when a recommendation was refused.

The two forward companies, under the commands of Archie "Lighthouse" Macdonnell and Duncan Stairs, who somehow never heard the withdrawal order, or ignored it, continued to enfilade the Boer ranks throughout the night. But the Boers kept up a steady fire in return. Then the Canadian guns fell silent as the men moved to more protective terrain to the right and occupied trenches evacuated by the engineers. This completely fooled the Boers who were certain the Canadians had retired to the rear. At daylight, the Boers began emerging from the trenches to survey the success they mistakenly thought they'd achieved. When they were fully exposed, the men of the Royal Canadian Regiment let go with everything they had. It proved too much for the Boers. At six o'clock that morning an Afrikaner soldier marched forlornly out of the laager carrying a white flag. The Canadians had not only "wiped out the shame" of Majuba Hill, they had avenged it.

The 9th Division commander, General Henry Colville, arrived to accept the surrender of General Piet Cronje, accompanied by his wife, along with 4,069 Transvaalers and Orange Free Staters, including 150 wounded soldiers and 100 more wounded women and children; they were led into captivity.

Lord Roberts credited the Canadians with being "instrumental in the capture of Cronje and his forces," and praised them for their gallantry. "Canadian," he told them, "now stands for bravery, dash and courage." Congratulations poured in from Queen Victoria, members of the royal family, the Canadian high commissioner to the United Kingdom, Governor General Lord Minto, Prime Minister Laurier, and many others such as authorities of Canadian towns and cities, provincial legislators, commercial, patriotic, educational and volunteer organizations. When the victory was announced in the British House of Commons, the mention of Canada's part brought members to their feet. At home the news of the Canadian victory erupted in wild celebrations and press headlines across the nation.

This had been the Canadian Contingent's first battle, the most celebrated British victory and the turning point of the Boer War. Forgotten in the frenzied excitement of the moment was the fact that it was also the first battle, the very first victory that Canadians had ever fought, and won, on foreign soil. Canada had attained that military renown which was to earn her the respect of the world.

7

AN EVENT UNPRECEDENTED IN THIS WAR

Liliefontein was certainly no victory, not for the British at any rate. Nor had it any particular military significance. Simply a bitter rearguard action. Still it was indeed a strong contest of wills and for Canada the most spectacular feat of arms of the Boer War. General Horace Smith-Dorrien, under whom the Second Canadian Contingent served, called it ''an event unprecedented in this war.'' Three of the five Victoria Crosses awarded to Canadians for valour during the South African conflict were won on that bright November day in 1900. At the time, the regiment was part of Smith-Dorrien's force in the Transvaal to the north-east, pursuing Kitchener's distasteful scorched earth policy, putting farms to the torch, expelling women and children and interning them in concentration camps. This was a direct follow-up to the British victories at Bloemfontein, Ladysmith and Pretoria, aimed at crushing further Boer resistance. But it only served to stiffen their resolve. Enemy resistance at Liliefontein was illustrative of their determination to fight fire with fire.

The area under exploitation by the Canadians was the Carolina region south of Belfast. Large enemy commando forces controlled the territory which served as a Boer depot and a marshalling point for raids in every direction. With a strong force gathered at Belfast, Smith-Dorrien's objective was to clear it. The first attempt failed miserably, principally because of appalling weather, mist, driving winds, thunderstorms and torrential rains.

A week later under cover of darkness and, this time, in clear weather, on November 6, the Canadians set out again. Their aim was to destroy farms suspected of hiding rail saboteurs, and two enemy laagers, one at Witkloof and the other at Carolina itself. The advance guard led by British Lieutenant Colonel John Spens included the Royal Canadian Dragoons led by Captain Edward Morrison with two field guns, all under the command of Major Harold Lessard. The main column was made up of the Canadian Mounted Rifles, a Royal Engineers section, five companies from the Shropshire Light Infantry along with six field guns. Bringing up the rear were several other British units along with the supply wagons. All told, the column stretched six miles.

The Boers were ready and waiting, certain the British would return after their earlier debacle. Four miles out of Belfast they ran into the enemy forward posts. Gradually, however, they were able to force the Boers back to Van Wyk's Vlei. In this initial encounter Edward Morrison's field gunners made such a fine account of themselves, firing from 4,000 yards so accurately, that other artillery officers asked him to establish their range. Sergeant Major Edward "Eddie" Holland's work with his Colt machine-gun was also highly notable as he kept up a rapid fire. By noon the British had driven the Boers back to Witkloof. The Colt was a particularly effective weapon. So light, that one horse could drag it at full gallop, it could be kept in position until the very last minute and withdrawn quickly.

While this initial encounter took place, the Boers from the Carolina laager had been busy placing themselves strategically along a natural defense formed by a steep, rock ridge overlooking the Komati River between Witkloof and Liliefontein. As soon as the British approached the Boers let fly with deadly rifle fire. At first Lessard's Dragoons and the Shropshires were helplessly pinned down. But as soon as Morrison's field guns and Holland's Colt pulled within range, the situation changed dramatically. They silenced the Boers' fire so quickly that Smith-Dorrien personally congratulated Morrison, one of whose gunners, Bombardier William Hare, received a slight shoulder wound.

Now the infantry, supported by Morrison's "Cow" guns, tried to move up the ridge but were still unable to dislodge the stubborn defenders. At about 2:00 in the afternoon, Smith-Dorrien decided on a plan to cut the Boers off between the ridge and Liliefontein. He ordered the Dragoons and two companies of Suffolks, along with a pair of pom-pom guns and Morrison's Cows, south-west to block the

Carolina road. When they reached a point 5,000 yards away, the British guns opened up forcing the Boers to evacuate their stronghold. By 4:00 the first phase of the battle was over.

In the meantime the Canadian Mounted Rifles busied themselves with the nefarious practice of scorching the countryside and skirmishing with roving bands of Boers. Lieutenant Thomas Wroughton's troop burnt down farmhouses and stole horses and cattle. Captain James Begin's unit surrounded a house, ordered the inhabitants to leave, then torched it. The British commandeered adjoining farms at Liliefontein and Goedhoop within sight of the Komati River and in command of the Carolina road.

The Boers calculated that the British would cross the Komati and continue south to Carolina where they would counter-attack. That was exactly what Smith-Dorrien hoped they would believe. He had decided to return to Belfast. The foray had not been decisive enough for him to remain in the field. While he had sufficient supplies and twice the number of men, he lacked the Boers' mobility and being so extended, was vulnerable to being cut off. He sensed that the Boer attack would single out his supply wagons and his guns, so he assigned their protection to his advanced guard and to Morrison's Cows.

At 7:00 next morning, Smith-Dorrien, anxious to put as much distance as possible between his force and the Boers, broke camp. It was an hour before the enemy realized what was happening and they immediately resolved to make for the ridge they had occupied the day before. The Canadian Mounted Rifles raced to get there first, and won. From that vantage point, they kept up a steady rain of rifle fire, trapping 300 Boers below them in the river bed, until artillery could be brought up to force the enemy to seek shelter on the opposite side of the Komati. The CMRs maintained their position until the convoy had retired for two miles, then they abandoned it, joining the main column.

Meanwhile, Smith-Dorrien ordered Spens, with a company of Shropshires and a squadron of cavalry, ahead to seize the high ground at Van Wyk's Vlei, leaving the Dragoons, three companies of Shropshires and Morrison's two guns, to protect the rearguard. Lessard had divided his men into two groups of 30 each, one to the left, the other to the right, spread out in a semicircle along a ridge with Morrison's Cows and Holland's Colt in the middle. The plan was to withdraw in stages using various ridges along the way as defense lines.

As soon as the Mounted Rifles left for the main body, a force of 200 Boers, with reinforcements clearly in view, swarmed towards the rearguard. The British infantry were woefully slow reaching the next ridge, and this left the Dragoons and the gunners to ward off the enemy assault. On the right, Captain Hampden Cockburn and his troopers were soon in trouble. Lessard told Morrison to move one of his guns in support. Morrison raced across the ridge and began opening up on the attacking horsemen who were firing from the saddle. It quickly became obvious that the Boers were determined to seize his gun. Lessard ordered Morrison to save it at all costs.

Cockburn's troops now faced a virtual stampede of enemy cavalry. To buy time Cockburn threw the last of his men into the fray, a deliberate sacrifice. This allowed Morrison to rescue his gun and drag it to comparative safety. But in the mêlée, Cockburn was wounded and he and his men taken prisoner. For his valiant action Cockburn was later awarded the Victoria Cross.

Morrison still had his problems trying to get both of his guns away. His horses had become exhausted and slowed to a walk. The Boers seized on the opportunity to make a spirited attack to capture the guns. Now things had became desperate, and Morrison had no choice but to turn his foremost gun on the attackers. It slowed, but failed to stop them.

With Cockburn's troop wiped out, Morrison had counted on the rearguard protection of Eddie Holland and his Colt. At one point he feared that Holland had been taken out of action. But Holland had stood his ground, keeping the mounted Boers at bay from 200 yards until he ran out of ammunition. He then coolly unscrewed the still hot gun barrel, then calmly tucked it under his arm, mounted his horse, and rode off. He too won the VC for valour that day.

In the meantime, Morrison's gunners dismounted and his horses broke into a trot. Things were looking up but then one of the horses was wounded though still able to plod along. Worse still, they had nearly reached the ridge, when the British infantry broke ranks and ran. With the Boers getting ever closer, Morrison sent his lone escort, a Dragoon, to Lessard asking for help. But it never reached him. It would not have made any difference if it had.

The battle by this time had fallen into a state of confusion. Riderless horses charged about in all directions. Seeing that Corporal Percy Price had lost his mount and was hiding behind a rock, Private William Knisley ignored the enemy fire, rode out and put him on his horse behind him, although he himself was severely wounded. Following his rescue Price retrieved one of the riderless animals and rejoined the fight, only to have that horse killed under him as well.

Though suffering from a badly shattered arm, Major Richard "Dick" Turner knew how desperate the situation was. He gathered 12 of his Dragoons about him and ordered them to dismount. "Never let it be said that Canadians let their guns be taken," he exhorted them, and promptly set up an ambush. The Boers knew it was now or never if they were ever to capture the Canadian guns and rallied for one last, frantic do-or-die assault. As the Boers charged across the field at full gallop, firing from their saddles, they reminded the Canadians of a western rodeo. They had advanced no more than a few hundred yards when both Boer leaders were killed, one shot through the mouth, the other struck in the head. The Boer horsemen rode on, right through Turner's ambush making for Holland's Colt. What they found instead was an empty gun carriage which so infuriated them they set it on fire.

Without leadership, the Boers quickly became disoriented, disorganized and demoralized. By the time the Mounted Rifles arrived on the scene to lend support, the enemy attack had already been broken. It was all over by 2:00 p.m. leaving Smith-Dorrien free to withdraw his force, without further molestation, to Belfast.

For such bitter skirmishing losses had been extraordinarily light. This was due chiefly to the fact that mounted solders had more mobility than the infantrymen, and the protection of their mounts' forequarters made them difficult targets, as well as poor shots. Two Canadians were killed in the battle. Seven were wounded, including Turner who was again injured, in the neck, during the final charge. Two Boers were killed, both losses critical to the outcome, and four wounded. Dick Turner received the third VC awarded to a Canadian for valour that day. Edward Morrison was awarded the Distinguished Service Order for his work with the guns, and William Knisley, the Distinguished Conduct Medal, for rescuing his comrade Percy Price while under fire.

Altogether 7,368 Canadians served during the South African War which ended with the signing of the Peace of Vereeniging on May 31, 1902. Canada's participation gave the country a military maturity that resulted in the expansion and modernization of the army militia, including new armouries, rifle ranges and a large camp at Petawawa, Ontario. Canadians found a new perception of themselves and the country's place in the British Empire assumed a new and greater prominence. But the downside was that the war damaged relations between English and French Canadians. The bitterness created by the conflict erupted into a three-day riot in Montreal. Consequently, although it had sharpened English Canada's identity, it left a lot of distrust and resentment in its wake. In fact it launched the twentieth century French-Canadian nationalist movement and broke Sir Wilfrid Laurier's power in Quebec.

8

DISINFECTION

The manhood of Canada shone out like pure gold...
The Bishop of London

The Canadians saved the situation
Field Marshal Sir John French,
British Commander-in-Chief in France

As we walked to the edge of the village...we noticed a peasant planting seeds in the garden in front of his little house.... To our "How do you do," he replied: "It is a fine day," looking up at the sun with evident satisfaction.

As we tramped along towards St Julien our attention was attracted to clouds of greenish-yellow smoke ascending from the line occupied by the French. We wondered what the smoke could be coming from in such volume close to the firing line. We seated ourselves on a disused trench and looked about us....Rising along the French line we could see this yellowish-green cloud ascending on a front of at least three miles and drifting, at a height of perhaps a hundred feet, towards us.

"That must be the poison gas we have heard vague rumours about," I remarked. The gas rose in great thick clouds as if it had been projected from nozzles, expanding as it ascended. Here and there brown clouds seemed to be mixed with general yellowish-green ones.

"It looks like chlorine," I said, and the captain agreed that it probably was.

Colonel George Nasmith
Canadian Military Historian

Following a short period of indoctrination in the trenches in front of Armentieres in Flanders, France, on April 5, 1915, 20,000 troops of the First Canadian Division began marching north to take over part of the defense of the Ypres Salient in Belgium from a French division. After a thoroughly miserable winter spent on Salisbury Plain in southern England, where they had been plagued with flu as well as spinal meningitis, they considered themselves ready for anything. But nothing had, or could have, prepared these citizen-soldiers for the ordeal that lay directly ahead. Eight months earlier they had rallied to the colours with exuberant enthusiasm. The outbreak of war on August 4, 1914 promised adventure and excitement. It would give commerce a boost, and besides, the boys would be home by Christmas. On the Western Front, the boys soon learned differently.

The Great War found Canadians taken by surprise and the country wholly unprepared. Even by today's jet measurements, Sarajevo is still a long way from Ottawa. When, on June 28, that year, a Serbian nationalist in the Bosnian capital assassinated Archduke Franz Ferdinand, heir to the Austrian throne, few in the dominion could relate to, or foresee that, an incident that distant could trigger the chain of events that led to the alliance of Austria and Germany against Russia, France and England, and ultimately to a world conflict in which Canada would play an integral part.

Unlike the start of the Boer War, when the country had been split over the issue of participation, in 1914 there was almost complete unanimity that Canada should play a role. Four years earlier the then-prime minister, Sir Wilfrid Laurier, had said, "When Britain is at war, Canada is at war. There is no distinction." Although the regular army had only 3,100 men, within a matter of weeks thousands of young Canadians crowded recruiting centres across the country anxious to serve. Within two months a force, gathered at Valcartier near Quebec City, had swelled to 35,000, and two months after that, the First Division of the Canadian Expeditionary Force had sailed for England.

Meanwhile, on the continent, the Germans had struck hard in the west, intent on a quick victory. By following the Schlieffen Plan to cut off the French armies, they hoped to bring about an allied defeat that would free up their own armies to concentrate on crushing Russia which was still in the process of mobilizing. But after sweeping through Belgium between Liege and Namur and turning south into France, the juggernaut had slowed down. When the British and French counter-attacked, they stopped the enemy at the Marne River, 40 miles short of Paris. There now developed a race to outflank each other in an effort to capture the Channel ports. It ended in a draw on the sands of Nieuport.

The war quickly stagnated into a stalemate, one of attrition, with each side digging in opposite the other. A line of trenches now corroded the countryside, stretching from the Swiss border to the Belgian coast, fortified with barbed wire entanglements, machine-gun nests, mortar batteries and field guns. The area in between known as ''No Man's Land.''

On October 29, the Germans made a desperate attempt to break the deadlock and at the same time reach the Channel ports. Driven back by the ''Old Contemptibles,'' during the First Battle of Ypres, the bitter fighting around the 17-mile salient had cost the British dearly. But an even more horrific struggle was to be fought over the same ground. And the apocalyptic Second Battle of Ypres was to cost the three brigades of the First Canadian Division a third of its strength in casualties. In their first battle of the war, the Canadians were also about to experience the introduction of the vilest, most wicked weapon unleashed by one nation against another on a battle-field: poison gas. No one was ready for it, though it certainly should have come as no surprise. There had been plenty of warning.

There was nothing unique or new about chemical warfare. In 429 B.C., the Spartans attempted to capture Plataea by using clouds of sulphur fumes. In 1485, Belgrade was saved from the Turks by an alchemist who created a toxic cloud from burning chemicals. During the American Civil War the United States entertained proposals for liquid chlorine gas shells. In Canada the Department of Militia and Defence had been delving into the possibilities of gas warfare for some time. In November 1914 it suggested ''that tubes of CS/2 highly charged with cacodylcyanide be thrown to burst in the enemy's trenches.''

Early in the war the famous French spy, Charles Lucieto, had reported from the Ruhr and the Rhineland that the Germans were producing poison gas at two Mannheim factories. Despite his reliable reputation, the French high command dismissed his report out of hand.

On March 28, 1915, a German officer captured by the British near the Zillebeke Salient southeast of Ypres, signed a statement that "gas cylinders were in No Man's Land to be used on us at the first favourable wind." This was confirmed in a bulletin from the French Tenth Army after they had vacated the salient. But that bulletin never reached the British.

On April 13, a German deserter, Private August Jaeger, who had become disgruntled with army life, slipped through the lines at Langemarch in the Ypres Salient. Under interrogation he revealed that an attack on the French trenches had been planned using asphyxiating gas released from buried cylinders as soon as the wind was favourable. When this information reached General Edmond Ferry, commander of the French 11th Division, he took what steps he thought necessary. He gave orders to thin out the lines to avoid casualties. He also warned the British 28th Imperial Division and the 2nd Canadian Brigade, under Brigadier General Arthur Currie, which was due to replace some troops that night. But at those levels and by his superiors, his information was received with some skepticism. The deserter was probably part of a ruse. And, after all, poison gas had been outlawed by the Hague Convention in 1907.

But the 28th Imperial Division had second thoughts and sent further information to General Sir Herbert "Daddy" Plumer's V Corps headquarters, which described how the cylinders worked, and enclosed a sample of the cotton waste from a crude cotton face mask that Jaeger had shown his captors. On the morning of April 15, a second German deserter confirmed the same information and that afternoon a Belgian agent sent a message warning of an imminent attack using cylinders of asphyxiating gas. "They are placed in batteries of 20 tubes per 40 metres," it read, "along front of XX1V Corps [sic XXVI]. A favourable wind is necessary." But all this information, which should in effect have been recognized as evidence, was in fact, disregarded as "rumour." French general headquarters went so far as to state that "all this gas business cannot be taken seriously."

This intelligence was not entirely lost on the more prescient, however. In his personal diary, Arthur Currie, whose 2nd Brigade had by this time occupied the trenches at Ypres, recorded: "Attack expected at night preceded by sending of poisonous gas to our line and then sending up three red lights (reported by German who came into French lines)." He took the precaution of having his brigade artillery fire on the German lines at intervals of 20 yards but without apparent result.

On Friday, April 16, after the "gas attack" failed to materialize, the Belgian agent reported to Allied Headquarters that a rush order had been placed with a firm in Ghent for 10,000 "mouth protectors." The mouth protectors, the signal stated, "soaked with a suitable liquid will serve to protect the men against heavy asphyxiation gas which the Germans intend to discharge towards the enemy lines, notably in front of the XXVI Reserve Corps."

Next day the 5th Imperial Division captured Hill 60, the refuse dump in the salient. When British mines exploded the Germans were seized with panic, "falling over one another in their struggle to escape into the communications trenches, others in their terror forcing their way through their comrades at bayonet point." They then desperately tried to retake the dump. The British reported "strong gas vapours" that stung the eyes. This along with all the enemy brouhaha, failed to produce the slightest suspicion that the Germans might be protecting something toxic. Without further investigation or thought, it was summarily accepted that the Germans were probably using tear gas shells. Annoying but hardly worth worrying about.

That very night, the First Canadian Division, under the command of British Lieutenant General Edward Alderson, completed its relief of the French 11th Division with all three brigades in place. On the following day Sunday, April 17, British reconnaissance planes reported a heavy increase in rolling stock in the direction of Wervicq where the Germans faced the Canadians and the French. Though no reinforcements were noticed it was plainly obvious that a bulk cargo of some importance was being delivered.

Some days later, a German document fell into British hands that would have sent a chill through Allied intelligence had they taken it seriously. It was a copy of a memorandum issued by the German Second Army back on October 16, 1914, listing the weapons available to their divisions. Among them were "flame and asphyxiating gas projectors."

In fact "poison" gas had already been used against the Allies on three different occasions, though they were unaware of it. On October 27, 1914, 3,000 non-toxic sneezing powder shells had been lobbed on British and Indian troops at Neuve Chapelle. But the victims did not even know they had been "gassed." On Sunday, January 30, 1915, the Germans began firing 18,000 explosive shells filled with xylyl bromide, a liquid irritant, at the Russians during the start of the Battle of Bolimos. These were rendered ineffective by the frigid Polish winter weather.

The shell was promptly modified to counteract the cold and the Germans again experimented with it in March against the French at Nieuport. But it proved just as ineffectual there as it had in the east. The Germans had begun to lose faith in the potential of gas warfare. It had certainly fallen far short of the objective of driving troops from inaccessible places. In the meantime, however, Dr (Captain) Fritz Haber, director of the Kaiser Institute for Physical Chemistry, had come up with the solution.

Germany was producing 37 tons of chlorine chemical gas per day for her dye industry. Here was a poison gas that was a potent toxic lung irritant. It was heavy and therefore not easily dissipated, and it left no visible residue. Haber calculated that it would only require a week's supply to launch a full-scale gas attack. Because of a severe shortage of artillery shells, he proposed using commercial cylinders from which the gas could be projected through the discharge valves. To Field Marshal Erich von Falkenhayn, German minister of war and chief of the general staff it presented the opportunity of seizing a victory, and a quick and decisive one, that so far had eluded the fatherland.

After accepting Haber's proposal, he assigned him to provide the necessary tools, and General Bertold von Deimling, commander of the XV Corps (part of the Fourth Army stationed along the Ypres Salient) to implement the attack. The operation was given the paradoxical, yet deliberately misleading title, "Disinfection." By late February the first gas cylinders were in the ground near the village of Gheluvelt on the southwestern curve of the salient. The deadliness of their new weapon became abundantly apparent to the Germans when, early in March, British shelling blew two of the cannisters open. Several infantrymen were badly gassed, one of whom died coughing up blood. A few days later, rifle fire punctured another cylinder. Three men choked to death and 50 others became seriously ill. These accidents indicated the need to cover the nose and mouth to avoid asphyxiation and gave birth to the mouth protector.

By the 10th of March 6,000 cylinders had been embedded along the front line. But the weatherman refused to cooperate; a favourable wind enabling an attack to be launched had failed to develop. To overcome this frustration, on March 25, the Fourth Army commander, Duke Albrecht of Wurttemberg, ordered the establishment of an "alternate gas front" on the north side of the salient between the villages of Streenstraat and Poelcappelle with new cylinders, while the original installations remained intact.

By this time a metamorphosis in thinking had permeated the German High Command. Victory in the west no longer took priority. That could wait until the Russians had been defeated. Von Falkehayn planned to deliver a knockout blow against them at Galicia. Disinfection now became an experiment in which the tactical objective was an advance of a mere one and a half miles. For the Russian campaign, von Falkehayn needed to divert as many troops as could be spared from the Western Front, particularly his crack units. He advised the Fourth Army that the XXVI Reserve Corps might soon be needed elsewhere. For that reason, he ordered that Disinfection should be implemented as soon as possible.

Following the debacle of Hill 60, the Germans were fearful, almost certain that their secret had been discovered. If not, with the British in control of the refuse dump, it was only a matter of time before it would be. Impatiently they waited for that elusive favourable wind. Finally, after interminable delays and the frustration of waiting, on the night of April 21, a faint northeasterly breeze began to develop. Duke Albrecht could wait no longer. He ordered Disinfection to begin next afternoon at 5:00 p.m. One of the most horrendous, most sordid battles ever fought, was about to start. It would change warfare forever.

Aside from the use of poison gas, the attack had been planned on a strictly limited scale. Carried out by two corps, the XXIII and XXVI Reserves, the objective was to seize the Pilckem Ridge at the apex of a V running south from Streenstraat on the east and Poelcappelle to the west, and dig in while flanking columns would provide support. The Germans were confident that the capture of this high ground would make it "impossible for the enemy to remain longer in the Ypres Salient."

The Canadian Division was positioned to the east of the St Julien-Keerselaere-Poelcappelle road running south-east for 4,250 yards. Two battalions, the Western Cavalry and the Winnipeg Rifles of Currie's Second Brigade occupied the right part of the line, with the British Columbia Battalion in close support near Fortuin and the Calgary-Winnipeg Battalion held in divisional reserve in battered Ypres — "Wipers" the Canadians called it — itself. To the left, the Third Brigade under Brigadier General Richard Turner VC, of Boer War fame, took its place with the Royal Highlanders and the 48th Highlanders of Canada up front, the 14th (Montreal) Battalion in close support at St Julien and the Canadian Scottish in divisional reserve also at Ypres. Behind the brigade on the right of the road stood the Third Brigade's 10th Battery of the Canadian Field Artillery. Brigadier General Malcolm Mercer's First Brigade was billeted in and around Vlamertinghe, a small village on the road directly west of Ypres.

On the left flank of the Canadians were two French Divisions. The 45th Algerian Division — Zouaves and Tirailleurs with their colourful blue jackets and red pantalons — occupied the position directly alongside on their left. To the North Africans' left was the 87th Territorial Division which held the line as far as Streenstraat on the Yser canal. It was made up of men between ages 36 and 43, ancient by military standards. On the Canadians' right flank were the 28th and 27th British divisions.

The Canadians were poorly equipped for battle. To begin with, they had no experience to speak of. Their apprenticeship in the trenches at Armentieres had been low-key, in other words they were not combat hardened. Their uniforms, greatcoats, and boots were of poor quality — so poor, they absorbed moisture. But worst of all, they were armed with the defective Ross rifle instead of the superior British Lee-Enfield. The bolt jammed, the gun misfired under rapid fire and shot off the bayonet. For this, the boys in the trenches could thank the irascible minister of militia Sam Hughes, whose unswerving faith was due to his friendship with its inventor, Sir Charles Ross. The division's machine-guns also were of questionable merit. Made in the United States, the Colt tended to jam when British ammunition was used. Arthur Currie put it mildly when he said: "I do not consider the Colt a very serviceable machine-gun."

The trenches the Canadians had taken over were waterlogged and poorly constructed. Built strictly for offense, they lacked the essentials, such as parapets, needed for defence. The French had left some of their dead buried under the mud and slime: heads, whole bodies in some cases, protruded in spots. Parapets had to be built and put up at night to avoid enemy fire. What the Canadians needed most was faith and confidence in their own ability and courage. They were soon to demonstrate those qualities in abundance.

Late in the night of April 21, the 48th Highlanders reported an unprecedented roar of wagons and gun carriages. At 2:50 that morning Richard Turner's Third Brigade heard a Zeppelin flying over the lines. Clearly something was in the offing. But what?

The day dawned clear and bright, with the temperature climbing into the seventies. Lieutenant Colonel George Nasmith, the military historian, then a medical officer, described it:

On that April day, the very essence of spring was in the air; the hedges of northern France were beginning to whiten with bloom, and the wild flowers were thick.... It was the time back in Canada when the spring feeling suddenly gets into the blood, when one throws work to the winds and takes to the woods in search of the first violets.

During the day, the Germans continued the shelling of Ypres begun the previous day. Many of the town's 17,000 citizens started leaving, while others decided to remain. They had become accustomed to it. But this was heavier, more intense than ever before.

There was noticeable aerial activity over the front lines although there was an absence of Allied airplanes. However, a French reconnaissance report noted an unusual amount of movement behind the German lines including a quarter-mile column at Poelcappelle. It made no mention of anything that indicated an impending gas attack.

That afternoon, the Canadian and French defences were subjected to a particularly strong bombardment. By three o'clock it had subsided and the German planes had vanished. The Front was now almost completely silent. A sense of foreboding pervaded. It was eerie, frightening. Then at precisely 5:00 p.m., the Germans opened the valves of the 5,730 cylinders allowing 149,000 kilograms of hissing chlorine gas to escape in less than eight minutes, and sending an ominous cloud of deadly yellow-green vapour in the direction of the French lines. The Germans had suddenly changed the face of war.

It all happened quickly, the olive-greenish wall of clouds wafted across No Man's Land, then sank down into the French trenches like a giant serpent. And at that very moment a cascade of shells descended on the Zouaves, the Tirailleurs, and the Poilus. Behind the gas attack, German infantry, their faces covered with gauze masks that resembled those that surgeons wear, advanced, firing their rifles to add to the hell.

In the trenches, the suffering was indescribable. The gas burned men's eyes and throats, seared their lungs bringing fearful pains to the chest. Men turned purple in the face, gagged and coughed up blood. They shrieked and they screamed. Some threw themselves to the ground in sheer agony, their bodies writhing spasmodically, convulsed in excruciating death throes. Those who did not choke to death, ran or staggered as best they could to the rear, gasping for water to soothe their torment. Some lived only to die a slow lingering, torturous death. The world had come to an end.

Incredibly, some of the French infantry managed to fight back, but it was a losing encounter. The immediate enemy objective was the village of St Julien to the south on the Poelcappelle road. But the gas had not reached the Algerian garrison at Langmarck, directly behind the front lines, and there the Zouaves and Tirailleurs put up a stiff fight before the Germans overwhelmed them. By six o'clock the town was in enemy hands but for the time being, the advance had been blunted. However, it had left the French in chaos. Lieutenant Colonel Edward Morrison, a former newspaperman with the 1st Field Artillery Brigade, reported:

> The French troops were in rout and were coming across the country in a very demoralized condition. Ambulances loaded with unwounded men, ammunition wagons, transport vehicles crowded with infantry, were galloping across country through hedges, ditches, and barbed wire. In many cases artillery horses had been unhooked from guns and limbers, and were being used for quick transportation, sometimes with two and three men on their backs. After this rabble came men on foot, without arms, singly and in groups, alternately running and walking, and only intent of getting away. At the time nothing was known regarding gas and the fugitives were quite unable to explain the cause of their terror.

Captain Paul Villiers at Third Brigade Headquarters recalled that the Algerians in flight were "suffering the agony of the damned, grey-green in the face, and dying from suffocation." It was a total defeat in which the Germans captured 57 French guns.

By some miracle, and for reasons never explained, the cylinders opposite the 3rd Canadian Brigade, just to the east of the Poelcappelle road, were never opened. But not all Canadians escaped the horror of poison gas that afternoon. On the immediate right of the Algerians, on the east side of the Poelcappelle Road, the 13th Royal Highlanders of Canada had spent an uneventful afternoon until, at 5:00 p.m., they heard a burst of gunfire from the French trenches beside and behind them. Ahead loomed the cloud of gas.

"At first we thought it was just the intense musketry that was creating the yellow haze," Lieutenant Ian Sinclair said later, "and then it began to come into us, and the French on the left...started pouring into our trench, coughing and bleeding and dying all over the place."

As the French began to collapse, the Highlanders were left totally unprotected. Major Robert McQuaig formed a new flank along the road, thinning out his own front line. Six hundred yards behind, the battalion's second in command, Major Edward Norseworthy, posted two platoons to the rear. But, standing in the way of a German effort to outflank the Canadian front line, they were doomed, overwhelmed by German infantry. All of them were either killed or captured. Norseworthy was among the dead. Their brave stand had not been in vain, however. With darkness falling and having suffered heavy casualties, the Germans halted their advance.

Although they had been spared the horror of a gas attack, the other Canadians were kept busy dodging shells from a fierce enemy artillery barrage that reached back to St Julien. By nightfall the French collapse had left a gaping hole four miles wide in the front line between the Poelcappelle road and the Yser Canal. Now the possibility existed that the 50,000 British troops, including the Canadians, would face a similar fate to the French. This would put Ypres, with its large garrison and 150 guns, in jeopardy. Unaware that the Germans had already halted, the Canadians made frantic attempts to close the gap. Meanwhile, refugees began fleeing battered Ypres in increasing numbers, in the hopes of boarding trains to the west, or failing that, by road away from the burning city. This exodus choked the roads and bridges with people moving in the opposite direction to troops headed north and east.

By eight o'clock, the situation had become one of both confusion and desperation. The road to St Julien lay wide open except for four 18-pound guns manned by Major William King's 10th Field Battery, positioned in an orchard between Keersselaere and the village. With Norseworthy's force wiped out, it remained the only obstacle to the Germans in the mile-wide gap between St Julien and the front line. King warded off a brief encounter with a column of German infantry. But undermanned, underequipped, and badly exposed, he knew he couldn't hold out for long once it turned dark. However he received a reprieve with the arrival of 64 Canadians from St Julien, among them Fred Fisher, a machine-gunner with the Royal Highlanders of Canada. When the Germans made a concerted attack to capture or destroy the guns, Fisher drove them back, time and again. All four of his crew were killed, but Fisher moved to a more forward post. Fully exposed to enemy shrapnel, machine-gun and rifle fire, he kept repelling the Germans until he was killed, an action that won him a posthumous Victoria Cross.

Fisher's tenacity and sacrifice bought Major King the time he needed to withdraw his group to the west side of the Yser Canal. The spirited defense had also convinced the Germans that they faced a far stronger Canadian opposition than was actually the case.

Meanwhile, throughout the evening, Currie and Turner's Second and Third Brigades did their best to stiffen their defensive positions. Turner called up two reserve battalions, the 10th (Canadian Scottish) and the 16th (Calgary-Winnipeg). The 14th occupied the front line near Mouse Trap Farm, the site of brigade headquarters. The entrenchment ended on the left at Mauser Ridge, now in German hands. On the right, Currie had called up his support battalion, the 7th (British Columbia) which he stationed at Location C on Gravenstafel Ridge directly to the east of St Julien.

At 8:25 p.m., the British commander of the Canadian division, Lieutenant General Edward Alderson, issued orders to Turner to clear the Germans off an oak plantation, a mile and a half west of St Julien, which the Canadians had nicknamed ''Kitchener's Wood.'' Ostensibly this was to support a planned French attack on Pilckem Ridge. In fact, not a single cohesive French unit existed; the troops were suffering so badly from the effects of the poison gas that they were incapable of action.

Not knowing this, excitement rippled through the ranks of the 1,500 Canadians about to take part. This marked the first time Canadians had attacked an enemy since the Boer War. Assembled in a field 500 yards north-east of Mouse Trap Farm and an equal distance from the objective, the battalions began their advance at 11:48 p.m. Each company of 200 men formed two ranks, 20 yards apart. Thirty yards separated the companies from one another. From the start, however, the battalions were handicapped. There had been no time for reconnaissance and artillery support was woefully inept; only 13 guns backed the assault. And the advance began in bright moonlight.

At the outset, the 10th Battalion commander, Lieutenant Colonel Russell Boyle, was guilty of a tactical error. Despite the pleading of his adjutant, Major Dan Ormond, he refused to capture Oblong Farm which swarmed with machine-guns.

At least there was the element of surprise — to begin with. The freshly plowed field absorbed the sound of soldiers' boots thumping against the ground. As they drew nearer, there was no indication the enemy was aware of their presence. Then, 200 yards from the wood, they encountered a six foot-high hedge bristling with barbed wire, which a reconnaissance would have revealed. Now the sounds of rustling, cutting wire, the clatter of bayonets, alerted the Germans. A flare arched above them, turning night into day.

The Canadians immediately dropped to the ground but one of the company commanders, Major James Lightfoot, brought them back to their feet when he shouted: "C'mon boys, remember that you're Canadians." However, the resulting charge was chaos; they ran into walls of enemy gunfire. "Our men were dropping thick and fast," Lieutenant Henry Duncan recalled, "the fire was coming from all directions." Canadians fell by the hundreds, but the advance continued.

On the south side of the wood, the Canadians swarmed over a shallow trench which, after moments of hand-to-hand fighting, they captured at bayonet point. Now the battalions swept into the trees. "Many Germans were encountered in the woods," Lieutenant Edward Lecki said, "some of whom surrendered, but the majority were bayoneted or shot. Many, however, escaped by dodging through the underbrush." The Canadians also encountered a series of sandbag forts defended by machine-guns. "It was all so mixed up you didn't know for anything," Private Sid Cox related later. "That's where I got the biggest scare of my life. I went into a bit of a hut there. I went to go in it, and a great big German stepped out, and he may have been going to surrender — I couldn't tell you — but I got out of there in a hurry. I pulled the trigger and ran."

Kitchener's Wood was soon cleared of Germans but it took some time for the battalions to regroup. They found that their losses had been horrendous. The 10th, which had gone into the battle with 816 men, had been reduced to 193. During the fighting, it had lost two commanders. Russell Boyle was mortally wounded when he took five bullets in the leg. He was replaced by the unit's second in command, Major Jack MacLaren. He, too, was wounded in the leg and later killed when his ambulance was struck by a shell. Command then passed to the adjutant, Dan Ormond. The 16th Battalion, which had started with nearly 900 men, had only 268 left.

By dawn from the standpoint of both position — in a shallow trench to the north of the wood — and numbers, they were extremely vulnerable to counter-attack by the Germans. Fortunately, they were soon relieved by two fresh battalions, the 2nd (Eastern Ontario) and the 3rd (Toronto). But they were too late to save Kitchener's Wood and had to withdraw to Mouse Trap Farm. The overnight action by the inexperienced, unblooded Canadian troops turned out to be the only successful attack by the allies during the entire Second Battle of

Ypres. A German prisoner told his captors: "You fellows fight like hell." The French general, Ferdinand Foch, praised it as "the finest act of the war."

On April 23, with his overwhelming manpower superiority of five to two and an artillery advantage of five to one, German Fourth Army Commander Duke Albrecht was confident he could easily overrun the Salient. He planned to maximize his gains by attacking west in the direction of Poperinghe and by overpowering the Canadian Division to the south.

His timing was perfect. The situation in the Salient was chaotic. The roads were clogged with refugees. The medics were hard-pressed tending the wounded. Evacuation was a problem under constant enemy shellfire. The collapse of the French had tripled the Canadian frontage. Turner was busy filling gaps in the line but the Third Brigade was still dangerously exposed. To stabilize the situation, another Canadian counter-attack had been planned. The French again declared their willingness to participate with their 54th Division. Alderson was skeptical, not without good reason. Where were they during the battle for Kitchener's Wood? For the assault, he picked the two Ontario battalions from Malcolm Mercer's First Brigade.

To hedge his bets, Alderson had the night before deployed a provisional British brigade on the left flank under Lieutenant Colonel Arthur Geddes. Also Currie's Second Brigade had rushed to Turner's assistance. Next morning, the Ontario battalions could clearly see the Germans 1,500 yards away, feverishly digging in on Mauser Ridge and laying barbed wire entanglements. But that worked both ways. The Germans could just as easily see the Canadians. At 5:30 a.m., Lieutenant Arthur Birchall, commander of the 4th Battalion, spotted troops through the trees on the left. At first, he mistook them for the French division, but soon realized that they were actually Germans and immediately gave the order to attack. But the flank was wide open; predictably, the promised French support had failed to materialize. When the Germans opened fire, it was nothing short of butchery. One survivor, Private George Bell of the 1st Battalion, described it:

"Forward," commanded our officers ahead of us. We kept on going. Ahead of me I see men running. Suddenly their legs double up and they sink to the ground. Here's a body with the head shot off. I jump over it. Here's a devil with both legs gone, but still alive. A body of a man means nothing except something to avoid stumbling over. It's just another obstacle. There goes little Elliot, one of the boys from the print shop where I worked in Detroit, only ten yards from me. Poor devil. There's nothing I can do for him. What's one man, more or less, in this slaughter.

By half past seven that morning, the attack had been stopped in its tracks. Watching his men being massacred, a frustrated Malcolm Mercer set out on foot to find Colonel Jacques Mordacq, commander of the 45th French Division. Mordacq assured him that he had five and a half battalions ready to join the assault. But Mercer was far from convinced. Disgusted and disillusioned, he returned to his post and when by 8:30 a.m., the French had still not taken up positions (it was noon before they finally did, but they still made no attempt to lend support) he ordered his men to dig in. With the enemy holding the high ground on the ridge, it still left them terribly exposed. Fortunately, the Germans failed to exploit the situation.

Still, casualties mounted steadily from the continuous shelling. Two of the battalions were losing three to four men at a time. At midday, Turner sent in two companies from the 14th (Montreal) Battalion to reinforce the line at Kitchener's Wood. It proved hopeless and they were quickly withdrawn. All day long, the Canadians awaited an impending attack. The signs were there. Heavy artillery bombardment, reinforcements being brought up. An estimated 25,000 troops had been assembled behind Kitchener's Wood alone. But the attacks that did materialize were minor forays — four against St Julien alone — and were driven off by small arms fire, despite the use of tear gas by the Germans.

The British and Canadians knew that if a full-scale attack did develop they were doomed and would be forced to withdraw. Field Marshal Sir John French, the British Army commander, considered abandoning the Ypres Salient altogether. It was true that it represented the only bulge in the entire Western Front trench lines and by stabbing into the German defenses, it posed somewhat of a threat, but that was debatable. Overall the terrain was generally even, the location of no special geographic significance, so that it offered little, if any, strategic or even tactical advantage. Symbolically, however, it harped back to the First Battle of Ypres that blunted a German drive to the Channel ports. And it was on Belgian soil, so that politically, in a sense, it had to be saved. And General Ferdinand Foch, the French Army commander, assured his British counterpart that his armies intended to make good the line lost by his two divisions the day before, by bringing up "large reinforcements." Foch had deliberately mislead Field Marshal French. The large reinforcements turned out to be a single division. But, French came away from their meeting feeling that Foch was acting in good faith.

Out of this developed a plan, if it could be called such, for the British 31st Brigade to attack in the direction of Pilckem. Somehow the Canadian 1st and 4th battalions, still clinging for all they were worth to the south slope of Mauser Ridge, were to form the right flank. "After the capture of Pilckem," the order read, "the attack will continue and the old French line occupied." Just like that!

Once again, as in the case of the attack on Kitchener's Wood, there was no time for reconnaissance. It was scheduled to start at 3:30 p.m., half an hour after the French were to move out. And the British 13th Brigade and the 45th Division had the same objective. Mercer was quick to recognize the flaw in such duplication and strenuously recommended cancelling the French attack. But Canadian Division headquarters ruled otherwise. On top of this, coordination between units was noticeably lacking. At 2:45 the artillery opened up believing the attack was to start at 3:00 instead of 3:30. When the attack by the Canadian First Brigade battalions began there was no ammunition left for artillery support. Three o'clock came and went with no sign of a French assault. Then at 3:45, the British Brigade announced that another half-hour was needed to get into position. In any case their assault was doomed.

There was no artillery support and a battalion of French Zouaves disrupted the advance by cutting in front of the British overcrowding the road, and presenting perfect targets for the Germans. Mayhem resulted. Watching, Private James Fraser of the 4th (Central Ontario) Battalion said, "They were simply bowled over like ninepins." Canadians joined in the fracas but accomplished little, except to add to the growing casualty list. In half an hour the fiasco was all over.

Canadian casualties for the day had been crushing. Of the two Ontario battalions, the 1st lost 404 men, the 4th 454 including the second in command, Lieutenant William Buell. Nothing expressed the gruesome, macabre aftermath of this grim fighting so well, and so pathetically, as the words of Gunner John Armstrong of the 3rd Field Battery who recalled seeing a horse meandering about the battlefield. "For three days after the attack he went around with just the lower part of a man's body in the saddle. From the waist up there was nothing. A good-sized shell had hit him."

If the Canadians had suffered heavily in their suicidal charges, the day had also been less than rewarding for the Germans. Duke Albrecht's bid to take Ypres had failed miserably due to his unrealistic aim of trying to capture Poperinghe, too far to the west, instead of lopping off the top of the Salient.

Albrecht knew now that an entire day had been wasted and his Fourth Army had achieved nothing. He also realized that if he was going to capture the Salient he would have to crush the Canadian Division. On this Friday evening he began marshalling his forces, 34 battalions strong, against the opposing eight Canadian battalions. But he was not content to rely on overpowering his enemy with numbers alone. To ensure success, next morning he would unleash the same weapon he had used to overpower the French: poison gas.

Fortunately, the Canadians had anticipated that gas would be used against them and had taken some precautions that doubtless saved lives and suffering. Water bottles and cans had been filled and placed at intervals along the trenches. Cotton bandoliers had been dampened to be held over the mouth and nose for protection. The diminutive medical officer, George Nasmith, had been busy developing a remedy, a pad soaked in hyposulfite of soda, but it would be some days before this was issued to the front lines. Meanwhile, Francis Scrimger, a surgeon with the Royal Montreal Regiment, who would win a VC the next day had evolved his own homespun, emergency antidote. "Urinate in your handkerchief," he instructed the men of his battalion, "and hold it over your mouth."

At 3:00 a.m., Saturday, April 14, Lizerne across the Yser Canal west of Steenstraat, fell to the Germans after an attack on the Belgian positions. What the official history called "a great and terrible day for Canada," was about to begin.

Exactly an hour later, a deafening artillery barrage pulverized the 8th and 15th Canadian battalions' front line trenches at the western end of the Gravenstafel Ridge and at St Julien village, on a front 1,200 yards wide. Simultaneously, gazing with dread over what was left of the parapets the Canadians could see a green cloud of vapour 15 feet high, blowing towards them. Within three minutes it had engulfed the trenches. Corporal William Thomas of the Winnipeg Rifles, remembered: "When I saw it coming, [I] just grabbed a towel, which was a big thick one, soaked it in water and covered my face, so I came off lucky."

Major Harold Mathews of the same battalion was not quite so fortunate. "When the fumes were first on us," he related, "breathing was most difficult, it was hard to resist the temptation to tear away the damp rags from our mouths in the struggle for air... all around men were coughing, spitting, cursing and groveling on the ground and trying not to be sick...[but] there was not a single officer or man who did not do his duty by manfully fighting down to the best of his ability the awful choking sensation and trying to stick to his post.''

The gas quickly penetrated the rear echelons as far back as the Second Brigade report centre near Fortuin where its commander, Arthur Currie, complained that it "made the nose and eyes run and our heads ache." The German infantry, equipped with primitive respirator masks, charged in behind the gas cloud fully expecting a quick and easy victory like the one they had enjoyed over the French two days earlier. They were in for a shock. In the first place, the Canadians were not surprised. They knew what they were facing. They had taken measures, no matter how rudimentary, to protect themselves against the gas. The Winnipeg Rifles (8th Battalion), known as the "Little Black Devils," were determined to fight back. And they did exactly that. Despite discomfort from the effects of the poison gas they stood their ground and mowed down the attackers. It was the only regiment in the British service to hold its trenches after being gassed. It also had the support of the 2nd Field Artillery Brigade which fired off rounds of shrapnel at the rate of half a ton a minute.

By contrast, the 48th Highlanders (15th Battalion) on the Little Black Devils' left suffered frightfully. Sergeant William Miller described it: "Imagine Hell in its worst form and you may have a slight idea what it was like." The Highlanders also lacked artillery support; the 3rd Brigade batteries were out of range. One company was almost completely annihilated. Out of 200 men, only six survived. The battalion itself was forced to retreat. Watching the chaos that ensued, Private Tom Drummond later reported, "the men on our left leaving the line, casting away equipment, rifles and clothing as they ran... [some fell] writhing on the ground, clutching at their throats, tearing open shirts in a last struggle for air, and after a while ceasing to struggle and lying still while a greenish foam formed over their mouths and lips." Captain George McLaren stated that, "Many were so weak they could not hold a rifle and others died in the trench from suffocation."

The Canadians were now in serious trouble. Having breached the 15th Battalion line, the Germans began pouring through it and by 6:30 in the morning had reached Stroombeek, threatening to envelope

St Julien. The Little Black Devils had done their best to plug the gap but it was hopeless. By this time they too had suffered heavily. Forces on either side of the breach were in grave danger. On the left the Germans had cut around the rear of the 13th Battalion (Royal Highlanders of Canada). On the right, enemy troops were within 300 yards of Locality C on Gravenstafel Ridge. If they captured it Currie's front battalions would be cut off.

Turner was coming to the rescue, but he'd gotten his signals crossed. Believing the Second Brigade to have been driven back, he ordered his 16th Battalion from Kitchener's Wood to the secondary defense position, the General Headquarters (GHQ) line, and the 10th to reinforce the Locality C defenders. Here, the 10th teamed up with the remnants of the 7th and 15th battalions to ward off full-scale German attacks. Lieutenant Walter Critchley of the 10th, said that, "all we could see was masses of Germans coming up in mass formations. Their officers were still on horseback then. They were just coming right up."

The Canadians withstood three such mass attacks. Dan Ormond, the 10th's third CO in two days, explained: "We stood up on our parapet and gave them three ruddy cheers and shook our fists at them. We gave them everything we had, and they figured it wasn't worth while and they just turned around and went back. They did that again and we did it again. We were quite happy about it. So then they did it a third time. When they went back a third time, we thought we'd won the war."

Among two fresh platoons from the 8th Battalion reserves brought into the line the night before, was Company Sergeant Major Frederick Hall. Hall earned the Victoria Cross that morning for rescuing a wounded comrade in an action in which he himself was killed while hauling the injured man to safety amid a hail of bullets.

At this point heavy fighting took place on the north-western edge of the line which was occupied by five battalions, the 2nd, 3rd, 7th, 13th, and 14th. Most of the sector escaped the effects of the poison gas due to the prevailing wind. But enemy pressure was strong and consistent. During the repeated attacks the Canadians became frustrated with the failure of their Ross rifles. They jammed after firing at most three rounds. To force the bolt open a man had to lie down and take his heel to it. Sergeant Chris Scriven vented his fury when he said: "It wasn't even safe to send a 14-year [-old] kid out rabbit-hunting in the fields with, never mind going into battle with." Major Peter Anderson of the 3rd Battalion put it in even angrier perspective:

"The Ross Rifle Company got the money; our brave men died for the aforesaid company's greed."

By 8:30 that morning, after the recurring enemy attacks were beaten back time and again, and failed to dislodge the defenders, the Germans called up their artillery, with devastating effect. It reached as far back as Fortuin where Arthur Currie was forced to evacuate his advance headquarters. But nowhere was it more shattering or telling than along a line north-east of St Julien. There, at Gravenstafel Ridge, the 7th and 13th battalions held on doggedly. Then a sudden German attack annihilated two platoons on the north side of the Poelcappelle road. The rest of the force was trapped, leaving the Germans free to force the Canadians' line. However, machine-gun officer, Lieutenant Edward Bellew brought up two of his machine-guns onto high ground overlooking Keerselaere. As the Germans tried to surround the weapons, Bellew's companion gunner, Sergeant Hugh Peerless, was shot dead. Bellew was wounded but kept on firing until his ammunition ran out. He then grabbed his rifle, destroyed the Colt, and warded off the enemy at bayonet point until his was finally subdued and taken prisoner. Only after the war did he learn that his action in saving the position had won him the Victoria Cross.

By noon a decision was reached to withdraw 300 yards to the bottom of the ridge. In the process, the 7th Battalion was virtually annihilated on the ridge. Major Percy Byng-Hall and Captain Thomas Scudamore reported that: "the enemy were advancing in large numbers...we were being cut down in masses by rifle fire." Private Percy Smith recalled: "The wounded and the dead were lying everywhere and there was everything in the German Army coming towards us over the fields for miles." Private Arthur Corker never forgot the experience:

They came over in masses. You couldn't miss if you could fire a gun. If our guns had been working, or just if we had good rifles. Some fellows picked up Lee-Enfields and threw the Ross away. There were some fellows crying in the trenches because they couldn't fire their damned rifles.

One company of the 15th was wiped out. But the 14th and 10th made it back with most of their wounded. At 12:30 the 10th's CO, Dan Ormond, considered a possible counter-attack but in view of the losses, shortage of ammunition, and lack of artillery support, it was quickly ruled out as unfeasible. Instead it was agreed to retire to some unused trenches south of St Julien.

At noon the Germans, outnumbering the Canadians by ten to one, descended on the defense line slightly forward of the village. It was garrisoned by one company of the 15th Battalion, and two from the 14th, as well as a few odds and sods from other units. They were quickly overwhelmed in fierce hand-to-hand combat, although part of one company of the Royal Montreals managed to escape on the left into a bunch of gutted buildings that were still standing.

Private William Thurgood of the 7th Battalion recalled bitterly:

Our rifles were jammed, and our machine-gun was clogged with mud. Then the enemy broke into the trench further along and started bombing their way towards us. One of our officers, Major Byng-Hall, it was I think, ordered us to surrender, and we threw up our hands....Though we held our hands aloft and were now unarmed, the cold-blooded crew started to wipe us out. Three of our men were bayonetted before an officer arrived and saved the rest of us. Even then our rough captors struck us with their rifle butts and kicked some of our men who were unfortunate enough to be laid out with wounds.

As they marched into captivity, the prisoners of war left St Julien behind them, now nothing but the shell of a once peaceful country village, lying in ruins.

Confusion in communications now complicated matters. Richard Turner received instructions from division headquarters to cancel a planned counter-attack by his Third Brigade in support of the Second Brigade line on the left. Instead he was instructed to use two British battalions to "strengthen your line and hold on." This illustrated the state of bewilderment pervading divisional headquarters as a result of conflicting reports from the various units of the German advance. In fact Third Brigade no longer held a line. It was therefore natural that Turner would interpret the directive to mean the GHQ line. He promptly issued the following command:

To the 5th Durham, 4th Yorks [British], 2nd, 3rd, 14th, 15th, 16th Canadian Battalions. You will hold GHQ Line from St Jean [St Julien] – Poelcappelle Road south.
From 3rd Canadian Infantry Brigade 1:40 p.m.

This created a gap between the GHQ Line and the line still held by the 5th and 8th battalions, nearly three miles wide. Nor did the withdrawing battalions know that orders for the Second Brigade to retire had been cancelled. Though this brigade had been reduced to half its initial strength (7th and 10th battalions having been transferred to Third Brigade) it still hung on tenaciously to its original position between Streenstraat and the Berlin Wood. However, both the 5th and 8th battalions had been stretched to the limit even with all their reserves thrown in. Arthur Currie knew that he had to fill the gap between his line and Locality C to avoid disaster.

But when he learned of the critical situation facing the Third Brigade, before the withdrawal to the GHQ Line, he abandoned his plan to close the gap, and instead decided on a counter-attack. At GHQ a supporting British battalion had been promised. The unit arrived at 2:00 p.m. but refused to budge without direct orders from its own brigade commander who was nowhere to be found. Adding to that frustration, Currie now learned that instead of joining in the offensive, the Third was withdrawing to a point three miles to the rear of his own brigade. By the time he tracked the British brigadier down, he found that the battalion had been assigned to the Third Brigade and was to proceed to the GHQ Line.

Currie then came across the 27th Imperial Division Headquarters, which controlled the reserves, to whom he now appealed for help. But they were under the impression that his right at Berlin Wood and his own command post had been overrun. It was clear he would receive no assistance to secure his left flank. By this time he had been away from his brigade for three hours and his absence had caused some concern. And no word had been received of the Third Brigade's impending attack. At 1:45 p.m. Currie's brigade major, Lieutenant Colonel Charles Betty, sent a bulletin to the Third Brigade:

How soon may infantry counter-attack be expected to reach left flank of Section 11 Locality C to relieve pressure on that flank? Upon your answer depends the decision of OC. 8th Battalion as to whether to hand on trenches or not. General Currie missing. Do you know his whereabouts? Last seen going to GHQ 2nd Line.

Back came an instant reply from Turner:

Have instructed troops to hold GHQ Line. Orders for counter-
attack cancelled.

Now what? With no brigadier in command, what to do? Fall back?
That would imperil the British on the right. Anyway, who would take
the responsibility? Fortunately Second Brigade already had in force
a contingency measure to be put into effect under such circumstances.
It was up to the four colonels of the unit to select a leader among
them. The logical choice was Lieutenant Colonel Louis Lipsett of the
8th Battalion who had been in charge of training in Western Canada.

At first Lipsett considered sticking it out. But soon two of the
artillery brigades had run out of ammunition and had been forced to
withdraw. This allowed the Germans to occupy Hill 32 between
Locality C and Boetleer Farm.

By 4:00 that afternoon, the British 27th Imperial Division had
arrived to fill the gap. But by then the Germans had overrun Gravenstafel Ridge as well as farm buildings to the left and had entered
the town of St Julien. By nightfall the firing had died down, but the
Canadians were still in a precarious position with a gap still wide
open to their left.

During the night, Currie mustered what troops he could from the
7th and 10th battalions to bolster the line on the left of Lipsett's 8th.
Next day the British 10th Brigade swept into St Julien but was soon
forced to withdraw. The attack had stemmed the German advance
but accomplished nothing else. At mid-afternoon that Sunday, April
25, a German assault completely wiped out a British battalion and an
entire company of the 8th Battalion.

The Canadian Army Medical Corps were hard pressed tending the
casualties. Francis Scrimger, the medical officer who had devised the
method of urinating into a handkerchief to protect the men of his
regiment, the Royal Montreals, from the effects of poison gas, was
in a farmhouse serving as a dressing station when it was set on fire
by enemy artillery and had to be evacuated. The road leading from it
had been rendered impassable by shelling so the wounded men had
to swim across a moat that surrounded the building. One man was in
such bad shape that this was impossible. To shield him from shrapnel
splinters flying all around, Scrimger stood over him protecting him
with his own body. He then dragged him to the edge of the moat out
of danger from the fire and curled himself around and above the
man's head and shoulders for protection until help arrived. For this

action Scrimger became the fourth Canadian to be awarded the Victoria Cross during the Second Battle of Ypres.

At this time, the all but decimated Second Brigade advanced to keep the line intact along the Gravenstafel Ridge. There it held on grimly until taken out on April 26, by which time both the First and Third brigades had also been relieved by the British.

The Second Battle of Ypres, one of the vilest demonstrations of man's inhumanity to man, continued officially until May 31, though the Canadians had been ordered back into reserve after six solid days of fighting and shelling, and 12 days in the front line. Nothing had been gained. The salient had not even been blunted; the town, though in chaos, was still in British hands, for whatever that was worth. The Germans had advanced a mere two miles on a front only six miles wide, overrunning a paltry six square miles.

The Germans had lost their chances of victory after the third day and due to the mix-up in command and orders, the British had blown any hope of regaining lost ground and the front again became static. Though the battle itself was in no way decisive nor had it been so planned (the Germans used it as a means to test chlorine gas and to mask troop movements to the Russian front), losses had been staggering. The British lost 59,275 men killed, wounded and missing, while the Germans admitted to 34,783.

But for Canada it emerged as an hour of glory. Her troops had not broken during the first three days of the battle and against superior numbers, they had held the vital left flank left open by the French. Had they failed, the two British divisions would have been cut off. They had paid a heavy price, however — more than 6,000 casualties. Out of the 5,000 survivors, 1,452 had thrown away their Ross rifles in disgust and picked up Lee-Enfields from their fallen British comrades.

Though poison gas never became a decisive weapon in World War I, gas attacks became commonplace. Altogether over the next three years the Germans lauched 24 such assaults, the French 20 and the British 150, one of which was mounted by the Canadians on March 1, 1917, six weeks before the assault on Vimy Ridge. One of the trench raids conducted by the Canadian Corps, was a "reconnaisance in force," the first time the phrase was used. Employing 1,700 troops, aimed at Hill 145 of the Ridge, it turned into a fatal fiasco. The Germans had prior knowledge of the attack. They were ready and their artillery shells burst some of the Canadians' gas cylinders. Once the poisonous phosgene and chlorine was released, the wind changed and blew it into the faces of the attackers. The Canadians suffered 687 casualties.

This exercise illustrated the futility of such operations. At Ypres, initially, there had been the element of surprise. That was never again duplicated. Furthermore the use of respirators offered some protection. Nevertheless, the eerie prospect of poison gas attacks on the civilian populace from the air remained to haunt Europe for a generation, through the Munich Crisis in 1938 and the first few years of World War II. Pictures of frightened, pathetic children shouldering gas mask satchels in the major cities of Europe come readily to mind. What prevented the use of gas was fear of certain reprisal. In this, it might well be likened to the deterrent effect of the atomic bomb.

Ypres brought home to Canada and Canadians the cruelty and horror of war for the first time. Hardly a community, large or small, was left untouched by the fearful cost in dead and wounded. But at the same time the heroism, which will never be forgotten, reached out to every heart with a sense of pride.

✦ 9 ✦

THE BYNG BOYS

...make sure every man knows his task. Explain it to him again and again; encourage him to ask questions. Remember also, that no matter what sort of fix you get into, you mustn't sit down and hope that things will work themselves out. You must *do* something. In a crisis the man who does something may occasionally be wrong; but the man who does nothing is *always* wrong.

> **Lieutenant General Julian Byng,**
> Commander, the Canadian Corps, to his officers

Things Worth Remembering. Thorough preparations must lead to success. Neglect nothing. Training. Discipline. Preparation and Determination to conquer is everything.

> **Major General Arthur Currie**
> Commander First Canadian Division.

What is today a peaceful hill, surmounted by twin commemorative pylons communing with the placid sky, was on that day a turmoil of moving men, spouting earth, drifting smoke and driving sleet....

> **John Swettenham,** Canadian Military Historian

...in Canada's history, one of the great days, a day of glory to furnish inspiration to her sons for generations.

> The *New York Times*

After two and a half years of war, in which millions of lives had been callously and shamefully frittered away to no avail, the time had come for a drastic change in thinking, policy, strategy and tactics. Trench warfare extending from Switzerland to the English Channel, at appalling cost in life and limb, had yielded gains that could be measured in yards. 1916 saw the calamitous battles of Verdun and the Somme in which more than two million men had been killed. By 1917, on the grand scale, the picture augured well for both the Allies and the fatherland.

On December 12, 1916, German Chancellor Theobold von Beth-mann-Hollweg had put out peace overtures. At face value the proposal seemed propitious. Naval blockades were starving both sides. But Paul von Hindenburg, chief commander of the Central Powers and David Lloyd George who had replaced the ineffectual, indecisive Herbert Asquith as prime minister of Great Britain, saw it quite differently. Hindenburg's answer was unrestricted submarine warfare. Lloyd George's policy was to continue the war until final victory.

At this time, two events occurred that were to have an eventual impact on the war, though at the time the effects were purely psychological. The first of these was the March Revolution which overthrew the tsar in Russia. This meant that in time the Germans would be able to free up fresh troops from the east for the decisive battle in the west. Then on April 6, 1917, the United States entered the war — the full benefit of which would not be realized for at least a year.

Whether these combinations of circumstances had a bearing on French commander-in-chief Robert-Georges Nivelle's decision to attempt a knockout punch to end the war is pure speculation, though the possibility cannot be ruled out. A champion of the great breakthrough, he had been acclaimed the "Hero of Verdun" for recapturing French forts. He now intended to use the same technique on a much larger scale against the German salient bulging south of the Somme and north of the Aisne.

Back in November, Joseph Joffre, Nivelle's predecessor, along with Field Marshal Sir Douglas Haig, British commander-in-chief in France, had drawn up a plan for an offensive in February. This amounted to a Franco-British extension of the Somme offensive but on a wider front. More of the same old grind, a strategy that reflected their inflexible, unimaginative personalities. It was just such rigidity that cost Joffre his job at Verdun.

Nivelle was able to persuade Haig that given the right support he could achieve an all out victory within 48 hours and at very little cost. It would begin with a British drive from Arras and Bapaume towards Cambrai. It was purely diversionary, intended only to tie the Germans down. Eight days later three French armies would attack to the south, east and north. Caught in the bulge from Peronne to Craonne, the Germans would be surrounded, leaving a gap through which the Allies could march into Germany. ''We have the formula,'' Nivelle crowed confidently, ''...victory is certain.''

Although Hague and Nivelle rarely saw eye to eye on anything, they had only a single disagreement over the Frenchman's grand plan, one that significantly affected the Canadian Corps in France: should Vimy Ridge, the front facing it, be taken or simply ignored? Nivelle wanted the heaviest concentration of manpower south of the Scarpe River in conjunction with his own attacks north of the Oise and he considered the taking of Vimy Ridge unnecessary, as well as nigh impossible. He predicted a Canadian attempt to capture it would end in disaster. After all, hadn't the French and British failed to dislodge the enemy from the escarpment at a fearful cost of 190,000 men killed over the past two years? The Germans boasted of their own impregnability. A Bavarian officer, taken prisoner in one of the pre-battle trench raids, declared, ''You might be able to get to the top of Vimy Ridge but I'll tell you this; you'll be able to take all the Canadians back in a rowboat that get there.'' However, Haig stuck to his guns and won his point. He was sure the Germans would never give up the ridge voluntarily despite the pressure from the main assault to the south, and its presence on his left flank was like an intolerable thorn in his side that would dangerously impede his advance.

During this period of Allied planning, the Germans had fallen back to a new fortification behind their forward trenches — the Siegfried-Stellung line, which the Allies later called the Hindenburg line. Stretching from behind the front at Arras, it extended through St Quentin to Vailly on the River Aisne and consisted of a labyrinth of barbed wire and concrete, artillery and machine-gun emplacements. Though it had been under construction for six months, the Allies were totally unaware of its existence.

It was a logical step. For a variety of reasons, the Germans needed to consolidate and shorten their defence line. Their troops were spread over three fronts: the Western, the Russian and the Italian. The most significant development arising at this stage — whether intentionally or unintentionally has never been determined — was the elimination of the German salient. The bulge, the cornerstone on which Nivelle had hinged his hopes for victory, simply did not exist anymore. In its place lay a ravaged land in which every tree, building, road and path had been obliterated leaving a desolate, impassable scorched stretch of earth, 25 to 50 miles wide.

Though it was like attacking a vacuum, Nivelle rigidly refused to alter his plan and his armies ran out of steam, eventually coming to a standstill. This placed the onus on the Arras front, and the spring offensive now became an all-British operation with particular emphasis on the Canadians. On January 2, 1917, General Sir Edmund Allenby, commander of the British Third Army, received orders from Haig to carry out an attack at Arras. In the same directive, General Sir Hubert Gough's Fifth Army was instructed to operate against the southern flank of the Bapaume Salient, while General Sir Harry Horne, commander of the First Army, which included the Canadian Corps, was ordered to coordinate his assault with Allenby and seize Vimy Ridge.

An imposing escarpment, the "Ridge" dominates the Flanders landscape in a shape that resembles a gigantic, solid earthen-clay porpoise bellyflopped onto the countryside between the flat Artois plain extending east towards Douai, and the broken, sometimes roly-poly country west in the direction of the English Channel. Looking north-west, its head has two bumps which represent its highest points, while the carcas is studded with five or six woods, a number of farms and two or three villages. Rising 450 feet above sea level, it is four miles long and at its thickest part, some 1,500 yards wide.

After the Germans captured it in the first three months of war they spent two years reinforcing its natural strength as a bastion (with interlacing honeycombs of forts, redoubts, tunnels and bunkers), by the beginning of 1917 Vimy Ridge had become the strongest defensive position in all of France. Some of the bunkers were deep enough to house an entire battalion. The forward defences, 500 to 700 yards deep, consisted of three lines of parallel trenches protected by dense barbed wire entanglements and a vast network of steel and concrete machine-gun emplacements connected by communication trenches and tunnels. To the rear was a similar second system of ditches, a secondary defence, 700 yards deep, a mile from the Canadian front to the north and two miles to the south. Behind these, out on the plain, was a third line of trenches interspersed between lines of self-contained, strongly armed fortresses.

Three German infantry divisions had been assigned the ridge's defence; the 1st Bavarian Reserve Division in the south; the 79th Reserve (Prussian) Division in the centre, around the village of Vimy at the eastern foot of the ridge; and the 16th Bavarian Infantry Division, to the north opposite the town of Souchez. All three units were thoroughly battle tested, the Prussians having recently been recalled from the Russian Front. The other two had fought the Canadians before and had a high opinion of their combat abilities. The commander of the 79th wrote: "There are no deserters among the Canadians.... It is very certain they will attack on a large scale in the immediate future."

Opposing this seasoned force of veterans was the Canadian Corps, made up of four divisions, poised to go into action as a complete unit for the first time. Its commander, Lieutenant General Sir Julian Byng, a British professional soldier who had fought in the Boer War and in India, would become governor-general of Canada in 1921. The four divisions of the corps were neatly arrayed at the foot of the ridge: the First Division under Major General Arthur Currie to the south; to his left the Second Division commanded by Major General Henry Burstall; on his left Major General Louis Lipsett's Third Division; and to the north the Fourth Division under Major General David Watson. The left flank would be supported by the First British Corps, the right by another British corps, the 17th. All told the force numbered 170,000 men. The Canadian Corps, among its ranks veterans of Ypres, Festubert, Givenchy, Courcelette and the Somme, was one of the finest fighting forces ever forged, as both its allies and enemies readily admitted. Most British Divisions numbered 15,000 men. Byng's divisions totalled 25,000. His corps was like a small army.

The confidence, high *esprit de corps* and morale of this force was in no small measure due to the inspirational personality of its commander. Julian Byng refused to stand on ceremony and in this he differed from most of his British counterparts, many of whom insisted on being saluted in the trenches. He had a casual manner with his men, communicated easily and informally with them, which suited the Canadian temperament. They soon began to call themselves "Byng Boys," after the popular London musical revue at the Alhambra Theatre. Byng's view that each man be thoroughly briefed on his part in battle, was popular. Even the training and retraining was tolerated. And he also knew how to pick leaders.

Determined to avoid bloodbaths like the Somme (where the British suffered 600,000 casualties, among them 24,000 Canadians) and

Verdun, Byng assigned Arthur Currie to study and analyze both battles and apply the lessons learned to tactics and training for the attack on Vimy. His choice of Currie for the job was right on target. Methodical, scholarly and thorough but also practical, the First Division commander had already shown an attuned appreciation of combat techniques. Currie abhorred many of the methods being used, considering most outmoded. He was also a perfectionist and even the slightest detail did not escape him.

From his inspection, Currie concluded that of primary importance, before any other consideration, was the need for proper, effective and in-depth infantry training before any assault could be attempted. This was divided into two exercises. The first of these was a series of "trench raids" to familiarize the troops with enemy defence dispositions and to gather information by taking prisoners for interrogation. This intelligence, together with Royal Flying Corps reconnaissance photographs, allowed them to build a scale model of the ridge with its multifarious defences. The duplicate "battleground," on terrain a safe distance behind the front, gave the troops a chance to rehearse their part in the coming assault. With the use of miles of coloured tape and thousands of flags, a full-scale replica of the German trench system was laid out in detail. Every infantryman practiced his role with full gear, again and again until he could walk it in his sleep. To avoid tedium, the two exercises, the trench raids and the duplicate rehearsals, were co-mingled.

To provide greater mobility and flexibility, the next thing Currie recommended was a return to the pre-war tactic of fire and movement in place of the "wave" attack against which a machine-gun defence could mow men down unmercifully. This manoeuvre consisted of part of the platoon keeping the enemy occupied with heavy fire, while the other troops moved around their flanks to the rear and bombed them into submission with hand grenades. This could also be useful in coping with pockets of resistance. Currie also recommended that each platoon be organized as a self-contained unit giving junior officers, NCOs and ordinary soldiers specific responsibilities — a first on the Western Front. With such flexibility, Byng issued orders that if a brigade or a division were held up, the units on its flanks were not to stop as they had at the Somme. Instead, the bogged down groups were to defend their own flanks and fight their way through with machine-guns. The emphasis in this operation was speed of advance. And this brought up the question of weaponry.

When Byng took over the corps in the summer of 1916, he and Currie quickly came to the conclusion that the armament available, given the change in battle conditions over the past two years, was not only being used ineffectively but that some weapons had long outlived their usefulness. To the British and French, the old standby was still the rifle and the bayonet. In reality it was a clumsy combination. During a struggle in the confines of a trench, pillbox or dugout, it was virtually impossible to take proper aim and it was as likely to stab a comrade as an enemy. A cliché went the rounds that the only man ever killed by a bayonet was the one who put his hands up first. Few soldiers could fire a rifle accurately anyway and what practice they did get was in the comfort of the rifle range, lying on their stomachs. After the first few trench raids, Byng and Currie quickly realized that the equipment the raiders needed were light machineguns and hand grenades.

The drum-fed Lewis gun was light, easy to carry and could be fired from the shoulder or from the hip. It shot 47 rounds in only five seconds, so infantrymen were advised to take short, sharp bursts. Backing them up were crews carrying extra drums of .303 calibre ammunition to feed them.

The Mills bomb was a wicked instrument, a real killer that spewed cast iron fragments in all directions. Shaped like an egg, it was about the size of a tennis ball. Holding the safety lever down, the bomber (as hand grenade throwers were called) pulled the pin then lobbed the missile into the enemy position where it exploded four seconds later. For extra range, these grenades were also fired from a launcher attachment on the muzzle of a rifle, propelled by the explosion of a blank cartridge. At first, the German grenade launcher had twice the range of the Canadians. This shortcoming was overcome quickly by the innovative Lieutenant Colonel Chalmers Johnston, the commander of the 2nd Canadian Mounted Rifles of the Third Division's 8th Brigade. "Whizzbang," as he was known, figured the culprit lay in the length of the Lee-Enfield rifle. Breaking regulations, he promptly sawed 11 inches off the barrel and, just as he had calculated, the shorter length that the cartridge gasses now had to travel provided twice the thrust and doubled the range. Byng immediately ordered all rifles assigned as launchers to be similarly sawed off, making him an accessory to "destroying government property."

And then there was artillery. It was two Canadians who brought it to a state of the art. On the Somme, Byng had been frustrated and dismayed at the failure of shrapnel shells to break down enemy barbed wire entanglements. The infantry had to force its way through with wire cutters, slowing its advance and resulting in heavy casualties. The problem was that the fuse used in the shrapnel shell burst too soon, killing hundreds of soldiers as it was intended to do, but making no dent in the barbed wire defences. Byng's chief gunner, Brigadier General "Dinky" Morrison, discovered that a new fuse would explode the shell on contact with the wire, shredding it to pieces and cutting wide swaths in the entanglements through which the troops could charge.

Morrison pushed hard through every possible channel in both England and France for supplies of the new fuse, until by mid-January of 1917, he and Byng were satisfied they had sufficient quantities to obliterate the German barbed wire obstacles.

At this time Byng appointed Andrew McNaughton as counter-battery staff officer and sent him south to study artillery techniques used at Verdun and the Somme. From the French he learned virtually nothing. The brass were pitifully out of touch with the front line. Furthermore they still clung to the old rifle and bayonet form of attack. With the English he was luckier; they told him of their experience with flash spotting and range sounding. This was something entirely new, and as such, appealed to the Canadian's scientific mind and his engineering background, and it steered him in the right direction. By war's end Andy McNaughton would be acknowledged as the top artillery expert in the British Empire. He was now about to bring science to the battlefield.

McNaughton's objective was to pinpoint the position of all the German field guns on the ridge so that they could be taken out of action prior to the actual attack. Flash spotting entailed setting up a series of telephone posts along the front line equipped with surveying gear. From gun flashes enemy positions were relayed back to headquarters, a system that proved so accurate that the Canadian artillery was able to locate the German gun batteries within a distance of five yards.

Sound ranging was a good deal more sophisticated and a lot more complicated. For his team of scientists, McNaughton had the temerity to import an oscillograph, a radar-like instrument of its day, onto the battlefield. As one British general remarked somewhat haughtily: "You Canadians take all the fun out of war." When a German gun opened fire, a man in a listening post set up in No Man's Land, pressed a lever activating the recorder at headquarters which picked up sounds from microphones all along the front and back a mile and a half. In this way the gun's exact location was indicated by monitoring the time intervals between microphones.

McNaughton also set up an electrical chronograph which could measure the time it took a shell to pass through an electrically charged wire screen enabling the Canadians to figure out the muzzle velocity of each weapon. There were problems: the variety of speeds of shells, the wind and the weather, to name a few. But McNaughton's band of scientists overcame them and were able to calculate not only the position of each gun, but also its type, calibre and the target at which it was aimed. In fact every key gun at Vimy would be individually calibrated. In addition to the expert, scientific data collected, information also flowed in from other sources: aerial reconnaissance photographs, observation balloons, deserters and spies. As well, the trench raids yielded captured documents, and German prisoners for interrogation.

The arsenal of artillery amassed for the Vimy assault was the largest ever assembled: a total of 983 guns, ranging from 13- and 18-pound guns to 4.2-, 6.8- and 9.2-inch howitzers, were brought up. The manpower required for the guns was also massive. Two hundred men were needed to operate a battery of four 18-pounders, for example. The firepower from this repository of armour was frightening to behold. The 8-inch howitzer could fling 180-pound shells. The smaller 4.2-inch model, angled at 45-degrees, could drop 35-pound shells with astounding accuracy into the enemy trenches, creating chaos. To devastate such defences as pillboxes, dugouts, concrete gun emplacements and batteries, the huge 9.2-inch howitzer, so big it had to be assembled in three sections, could hurl a 290-pound shell that smashed everything on which it landed to smithereens. When all the guns were in position there was one heavy weapon for every 20 yards of front, and one field gun every ten yards.

Augmenting this awesome array of artillery was the introduction of the machine-gun as a weapon of "indirect" firepower, the brainchild of Raymond Brutinell, a one-time French army reservist, who migrated to Western Canada in the early 1900s where he amassed a fortune as a land developer. Largely at his own expense, he created the 1st Canadian Motor Machine-Gun Brigade which became attached to the First Canadian Division. In fact Canada had entered the war with a larger machine-gun arsenal than the British.

Brutinell's "indirect use" of the machine-gun was a back-up operation instead of a direct firing attack. In effect, he converted the use of the machine-gun to light artillery. Firing over the heads of the advancing troops, it supplemented the artillery barrage by filling in the gaps left by the shelling, prevented the Germans from repairing the holes made in the barbed wire, harassed road crossings, and hampered supply deliveries. By March 1917, 64 machine-guns were constantly firing across No Man's Land at the Germans all-day long and another 64 kept up a steady stream all-night.

While all these activities and preparations for the attack on the ridge (now scheduled for Easter Monday, April 9) got underway, a vast, eerie, nightmarish, underground war was being waged. When the British took over the Vimy front from the French in March 1916, they knew they could never hope to wrest the ridge from the Germans. But at least they could make life uncomfortable and uneasy for them by countering the tunneling warfare that the enemy had perfected to the point where they could explode mines under the British front lines with impunity. What now developed was a war of nerves in which the British dug six miles of tunnels in the soft clay 23 feet below ground. Arteries branched off from the main shored up substructure which led to the front where chambers, used as communications centres, headquarters and medical dressing stations, had been gouged out. The entire complex was serviced with electric powered lighting and a narrow gauge railway for emptying the excavated soil. The longest tunnel was a mile long and, with the others, provided access to the front without the threat of exposure. But it was nerve-racking work with the ever present prospect of both sides tunnelling into one another or blowing each other up. When the Canadians moved into the sector later in October 1916, they continued to expand and improve the underground network, actively tunnelling corridors they called "saps" after the French meaning "an undermining," under German positions. Their objective was to eavesdrop on the enemy's plans through the tunnel walls, or plant explosive charges to blow them up.

By late March 1917, the Canadians had completed 12 subways towards the forward line and in some cases past it. The total length was just under six miles. With the end of the subways sealed off, they would now become a launching point for part of the assault wave. At Zero Hour, charges would blow open the tunnels from which the attackers would pour into the heart of the battlefield with the complete element of surprise.

When the time finally arrived for the assault on Vimy Ridge, the Canadian Corps was the most finely tuned allied force ever seen on the Western Front. Its men were better equipped and better prepared than any other group had ever been. Troops had been trained and rehearsed for battles before, but never with such care, exactness, precision, split second timing and the downright doggedness that Byng and Currie insisted upon. Planning for the assault had been worked out to the smallest detail. Every possibility had been considered; nothing had been left to chance. In short the preparation had been a model, a lesson in how to ready for an attack. All the elements of a successful operation were coming together: the build-up, the barrage, surprise and, most important of all, the high morale of the Canadians themselves, every man jack of them full of confidence and anxious to do battle.

On the sunny morning of March 20, with a deafening thunderclap, 500 guns opened up with a barrage that set aflame a line running from the Scarpe River to the Souchez. From that moment until April 2, 275,000 shells smashed into the ridge, destroying barbed wire, tearing into trenches, blasting apart pillboxes and cutting off the defenders from their food and ammunition supplies. The field batteries alone fired 500 rounds a day. During that time the Canadians carried out trench raids every night and knew from first-hand enemy reports just how devastating the shelling had been. But these forays took their toll: 327 dead and 1,316 wounded.

For the Germans it was a catastrophic crescendo of carnage, yet worse lay in store. During that 13 day holocaust, to conceal the total artillery strength, only half the guns had been used. But now, for the next seven days, every gun available, nearly 1,000 in all, went into action to batter the ridge with nearly a million rounds. Fifty thousand tons of high explosives rained down on the Bavarian and Prussian defenders who aptly described the period: "The Week of Suffering." With 82 percent of his guns destroyed, German chief of staff, Erich Ludendorff ordered new batteries moved into position. But the relentlessness of the Allied barrage, day and night, prevented any such rescue attempt.

By April 6, Good Friday, the date of the attack had been set for Easter Monday, April 9. A day later, Zero Hour had been decided upon for 5:30 a.m. that morning. Feverish last minute preparations took place over the Easter weekend, as more than 30,000 men, stretched out over nearly four miles of front moved into battle positions. Twenty-three battalions were in the forward line, 13 behind them in direct support and another nine, with three British battalions, in reserve.

There was no let-up in the artillery barrage but there was no intensification either and as Easter Sunday came to a close, the guns were all but silent. Previous assaults had always been heralded by a fierce shelling preceding the assault itself. This gave the enemy ample warning of an impending advance and they could prepare for it, ready to mow down their assailants with machine-gun fire the moment they went over the top. Currie avoided such forewarning; there would be no concentration of artillery until Zero Hour which, he hoped, would catch the Germans off guard. It did.

The enemy knew an attack was coming — all the signs were there — but they had no idea when. The Canadians moved undetected into the trenches through the subterranean system. The Germans had no idea that on Easter Monday, 15,000 front line troops faced them, some of them as close as 100 yards away — within pistol range.

In every military engagement there is chaos and confusion. That these factors were kept to a minimum at Vimy Ridge was entirely due to the meticulous planning and intense training. As a result, every man, from private to divisional commander, knew exactly what he was supposed to do, how he was to do it, where he was supposed to be and when. Objectives had been carefully delineated on maps in colour, and set to a rigid timetable. If all went according to plan, the escarpment would be in Canadian hands in less than eight hours. Deadline: 1:18 p.m.

Each division had its specific task to perform over a particular part of the ridge. What was about to take place was four mini-battles within one large operation. Assaults by all four forces would be covered by the creeping artillery barrage as well as continuous "indirect" machine-gun fire over the infantry into the face of the defenders. The shelling was timed to move ahead at the rate of 100 yards every three minutes.

Around midnight, each man in the assault force was given a last hot meal and a generous ration of rum. They needed it. In contrast to the bright, sunny Sunday, the night had turned chilly. In the early morning hours of Easter Monday, clouds moved in obscuring the moon, followed by a light, cold drizzle. Then a breeze sprang up and the drizzle turned to rain mixed with snow. A sharp frost hardened the upper soil of the ground, and as dawn approached, the snow became a blizzard blowing from the east right into the face of the attackers. As Zero Hour loomed, anxiety and apprehension approached apocalyptic proportions. There were jangled nerves, shaky hands, time for the last, quick pee, or a final tug on a cigarette.

Two minutes to go. The word passes along to fix bayonets. An ominous hush all down the line, save for the click-click-click of muzzle lockings. Then at precisely 5:30 a.m. — All Hell breaks loose! Brimstone and Fire! Steel and Flame! Armageddon! A world gone completely mad! With a thunderclap that could be heard all the way to England, the greatest artillery barrage in the history of warfare erupts all along the four mile front as 23 Canadian battalions, 15,000 men strong, surge over the trench parapets and charge into blinding sleet across the mire and murk of a shell torn No Man's Land.

Though the enemy had been so taken by surprise there was little return fire at first, the ravaged, pockmarked earth made for tough slogging. Stumbling up the slopes over the quagmire, some men got bogged down temporarily, many waist-deep in the mud and water. One of them wrote: "In one place I had to get out of my boots, climb on the bank of a sunken road and then pull my boots out after me."

But these adverse conditions failed to upset the carefully scheduled timetable. The German first line of defence was quickly overrun, some of the enemy captured still in their underwear.

There was one complication. Arthur Currie's First Division was flanked on the right by the British 51st Highland Division commanded by the inflexible Major General George "Uncle" Harper, a Colonel Blimp who opposed, among other things, the use of machine-guns by the infantry and had a complete mistrust of the newfangled tanks. He steadfastly refused to cooperate with the 5th Saskatchewan Battalion on his left so that his intentions and movements went unknown to his immediate allies. That he chose to fight his own little war in his own little way was to have unfortunate consequences.

Early on in Currie's sector, William Milne, a private with the 16th Canadian Scottish Battalion, won the Victoria Cross, one of four Canadians to be awarded the coveted medal at Vimy. With a bag of hand grenades slung over his shoulder, he found himself in the vanguard of his unit which had been halted by an enemy machine-gun. Creeping forward he single-handedly overcame it by hurling hand grenades into the nest, killing and wounding the gun crew.

After a brief pause, at exactly 6:55 a.m. the First Division, supported by a renewed creeping barrage, moved forward to assault the Zwischen Stellung entrenchment, their first objective, crossing a half mile of shell-torn ground to do so. Here Milne repeated his earlier performance, taking out a machine-gun post by himself. This time the entire enemy garrison surrendered to him. But Milne's VC had to be awarded posthumously. That afternoon he was killed.

It took only 28 minutes for Currie's forward battalions to complete their conquest of the primary goal. And, small wonder, the Germans were surrendering in droves. The fearful shelling had smashed their guns, shattered their trenches, killed every horse and knocked the fight right out of them. As the Canadians overran their positions the Germans threw down their rifles and offered their wristwatches and other possible souvenirs.

At times their willingness to give themselves up caused frustration for the Canadians. Jim Church of the Saskatchewans spotted 60 Germans emerging from a crater dead ahead of him. He pulled the pin on a Mills bomb and got ready to throw it when an enemy officer waved a white flag and shouted ''Don't throw it!'' as his comrades threw down their rifles. But the bomb was about to go off in a matter of seconds. Church tossed it as far away as he could. But when it exploded another batch of Germans rose out of another crater with their hands up, yelling: ''*Kamerad! Kamerad! Kamerad!*''

At Zero Hour, Henry Burstall's Second Division attacked on a front about half a mile wide which gradually broadened to a mile and a quarter at the site of the final objective, the Goulot Wood at the foot of the eastern slope. It was very much an echo of Currie's assault — a battlefield churned up by the devastating pre-attack shelling, prisoners surrendering by the score. And the award of another VC. Sergeant Ellis Sifton's C Company of the 18th Battalion (London, Ontario) with the Fourth Brigade on the right flank, was held up while advancing on the second German trench line, by a hidden machine-gun nest. His men were being mowed down unmercifully. Sifton spotted the gun barrel over the parapet and ran forward lobbing Mills bombs in the general direction of the weapon. Racing through a hole in the barbed wire conveniently laid open by the artillery barrage, he attacked the gun crew with his bayonet killing them all. But meanwhile another party of Germans had charged down the trench towards him. He managed to stave them off with his bayonet and held them at bay by clubbing them with his rifle butt, but it wasn't enough to save his life. One of the wounded enemy soldiers gathered enough strength to level his rifle and killed Sifton. However, his sacrifice saved countless lives and allowed the advance to continue.

Captain Bob Manion, the medical officer of the 21st Eastern Ontario Reserve Battalion and a future leader of the Canadian Conservative Party, found himself stranded in a dugout before the Zwischen Stellung trench with a wounded colonel and a badly disoriented padre. They had started out with 30 officers to set up a headquarters at the trench line. Now they had to turn back. By crawling from shell hole to shell hole they finally made it. Manion's part in the action earned him the Military Cross. When he eventually made it to the Zwischen Stellung trench, he passed a number of tanks bogged down in the mud. They were supposed to support an attack on the battered village of Thelus on the right flank, a veritable beehive of machine-gun nests. It was small wonder that a number of senior British officers, among them as aforementioned, "Uncle Harper" of the 51st Highland Division, had little faith in tanks.

The advance on the German defensive line, known as the Turko Graben Defence, progressed steadily, yet even at the relentless pace to keep to the timetable, the attackers could not ignore the horror and ravages of war around them. In shell holes, mine craters, abandoned trenches, ditches and dugouts, wounded men, friend and foe, sprawled about everywhere hideously mutilated. Some screamed to high heaven in pain, others merely moaned or sobbed. Captain Claude Williams of the 27th Reserve Battalion (City of Winnipeg) passed one man in a deep shell hole who cried out plaintively for "Water! Water!" The top of his head was missing. To one observer, the exposed brains seem to resemble fish roe. Then there were the dead, now beyond hope or help, their bloodstained uniforms a gruesome enough sight, but some so badly butchered and mangled that they were unrecognizable as human beings. Overworked stretcher-bearers carrying the wounded back to the dressing stations seemed to convey the sole sense of humanity to this macabre scene.

The Third Division's final objective, La Folie Wood at the foot of the eastern slope of the ridge, was only 1,200 yards from its start line. This was child's play by comparison to the two to three miles the First and Second divisions had to advance to the far side of the escarpment. By eight o'clock that morning the Third had overrun the three German defence lines in half an hour — right on schedule. The attack was over in two and a half hours, but it was far from smooth sailing.

On the left flank, the 7th Brigade had run into trouble. The Fourth Division had failed to capture Hill 145, one of the two bumps on the porpoise's head. From this highest point on the ridge, the Germans rained down merciless machine-gun fire on the advancing Canadians: the Royal Canadian Regiment, the Princess Patricia's Canadian Light Infantry and the 42nd Battalion (the Black Watch). For the latter the carnage was frightful. In four hours of fighting, the regiment lost 200 men. This resulted in a hold-up that left a gap between the division's two brigades, the 7th and 8th. What had happened?

By this time, according to the planned schedule, Hill 145 should have been in the hands of Brigadier General Victor Oldum's 11th Brigade. Five factors prevented it. One: the strength of this well defended bastion had been thoroughly underestimated. Two: the artillery had failed to penetrate the deep concrete tunnels and dugouts, leaving the inmates of the fortress intact. Three: the Germans had cleverly camouflaged a network of machine-guns on the crest of the ridge which remained hidden until the Canadians attacked. Four: the Fourth Division was the weakest in the corps as a result of the poison gas trench raid of March 1 that had backfired, causing 700 Canadian casualties. Five: Major Harry Shaw had asked the artillery to leave the nearest German trench undamaged for his regiment, the 87th Battalion, Grenadier Guards, to occupy and use as a shield. This was a major miscalculation for which Oldum, who had given Shaw his permission, had to share the blame. It was a misjudgement of the worst magnitude, one that resulted in utter slaughter — 60 percent of Shaw's Guards were wiped out in less than five minutes. The advance stopped in its tracks, one battalion after another stumbling into each other. Unable to keep to schedule the troops lost the protection of the creeping barrage. The situation quickly became so confused and reports so conflicting, that Oldum's headquarters and Oldum himself, had no idea what was happening.

What transpired was what all commanders dread. The enemy was able to form a salient from which it could open fire on the 10th Brigade to its left and the 12th Brigade on its right. That unit had enough problems just trying to advance across the quagmire, the soggiest terrain on the entire ridge. Wounded men slid into shell holes full of muddy water and drowned. The troops had trouble keeping up with shelling and lost its protection also. The 38th Battalion (Ottawa) found itself under fire from the front, the left and the rear, and most of the men became separated from their leaders.

Captain Thain MacDowell was left with only two runners. From his position he was able to make out the enemy dugout he had selected to capture for his headquarters. He first bombed out two machine-gun posts. When the Canadians reached the dugout, they found a flight of 50 steps leading to the bottom. MacDowell yelled down for the Germans to surrender. When there was no reply, he descended the stairs and was suddenly confronted with 77 Prussians.

MacDowell now decided on a bluff. He shouted back to an imaginary force to give the enemy the impression they were facing a substantial number of troops. Up went the hands in surrender. His problem now was to get the Germans to the top without giving away the ruse. This he accomplished by dividing them into small groups of a dozen each. But when the enemy discovered they'd been tricked, one of them grabbed a discarded rifle and fired at one of the runners. Luckily he missed and was shot on the spot for his pains. For this quick thinking, horrendous hoax, MacDowell added the Victoria Cross to the Distinguished Service Order he had won a year earlier at the Somme.

Of the four battalions in the 12th Brigade, only the 73rd Royal Highlanders reached their objective and that was due to the support of the 10th Brigade on the left flank acting as a hinge between the Canadians and the British 1st Corps. Its objective was to seize the Pimple, the other bump on the porpoise's head, at the very northern point of the ridge and the second highest elevation, the following day. But the calamitous failure to take Hill 145 now scrapped that plan. If total disaster was to be avoided, the bastion had to be overrun, and quickly. Oldum's dilemma was not so much as how to accomplish it. But with what?

Just before 10:00 a.m., much to the relief of the First and Second Divisions, artillery pounded the machine-gun infested ruins of the village of Thelus into rubble. Now the barrage began to move ahead again as the advance continued on to the next objective, known as the Chain Trench. There were some grisly moments: some of the shelling in the First Division sector fell short of the mark, the explosives killing their own men. A dud shell whizzed by Bill Green of the 1st Brigade, barely missing him but decapitating a gunner next to him as well as cutting the leg off another. The head went flying, hitting another man, almost knocking him off his feet, while the headless soldier, spurting blood like a broken water pipe, actually took two steps forward before flopping into the muck.

Between 11:15 and 11:45 the brigade had secured the Chain Trench from where they could see the plain beyond the ridge. The Germans were in full retreat lugging their guns with them. By this time the weather had cleared and the Royal Flying Corps was taking an active part in the advance. Flying a Nieuport scout fighter plane, Billy Bishop, who had become an ace the day before by shooting down his sixth German plane, described the scene from the air:

It seemed that I was in an entirely different world, looking down from another sphere on this strange, uncanny puppet show.

Suddenly I heard the deadly rattle of a nest of machine-guns under me, and saw that the line of our troops at one place was growing very thin, with many figures sprawling on the ground. For three or four minutes I could not make out the concealed position of the German gunners. Our men had halted, and were lying on the ground, evidently as much puzzled as I was. Then in the corner of a German trench I saw a group of about five men operating two machine-guns. The sight of these men thoroughly woke me up to the reality of the whole scene beneath me. I dived vertically at them with a burst of rapid fire. The smoking bullets from my gun flashed into the ground, and it was an easy matter to get an accurate aim on the German automatics, one of which turned its muzzle toward me.

But in a fraction of a second I had reached a height of only 30 feet above the Huns, so low I could make out every detail of their frightened faces. With hate in my heart I fired every bullet I could into the group as I swept over it, then turned my machine away. A few minutes later I had the satisfaction of seeing our line again advancing, and before the time had come for me to return from my patrol, our men had occupied all the German positions they had set out to take. It was a wonderful sight and a wonderful experience.

Predictably, "Uncle" Harper's 51st Highland Division failed to keep up, leaving the First Division's right flank exposed to heavy German machine-gun fire. But, in any event, the 1st Brigade left the Blue Line at 12:25 p.m., as the creeping barrage swept ahead to shatter the final objective, the Farbus Wood.

Earlier, at 10:40 that morning, the forward battalions of the Second Division had occupied battered Thelus village. It was a strange, ironic sight. Amid the ruins, in which no wall higher than six feet was left standing, an inn was left intact; there was an unscratched wallpapered bedroom with a feather bed on which the sheets had been turned down, a fully equipped unshattered bar, and a dining room table set for lunch complete with five waiters in attendance who were quickly shuttled to the rear as prisoners of war.

By 11:30 the 6th Brigade, and on its left flank, the 13th British Imperial Brigade, had reached their secondary objective where they waited for the barrage to continue so as to begin their advance to take the final goal, the bottom of the eastern slope of the ridge.

The Third Division made steady progress, although the 7th Brigade continued to be enfiladed by machine-gun fire from Hill 145. However, most of the unit, and the whole of the 8th Brigade, advanced steadily toward the final objective, La Folie Wood.

By early afternoon Victor Oldum realized there was only one source of fresh troops in the Fourth Division with which to dislodge the Germans from Hill 145. His own 11th Brigade and the 12th, both badly mauled, were already fully committed. The 10th, on the left flank, could not be spared if it was to capture the Pimple next day as scheduled. That left only the 85th Nova Scotia Highland Battalion, under any other circumstances one that Oldum would never have chosen for the job. It was a work battalion that had been assigned the task of digging a new communications trench. Now it was to go into battle for the very first time, with no combat training whatsoever, to take Hill 145 with two of its companies.

At 1:30 p.m., the First Division had seized the German battery positions in Farbus Wood. The enemy had beaten such a hasty retreat that meals had been left uneaten. At the same time the Second Division had reached the Brown Line and stared incredulously across the plain towards Douai where the Germans were retreating, well out of artillery range. The Canadians were helpless to exploit their success. The ridge had been so thoroughly pulverized into watery shell holes that it was impossible to move guns or tanks across the captured ground into firing position. It was the same story with the Third Division which occupied La Folie Wood. To the delight of the Canadians, the Germans had evacuated so hurriedly that they left all their rations behind.

At 6:35 that evening, Captains Harry Crowell and Percy Anderson of the Nova Scotia battalion, led their companies "C" and "D," through the melting snow to the jumping off trenches for the assault at dusk on Hill 145. It was to have been preceded by a 12-minute artillery barrage which was cancelled at the last minute for fear of hitting scattered troops of the 38th Ottawa Battalion. But neither Crowell nor Anderson had been made aware of it. However, the Canadians still had one strong advantage. The setting sun in the west was glaring right into the eyes of the enemy.

As Zero Hour arrived and passed with no shelling support, Crowell and Anderson were uncertain what to do. However after a minute went by, Crowell decided to go ahead with the attack. Anderson followed suit. Without the barrage, the German machine-gunners responded in force with devastating effect. With the men falling on their stomachs and into shell holes to protect themselves, the assault was in danger of completely coming apart. But as so often happens on such occasions, a single action, a compulsive act of individual courage and daring, turned the tide of failure into success.

Suddenly, Corporal Martin Crull of ''C'' Company leaped out of a shell hole firing a grenade rifle from the hip. It had two immediate effects. It completely demoralized the German machine-gunners who turned tail and tried to run; but they were at once cut down by Crull and two others in his platoon. At the same time his example put new heart into his comrades who quickly followed him. This single feat marked the turning point in the battle for Hill 145. The Germans quickly panicked and, as the 85th swarmed over the hill, firing rifles and Lewis machine-guns from the hip, they killed 75 of the fleeing enemy. Within an hour, the Nova Scotians had captured the hill, though pockets of resistance still remained down the steep eastern slope and at the base of it. Almost all of Vimy Ridge was in Canadian hands, save for the Pimple and the German remnants at Hill 145.

The next day was spent mopping up Hill 145, a task that fell to the 50th (Calgary) and the 44th (Winnipeg) battalions of the 10th Brigade. This meant that the attack on the Pimple had to be delayed. Oldum insisted on artillery to support the assault, which began in the mid-afternoon. During the deadly skirmish that followed, yet another Canadian, the fourth of the battle, won the Victoria Cross. Private John Pattison, who also had a son serving with the 50th, single-handedly wiped out a machine-gun nest that was holding up the advance. First he immobilized it with an accurate bombing attack then, charging forward, he killed all five of the gun crew.

An hour after the assault began, the enemy positions had been secured and the troops began to dig in. But the cost had been high. The Calgary battalion alone had lost 228 men killed, wounded and missing, more than a quarter of its total strength.

After a day in which the exhausted front line troops were allowed to catch their breath, the final assault on the ridge to capture the last vestige of enemy resistance, the Pimple, began at dawn on Thursday April 12. The attacking force, made up of part of the 44th and 50th battalions along with the 46th (Regina and Moose Jaw), advanced behind a creeping barrage in a blinding snowstorm. The German machine-gunners were unable to see the Canadians coming towards them and despite the fact that they had been able to bring up fresh troops, it was all over in two hours.

No one in the Allied military hierarchy had expected such a quick, stunning victory — or a victory period! Certainly not Robert-Georges Nivelle, who had written off any chances of the Canadians taking Vimy Ridge. Probably, and most likely, Sir Douglas Haig shared those doubts. In a way, that was understandable in view of the fact that for two years, the French and British had hammered themselves into insensibility against the escarpment with paralysing losses. If they couldn't handle it, what could you expect from an unruly — brave enough but unruly all the same — bunch of colonials? But it also showed an appalling lack of flexibility and initiative. Haig had at his disposal a mass of cavalry in the Arras sector. Why wasn't this employed to exploit the situation which was ripe for a breakthrough?

True, the guns could not be brought forward. But the Germans, in a panicky retreat had left their own artillery behind. This could have been turned on them. But consolidation, not exploitation, became the order of the day, and indeed this was successfully established; the Germans never attempted to recapture the escarpment. Yet, the Battle of Vimy Ridge had no impact on the military conduct of the war — none whatsoever. It was, after all, only a part of the Battle of Arras which had also been successful, even though the Spring Offensive was a failure. During the Second Battle of Aisne, which ended on May 9, the French lost another 200,000 men and the Germans 163,000, for a ground gain of only four miles. Nivelle was fired and replaced by Marshal Henri Petain. This hardly improved matters. The French Poilu had become so thoroughly disillusioned and fed up that open mutiny broke out. For the allies, for the time being at least, it was back to square one — and then some.

That digression aside, as far as Canada was concerned, the Battle of Vimy Ridge marked the birth of the country's nationality and a decisive step in its coming of age. There was no longer a question of secondary ''colonial'' status; Canadians had proved themselves to be among the best, if not *the* best, soldiers on the Western Front. It is significant that from that point on, the Canadians were chosen as the assault troops for all the battles that followed.

Vimy had set an example — a lesson, if you will — in enterprise, ingenuity, innovation, organization, planning and skill, not to mention bravery and determination, that reflected the Canadian character.

It had been costly; one Canadian in ten had been killed or wounded during the four day battle. Total casualties numbered 10,600 of which

3,598 were killed. Fifty-four German guns, 104 mortars and 124 machine-guns had been captured, along with 4,000 Bavarian and Prussian prisoners. Significantly, Arthur Currie, who was knighted in the field by King George V, was also appointed as the first Canadian commander of the Canadian Corps, replacing Sir Julian Byng, who, in parting, said: "the good old Canucks behaved like real, disciplined soldiers."

Other accolades came from the British press: "Canadians Sweep Vimy Ridge," blared the *Morning Post*; the French: "Canada's Easter Gift to France," the Americans: "Well Done Canada," and of course at home: "Canada Captures The Famous Vimy Ridge," the Montreal *Gazette* boasted. But probably the greatest compliment to the corps' success was the visit to the battlefield by members of the French general staff to learn how the fight had been won.

In 1930, the Canadian Government made certain that the Battle of Vimy Ridge would never be forgotten by commissioning architect Walter Allward to build a monument to commemorate the battle and pay tribute to the memory of those who fell. On Sunday July 29, 1936, the uncrowned King Edward VIII unveiled the monument described as "the most beautiful work in the world," before a crowd of 8,000 Canadian veterans and war widows, many of whom had paid their own way across the Atlantic.

The most striking, most massive monument of its kind anywhere, it stands on a concrete plinth, 4,000 feet square, on the site that was once Hill 145. It is the highest point of the escarpment and can be seen for miles from all directions. Huge twin spires, representing Canada's founding races, rise 226 feet, adorned with sculptures at the top and at the base, the largest of which is a mourning mother. The stone from which it is built and carved is the same marble used to build the Diocletian Palace on the Dalmatian coast of the Adriatic, chosen by the architect to last "for all time." Around the monument itself are shell holes and trenches preserved in concrete.

Haunting in a way, yet all about it a strangely incongruous aura of tranquility pervades. The effect is oddly pastoral. The rising majestic maple and pine trees, the cultured, carefully tended green grass, the winding road, all seem out of place with war. Still, on the quietest morning one senses the faint, phantom sounds of distant guns that once ravaged what is now this peaceful park. Every year, half a million tourists treat themselves to this awesome spectacle. And as each year goes by, the Battle of Vimy Ridge recedes a little further into our nation's history. We can be thankful that this magnificent monument will never allow the memory of Vimy Ridge to die.

✦ 10 ✦

THE DUCK'S WALK

I carried my protest to the extreme limit...which I believe would have resulted in my being sent home had I been other than the Canadian Corps Commander. I pointed out what the casualties were bound to be, and asked if a success would justify the sacrifice. I was ordered to go and make the attack.
Lieutenant General Sir Arthur Currie

No battle in history was ever fought under such conditions....
Major General Sir Hubert Gough,
Commander, the British Fifth Army

...a triumph of what might be called aquatic engineering.
John Terraine
Leading authority of the Great War

What greeted Canadian veterans of Ypres, the Somme, Vimy and Hill 70, along with yet untested fledgling infantry, in late October, 1917, was a scene so grisly and grotesque, that those fortunate enough to survive the forthcoming struggle would never forget it for the rest of their natural lives.

Since the last day of July, the struggle to capture the ruined village of Passchendaele in Belgium and the small ridges that break up the otherwise flat Flanders countryside around it east of Ypres, had already cost the British 200,000 casualties. Now the Canadian Corps, 100,000 strong — making up four divisions — was to be thrown into the breech. That prospect was fearsome enough but worse still were the sickening conditions under and over which their assault would have to be fought.

Heavier than normal autumn rains of torrential proportions (which the Germans described as their most effective ally) had turned the loose clay soil into a morass of mud and water. Artillery bombardment, which had wrecked the drainage system, further adding to the deluge over a land already swamped by swollen streams, had created a lunar-like scape of shell holes filled with water in which bodies floated. Other corpses were simply sucked down into the slime that had become a giant, tormented bog. Here and there blood oozed to the surface. In the craters it gave the mud a crimson texture. The land was all but impassable. It took all day to move a distance that would normally be covered in an hour's march. Men dragged themselves through waist-high gooey muck, now and then finding a firm footing which in reality was a dead body, from which often came strange moaning sounds. Horses and mules became hopelessly mired and had to be destroyed, causing great anguish for those who had to perform the task. Conversely the story of Lieutenant Howard Sutherland of the 97th (Grenadier Guards) Battalion illustrates just how far the affection between man and animal could extend. When a shell burst knocked him off a plank road, Sutherland was blown into an icy water filled shell hole and had just about given up the ghost when his faithful mule clutched the collar of his uniform in its teeth and pulled him from the crater.

Everywhere about that desolate landscape, which had been reduced to a few tree stumps, there was the vomit inducing smell of decay and death. It was impossible to dig trenches or hide except for the odd rise. The mud also gobbled up the guns. The only answer was to build duck walks — "bath mats," the Canadians called them — and these became prey to the German artillery. Under such conditions the heavy, lumbering tanks would never have stood a chance.

This sector assigned to the Canadians was located exactly a mile south-west of Passchendaele village itself on a 3,000-yard front through which ran the overflowing Ravebeek River. On the right was the Ypres-Roulers railway line. Once the objective had been taken, British commander-in-chief, Field Marshal Sir Douglas Haig planned on a cavalry charge through Roulers north to overwhelm the German submarine bases at Ostend. It sounded simple enough, but first just take a look at those German defences.

There was certainly no element of surprise. The enemy had been expecting an attack. From their vantage point they could easily see the build-up and had prepared accordingly. Trenches had been abandoned in favour of strong concrete machine-gun emplacements called "pillboxes" for their similarity in shape to the apothecary items. These were well concealed with mud and were difficult to spot from any appreciable distance. Strategically placed, they could provide a withering crossfire. What farm buildings that had been spared were reinforced with concrete, and these too presented sturdy fortifications.

German artillery support behind the village was also a powerful counter threat. And from the air, where the Germans had superiority at this stage of the war, the large enemy Gotha bombers escorted by fighters could raid the Canadian munitions supplies and headquarters, particularly at night. This marked the first time the Canadians had been harassed from the sky and the experience was harrowing.

The attack began at 5:40 a.m. after the men had received their warming tot of rum on the chilly, misty morning of October 26. Rain had fallen steadily overnight insuring that the battlefield would be effectively gummy. This meant that the creeping artillery barrage, normally moving 100 yards ahead ever four minutes, would be slowed to half that. The shelling had been continuous, every morning and afternoon for the past four days. The key to the entire operation lay in taking the heavily defended Bellevue Spur, the main German trench line defending Passchendaele, which the Australians and New Zealanders had failed to capture earlier in the month.

On the left, the 4th Canadian Mounted Rifles, entering what they later described as "the bloodiest battle in their history," were in trouble only eight minutes after the assault began. It had started to drizzle and that upset the timetable. The advance slowed down and now Canadian shells began to fall into the midst of the CMR. Then the German machine-guns opened up. Men fell and were helplessly swallowed by the mud. The advance quickly bogged down between Wallomolen and the Bellevue Spur, chiefly from the fire of one German pillbox. No one could get within 50 yards of it. No one, that is, except Private Tommy Holmes. Holding a Mills bomb in each hand, he charged forward across the mud infested ground and took cover in a shell hole just as machine-gun fire from two German crews erupted all around him. Then, at the moment the gunners began to reload, he lobbed his grenades so accurately that he took out both enemy positions. Now for the pillbox itself: Holmes ran back to his front line, rearmed himself with more bombs, and raced ahead, bullets blazing all around him. Manoeuvring behind the fortification, he tossed the explosives inside through the entrance. There was a loud burst, then 19 terrified Germans emerged from the pillbox with their hands raised in surrender. This valiant action won Holmes the Victoria Cross and allowed the CMRs to continue their advance. By 11:00 they had reached their intermediate objective, the Wolfe's Copse but murderous enemy fire prevented them going any further.

The battalion had already suffered such crippling losses — only five of its 16 officers were still alive — that the commanding officer, Lieutenant Colonel William Patterson, ordered his men to dig in as best they could in the muck and mire, to consolidate their modest gain. There they beat off counter-attack after counter-attack, capturing 12 machine-guns and taking over 200 German prisoners. But the cost had been horrific. Next day, by the time they were relieved, their losses had climbed to 312.

On the Third Division's right flank, the 43rd Cameron Highlanders of Canada and the 58th Central Ontario battalions easily overran the forward pillbox concentrations but soon came under intense enemy artillery fire. The 58th was forced to retire but meanwhile a detachment of the 48th, led by Lieutenant Robert Shankland, had reached the crest of the Bellevue Spur. However, the withdrawal of the 58th left their right flank exposed. On the left flank, the halt of the CMR short of their main objective left the right side naked as well.

With the Germans threatening and under severe shelling, Shankland turned his command over to a subaltern and wove his way back to battalion headquarters to explain the situation first-hand and point out the need for an immediate counter-attack with the aid of reinforcements. That done he returned to the front line while a company of the 52nd Ontario Battalion, led by Christopher O'Kelly, moved forward to support Shankland, just in time to mow down German troops advancing on the Highlanders' position, routing the enemy force completely. Next, O'Kelly led the capture of six pillboxes taking 100 prisoners and ten machine-guns. For their stalwart efforts, both Shankland and O'Kelly were awarded the Victoria Cross.

On the corps' extreme right, working in conjunction with Australian troops, the 46th South Saskatchewan Battalion of the First Division's 10th Brigade not only encountered fierce German machine-gunfire but also fell victim to their own Canadian artillery shelling. Luckily, ground conditions prevented what might otherwise have been severe casualties. ''We were wading in mud and falling in shell holes,'' Private Don McKerchar recalled:

...if you were a casualty...you'd probably drown in the mud and dirt — many of them, all kinds, drowned in this mud. [Fortunately], a lot of shells would bury in the soft mud — many of them were duds — and if they did explode, they were down so deep that the shrapnel wasn't too effective.

Despite this untoward shelling along with the German artillery and the merciless fire from the pillboxes, by 7:10 a.m. the 46th had managed to reach its objective, the Decline Copse, a shattered wood lying adjacent to the Ypres-Roulers railway line. But it was impossible to dig in due to the soft mud and the men had to consolidate positions in the water filled shell holes, expecting a major enemy counter-attack at any moment. That did not take place until 4:34 in the afternoon and it came from three different directions: Crest Farm, Passchendaele village, and Tiber House, supported by a heavy artillery barrage. The battalion sent up signal flares for artillery assistance of their own but 20 minutes went by before the Canadians' shells started falling. By then it was too late, the overpowering German force was already on the Canadians' doorstep.

The assault proved too much for the outnumbered 46th, and despite a spirited attempt to hold on, the defence soon crumbled and the men were seized with panic. However, two officers, Major John Hope and Captain William Kennedy, rallied what was left of the decimated battalion. The German attack had begun to falter in the mud and with the help of the supporting 10th Canadian machine-gun company, the small band of Canadians was able to force the Germans to give ground. They were able to recapture the rise near the Decline Copse, though they were unable to retake the battered wood. It had been a deadly day for the 46th. Of the 600 men who took part, 70 percent became casualties: 18 officers and 426 other ranks.

In spite of this demise, the 10th Brigade commander, Brigadier General Edward Hilliam, was adamant that the copse be retaken and quickly. He relieved the 46th with the 44th Manitoba and the 47th British Columbia battalions and ordered them to go to it. That night they made a joint attempt that, in the confusion of the darkness, failed. However, at 10:00 p.m. the following night, October 27, in a renewed attack, the 44th recaptured the Decline Copse as well as the wood at bayonet point. At this time they were relieved by the 85th Nova Scotia Highlanders battalion, and the Germans took advantage of this midnight turnover to recapture some of the lost ground. However, the fresh battalion soon routed them and the position remained in Canadian hands from then on.

Thus ended the first phase of the Passchendaele campaign. Casualties for the period totalled 2,481. Against only seven battalions with an average of 600 men, it represented a horrendous, virtually unacceptable level. The Canadian Corps medical service and stretcher-bearers working under the most difficult conditions — in some cases it took ten men to carry one stretcher — treated 1, 207 wounded Canadians and 55 Germans.

The key to the next stage, as before, was the capture of the Bellevue Spur which the Germans (the 11th Bavarian Division) were doggedly determined to hold. The Canadians were now in a much more advantageous tactical position to take such objectives. They were on higher, drier ground with more room to manoeuvre. Major General David Watson's Fourth Division, for example, could now deploy three battalions from the Decline Copse instead of the one that it took to secure it. And at Zero Hour, 5:50 a.m., Tuesday, October 30, the weather was clear. In fact it hadn't rained for three days.

The immediate objective was the Blue Line, 600 to 700 feet directly ahead. This included the Vienna Cottage and Crest Farm in the Fourth Division sector and Meetcheele and Vapour Farm in the Third's territory north of the Ravebeek River. North of the Ypres-Roulers Railway from right to left were the 85th Nova Scotia Highlanders, the 78th Grenadiers and the 72nd Seaforth Highlanders of Canada and battalions from the 12th Brigade. North of the Ravebeek in the same order were the Princess Patricia's Canadian Light Infantry, the 49th Edmonton Regiment Battalion from the 7th Brigade and the 5th Canadian Mounted Rifles from the 8th Brigade.

When the Nova Scotians began their charge, to their horror they found they were without artillery support. Anyone advancing higher than crouch level was cut down by the raking German machine-gun and rifle fire. In retaliation, the Canadians brought their Lewis guns to bear, allowing the infantry to hopscotch from shell hole to shell hole. In the face of this determined onslaught, the Germans broke and fled in disarray with the maritimers in hot pursuit. By 6:35 a.m. the 85th had reached its Blue Line objective. Here the ground was firmer and they were able to entrench themselves solidly for the first time since the battle began.

In the centre of the 12th Brigade advance, the Winnipeg Grenadiers made the assault in four waves, 50 yards apart. Though unimpeded by German shelling which was sporadic, ineffective and landed mostly behind Canadian lines, the battalion ran into a dense wall of small arms fire that riddled the ranks and brought the attack to a halt. Major John McEwan, the second in command, quickly mobilized the force of survivors and led a charge straight ahead to the objective, 800 yards away. His uniform ripped to shreds by enemy bullets, he miraculously escaped unscathed. For his dash, daring and example to his men, he received the Distinguished Service Order.

By 7:30 that morning, the 78th had dug in. Here again the ground was dry, and hard enough to build proper trenches six feet deep by three feet wide. During the day the Winnipegers repelled several counter-attacks but nothing could dislodge them now.

The principal objective of the 72nd Seaforth Highlanders of Canada on the left flank of the 12th Brigade, was Crest Farm. To achieve it, because the battalion's front was so badly flooded, the commanding officer, Lieutenant Colonel James Clark, had to squeeze three companies in single file through a gap a mere 50 yards wide. Unlike their comrades in the 85th battalion, they had full artillery and machine-gun support. Haalen Copse on the left was quickly taken after a heated skirmish in which 50 Germans were killed and 25 taken prisoner.

Next to fall to the Canadians was the main goal of Crest Farm. Here they killed 40 more of the enemy and took another 30 prisoner. Corporal Stuart Irwin distinguished himself by wiping out three machine-gun crews preparing to enfilade his comrades at Haalen Copse, in a matter of seconds with his own Lewis gun.

To the right, another company captured the high ground east of the farm. A patrol went forward to probe Passchendaele and found it deserted. But taking no chances — highly vulnerable, out in the open — the detachment cautiously withdrew.

By 9:30 a.m., the battalion had solidified its gains and was well dug in. Now it came under a continuous, heavy enemy artillery barrage that lasted 18 hours. During the night the Germans attacked in company strength but were finally repelled, 30 of the survivors surrendering to the Canadians at daybreak. Losses to the brigade had not been light: a total of 1,028 casualties out of an attacking force of 1,800 men. Two of the battalions, the 72nd and 78th, lost over 50 percent of their total strength.

North of the Ravebeek River it had been planned for the Princess Patricia's Canadian Light Infantry, with the 49th Edmonton Regiment Battalion on the left, to capture a strong point known as Duck Lodge, take Meetcheele, a small shell torn hamlet on the road to Passchendaele, then overrun Graf House. It didn't quite work out that way. Each man carrying, among other things, 270 rounds of small arms ammunition, three sandbags, two rifle grenades and a shovel had to wade through swamp up to his knees. Forward progress was reduced to 750 yards an hour, what the PPCLI battalion history described as "the low record for a charge in all the history of war." The creeping barrage crept forward at the rate of 50 yards every four minutes to keep pace, such as it was, with the infantry advance.

Soon the PPCLI found itself facing accurate and rigorous fire. Almost all the battalion officers and men were either killed or wounded. But by 7:00 that morning they had captured the Duck Lodge. The next objective, Meetcheele, lay straight ahead. But where was the 49th, which was to have supported the Patricias for this next attack? That regiment had run into trouble from the outset. Canadian artillery had not only proven to be ineffective, it had created carnage. Shells fell too far short, wounding and killing scores of the Edmontonians. Joining in this slaughter, the German artillery, their range dead on, was perfectly timed and coordinated with wicked small arms fire. Nearly all the battalion's officers were either killed or wounded. It was during this deadly mêlée that Private Cecil "Hoodoo" Kinross won the Victoria Cross.

Seeing his comrades halted by a German machine-gun, he decided to take matters into his own hands without any orders or prompting. He stripped off all his gear, then with rifle and bayonet he charged the position, dodging enemy bullets. He reached the pit, leapt into it and killed all six of the gun crew. His courageous act was not enough to allow the regiment to pursue its attack. Although the Edmontonians, with more losses, managed to reach their intermediate objective, Furst Farm, it was clear that, with their ranks so decimated, they could continue no further. The casualty rate of 75 percent was the worst in the battalion's history. Going into the battle that day with 567 men, it had lost an appalling 443. The order went out to dig in. If the Princess Pats were going to take Meetcheele, they would have to go it alone.

From Duck Lodge, the PPCLI surged forward in the teeth of relentless, withering enemy fire with the aim of first overcoming a pillbox on the rise of a hill, the key to capturing the ruined village. It proved to be a stubborn redoubt, pinning down as many as 40 men. Investigating the problem, Lieutenant Hugh McKenzie of the supporting 7th Machine-Gun Company, went forward to take charge. McKenzie sent out several small parties, one of them led by Sergeant

George Mullin, to circle around behind the concrete stronghold and attack it from the rear while he himself led a frontal assault to distract the German gunners.

In the meantime, Mullin had decided to rush the pillbox head-on. He blasted it with hand grenades, then climbed on top of the emplacement, reached through the gun aperture and shot the two enemy machine-gunners through the head with his revolver. At this point McKenzie was killed with a bullet through his head. Mullin proceeded to force his way into the fortification, where he took the remaining occupants prisoner. Both McKenzie and Mullin received the Victoria Cross. Their gallantry allowed the PPCLIs to capture Meetcheele but they went no further.

With less than 200 survivors — casualties amounted to 363 — Colonel Agar Adamson, the commanding officer, called off all further operations and decided that the final objective, Graf House, could, for the time being, remain in German hands. Having entrenched themselves, the Patricias now braced themselves for the inevitable enemy counter-attacks. They didn't have long to wait. The first occurred at 8:00 a.m. followed by two others. But all three assaults were beaten off by Canadian artillery and the battalions' Lewis guns. That afternoon, reinforcements from the Royal Canadian Regiment arrived bringing water and ammunition and helping evacuate many of the wounded.

On the left flank, the 8th Brigade's 5th Canadian Mounted Rifles scored a resounding success thanks to the gallantry and leadership shown by Major George Pearkes who posted the fourth Victoria Cross for the day. But he nearly bought the farm before the attack even got underway. A piece of shrapnel from the German counter barrage struck him in the thigh so forcibly it knocked him down. For a desperate few moments his men wondered whether they should call off the operation. Struggling to his feet, Pearkes assured them he was able to continue and led his men forward.

It was heavy slogging through the mud filled shell holes, particularly for Pearkes who was in some pain. Worse still was the punishing enfilade machine-gun fire from the battalion's undefended left flank which had been abandoned by a British supporting unit. But the 2nd CMRs plunged ahead toward the intermediate and final objectives, Vapour Farm and Vine City. With some 50 men, Pearkes stormed the intermediate target and secured the farm at bayonet point. (Farm was a misnomer, the position turned out to be nothing more than a deteriorating haystack.) Digging in, the Canadians warded off countless counter-attacks. Reinforcements — the 2nd CMR — rushing to relieve Pearkes' party were so badly cut down by enemy enfilade machine-gun fire that they were forced to abandon the rescue until after dark. Meanwhile Pearkes' company stubbornly hung on. By the time help arrived at dusk, German machine-gun and sniper fire had reduced the company to 12 men, many of them wounded.

Battalion casualties amounted to 416 out of a total strength of 590. Only the 49th's losses were heavier, but the 5th CMR had at least attained most of its objectives. Total corps casualties for the day were 884 killed, 1420 wounded and eight taken prisoner. The battle for Passchendaele was indeed proving to be a costly one for the Canadians. And there was more to come.

Nevertheless, at this point, the gains outweighed the losses. The Canadians had gained 1000 yards. It was now time to regroup and restructure for the next phase of the battle. Canadian Corps commander Lieutenant General Sir Arthur Currie set the date of the next attack for November 6. In the meantime, sporadic exchanges between the Canadians and Germans took place, mostly search patrols to keep each other on their toes and take prisoners for interrogation. In one foray, the 42nd Royal Canadian Highlanders captured the Graf House which the 49th Edmonton Regiment had failed to take on October 30. The triumph was short-lived, however. Under heavy enemy pressure, the battalion soon had to abandon it. But the Canadian assault had not been a total failure. It had upset plans by three German raiding parties to attack the 42nd's left flank.

On Saturday, November 3, the Germans staged a heavy barrage with a simultaneous assault on the Canadian line, but it was quickly subdued and several enemy prisoners fell into the defenders' hands. The Germans demonstrated that they were not going to give up Passchendaele without a serious fight. The high command had issued a directive that the village must "be held or, if lost, recaptured at all costs." They had also reinforced their 4th Division with the 11th brought from Champagne in northern France.

On the Canadian side, fresh troops were also brought in. The First and Second Divisions replaced the weary Third and Fourth at 4:00 a.m., a mere two hours before Zero Hour on Tuesday, November 6. The main Canadian objectives were the battered villages of Passchendaele, Mosselmarkt and Goudberg, or what was left of them. Deployment placed Major General Archie Macdonell's First Division on the right and Major General Harry Burstall's Second on the left. The attack was preceded by a deafening two minute barrage from every available gun which, at Zero Hour, began to creep forward. Close behind it, on the extreme left flank, the 3rd Toronto Regiment Battalion from the 1st Brigade made straight for the Vine Cottage stronghold, while on the right of the Second Division sector, the 1st Western Ontario and the 2nd Eastern Ontario Divisions advanced on the hamlet of Mosselmarkt, to the north of Passchendaele.

At first the 3rd Battalion knocked out two pillboxes defending the approaches to the Vine Cottage, and at the same time overcame a third where 30 Germans surrendered. A piece of cake. But now the unit became pinned down by fire from the pillbox inside the shattered Vine House itself. At this point Corporal Cecil Barron took over. Inching forward on his stomach, when he drew within point-blank range he hurled several Mills bombs at the emplacement. The explosion killed most of the gun crews and Barron took the rest prisoner. Chalk up another Victoria Cross, and with the fortification out of action, the battalion was now able to proceed towards the Goudberg Spur.

As the men struggled through the quagmire they encountered other machine-gun nests but in every case were able to put them quickly out of action. By mid-morning Goudberg was in Canadian hands at a price of 240 dead, wounded and missing.

At the outset, the 2nd Battalion suffered its only real setback for the day when a routine German bombardment caused casualties, many of them officers, before the unit even went over the top. But from then on, alongside the 1st Battalion, it experienced few difficulties. The mud was not nearly as thick as had been expected and the Germans were taken completely by surprise. Their defensive artillery came too late to be effective and was therefore practically useless; most of the shelling landed well behind the advancing Canadians. Although the Graf House, which the enemy had recaptured three days earlier, put up some resistance, it was soon quelled. Finally, by 7:45 a.m., Mosselmarkt fell with virtually no opposition. Most of the defenders had been killed by the Canadian barrage. Archie Macdonell could well be pleased with his division's performance that morning. "You can't beat them," he said.

The Second Division had even greater success. To capture Passchendaele, Harry Burstall had assigned four battalions: one, the 26th New Brunswick from the 5th Brigade and three others, the 27th Winnipeg, the 31st Alberta and the 28th Northwest from the 6th. Fine work by the artillery made the initial advance sure and swift. By 7:30 a.m., the 26th on the right flank, had reached the high ground to the south of the village. The seizure of this mass of rubble and ruins, with not a single house left standing, was the objective of the three battalions from the "Iron Sixth" Brigade. To reach it, they had to work their way across a porridge of mud and water. The 27th, on the right of the 6th Brigade assault, had to slosh through a morass, in some places waist-deep.

On the outskirts of Passchendaele, the 27th's left hand platoon was being decimated by fire from a German machine-gun nest surrounded by barbed wire which made it virtually impregnable. The unit commander called for volunteers. Private James Robertson was one of the first to reach the nest. Charging boldly forward in the direct line of fire, he hurdled the barbed wire and killed four of the enemy gunners with his bayonet. When the others tried to flee, he mowed them down with their own gun. Carrying that same weapon, he led the volunteers in a charge into the village. When they returned to their own line, they discovered that two of their wounded had been left in No-Man's Land. Robertson went to bring them in. He managed to rescue one of his comrades but when he returned for the second he was struck by a bullet. Still, he was able to carry the second man to safety before a shell exploded, killing him instantly. Robertson's courage was rewarded with a posthumous Victoria Cross.

Private Harry Badger of the 28th on the 6th Brigade's left flank was in a bloodthirsty frame of mind and would have tackled the entire German army if he could. The first in his battalion to reach the enemy's forward posts, he took on a pair of German pillboxes. He called on the occupants of the nearest one to surrender, whereupon six of them emerged with their hands up. Badger was in no mood to respect the conventions of war and he cold-bloodedly bayoneted them on the spot. The second pillbox then promptly surrendered as well. This time compassion took over from the moment of cruelty and Badger made the gunners his prisoner. When one of them pointed out another stronghold, Badger demanded its surrender also. His score for the day: six enemy executed, 15 captured. As the saying goes, war is hell.

In the centre of the brigade's assault, Lieutenant John Cameron of the 31st Battalion went on his own kind of rampage. When his platoon became pinned down by an enemy machine-gun strongpoint which the creeping barrage had not yet reached, Cameron saw red. Charging through his own artillery fire, he reached the emplacement, bayoneted seven of the German gun crew and captured 12 more along with the weapon. Tally: seven killed, 12 prisoners, one Spandau souvenir. *C'est la guerre.*

By 7:40 that morning Passchendaele was in Canadian hands. The Germans had fled rather than surrender, leaving the 6th Brigade with only token pockets of resistance to be cleared out from the rubble filled cellars. All the objectives had been taken at relatively small cost compared to the October attacks, although by any measurement it was still expensive enough. Corps losses for the day totalled 2,238, including 734 dead. This was from only seven battalions at an approximate strength of 4,200 men.

Passchendaele had been a bitter strategic loss for the Germans, who considered an immediate offensive to retake it. However, circumstances mitigated against it. Oberste Heerseleitung (OHL) lacked confidence in the infantry's ability to carry out such an operation and settled instead for a protracted artillery bombardment of the Canadians in and around the village. Most of the 250 casualties incurred by the 28th Battalion that day resulted from that retaliatory shelling. Heavy rain did not lessen the discomfort.

Over the next two days, relief battalions arrived. They could hardly believe the fearful spectacle that confronted them. The 13th Royal Highlanders of Canada regimental history described it:

> The mud was in many places waist-deep, torn and twisted wire lay everywhere, water filled shell holes were numerous while all about bodies of the dead, the whole area presenting a picture of desolation and horror hard to equal and surpass.

Private Jacques Lapointe, a signaller with the 22nd French-Canadian Battalion, which relieved the shell-shocked 28th, never forgot the sight. He wrote:

> In a flooded trench, the bloated bodies of some German soldiers are floating. Here and there, too, arms and legs of dead men stick out from the mud, and awful faces appear, blackened by days and weeks under the beating sun. I try to turn from these dreadful sights, but everywhere I look bodies emerge, shapelessly, from their shroud of mud. It would seem life could never return to these fields of abundant death.

The final stage of the Battle of Passchendaele was, characteristically, fought in the worst weather of the entire campaign. Saturday, November 10, dawned misty with low clouds, but by 7:00 a.m. 55 minutes after the Zero Hour, a driving, raging rainstorm enveloped the battlefield, the rain falling so heavily that many of the troops could only crawl forward.

The assault was directed towards the high ground north of the village, the two specific objectives: Vindictive Crossing, 1,000 yards from the town, and Hill 52, the highest point of the ridge. In the vanguard were two battalions from Brigadier General Frederick Loomis's 2nd Brigade (First Division), the 7th — 1st British Columbia Regiment, and the 8th — 90th Winnipeg Rifles. In support on the right was the 20th Central Ontario Battalion from the 4th Brigade, on the left a British brigade.

As early as 3:40 that morning the two spearhead battalions came under German artillery shelling, obviously in anticipation of an attack. By 5:00 a.m. it had intensified. This barrage, which came to a halt only a few minutes before Zero Hour, caused 132 casualties among the two units. Given that and the atrocious weather conditions, it was a wonder the day's operations succeeded as well and as quickly as they did. But it was by no means easy, and the cost was, in some cases, frightful.

The British Columbians quickly achieved the primary objective, Vindictive Crossing, but one company lost all its officers in the assault, and one platoon was virtually wiped out, only a lance corporal and seven privates being spared. Having consolidated the position the battalion now faced heavy fire from a nearby trench. This was soon subdued but then the unit came under fire from a pillbox. Private Crosby Dorais neutralized it with his Lewis gun and prevented reinforcements from reaching it. This allowed the Canadians to overrun the emplacement taking 18 Germans prisoner and capturing two machine-guns.

Losses prevented the 7th from advancing any further and the reserve battalion, the 10th Canadians, moved in to renew the attack. Meanwhile the 20th Central Ontario Battalion reached its objective on the right flank at 7:00 a.m. Shortly afterwards a gap opened up between the 20th and the 7th. Two platoons were promptly dispatched to fill it and during the subsequent encounter, they overran a German pillbox, which had laid low during the advance and been bypassed. In the process, the Canadians took 24 prisoners.

More serious was an opening created on the left flank by the faltering 2nd Brigade of the British First Division. After capturing Ventura Farm in textbook fashion, during which the 90th Winnipeg

Rifles seized four 77-millimetre guns, the battalion found itself enfiladed by enemy fire on the left flank then subjected to prolonged shelling by artillery batteries from five German corps. General Currie was irate and with good reason. The British failure and ineptitude threatened the Canadian victory. "The British," he charged, "retired in very bad and pronounced disorder, amounting to panic."

But the Canadians hung on. With the help of the 5th Western Calgary Battalion, the 80th soon had the situation under control. The shelling persisted but the battle had already been won. At dawn next day, Hill 52, the highest point on the ridge, was in Canadian hands. Now they could look across the rolling green Belgian countryside, at roads, villages and farms unravaged by war. Casualties on November 10 totalled 1,094, including 420 who gave their lives. For the next few days the Germans made sporadic raids against the consolidated Canadian positions, but they were half-hearted and soon petered out altogether.

Once again Canadian energy, grit, skill, technology and superior planning had won the day, this time under the worst of conditions imaginable. And to what avail? General Currie had never considered the grubby little war-torn crossroads town of Passchendaele worth the candle either strategically or tactically. And a miserable, paltry ground gain of four and a half miles after 12 days of bitter fighting scarcely justified casualties amounting to 15,654 only marginally lower than Currie's estimate of 16,000. Winston Churchill, then British minister of munitions, best described it as "a forlorn expenditure of valour and life without equal in futility." That being so, why had it ever taken place? And why had the Canadians been picked as the sacrificial lambs?

The answer to that last question is simple, easy and straightforward. The Canadians were the best damned troops on the Western Front, respected by friend and foe alike. Ever since Ypres and Vimy Ridge, whenever a tough job presented itself, it was given to the Canadians.

Explaining the reason for Passchendaele is far more complicated, and in a sense devious, and not without political under- and overtones. Its genesis arose out of the French army mutinies following Marshal Roger Nivelle's disastrous 1917 spring offensive. To draw attention away from the insurrections, Nivelle's successor, Marshal Henri Petain, urged British Commander-in-Chief Sir Douglas Haig to take the offensive against the Germans in the north on the Flanders Front. For this he promised the eventual support of French divisions. Haig was only too happy to comply. He had long had his heart set on destroying the enemy submarine bases on the Belgian coast.

On June 7, 1917 he launched what was in effect the kick-off to the Third Battle of Ypres, with the capture of the Messines Ridge. This gave the British Second Army under Lieutenant General Sir Herbert Plumer, a position overlooking the southern part of Passchendaele Ridge. This, in turn, dominated the low-lying ground over which Haig planned to advance to the Belgian coast.

The offensive resumed on July 31 with Haig confident that he could smash his way through to the Belgian coast that summer. But in the meantime the British Prime Minister, Lloyd George, had begun to have second thoughts. He was convinced that 1918 would be the critical year for the war and believed that a policy of defence should be implemented to conserve British army strength and await the arrival of American troops. He regarded Haig's plans as an expensive waste of manpower and his goals as unnecessary. After all, the U-boat menace had been overcome with the use of convoys. He also believed that the army should support the Italians on the Austrian front. However, without French support Haig knew that Lloyd George would be unable to transfer British troops if he continued his "duck's walk," as Marshal Ferdinand Foch called it, across Flanders. So he determinedly and stubbornly continued his offensive, although for limited gain and under deteriorating field and weather conditions.

During the first phase, between July 31 and August 2, Lieutenant General Hubert Gough's Fifth Army captured the villages of Bixschoote and St Julien and the Pilckem Ridge. But tough German counterattacks robbed the right wing of solid gains. The artillery barrages — four million shells landed in the Ypres area — destroyed the drainage system and turned the battlefield into a muddy morass. It would get worse as the month progressed and the heavy rains began to fall.

After three successful battles — Menin Ridge, Polygon Wood and Broodseinde — Plumer's troop managed to get a foothold on the Passchendaele Ridge, but only briefly. Then the rain came down and the mud made any further advance impossible. Most of Haig's staff recommended consolidating their position and calling off the offensive until spring. But Haig insisted that all that had to be done was to take the Passchendaele Ridge, then the way would be open to the German held Belgian ports and the war would be over. He persisted in carrying on and nothing could stop him, certainly not his own field commanders. And his glowing communications with the war department was so enthusiastic and optimistic that Lloyd George was unable to persuade his cabinet to halt the offensive. However, further attempts to accomplish Haig's aims ended in failure. By this time, he had committed every division available to him.

But Haig still had an ace in the hole — his admiration and faith in Sir Arthur Currie and the Canadian Corps who most recently had captured the well-defended Hill 70. He was now about to play that card. On October 13, Haig ordered Currie to move his corps to the Ypres sector and submit a plan for the capture of Passchendaele "as soon as possible." It was far from a welcome assignment. Currie had bitter memories of Ypres, going back to the 1915 gas attack, and after reconnoitering the battlefield he regarded the Passchendaele operation as impossible, except at heavy cost, and futile. Although he both liked and admired Haig, he had no hesitation in voicing his objections in the strongest terms.

Haig overruled Currie's protestations. "Some day I will tell you why," he said to him, "but Passchendaele must be taken." Orders were orders but on one point Currie put his foot down. He refused to have his corps attached to Gough's Fifth Army. After the Somme, where his men had never been given proper artillery support and the planning had been incompetent, he swore he'd never serve under Gough again. On this point at least Haig acquiesced and for this operation the Canadian Corps became part of Plumer's Second Army.

Currie may have had strong misgivings about the Passchendaele assignment, but he began preparing for it in his usual meticulous and thorough manner, not leaving anything to chance down to the last detail. Nothing escaped his eagle eye: for example, he ordered that all units be provided with muzzle protectors and breech covers to protect the guns from the mud and rain.

The result, of course, was a brilliant victory, if at horrendous cost, that only the Canadians were able to achieve, and it won the respect of all the Allies. But it was a hollow success. Capture of the ridge came too late in the year for the breakthrough charge across Flanders fields. Haig's ambitious, high-minded offensive for the most part ground to a halt. A year, to the day, of war still lay ahead. Ironically the Germans recaptured the ridge the following spring. After the war, at the Versailles Peace Conference in Paris on February 12, 1919, Haig told Currie that following the victories at Vimy and Messines, it had been necessary to keep the offensive rolling to prevent the Germans from attacking the French and to raise the morale of both the British and French armies and governments. Therefore, the ridge had to be taken. But Currie still didn't buy it.

His feelings as reported by Canadian prime minister, Sir Robert Borden, are instructive.

> Currie tells me, and I believe he is right, that it had no useful result, as the British Army immediately went on the defensive and the campaign ceased for a year. No advantage in position was gained and the effort was wasted particularly when the ridge was simply handed back to the enemy six months later. [In Currie's opinion] the venture was by no means worth the cost: and that it was won to save the face of the British High Command who had undertaken all through the autumn most unsuccessful and highly disastrous attempts.

Personal feelings aside, objectively and without prejudice, Passchendaele must be viewed apart from those who engineered and executed it, and in some ways from those who fought it. Passchendaele may be judged as a tragic triumph, but a triumph over adversity and the enemy nevertheless. It must be remembered as an important, very gallant part of Canadian military history. It must never be dismissed or forgotten.

John Swettenham, the noted Canadian military historian, wrote what would seem a fitting epitaph to the whole grim business: "Canada...had been given a job to do and had done it well: but at a grim price. In this Ypres Salient and especially at Passchendaele, her sons had proved her right to call herself a nation." Swettenham added this postscript:

> For weeks the dead lay buried amid the mud. In the spring, when the Newfoundlanders held the ridge, corpses rose out of the softening ooze and were cleared away. One morning stretcher parties blundered into a pair of bodies, perhaps symbolic of the whole campaign. One was Canadian, the other German, grappling still in death. They had fought desperately and, sucked into the swamp, had died in one another's arms. All efforts to part them failed and so a large grave was dug in which to bury the pitiful remains.

✤ 11 ✤

THE MARCH TO MONS

Reference map "Operations — Canadian Army Corps."

A close shave! In March, 1918, the fatherland came within a whisker of winning the Great War. Logistically, General Erich Ludendorff's armies should have succeeded hands down. The Russian Revolution had earned peace with the Bolsheviks. That freed up enough German troops from the east to bolster their Western Front strength to a total of 177 divisions. This seriously upset the balance between the German and Allied forces. The British (who had lost heavily during the Third Battle of Ypres) and the French had jointly transferred 11 divisions to the Italian Front and were now thinly spread with few reserves. American involvement amounted to only six divisions with no battle experience. British commander-in-chief Field Marshal Sir Douglas Haig asked for 605,000 reinforcements available in England. But after the shocking losses suffered at Passchendaele, Prime Minister Lloyd George had lost faith in Haig and to avoid further attrition, he limited the fresh troops to 100,000.

With his new superiority, towards the end of March when the weather cleared and the ground dried, Ludendorff decided on one last desperate throw of the dice to deliver a knockout blow by striking at the Allies' weakest point splitting their forces in two before the American presence could be felt. Aided by a thick fog, which blinded the defenders, at 4:40 a.m. on March 21, the Germans attacked on a front 50 miles wide at the heart of the British sector roughly between Arras in the north and St Quentin in the south. The immediate strategic

147

objectives were the key railhead centres at Amiens, on the Somme River, and Hazebrouck.

The Germans very nearly succeeded. By noon they had broken through the British Fifth Army into open country. At nightfall next day they were on the Somme. The French commander-in-chief General Henri Petain lost his nerve and pulled back his forces to defend Paris. But Ludendorff failed to exploit this and his own early gains. Only one of his three armies, the 17th, had broken through. Ludendorff played it safe by ordering that force to stay in pace with the other two. It was a mistake. The British Fifth Army was shattered and the Germans could easily, given the circumstances and opportunities open to them, have split the British and French and that would have been it, Americans or no Americans. But events were moving rapidly. At Haig's instigation, all Allied forces came under the unified control of the aggressive Marshal Ferdinand Foch. As the German assault lost steam, the Western Front fell once again into a stalemate. But only temporarily and with a big difference. By summer the Germans had lost 348,300 men — slightly more than the British who were now receiving reinforcements — and the Americans by now had 179,000 men in France and that was only the beginning. Haig and Foch now prepared for a final Allied offensive aimed at bringing the war to an end.

During the German onslaught, the Canadian Corps holding part of the line on the Lens-Arras Front had been virtually inactive. This was in no small measure due to Lieutenant General Sir Arthur Currie's insistence that his corps remain intact and his refusal to allow his divisions to be attached to various British formations. Most Canadian units were held in reserve and because Conscription had been implemented in Canada, the corps was guaranteed replacements. By the time preparations for the Allied offensive were in place early in August, the corps was the strongest, best trained, best equipped of any formation in Europe. It was no surprise that it had been selected to spearhead the final Allied offensive.

PART 1 — AMIENS

For the initial phase of this assault, to clear the Amiens railhead, the Canadians were attached to Lieutenant General Hugh Rawlinson's Fourth Army along with the Australian Corps which formed the left flank, the 31st Corps of the First French Army on the right, on a front some 14 miles long. Two fresh elements were brought into play for the forthcoming battle — surprise and tanks. Because to the Germans the sudden appearance of Canadians spelled an imminent attack, part of the corps had moved to Ypres as a deception a few days earlier. None of the four divisions were moved into the attack area until the night before. There would be no pre-shelling. Instead tanks — 450 of them — which had been used so successfully at Cambrai the previous November, would charge in ahead of the infantry chewing their way through the barbed wire and mowing down enemy installations with their own firepower. The rumble of assembling the tanks was drowned out by the noise of Royal Air Force planes constantly buzzing overhead.

Weak defences faced the Australians and British — only seven German divisions, all understrength at about 3,000 men each, and poorly constructed and prepared fortifications. The Canadians were to attack between the Amiens-Roye road and the Amiens-Chaulnes railway, the Australians between the railway and the Somme River. What was to become famous as ''Canada's 100 Days'' began at 4:20 a.m. on Thursday, August 8, 1918, as the 450 tanks lumbered forward followed by the infantry to the thunder of 3,000 cannons and mortars.

Three of the four Canadian divisions (working together in action for the first time since Vimy), each accompanied by 40 tanks, led the assault: on the left, the Second under Major General Sir Henry Burstall, in the centre, the First commanded by Major General Archie Macdonell, and on the right Major General Louis Lipsett's Third. In reserve was Major General David Watson's Fourth Division in conjunction with the 3rd British Cavalry Division which included the Canadian Cavalry Brigade. Its assignment was to advance through the Third Division once Lipsett's objectives had been reached.

The Canadians attacked on a front 8,500-yards wide in dense fog which, as it had the British earlier, blinded the Germans. The premium was on speed as well as surprise. For the first time the infantry (which included the Australians) went into battle in light order carrying a minimum of equipment — ammunition, rations, a water bottle, gas mask, a light spade, and two Mills bombs. The Dominion troops went into battle that day thirsting for revenge; on June 27, a U-boat had sunk the Canadian hospital ship *Llandovery Castle* with 234 men and women being lost.

The attack went like clockwork from the start despite the heavy ground mist and the smoke. In fact few enemy machine-guns even opened fire. The Luce Valley posed no problem. By 11:00 that morning the engineers had thrown two bridges across the stream. The most precarious task fell to the Third Division. The French on its right flank had no tank support and had to rely on an artillery bombardment to pave the way. This took 45 minutes during which Lipsett's right flank was completely exposed. But thanks to Currie's prescience, the Canadian Independent Force he had formed to cope with just such a situation commanded by the Corps' machine-gun expert, Brigadier General Raymond Brutinel was dispatched to cope with the situation. This it achieved nobly, taking 30 enemy prisoners and capturing a dozen German machine-guns.

Generally speaking the assault that day was picture perfect. Troops accustomed to trench warfare, slogging it out foot by foot to measure ground gains in terms of yards, were mesmerized by the speed and distance of tank warfare. The work of the corps artillery of 646 guns under the brilliant direction of the corps counter battery commander, Colonel Andrew McNaughton, who Currie labelled "the greatest gunner in the world — not in the British Empire alone, but in the world," was especially noteworthy, a model of efficiency and destruction. Some batteries moved ahead to support the advancing tanks and infantry, as often as four times that day.

German prisoners were giving up in droves. By nightfall, the British Fourth Army had taken 17,600 enemy captive, 8,000 of them surrendering to the Canadian Corps alone. Some instances were comical, others ironic. There were instances of treachery and others of sheer drama. All of the following took place within the First Division.

In search of a forward battalion headquarters, Captain William Murray and Sergeant Alex Sample of the 22nd Eastern Ontarios came upon a dugout that seemed suitable but Sample took the precaution of first firing his rifle down the stairs. An immediate cry of "*Kamarad*" was followed by the surrender of 13 Germans. Covering them with his revolver, Murray suddenly came to the shuddering realization that he was in a highly precarious situation. His weapon was empty. He'd forgotten to load it that morning. However, he kept that discovery to himself and his prisoners were none the wiser.

The Honorary Lieutenant Colonel Frank Scott, the division chaplain, suddenly came face-to-face with three Germans with their hands held high in surrender after climbing out of a shell hole. Scott explained that as a non-combatant he could not accept their surrender. But the enemy insisted on being taken captive. Scott had no choice but to march them back until he could find some troops who could take over.

Lieutenant Walter Mackie from the 16th Canadian Scottish Battalion and his Lewis gunner had manoeuvred behind a trench from which their platoon had become pinned down by four enemy machine-guns. They quickly subdued the nest with enfilade fire of their own, whereupon a German officer stood up as if in surrender. Far from it. As he reached for his revolver Mackie killed him with his own. Shades of a shootout at the O.K. Corral!

Infantrymen of the 13th Battalion (Royal Highlanders) had outflanked a German position with the help of withering Lewis machine-gun fire and continued to storm it from both the flanks and the rear. The enemy finally raised the white flag in surrender. But when several Canadians stepped forward to take prisoners they were gunned down in cold blood. This resulted in a vicious mêlée at the end of which the Germans again raised the white flag. Two could play at that game. This time the 13th wiped out every last man in the stronghold.

In comparison to the other battles on the Western Front in which the Canadian Corps had been engaged — Ypres, the Somme, Hill 70, and Passchendaele — the first day of the Battle of Amiens was a romp. It was fought on open ground, a lot of it undefended. The action had been swift and the distance covered great. By day's end the Canadians had advanced nearly five miles. But it had not been without cost nor without some incredible acts of bravery. Casualties for the day amounted to 4,000, among them two of the three Canadians who won the Victoria Cross.

At the outset, three battalions from Brigadier General George Tuxford's 3rd Brigade with the First Division, the 13th Royal Highlanders flanked by the 14th Royal Montreal Regiment on the right, and the 16th Canadian Scottish on the left, formed the vanguard of the onslaught. About two hours after the attack began and a mile and a half ahead, as the fog started to clear, the brigade found itself under heavy enemy machine-gun fire which threatened to hold up the advance. That this was overcome was due to the boldness and dash of two members of the 13th battalion, Private John Croak, and Corporal Herman Good, both of whom received the Victoria Cross for their efforts.

Croak single-handedly took on a German machine-gun nest after becoming separated from his platoon. He hurled several Mills bombs into it, then attacked at bayonet point, putting the weapon out of action and taking its crew prisoners. In the process a bullet ripped into his right arm. Croak ignored it and, catching up with his platoon, which was being held up by another enemy stronghold, he dashed forward and charged the fortification, once again routing the enemy at the point of his bayonet and putting the guns out of action. But he was again wounded, this time fatally.

Meanwhile, Good's company was also halted in the face of a nest of three German machine-guns. Without waiting for orders, Good rushed the enemy position, killing every one of the gun crews. His next exploit occurred when the unit was again stopped, this time by a battery of three heavy 5.9-inch guns firing at point-blank range. Gambling that the gunners would be inexperienced in hand-to-hand fighting, the *métier* of the Highlanders, Good gathered three of his comrades and charged. Surprised and having no appetite for the close-in style of combat, the Germans quickly surrendered.

On the left flank of the assault, the Second Division was held up temporarily at the village of Mercelcave abutting the Amiens- Chaulnes railway line. It came in for special attention because it was well defended and a German Regimental Headquarters was quartered there. Since it was beyond the range of the field artillery, it was subjected to a 45 minute barrage from the long-range guns of the corps' artillery. After some street fighting, the town finally fell to Brigadier General Robert Rennie's 4th Brigade. The enemy regimental HQ was captured intact by the 18th Western Ontario Battalion, whose officers treated themselves to a still warm and untouched breakfast of porridge and coffee.

While the Second Division's advance slowed as the units consolidated their gains, the First Division forged ahead. At 8:00 in the morning, the 1st Brigade under Brigadier General William Griesbach swung into action. All three of his battalions, the 2nd Eastern Ontario, the 3rd Toronto Regiment, and the 4th Central Ontarios, had reached their primary objective, the "Red Line," by 11:30 although the 2nd had been slowed down for a while when part of the battalion got lost in the fog. Here the Canadians looked east towards a pastoral scene devoid of trenches and barbed wire entanglements. Fresh green fields and the peaceful Luce River seemed in sharp contrast to the havoc of the war.

Brigadier General Frederick Loomis' 2nd Brigade completed the First Division's advance for the day. At noon the 7th British Columbia Regiment and the 10th Canadian Battalion advanced to the Blue Dotted Line objective, a short distance east of the village of Caix which they reached by 11:30 that afternoon and proceeded to dig in. This left both flanks temporarily exposed. The Second Division was still catching up and it was not until 7:15 that the 29th Vancouver and 31st Alberta battalions from the 6th Brigade arrived at the Blue Line.

It had been a spectacular achievement. In one day, the two divisions had advanced an unprecedented total of eight miles, an accomplishment unmatched during the entire Great War. But the Third Division on the right did not have it so easy. In contrast to the flat terrain to the left, Louis Lipsett's troops faced a formidable barrier in the form of the Luce River at the outset. It had to be crossed before the enemy detected the Canadian presence. At first glance, the Luce looked like an ineffectual little stream. But marshes on either side of it widened it to 200 yards presenting a formidable barrier which could only be spanned by existing bridges and those thrown across the river by Canadian engineers.

The innovative division commander showed himself up to the challenge. Gambling on surprise, he assigned his 8th Brigade under Brigadier General Dennis Draper to clear the high ground north of the river and occupy the fortified village of Hangard. Brigadier General David Ormond's 9th Brigade was ordered to break out of the bridgehead with his three battalions and 14 tanks. One battalion was to make a frontal assault along the Amiens-Roye road on the far right to distract the Germans, while his other two battalions outflanked the enemy defences at Demin village and the Hamon Wood.

Fog threatened the operation at first, but only momentarily. Some units failed to reach the start line until 20 minutes after the Zero Hour. All 40 of the division's tanks got lost. But Ormond's 43rd Cameron Highlanders of Canada followed the creeping barrage along the Amiens-Roye road for 1,000 yards to a point where, although the Germans were totally distracted by their presence, they were unable to do anything about it. The Highlanders had reached a blind spot, rendering themselves immune to enemy small arms fire.

The 58th Central Ontario Battalion struck toward the village of Demuin to allow the troops of Draper's 8th Brigade to cross the Luce. It was during this action that Corporal Harry Miner earned the Victoria Cross. At the start of the advance he had been badly wounded in the head, face and shoulder. He refused to leave the field, however, and led his platoon in an attack on a German trench. Later, when a machine-gun held up the advance, Miner single-handedly assaulted it, killing the crew and turning the weapon on the Germans. Then, with two others, he overwhelmed an enemy grenade post, bayoneting two of the Germans and putting the rest to flight. In the encounter, he was again wounded, this time so seriously that he died.

On the right, the 116th Ontario County Battalion, led by Lieutenant Colonel George Pearkes, who had won the Victoria Cross at Passchendaele, had one of its companies practically decimated and all its officers killed. When the attack became stalled by an enemy trench atop a hill defending the objective, the Hamond Wood, Pearkes took personal charge. A quick visual survey of the situation revealed a hollow to the right from which it would be possible to make an assault encountering a minimum of enemy fire. In the subsequent onslaught, the Germans were routed and the battalion took 450 prisoners and captured 40 machine-guns along with 16 field guns. These joint operations by the 58th and 116th broke the German resistance in the sector, enabling the Cameron Highlanders from the 9th Brigade to sweep through to the primary Red Line objective at the Dodo Wood. It was now time for the second phase of the Third Division's assault which began at precisely 8:20 a.m.

Three battalions from Brigadier General Hugh Dyers' 7th Brigade, the 42nd Royal Highlanders of Canada, the Royal Canadian Regiment and the 49th Edmonton Regiment, made up the attacking force. The stiffest resistance came from a German position known as Hill 102, batteries of field guns firing at point-blank range. Captain Harold Trent of the Royal Highlanders, led his company in a series of section attacks until they reached a point 150 yards from the enemy position. Then, firing rapidly, the Highlanders quickly overran the Germans, killing or capturing them all. Similarly Captain John MacLeod led his company in a flanking assault against a German gun battery, routing most of the enemy and taking the rest prisoner. With Hill 102 in Canadian hands, the battalion reached the Red Line objective by 10:20 that morning. The other two battalions on either flank arrived shortly afterwards. By noon, the 7th Brigade was dug in. It was now the calvary's turn.

At noon, three brigades from the 3rd British Cavalry Division, which included the Canadian Cavalry Division led by Brigadier General Roy Paterson, galloped forward towards the next objective, the Blue Line. It was a spectacular sight. But in the words of the French general Pierre Bosquet at Balaclava: "*C'est magnifique, mais c'est ne pas la guerre!*" Ironically, the tanks, even the relatively speedy Whippets, were unable to keep up with the horses they were destined to replace. As a result, in the attack on Beaucourt, the Royal Canadian Dragoons were forced to go it alone. All but 50 were wiped out and the men were forced to dismount and fight their way forward with revolvers and lances. Eventually the Fort Garry Horse captured the village on foot. It was clear the cavalry's days were numbered. Late that afternoon they were relieved by infantry from the Fourth Division.

Passing through the Third Division at 12:40 p.m., the Fourth Division attacked, with the 11th Brigade under Brigadier General Victor Oldum and Brigadier General James MacBrien's 12th Brigade soon reaching the dismounted cavalry. MacBrien's battalions, the 38th Ottawa and the 87th Nova Scotia, arrived at the Dotted Blue Line objective shortly after six o'clock that evening having met only sporadic, token opposition. MacBrien's other two battalions, the 72nd Seaforth Highlanders of Canada and the 78th Winnipeg Grenadiers became embroiled in a bitter battle when they came under heavy enemy fire from a wood just east of Beaucourt-en-Santerre. Finally subduing this resistance, they advanced north-east towards Le Quesnel where the Germans had brought up reserve troops and established a pair of machine-gun nests. Lieutenant Colonel John Clark, the 72nd's commanding officer, personally led a platoon against these nests and overpowered them. The battalion reached the Blue Dotted Line objective before nightfall.

But the 11th Brigade failed to get that far. Both the 54th Central Ontario and the 102nd Central Ontario battalions became engaged in a fierce firefight in front of the woods east of Beaucourt where the cavalry was carrying on an uneven battle in the village. Three tanks finally arrived but they were quickly knocked out. So much for tank warfare at Amiens. Lieutenant Colonel Arthur Carey, the scrappy commander of the 56th, led two platoons in a desperate, suicidal drive without any artillery or machine-gun support against the enemy position. Though the casualties were frightful, the Canadians managed to penetrate one corner of the wood which allowed the 105th Battalion to capture it, taking a total of 159 prisoners. But that was as far as the brigade got. German machine-gun and artillery defences at Le Quesnel stemmed any further advance. This was the only section of the Blue Dotted Line that the Canadians failed to reach. But this in no way detracted from the spectacular victory achieved, the decisive engagement of the First World War. Ludendorff described it as "the black day of the German army...the worst experience I had to go through...."

The Germans had been thrown back eight miles. The Canadians had taken 8,000 prisoners and captured 161 guns at a cost of 4,000 casualties. In total that day, the enemy had lost 27,000 men, 400 guns and countless rounds of ammunition to the British Fourth Army.

Small wonder that Kaiser Wilhelm confided to Ludendorff: "the war can no longer be won." The chief of staff agreed and acknowledged that his war machine was: "no longer efficient."

On August 9, the first order of the day was the capture of Le Quesnel and consolidation of the Blue Dotted Line on that part of the front before the main assault could take place. At 4:30 a.m. the 75th Mississauga Battalion from the 11th Brigade began advancing on the village behind a heavy artillery barrage. Despite this accurate shelling, just west of the outskirts, the battalion ran into frenzied enemy machine-gun fire that threatened to stop the Canadians cold. But a furious, breakneck bayonet charge did the trick; after a quick hand-to-hand struggle, Le Quesnel fell to the attackers with a German divisional headquarters intact. Protected by the 87th Canadian Grenadier Guards on its right flank, the 75th now forged ahead, clearing the enemy trenches west of the town, and finally reaching the Blue Dotted Line at 11:00 that morning. As it turned out, that coincided with the main assault, though it had not originally been planned that way.

That had been scheduled to begin at dawn, but due to changes in the British Fourth Army's plans, had been delayed until ten o'clock. It had been postponed again until 11:00. Even at that, only one brigade got off the deck on time; most of the rest did not get started until after 1:00 p.m. Thus the entire day's operation was disorganized, disjointed and sporadic, creating support problems; artillery barrages were feeble and spasmodic. It is a wonder it came off as well as it did.

Brigadier General Arthur Bell's 6th Brigade of the Second Division was first off and two battalions strong, with the 29th Vancouver and the 31st Alberta focusing on the railhead town of Rosieres-en-Santerre flanked on the left by the Amiens-Chaulnes railway line, 1,000 yards from the start line. Terrain over that distance was so flat it offered no cover whatsoever and provided the enemy with an unrestricted field of fire. A grim battle ensued with predictably heavy casualties. Once more the use of tanks proved almost futile. Of five assigned to the brigade, three were immediately knocked out. Nevertheless, by following in behind one of the surviving vehicles, one infantry company of the Albertans was able to penetrate the village after a ferocious three hour stand-off machine-gun/rifle fire exchange on the outskirts. After a door-to-door battle that lasted a half hour, the town fell to the 31st battalion at 4:30 in the afternoon. The encounter had its ironic side as well. During the fighting, a German troop train pulled into the station to deliver fresh reinforcements. As they stepped off the train, the Canadians welcomed them by taking all 527 officers and other ranks prisoner.

At 11:45 a.m. on the right of the 6th Brigade south of the Luce River, the 5th Brigade opened its attack with the 22nd French-Canadian Battalion, advancing through the village of Vrely south of Rosieres and into Meharicourt to the south-east. During this action Brigadier General James Ross received a bad shrapnel wound and was replaced by Lieutenant Colonel Thomas Tremblay. Tremblay turned over command of the 22nd Battalion to Major Georges Vanier, a future governor-general of Canada.

Among the French Canadians that day, Lieutenant Jean Brillant was the star of the show. When his company was halted by German machine-gun fire at Meharicourt, Brillant ran forward, captured the weapon and killed two of the gun crew. Wounded, he refused to leave his command, and subsequently led a charge in which 150 Germans were taken prisoner and 15 machine-guns were captured. Brillant himself accounted for 15 of the enemy killed. Wounded again, he insisted on continuing and led an attack on a field gun firing at his men. After running ahead for 600 yards he was wounded a third time. He managed to rush forward for another 200 yards before collapsing from loss of blood and exhaustion. Brillant, who died two days later, was awarded a posthumous Victoria Cross.

After enduring a heavy German bombardment during the morning, the First Division's 1st and 2nd brigades mounted their attacks around 1:00 in the afternoon. The success of the 2nd Brigade that day was in no small measure reflected in the winning of three Victoria Crosses. Sergeant Raphael Zengel of the 5th Western Cavalry Battalion distinguished himself by leading two critical attacks against enemy machine-gun posts. The first was against a position east of Warvillers, south of Vrely which he wiped out all by himself. Later in the day when the entire battalion was held up by relentless machine-gun fire, Zengel directed the return fire so accurately it knocked out all the German gun crews. Thanks to his efforts Warvillers not only fell to the Westerners, but the battalion was able to reach the Meharicourt-Rouvroy-en-Santerre road beyond it, where it dug in for the night.

Two Victoria Crosses went to the companion 90th Winnipeg Rifles on the 5th's left flank. Near Abrecourt, Alexander Brereton's platoon was caught in the open, exposed to German machine-gun fire with no place to take cover. As man after man fell, without hesitation Brereton sprang to his feet and attacked the nearest nest, bayoneting the enemy gunners. His grittiness so unnerved the Germans that nine other gunners immediately surrendered to him.

When the battalion ran into trouble at Hatchet Wood, Corporal Frederick Coppins led four of his comrades forward in a desperate charge to clear an enemy machine-gun nest. Coppins was seriously wounded and all four of the others were killed, but the German position was overrun. Coppins killed four enemy gunners and captured four others. This bold assault allowed the Winnipeggers to continue their advance. But another battalion casualty that day was the commanding officer, Lieutenant Colonel Tom Raddall, who succumbed to machine-gun fire. Major Arthur Saunders promptly took his place. The unit's total casualties for the day were frightful: 15 officers and 420 other ranks.

The 5th Brigade's advance was somewhat smoother, the 1st Western Ontario and the 2nd Eastern Ontario battalions reaching their initial objective of Beaufort village with comparative ease. The day's final action fell to Dennis Draper's 8th Brigade on the Canadian right flank. The 4th Canadian Mounted Rifles overran the Rouvroy-Bouchier road in fast order. The 5th CMR went over the top 45 minutes later, after encountering some resistance, and finally fought their way into Bouchoir at five o'clock in the afternoon. Then, when the Germans began evacuating Arvillers on the south side of the road leading to Amiens (actually in the French sector) the 5th occupied it temporarily until the French finally caught up later that evening.

On August 9 the Canadians had advanced another four miles, only half what they'd gained the day before. Casualties of 2,574, however, were lighter. It had not been a spectacular day, only the Australians had kept pace with the Canadians. But then resistance had been considerably stiffer. The night before, the Germans had rushed in reinforcements — five fresh divisions.

Currie's objectives for the following day, August 10, were limited to clearing the network of trenches, once occupied by the British, directly in front of the corps. Only two divisions were involved, the Third and the Fourth, the First and Second going into reserve. At 4:30 a.m. the 1st and 2nd RCMR went over the top and two hours later had cleared the village of Le Quesnoy-en-Santerre of all enemy defenders. For the next three hours, the 1st Battalion cleared trenches to the north. Then at 9:30, the Third Division was withdrawn for a rest. Its sector was taken over by the British 32nd which immediately ran into heavy resistance and could advance no further.

Meanwhile David Watson's Fourth Division, employing the 10th and 12th brigades, managed to gain two miles even in the face of determined German opposition. James MacBrien's 12th faced three villages guarding the labyrinth of trenches to the east. The first of these, Maucourt, fell easily. Chilly was captured next by the 72nd Seaforth Highlanders. At noon the position was taken over by the 78th Winnipeg Grenadiers who, by two o'clock, had occupied Hallu. During that action Lieutenant James Tait single-handedly subdued an enemy machine-gun post, took 20 Germans prisoner and captured 12 guns. The quick capture of the towns had left the two battalions badly exposed. On the left, two other battalions, the 38th Ottawa and the 8th Nova Scotia, which had advanced between Maucourt and the Amiens-Chaulnes railway line to the north, came under extremely heavy German fire when the Australians were unable to take Lihons north of the railway line and were finally brought to a halt.

Now the Germans counter-attacked against Chilly and Hallu managing to penetrate the latter town. There, James Tait, who had distinguished himself earlier, saved the day. Rallying the survivors in a spirited defence, he stopped the Germans cold. During the fierce fight that took place, Tait was killed. For his gallantry that day, he was awarded a posthumous Victoria Cross.

On the 10th Brigade's front at Fouquescourt, midway between the Amiens rail line and the road to the city, the 4th New Brunswick and the 46th South Saskatchewan battalions, leading the attack, ran into heavy machine-gun and artillery fire respectively, as they leaped from trench to trench. Hugging the ground in front of Fouquescourt they called for barrage support. That did the trick—momentarily. It allowed the 44th to take the village with no trouble at all. But, due to garbled communications, the shelling started again and the Canadians were forced to evacuate the town. The Germans quickly reoccupied it. Later, with the help of two Mark V tanks, the 44th recaptured Fouquescourt and this time the Canadians were there to stay. By six o'clock that evening they had established an outpost just east of the village.

By this time the 47th Western Ontario and the 50th Calgary battalions had got into the act, the Calgarians advanced on the trenches south of Chilly which proved to be too hot for comfort. The unit later retired, leaving the Seaforth Highlanders to hold Chilly. Over the next few days it now became a question of the Canadians, and the Australians to the north, tenaciously holding onto their hard fought gains.

A change in thinking now developed following a visit to the front lines by Sir Douglas Haig. It was obvious from the state of the enemy's defences — trenches abandoned by the British in 1916 and beyond, the vast churned up, virtually impassable terrain — that a renewed offensive could meet, if not with total disaster, certainly with unacceptable losses. A repeat of the debacle of the Somme hung heavily in everyone's mind. Sir Arthur Currie at once opted to bring down the curtain on the successful Amiens campaign and move the Canadians to a new theatre where another speedy victory could be achieved before the corps was sundered by attrition.

The Allied commander, Ferdinand Foch, did not agree — at first. He wanted the Amiens offensive continued. But he was scarcely in a position to press his point. It was the British who were carrying the load on the Western Front at the moment. The French armies were still in poor shape and during the Amiens battle, had proved incapable of keeping pace with the advance. And the Americans, untested in combat, were far from a force to be reckoned with. So, Foch had no choice but to bend to Haig's demands.

On August 14, Haig issued orders for the Canadian Corps to move north to the Arras Sector as part of Lieutenant General Sir Henry Horne's British First Army. The Canadians did not withdraw until the 16th and in the meantime were charged with straightening out and strengthening the front line. This was the last time they fought as a volunteer force: reinforcements in the form of conscripts had begun to arrive.

The Amiens offensive had cost the Germans dearly: 75,000 casualties. The 22,000 prisoners taken by the British created a front line crisis for the Germans; it necessitated breaking up the divisions to provide reserves. "The war must be ended," Ludendorff declared flatly, a proclamation not taken lightly by Kaiser Wilhelm who ordered his foreign secretary to start initiating peace negotiations through neutral representatives immediately.

PART 2 — THE HINDENBURG LINE

A new Allied strategy called for Sir Julian Byng's British Third Army, holding down the front at Albert, to push the Germans back at Bapaume while the First Army, with the Canadian Corps in the vanguard, struck from Arras towards Cambrai. Meanwhile the Fourth Army stood ready to advance at the first sign of a German withdrawal from the Somme. This dovetailed perfectly with French plans to drive north from the Aisne River. On August 21 the French Tenth Army attacked between Compiegne and Soissons, gaining four miles in two days. On the 21st the Third Army advanced on the left. On the same day Byng's Third Army moved on Bapaume and by the following day, had advanced two miles and taken 5,000 prisoners. Next day the Fourth Army joined the assault astride the River Somme. Things had got off to a good start. It was now the turn of Sir Henry Horne's First Army and the Canadians.

German defence positions facing Horne's army were formidable, strong and in-depth. Immediately facing the Canadians were the British trenches, 5,500 yards long and abandoned during the March German offensive. Overlooking them were the three heights, the village of Monchy-le-Preux, Chapel Hill and Orange Hill. Behind these fortifications lay the German front line. Two miles east of Monchy was another trench system, the Fresnes-Rouvroy Line. A mile to the east of that loomed the elaborate Drocourt-Queant Switch, an extraordinarily powerful defence system that had been under construction for the past two years and was considered virtually impregnable. Haig feared it might be too tough a nut to crack. "Do you think it can be done?" he asked Currie, who assured him that "we will break it." Between this trench line and Cambrai another barrier, the Canal du Nord, formed an almost impassable obstruction. All these defences had to be breached before the Siegfried-Stellung (*stellung* meaning position), named Hindenburg Line by the British, the last German bastion, a series of fortified emplacements, and positions, broadly encompassing the area, including hamlets, around and before the textile town of Cambrai, could be reached.

Currie knew that the Germans would expect a dawn attack so he decided on the element of surprise by assaulting in the dark, despite the risks involved. With the assault scheduled for 3:00 a.m., August 26, the initial objective was to recapture the abandoned British trenches west of the three hills. On the right the Second Division was to attack south of the Arras-Cambrai road then push on to take the heights around Monchy-le-Preux. On the left, the Third Division was to strike between the road and the River Scarpe and take Orange Hill as well as Monchy. Protecting the Canadians' flank north of the Scarpe would be the British 51st Highland Division, while on the right would be the British XVII Corps (Third Army). Seventeen brigades of artillery were arrayed to provide barrage support and each division would be accompanied by nine tanks.

The attack began under heavy clouds and in a drizzle but the surprise was complete. The Canadians quickly overran the enemy positions all down the line. By 7:30 a.m. Monchy-le-Preux fell to the 1st and 5th CMR battalions of Dennis Draper's 8th Brigade. During that charge, Lieutenant Charles Rutherford of the 5th CMR earned the Victoria Cross for single-handedly taking 75 German prisoners and capturing three enemy machine-guns. After overcoming a pocket of resistance, Rutherford led his men up the hill towards the village, then left his own company to check on the progress of another. When he went to return to his own unit, he couldn't find them. Stumbling on an enemy pillbox, he demanded that the occupants surrender. Forty-five of them put their hands up and turned over their machine-guns to him. Later, Rutherford captured another 30 Germans, once again, all by himself.

By four o'clock that afternoon, the Second Division had captured the villages of Wancourt and Guemappe on the high ground south of the main road. They then forded the steep banks of the River Cojuel with the objective of taking a German trench named Egret beyond it. This attack fell to the 27th Winnipeg and 28th Northwest battalions of Arthur Bell's 6th Brigade. It was not as easy as it sounded; the battalions encountered furious enemy fire that made its capture impossible. But Bell was determined to secure it as a jumping off point for the following day. Borrowing from the experience of the initial onslaught, the Canadians held their fire until after dark. Then they successfully captured the trench in a quick night assault that took the Germans completely by surprise.

North of the road the fighting was also intense. Two battalions, the Royal Canadian Regiment and the Princess Patricia's Canadian Light Infantry of Hugh Dyer's 7th Brigade, overran the woods east of Monchy and south of Pelves. Well fortified defenses compelled the Canadians to battle their way through a seemingly endless series of trenches and barbed wire entanglements. Now, for the first time that day, the Germans were able to launch a strong counter-attack, so effective it stopped the battalions in their tracks. Though this was dispersed by the artillery, it marked the end of the Canadian advance for August 26.

All told, the score sheet was impressive. The two divisions had advanced nearly four miles and had taken 2,000 prisoners. But the price had not been cheap. The capture of Monchy-le-Preux alone had cost Draper's 8th Brigade 1,500 casualties, evidence of how important the enemy considered that position to be.

Next day, Tuesday, August 27, the Canadians renewed their drive with the objective of piercing the Fresnes-Rouvroy Line and hopefully breaching the powerful Drocourt-Queant Switch as well. Currie was in a hurry. His aim was indeed ambitious, taking into account that it covered a distance of five miles and was well defended with interlocking trench systems, countless machine-gun posts, and barbed wire. And overnight, the Germans had rushed in two more divisions to bolster their defence formations.

This aspiring undertaking did not get off to a very auspicious start. Fresh Third Division troops, the 52nd New Ontario, 56th Central Ontario and the 116th County Ontario battalions took two small woods by force. But the initial objective, the village of Boiry-Notre-Dame, the pivotal point of the Fresnes-Rouvroy Line, remained in German hands despite determined assaults by the 116th. Machine-gun fire from Pelves and the Jigsaw Wood blunted every attempt. The fact that his front had been stretched to 7,000 yards, twice that of the day before, further complicated Louis Lipsett's problems. But the division at least enjoyed one success when the 48th Highlanders of Canada and the 18th Western Ontario battalions penetrated and captured Vis-en-Artois along the Arras-Cambrai road.

The Second Division did not go over the top until 10:00 that morning due to a delay in bringing up reserves. In spite of an encouraging jump off it too soon became pinned down by remorseless enemy fire. The 22nd French-Canadian Battalion and the 24th Victoria Rifles took Cherisy village on the right flank, while the 26th New Brunswick Battalion managed to get across the River Sensee. But there the march ended, the Germans offering stiff resistance with their machine-gun and shell fire. Negligible artillery support didn't help either, nor did a squadron of Royal Air Force Sopwith Camels which straffed the Canadians by mistake.

Abundantly aware of the improved calibre of the German machine-gun and field battery defences, Currie limited his objective for the next day to the capture of the Fresnes-Rouvroy Line. Wednesday, August 28 was an ideal day for the enterprise, warm and bright. The Third Division went over the top at 11:00 a.m., the Second an hour and a half later. Lipsett had carefully planned the manner in which the Third would make its attack. He had the artillery concentrate on the enemy machine-gun positions which had been the division's main concern the day before. Overwhelming shelling support paid big dividends.

Attacking on a 1,000 yard front, Ormond's 9th Brigade broke through the shattered F-R Line smoothly and easily, securing Boiry-Notre-Dame and the heights surrounding it. At 12:30 p.m. the 7th and 8th Brigades got into the act, both meeting with equal success. On the left, the 49th Edmonton Regiment took Pelves which had been such a thorn in the Canadians' side earlier, while the PPCLI, the Royal Canadian Regiment and the 42nd Royal Highlanders of Canada joined forces in an assault on the Jigsaw Wood. After some hand-to-hand fighting the Germans were soon subdued and the Canadians in control of the position. On the right, the 5th Canadian Mounted Rifles and the 43rd Highlanders of Canada (which had been assigned to the 8th from the 9th in exchange for the 4th CMR), crossed the River Sensee and captured the heights beyond it. It had been a fruitful two hours. The Third Division had completely smashed the Fresnes-Rouvroy Line between the River Scarpe to the north and the Arass-Cambrai road to the south. But it was a different story on the other side of the road.

By comparison, the fortunes of Henry Burstall's Second Division that day were depressingly dismal. They had suffered so badly the day before that Currie would have taken the division (along with the Third) out of the line had not logistics prevented it. Both Rennie's 4th Brigade, assigned to attack down the main road, and Tremblay's 5th, on the right, were dog-tired and understrength; they were in no condition to face the yards of uncut barbed wire and strongly manned trenches confronting them. Their luck ran out from the start. All the officers in the 5th Brigade's 22nd French-Canadian Battalion immediately became casualties, including the acting CO, Major Georges Vanier, who suffered a leg wound necessitating an amputation. All the other battalion commanders in that brigade became casualties as well. Colonel William Clark-Kennedy of the 24th Victoria Rifles was wounded but refused to leave the field. Colonel Bill Mackenzie of 27th New Brunswick Battalion was killed by machine-gun fire. The Second Division got nowhere. It had too few troops to begin with and sustained too many casualties, killed and wounded. Its failure to take the southern part of the Fresnes-Rouvroy Line left that section of the fortification intact. Its capture was critical to completing the jumping off point for an attack on the Drocourt-Queant Switch. Until it could be taken, the assault had to be put on hold.

In three days of hard fighting the Canadian Corps had gained five-and-a-half miles and had cracked the northern section of the Fresnes-Rouvroy Line. During that time the casualties totalled 5,801. Two battalions of the Second Division, the 20th Central Ontario and the 22nd French-Canadian accounted for 1,000 of those losses. Both the Second and Third Divisions were worn out. That night Currie had them withdrawn to be replaced by the First Canadian and the 4th British Divisions.

Archie Macdonell, the First Division's commander, assigned the task of clearing the remainder of the Fresnes-Rouvroy Line to his 1st Brigade commander, Brigadier General William Griesbach. It was a wise choice. Griesbach was a master of ingenuity and innovation. Faced with the capture of the Vis-en-Artois switch line, Ocean Work, Upton Wood, the village of Enterpigny and several small hamlets that stood in the way of the Drocourt-Queant Switch, Griesbach laid out a carefully coordinated operation. He proposed to use three of his battalions, the 1st Western Ontario and the 2nd Eastern Ontario, which assembled in the British held village of Hendecourt-lez-Cagnicourt, and the 3rd Toronto Regiment. The Canadians again went over the top in darkness, at 4:40 on the morning of Friday, August 30, without any warning bombardment to achieve ultimate surprise.

Then with heavy artillery support, the 1st and 2nd battalions attacked in a northerly direction, while the 3rd advanced to the southeast. By mid-morning the brigade had captured the Upton Wood, taking 1,000 prisoners and capturing 99 machine-guns at a cost of 625 casualties. Local fighting continued for the next two days and on August 31, the Ocean Work stronghold fell to the Canadians. Next day George Tuxford's 3rd Brigade secured the Vis-en-Artois switch line. North of the Arras-Cambrai road, the British 4th Division captured Haucourt, Remy, and the redoubtable Enterpigny. But heavy losses, the difficult, heavily wooded country, and an extended front line of 2,500 yards, indicated any attack on the Drocourt-Queant Switch from that area might well meet with disaster.

On the basis of this assessment Currie wasted no time in making two significant moves. On the night of August 31, he sent a brigade from David Watson's Fourth Division into the front line between the First Division on the right and the British 4th Division. Then by bringing in a second brigade, he reduced the British front to 1,000 yards. All this took place while the Germans made a series of counterattacks, many of them resulting in fierce hand-to-hand combat. The enemy knew that an assault on their vaulted D-Q Line was imminent.

The plan to smash the powerful fortification was simple and straightforward. Three divisions, the British 4th on the left, the Fourth and First Canadian on the right, supported by 741 guns and howitzers, would take the stronghold head-on in a frontal attack. Further, Currie intended to send in Raymond Brutinel's Canadian Independent Force, an assortment of armoured cars and cavalry, charging down the Arras-Cambrai roads, across the Canal du Nord to seize the heights beyond it, in the highly ambitious and optimistic, yet unlikely, hope that the action would force Cambrai, the centre of German communications for all of northern France, to fall.

On the eve of the attack the Canadian Corps never looked, or felt, better and Currie was confident that no German position could withstand a Canadian attack. He had good reason for such high spirits. His corps stood at 148,090 strong and morale had never been higher. The infantry began their assault at 5:00 a.m. on Monday September 2, a beautifully clear autumn day, as the artillery opened up to pound the enemy defences into rubble. Where the shelling failed to scramble the barbed wire entanglements, the tanks — 50 all told — succeeded. By eight o'clock that morning the forward German lines, as well as some of the support trenches, had fallen. Prisoners gave up in droves. And when one German officer refused to surrender his platoon, he was shot dead by one of his own men.

As the morning wore on, resistance stiffened. By this time the Canadians had outdistanced themselves from their own field guns and could no longer rely on artillery to support them. As well, most of the tanks had been knocked out. The assault now developed into bitter close-in fighting but the Canadians so acquitted themselves on this "red letter" day that seven of them were awarded the Victoria Cross.

Sergeant Claude Nunney of the 38th Ottawa Battalion was badly wounded in the arm but refused to leave the field. Instead he positioned himself ahead of his men, sometimes by as much as 50 to 75 yards, single-handedly taking on every enemy soldier facing him, assaulting four machine-gun nests and wounding or killing the enemy gunners in the process. During the day he killed 25 Germans. He was wounded again that afternoon and this time had to be carried to a dressing station by stretcher. He died 16 days later.

When the right flank of Lance Corporal Bill Metcalf's 16th Canadian Scottish Battalion was held up by German machine-gun fire, it was decided to wait for a tank before trying to advance any further. When one finally did appear, the crew failed to see the infantrymen waving their helmets at it. When it reached a point 300 yards from the enemy barbed wire, Metcalf leaped up from a shell hole and began directing it forward with his flags pointing the way to the

German trench and then along it. The enemy responded with fire from no less than 17 machine-guns and clumps of grenades. Metcalf continued to point the way until the trench was subdued, receiving a wound in the process. But he stayed with his platoon until ordered into a shell hole to have his injury dressed.

Lieutenant Colonel Cy Peck, commander of the Canadian Scottish, who reintroduced the playing of bagpipes in battle, became the second 16th Battalion recipient of the Victoria Cross that day. When the Germans blocked the unit's advance at Villers-lez-Cagnicourt, Peck personally reconnoitered the area in the face of relentless machine-gun and rifle fire. He then reorganized his battalion so that both flanks were covered and charged forward at the head of his men. He next sought out the tanks and directed them to the final objective, the D-Q support line, the Bussy Switch.

Following an unsuccessful attack against a German trench west of Cagnicourt by the 10th Canadian Battalion, Sergeant Arthur Knight led his men under heavy fire in a grenade attack. When this failed, he charged forward alone, bayoneting several enemy machine-gun-ners and mortar crews and forcing the rest to retreat. Later, again all by himself, he routed another German party that was holding up the advance. However, this time he was so severely wounded he had to be carried from the battlefield. He died two days later.

At the height of the battle, Captain Belenden Hutcheson, the 75th Toronto Scottish medical officer, remained in No Man's Land to dress the wounded until all of them had been taken care of. During this time many of the stretcher-bearers themselves became casualties. After bandaging a wounded officer, with the help of some German prisoners, Hutcheson evacuated the man to safety by running the gamut of enemy bullets. He then returned to the battlefield, again under heavy fire, to tend to the others.

Having penetrated the D-Q Line, the 87th Canadian Grenadier Guards, in the process of assaulting a German ridge at Dury, became badly exposed to fierce enemy fire and heavy casualties resulted. Private John Young, a stretcher-bearer, ignored the hail of bullets to minister to the wounded. When he ran out of bandages he braved the storm of fire to race back to his headquarters for fresh supplies. He then dashed forward onto the battlefield once more. It took over an hour to tend to all the injured, then later in the day he organized rescue parties to carry the wounded back to a dressing station.

Shortly after the attack began, Corporal Walter Rayfield of the 7th British Columbia Regiment, rushed a heavily occupied German trench, bayoneting two enemy soldiers and taking ten prisoners. Later, under continuing rifle fire, he pinpointed a German sniper. Charging that section of the trench, he so demoralized the Germans that 30 of them threw up their arms in surrender. Still later, Rayfield rescued a badly wounded comrade from the battlefield, defying heavy artillery shelling and remorseless machine-gun fire.

Those "magnificent seven" had written an unprecedented chapter in the march of Canadian military history. For their deeds, and sacrifices, in one day the Victoria Cross was awarded to more men than on any other date on record.

However, along with bravery, acts of treachery and revenge went hand-in-hand. When the Royal Montreal Regiment attacked Cagnicourt, Lieutenant Alastair McLean led an assault on a German machine-gun nest. After a furious fight, two of the gunners stood up and raised their arms in surrender. When McLean stepped forward he was shot and killed. Enraged, the rest of his platoon assaulted the nest, bayoneting every last one of the defenders. But their thirst for vengeance was far from slaked. Minutes later when a group of Germans emerged from the village, presumably ready to surrender, the Canadians cut them down unmercifully.

The battle for Cagnicourt ended soon afterwards. Meanwhile Frederick Loomis' 2nd Brigade cleared the supporting Bussy Switch, the 7th British Columbia Regiment leading the assault in which Walter Rayfield won his Victoria Cross. The 10th Canadian Battalion took over at 8:00 that morning accompanied by four tanks. It was an unimpressive performance. After 45 minutes all four were disabled. It was a day of bitter fighting for the 10th during which Arthur Knight won his Victoria Cross. The climax came at 6:00 in the evening with the capture of Villers-lez-Cagnicourt. A rewarding victory: at a cost of only 233 casualties, the 10th had captured 700 prisoners and 150 machine-guns.

On the other hand, the performance of David Watson's Fourth left a lot to be desired. Originally planned as a single brigade assault along the Arras-Cambrai road, where Currie hoped to exploit the victory with a breakout by Brutinel's force of armoured cars and cavalry, due to heavy losses sustained by the British 4th Division, an extra brigade had been thrown in. It was a mistake. Watson and Currie, in haste, had exercised poor judgement which resulted in the front becoming overcrowded with troops. On the left, Ross Hayter's 1st Division planned to attack the village of Dury. On the right, James MacBrien's 12th Brigade would employ three battalions to take Mont

Dury along the road. And with Victor Oldum's 11th Brigade in support and Brutinel's brigade behind him also, like a marketplace on shopping day, Watson's constricted frontal sector had suddenly become a very congested and busy place.

Because the arrangements were all last minute, the 10th Brigade had to make a four mile forced march to take up its starting positions, which it quickly discovered were in German hands. Nevertheless the 47th Western Ontario and the 50th Calgary battalions broke through the Drocourt-Queant Line. Meanwhile the 46th South Saskatchewan Battalion swept into Dury and by 7:45 a.m. had secured it. So far so good.

At noon, however, the Germans made a determined counter-attack taking the Saskatchewans completely by surprise. A pitched battle ensued with heavy casualties on either side. Finally the Canadians stopped the enemy assault and once more took command of the town. But by this time, on the right, the 12th Brigade was in trouble. The 38th Ottawa Battalion was halted by enemy small arms fire. Once again the tanks proved to be absolutely useless; they were quickly put out of action. It was here that Claude Nunney rescued the situation in the action that earned him the Victoria Cross.

At the same time, the 72nd Seaforth Highlanders of Canada was one of the few battalions for which tank support played a significant role. They made it possible for the Seaforths to capture Mont Dury astride the Arras-Cambrai road. In one firefight, Sergeant Kenneth Campbell and two others took 50 Germans prisoner. But by the time the battalion reached the bottom of the hill on the east side, it was stopped cold by accurate long-range machine-gun fire. This was due solely to the fact that at this point the Canadian artillery stopped shelling along the 1,000-yard front to allow Brutinel's force to break-out across the open country. The problem was, it was anything but open and Currie's ambitious plan for a coup quickly fell apart.

Barbed wire, a sunken road, fences, trenches and field and machine-gun fire from point-black range soon blocked the brigade of cavalry and armoured cars forcing them to confine themselves to the road itself.

Failure to reach the Canal du Nord was one thing but more catastrophic was the absence of Canadian artillery shelling which allowed the Germans to retaliate with their own batteries, causing disturbing casualties among the Fourth Division ranks. By early afternoon, they were stopped in their tracks. Because there was now no hope of the armoured cars and cavalry reaching the Canal du Nord, Currie issued orders for an artillery barrage to be reorganized the following morning to support an infantry advance on the waterway.

This proved impossible to implement on such short notice. Beyond the D-C line the Canadians were in a shambles. And there was insufficient time to reform the artillery batteries into a cohesive force by dawn. Then fate intervened.

Overnight the Germans withdrew to the far side of the Canal du Nord. By nightfall next day, the Canadians had cleared the east bank. Despite all its last minute shortcomings and the disappointment of not seeing Currie's scheme to topple Cambrai realized, the offensive had been a signal achievement. Since August 26 the Canadian Corps had advanced 12 miles and had won back all the ground gained by the Germans in their spring offensive. It had taken 10,492 prisoners and captured 123 field guns and 927 machine-guns. Losses totalled 11,423 killed and wounded. The artillery which had played such a critical part had fired 847,990 rounds of shells of all sizes, weighing 20,424 tons. Overrunning the vaunted Drocourt-Queant Switch Line had been a banner accomplishment, what Haig described as "a great and glorious success." A dejected Kaiser Wilhelm put it another way: "We have lost the war!" he moaned. "Poor Fatherland!"

PART 3 — CAMBRAI

On the day the Canadians reached the Canal du Nord, Marshal Ferdinand Foch outlined his future plans for the Allied offensive on the Western Front. To prevent the Germans from massing their reserves, his strategy called for a huge, simultaneous attack by the British, Belgian, French and United States armies on a front stretching from Bruges in the north to St Mihiel in the south. It called for four simultaneous blows: by the British against Cambrai and St Quentin to the south; by the French beyond the River Aisne; by the Americans against the St Mihiel Salient, and later combining with the French in a strike against St Mezieres; and by the British and Belgians towards Ghent and Bruges. The key to this campaign was the crossing of the Canal du Nord by the British First Army and the capture of the vital communications and rail centre of Cambrai. Spearheading the assault would be, who else, the Canadian Corps.

On September 4, Arthur Currie climbed a ridge overlooking the waterway where he could make note of the formidable barrier he would have to get his troops across. The canal was only 100 feet wide but the Germans had flooded the marshes on either side broadening it to two or three times that at its widest point. Its defences consisted of concentrated machine-gun nests close to the east bank. A mile behind was the Marquion defence line, and behind it atop a hill, the Bourlon Wood. From aerial reconnaissance photographs, the Canadians had learned that between it and Cambrai lay another system of trenches, the Marcoing Trench Line.

Currie knew that the Germans would never give up Cambrai without a fierce struggle. He also knew that a frontal attack across the Canal du Nord would be difficult and costly. Bridges would have to be thrown over the waterway, making his troops highly vulnerable targets. As usual Currie's military genius solved the problem.

The Canal du Nord had still been under construction when the war broke out. Navigably it ran only 800 yards along the Canadian Corps front, ending at the canal lock near the village of Sains-lez-Marquoin. From then on it was dry, its bed at ground level running for 2,600 yards. Currie conceived of the idea of pushing his men across this stretch as fast as possible then fanning them out in a north-easterly direction to quickly expand the front to 15,000 yards. It was daring and depended upon proper planning, discipline, leadership and luck to succeed. But it was risky. The congestion of 50,000 troops squeezing forward through such a narrow space in a short time presented the inevitable danger of an artillery attack. The element of surprise was essential.

Henry Horne, the First Army commander, was highly skeptical and tried to talk Currie out of the scheme; he considered it too complicated. But the Canadian Corps commander was adamant and had Haig's blessing. Currie knew his reputation and military future were on the line but refused to budge. Horne finally gave in, with the proviso that supporting units be delayed until the leading divisions had firmly established themselves across the canal.

Surprise was almost impossible to achieve. The Germans were expecting an assault and from the heights of the Bourlon Wood had a virtually unrestricted view of preparations for the attack: the camps, horse lines, vehicle assemblies and artillery formations. Currie and his staff feared an artillery barrage in the concentrated area. None took place, probably because of the efforts of Lieutenant Colonel Andy McNaughton's counter-artillery shelling from time to time. Only darkness could hide the last minute arrangements before Zero Hour. On the soggy evening of September 26, the Canadians tumbled out of their dugouts in the recently captured Drocourt-Queant Line and began moving forward to the crowded start line, which had become so crowded that the artillery could not be brought up until the troops were ready to jump off. That occurred at 5:20 a.m., just before dawn, in light drizzle as the First Division on the left and the Fourth on the right began their advance over slippery terrain under cover of a thunderous artillery barrage the like of which had not been seen or heard since Vimy.

Everything went like clockwork. One entire German infantry regiment was annihilated, the 188th. Of the 230 enemy artillery guns assembled at the Bourlon Wood, 113 were knocked out by the corps' counter-artillery only a few minutes after Zero Hour. The main objective of September 27 was capture of the wood, a task that fell to the Fourth Division. David Watson assigned all three of his brigades, the 10th, 11th and 12th, to the job. Basically the strategy was to outflank the wood and attack from the rear instead of risking an almost suicidal head-on assault.

But things failed to go according to plan. The projected pincer movement broke down when the British 52nd Battalion failed to keep up, exposing the Canadian flank to deadly enfilade fire. It meant that the 102nd Central Ontario Battalion had to abandon its planned turning movement on the south side of the wood, because it was forced to take up a defensive position along the Bapaume-Cambrai road. To complicate matters, the battalion's commanding officer, Lieutenant Colonel Fred Lister, was wounded. A bright spot was the action by Lieutenant Graham Lyall who stormed a German strongpoint taking 13 prisoners and four machine-guns. He covered himself with even more glory later by capturing 92 more prisoners and another five machine-guns.

On the other side of the wood the Canadians were completely successful. The 87th Canadian Grenadier Guards, supported by the 78th Winnipeg Grenadiers, fought their way right into Bourlon village. During this action, Lieutenant Samuel Honey of the 78th, so distinguished himself, he was awarded the Victoria Cross. When all the other officers of his company were either killed or wounded, Honey took charge and rallied his men forward, personally capturing an enemy machine-gun nest and taking ten prisoners. Later he helped repel four particularly vicious German counter-attacks.

Now the heights fell with ease. The 45th Central Ontario Battalion advanced through the village, skirted the wood and captured the heights to the rear. Supported by the 75th Mississauga Battalion, the unit then pressed on towards Fontaine-Notre-Dame encountering in a dugout a German regimental commander and his staff who surrendered. Caught by surprise, they were under the impression that the Bourlon Wood had been retaken. Darkness prevented any further advance, but the crucial Bourlon Wood heights, from which the Germans had dominated the battlefield, was now solidly in Canadian hands.

North of the wood, the 85th Nova Scotia Highlanders helped clear the village while the 38th Ottawa Battalion struck at the railway line leading north to Sauchy-Lestree. However, a sunken road, heavily defended by machine-guns, temporarily checked their progress. When Lieutenant James Knight and Private Colin Graham of the 72nd Seaforth Highlanders saw the predicament, they rushed to the rescue. Armed with a Lewis gun they began pouring lead into the nest. The Germans had no taste for it and 50 of them quickly surrendered, allowing the Ottawans to continue their advance. After some confusion due to smoke and noise, they finally consolidated their position along the rail line and from there the Seaforths picked up the advance. The 72nd met with heavy enemy field gun fire at point-blank range. Led by Captain William Ross, who crept within 50 yards of the German battery, his men overcame the Germans, capturing 119 of the enemy along with eight 77-millimetre guns. The battalion now turned its attention to a hill called Pilgrim's Nest, a half mile to the east. The time was 2:45 in the afternoon and two companies, yelling at the top of their voices, launched a bayonet charge that so unnerved the defenders, all 200 of them immediately surrendered. The battalion now settled down and for the rest of the day sent out reconnaissance patrols to set up outposts.

On the left, to the west, Archie Macdonnell's First Division was fighting four different battles in four different directions, east, northeast, north and west, and fighting them very well. Progress was steady and casualties light. However, just before midday the 13th Royal Highlanders of George Tuxford's 3rd Brigade became pinned down in their advance on Marquion, situated on the Arras-Cambrai road. They were helped by the Manchester Regiment from the British 11th Division (assigned to the Canadian Corps) which rescued them from a ticklish spot and joined the Canadians in capturing the village.

On the right flank, to reach its final objective for the day, the 1st Brigade's commander William Griesbach assigned the 2nd Eastern Ontario and the 3rd Toronto Regiment battalions; their advance was stemmed by machine-gun fire from an embankment along the Bourlon-Sauchy-Lestree railway line. But not for long. From its vantage point atop Pilgrim's Nest, the 72nd quickly routed the German gunners.

This enabled the battalions to continue their advance although they were constantly harassed by German machine-gunning enroute. At Raillencourt, close to the Arras-Cambrai road, George Kerr of the Toronto Regiment single-handedly subdued four enemy nests and took 37 prisoners, a feat for which he was decorated with the Victoria Cross. By the time the 2nd battalion reached its objective, La Maison Neuve farm, north of Pilgrim's Nest, the troops could see a convoy of German infantry, wagons and gun carriers escaping along the road toward Cambrai. But none of the enemy artillery eluded capture. The 1st Brigade overran 56 field guns, the artillery support for an entire division.

By mid-afternoon the corps began exploiting their earlier successes. However, this was not as extensive as it might have been had the British XVII Corps kept pace with the Canadian advance. Because it did not, it was impossible to throw in the Third Division on the right of the Fourth, without exposing it to deadly enemy fire. As a result all hopes of crossing the Canal de L'Escaut at Cambrai were quickly dashed. But on the left flank, the British Third Division and the First Division enjoyed substantial successes. The British took the village of Epinoy just short of the Canal de la Sensee, and this enabled the Canadians to reach the Douai-Cambrai road east of Hayencourt. That was as far as they could go, however. Any further advance by the 10th Canadian Battalion was prevented by a deep barrier of barbed wire entanglements facing them, heavily protected by a series of machine-gun nests. The commanding officer, Colonel Edward Mac-Donald, ordered his men to dig in. All evening long the Canadians were badgered by German counter-attacks aimed in the direction of Hayencourt, where troops of the 5th Western Cavalry Battalion had a tough time hanging on until the 8th Winnipeg Rifles arrived to reinforce them.

Canadian engineers came in for special praise for their work. Prior to the attack, they had repaired 18 miles of road. Following the jump off, they built seven footbridges across the Canal du Nord for the supporting infantry to cross, as well as ten larger bridges for the artillery. All this was accomplished under fire.

In fact, but for a few misgivings and shortcomings, September 27 had been one of the most fruitful dates enjoyed by the Canadian Corps. Significantly it also marked the halfway point of ''Canada's 100 Days,'' as well as that of the Great War's last 100 days. Germans captured, numbered 3,500. Currie's gamble, fraught with all its difficulties and dangers, not to mention the misgivings of his superiors as well as members of his own staff, had paid off and paid off handsomely. A distance of 6,000 yards had been gained. Foch praised the battle of the Canal du Nord, as a "magnificent dash."

Overnight the Third Division moved into the line on the Bapaume-Cambrai road east of the Bourlon Wood with the objective of capturing Fontaine-Notre-Dame. Next day the First Canadian and the 4th British divisions began advancing on the left to the north-east and the Fourth Division, whose front had been narrowed down to a width small enough to accomodate a brigade, directly east. The overall goal was the breaching of the Marcoing Line, the last trench bastion before Cambrai.

It was no piece of cake. The countryside north of Cambrai was almost bucolic, rolling and clear, with no place to take cover. Furthermore, geographically the corps was gradually hemming itself in between the Canal de Sensee on the north, and the Canal de L'Escaut on the south. The ability to manoeuvre was being sharply reduced.

By the following day, September 29, the Canadian Corps was suffering a "victory hangover," characterized by disorganization, disorientation and disruption, interrupted and uncertain communications, delays, confusion and uncoordinated, piecemeal attacks due to lack of proper reconnaissance.

The Third Division had a special problem of its own. All its senior officers were rookies. Major General Frederick Loomis had replaced Louis Lipsett (who had been transferred to take over a British division) only two weeks before. And both his brigade commanders were novices: Brigadier General John Clark had been in charge of the 7th for merely three weeks, and the 9th had been placed in the temporary command of Lieutenant Colonel Donald Sutherland.

Despite that situation, however, the division captured Fontaine-Notre-Dame. The entire German garrison surrendered to the 9th Brigade's 43rd Canadian Highlanders of Canada with only fractional resistance. In fact, many of the Germans escaped in such haste that the Canadians giving chase couldn't catch up to them. Beside the Highlanders, the Royal Canadian Regiment, supported by powerful shelling, and accompanied by four tanks which the commanding officer typed as "useless," reached the Marcoing Line. There they encountered a heavy uncut barbed wire entanglement defence that had escaped aerial detection due to the vegetation that had grown around it.

This, and strong machine-gun fire from both flanks, held up the advance of the battalion. Lieutenant Milton Gregg, a future Canadian cabinet minister, crawled forward alone and explored the wire until he found a small gap through which he led his men into the enemy trench. The Germans counter-attacked in force and without grenades, the Canadians were on the spot with the situation rapidly becoming critical. Although wounded, Gregg ran back under heavy fire and collected a supply of bombs. Rejoining his company, which had been greatly reduced in numbers, he reorganized his men and led them in an attack that cleared the enemy trenches. He personally accounted for 11 Germans killed or wounded and took 25 prisoners, in addition to 12 machine-guns. This gallant feat won Gregg the Victoria Cross.

That was the RCR's only success. They were unable to make any more headway against the barbed wire. John Clark, the brigade commander, sent in a fresh battalion, the Princess Patricia's Canadian Light Infantry to the rescue. Early in the afternoon the PPCLI, together with what was left of the RCRs, under a heavy artillery barrage, overcame the Marcoing Line's outer support defences. But that was as far as they got. In the south, having captured Fontaine-Notre-Dame, the Cameron Highlanders combined with the 52nd Nova Scotia Battalion to assault the Marcoing Line but were quickly brought to a standstill by withering enemy machine-gun fire. The failed attack cost the 52nd 259 casualties.

In the centre of the front, the Third Division's commander, Fred Loomis, was determined to reach the Douai-Cambrai road beyond the Marcoing defences, the objective of Clark's 7th Battalion, as well as the hamlet of Sainte-Olle, the objective of Donald Sutherland's 9th Brigade. At 3:00 p.m. reinforcements were brought up but the attack had to be postponed for four hours until the artillery was supplied with sufficient ammunition to provide an effective barrage. When the assault was finally launched, it got nowhere. Although some gains were made here and there, determined enemy counter-attacking forced the Canadians to give them up.

The Fourth Division fared little better. Only one battalion, the 47th Western Ontarios, attained its objective before nightfall, by capturing the stoutly defended village of Raillençourt and reaching the Marcoing Line. But due to heavy German resistance, the advance ended there. That night the 10th Brigade's 44th New Brunswick and the 46th South Saskatchewan battalions, reached the Douai-Cambrai road and dug in. It took the 44th, with only 100 men left, until three o'clock in the morning to fully consolidate the position.

To his amazement and utter disdain, Edward MacDonald's 10th Canadian Battalion, which had been stalled the day before at the Douai-Cambrai road east of Hayencourt by thick barbed wire entanglements, received the order to advance. MacDonald had clearly recommended standing fast until troops could be brought up to protect his flanks and the wire had been cut. It was ridiculous. The order should never have been given. The battalion was totally exposed on both flanks with high ground on either side.

To make matters worse, the artillery began its shelling right on the battalion's line. MacDonald hastily withdrew his men, but under fire from the Germans, they suffered 50 "unnecessary" casualties. Then when the barrage did begin, it was so weak, it was of no value at all. For two hours the battalion struggled through the barbed wire cutting it by hand. By the time MacDonald furiously called a halt to the operation, orders or no orders, the unit had sustained 100 more casualties.

It was not one of the Canadian Corps' greater days, and the next day's performance wasn't a whole lot better. The corps was starting to run out of steam, and resistance promised to stiffen. The Germans had brought in an extra division, bringing the total to eight, with five more on the way. From now on, matters would get progressively worse for the Canadians. Sunday, September 29, saw five brigades go into battle: the 7th, 8th, and 9th from the Third Division, the 12th from the Fourth Division, and the 2nd from the First Division. An omen of what they might expect was the warning to several battalions that they would receive only light artillery support due to the shortage of guns. This, coupled with an inexplicable lack of coordination, was to plague the Canadians all day long.

At 6:00 a.m. to the south, the 8th and 9th brigades kicked off the morning's offensive. The latter, on the right, dispatched the 58th Central Ontario Battalion to the Bapaume-Cambrai road to assist the British 57th Division. The Canadians cleared the Marcoing Line that had been blocking the advance to the Canal de L'Escaut.

At the same time the 116th Ontario County Battalion renewed the previous day's assault on Sainte-Olle, astride the road. It took until noon to secure it. The Germans met the assault from a trench on the outskirts of the village with resolute machine-gun fire that all but wiped out two companies. Major George Pratt, who commanded the battalion, called on a field battery for help. A battery of 18-pounders pin-pointed the trench perfectly, holding the enemy down, while Pratt led his two remaining companies in a flanking movement that quickly captured it and took 100 German prisoners. They then proceeded to occupy the town. It had cost them 250 casualties.

Meanwhile two battalions from Dennis Draper's 8th Brigade zeroed in on the Cambrai suburb of Nerville-Saint-Remy. As they deployed across the open fields, the 1st and 2nd Canadian Mounted Rifles were subjected to machine-gun fire from the vicinity of Saint-Olle which was yet to fall. But this did not impede their progress, until they were held up by machine-gun fire on the Bapaume-Cambrai road. Ignoring the danger, Captain John McGregor of the 2nd CMR, dashed forward by himself, located the machine-guns and put them out of action. With his rifle and bayonet he killed four Germans and took eight prisoners; although he was himself wounded in the action, he won the Victoria Cross. By nightfall the two battalions had reached the edge of the Canal de L'Escaut directly across from Cambrai, the final objective. So near, yet so far. Two more brigades joined in the fracas at 8:00 that morning: John Clark's 7th Brigade and the Fourth Division's 12th Brigade on the left, commanded by Lieutenant Colonel James Kirkaldy who had replaced James MacBrien the day before when the latter was wounded.

The 7th's objective was the village of Tilloy, on the edge of a low plateau that overlooks Cambrai from the north. Two battalions, the 49th Edmonton Regiment and the 42nd Royal Highlanders of Canada advanced under an almost pathetic artillery barrage across open field that offered no cover whatsoever; casualties began to mount immediately. The 49th reached the Douai-Cambrai road but couldn't get across due to the enemy fire. They had taken 150 prisoners but their own losses had been so heavy that part of the 2nd CMR had to reinforce them to hold on to what little ground they had gained.

The predicament of the Royal Highlanders was even worse; they encountered the same barbed war that the PPCLI had struggled with the night before. They had to clip their way through it by hand, while well concealed German machine-gunners waited patiently until the Canadians were thoroughly enmeshed in the entanglement, then opened up with everything they had. It was murder; how anyone survived was a miracle. Most were killed or wounded but some got through to exact vengeance on the enemy gunners, many of whom fled in panic.

Both the 42nd and 49th managed to get as far as the road but that was it. German machine-gun fire, from a railway embankment 300 yards ahead, pinned them down so effectively, it was suicidal even to lift one's head. There was only one way out of the predicament:

call on the field artillery for assistance. But even that shelling failed to dislodge the enemy gunners from the embankment. In fact the Germans even mounted a counter-attack, which the Canadians repulsed.

Kilkardy's 12th Brigade's luck was no better. With the 38th Ottawa Battalion on the left and the 72nd Seaforth Highlanders on the right, it began its attack from positions along the Douai-Cambrai road. The 38th's advance was stalled within minutes by enemy machine-gun fire.

However, the 72nd almost met with some success, albeit short-lived. Crossing the road, the infantrymen stormed the village of Sancourt, which surrendered after a brief skirmish, the battalion taking 250 prisoners there, and another 150 in a nearby sunken road, along with 20 machine-guns. The Seaforths then proceeded towards the next objective, the village of Blecourt, but were held up by vicious German crossfire. However, one company managed to steal away to take Blecourt, along with 150 prisoners — momentarily. With the Germans preparing a counter-attack, the Highlanders knew they were too few in number to sustain it. They quickly withdrew to the railway line where the rest of the battalion, even though reinforced by the 85th Nova Scotia Highlanders, was in deep trouble. They had to retreat back to Sancourt where the situation was even worse. A tremendous German artillery barrage left them no choice but to retreat to the Douai-Cambrai road from where they had started.

Now came the turn of the 2nd Brigade, the final attack of the day, one that should never have taken place. To his complete chagrin, Lieutenant Colonel Alan Saunders, commanding the 90th Winnipeg Rifles, received orders to drive on the village of Abancourt, due north of Blecourt. Saunders was appalled. This would take his battalion down the same valley in which Edward MacDonald's 10th Canadians had met with barbed wire disaster the day before. It was as if Archie Macdonnell and his staff had learned nothing from previous mistakes or simply ignored front line field reports. But the First Division commander assured Saunders that his left flank would be covered by the British 11th Division and that the 72nd Seaforth Highlanders would be on the right. He delayed the attack scheduled to start at 6:00 in the morning until 8:00 a.m. By that time the 72nd was on its way to capture Sancourt but after two attempts, the British never made it past the Douai-Cambrai road. Macdonnell decided to wait no longer and at 8:36 the Winnipeggers were sent over the top after a brief pre-shelling barrage.

Four tanks that were to support the battalion never showed up. However, the barbed wire that had been the nemesis of the 10th Canadians was found to be well cut. But, the attackers never got through it. Devastating machine-gun fire on both sides (from the left where the British had failed to reach the high ground, and from the right, unprotected by the 72nd's withdrawal) mowed down the 90th unmercifully, one company losing all its officers and senior NCOs.

It figured. It was one more near calamitous incident to climax a day of almost total failure and frustration for the Canadian Corps. And if Sunday had been a day of bitter disappointment, Monday, September 30, came close to disaster.

For the third consecutive day, Hugh Dyer's battered and bruised 7th Brigade spearheaded operations on the Third Division front. In the wake of a pulverizing artillery barrage, the PPCLI and the RCR battalions quickly and easily overran the railway embankment redoubt, east of the Douai-Cambrai road, and captured 67 enemy machine-guns, all of them concentrated in only 100 yards. But crossing the railway track was another matter. The PPCLI got through all right and handily took the village of Tilloy immediately north-east of Cambrai, by 7:30 in the morning, along with a battery of 77-millimetre guns and 50 machine-guns. Reinforced by the 49th Edmonton Regiment, the Canadians had consolidated their hold on the town by mid-morning. It was a fine achievement of vital importance and put Cambrai right on the doorstep. But it was the only success of the day.

On the left flank of the PPCLI, the RCRs ran into a hail of machine-gun bullets from the direction of Blecourt, which the 72nd had momentarily occupied the previous day. There, the Fourth Division was bogged down when its advance faltered due to an inadequate smokescreen that was supposed to have blinded the enemy. Instead the Germans were able to concentrate a wicked wall of fire into the ranks of the advancing Canadians.

Two battalions, the 75th Mississauga and the 54th Central Ontario, had been heavily shelled on their way to the jumping-off point, but the 75th managed to fight its way through to capture Sancourt, then advance upon the railway embankment where it was met by fierce fire from both Blencourt and Abancourt. The 54th, intent on taking Blencourt, suddenly faced a strong enemy counter-attack forcing them back. The 87th Canadian Grenadier Guards, which had been held in reserve to exploit the 11th Brigade's success, now found itself in a reinforcing role. Though losses were frightful, the 87th alone was quickly reduced to company strength; all three battalions managed to beat off the enemy assault, but were compelled to retire to the railway embankment.

It was clear that the Canadians had not only badly underestimated the enemy strength, they were rapidly reaching a point of exhaustion. Some men had been fighting for four consecutive days. Currie at once called off all further operations for September 30. He now gambled that the Germans were probably just as tired and had suffered such severe losses, that they would not find it worthwhile to risk further casualties by holding their positions. He decided to throw in everything he had the following day with the Zero Hour set at 5:00 a.m.

His plan called for a simultaneous assault by four of his divisions, from north to south, the British 11th and the Canadian First, Fourth and Third. The first objective was for the British to seize the high ground between Aubenchel-au-Bac and Abancourt. The Second Division and Brutinell's brigade stood in reserve to exploit any breakthrough.

Things got off to a poor start. The 11th Division was brought to a virtual standstill by heavy, uncut barbed wire. The British failure created problems on the right flank. William Greisbach's 11th Brigade from the Fourth Division, under a solid artillery barrage, reached the railway line blocking the way to Abancourt just before daylight. Then they became pinned down by German machine-gun fire. George Tucker's 3rd Brigade also made good progress in the dark, capturing Bantigny and Cuvillers. When it turned daylight, its battalions were besieged with German machine-gun fire. Practically cut off and running out of ammunition, they were forced to retreat to a point only 600 yards from where they had jumped off.

Meanwhile, things were going much more smoothly for the Fourth Division. Victor Oldum's 11th Brigade reached the road between Cuvillers and Ramillies. The 102nd Central Ontario Battalion took 403 prisoners, Lieutenant Graham Lyall accounting for 82 bringing his personal total to 185, and a great number of machine-guns, a feat that won him the Victoria Cross. The crippled 87th Canadian Grenadier Guards joined in the battle, both sides fighting to a standstill.

Donald Sutherland's 9th Brigade launched the final attack on October 1. The plan was to strike out to the east of Tilloy then capture the high ground, 1,000 yards dead ahead. The 52nd New Ontario and the 43rd Cameron Highlanders battalions made good progress at first but when they reached the ridge, there was no place to take cover and they ran into a storm of fire. The 52nd lost every officer and most of its NCOs, though somehow it managed to take 250 prisoners and 33 machine-guns. But it proved impossible to move forward. To break the deadlock, Sutherland committed his other two divisions, the 58th Central Ontario and the 116th Toronto County. The latter captured 100 prisoners, several machine-guns, and three field guns, but it had been cut in two, losing half its battalion strength. It was the end to another disappointing day.

Currie quickly realized that his belief that the Germans would rather give up their positions than incur more casualties, was totally incorrect. They obviously had no intention of giving in without a tough fight. The redeeming factor was that the 7,000 rounds the artillery fired off that day, was twice the daily average. But in the face of the small gain — an average of one and a half miles on October 1 — at such high cost, Currie decided to postpone any further engagement with the enemy until his troops had had time to recuperate.

On the plus side, during the five days of fighting (September 27 to October 1) the Canadian Corps had taken 7,500 prisoners and 205 guns. With its four divisions the corps had faced 13 enemy divisions and 13 independent machine-gun units on a front of five and a half miles, a clear indication of the regard in which the Germans held the fighting quality of the Canadians. In fact, a captured document revealed that they thought they were fighting at least 12 Canadian divisions. With good reason: since August 26, the corps had captured a total of 18,585 prisoners, 371 guns, 1,923 machine-guns, and had advanced 23 miles into enemy territory encompassing an area of 116 square miles. Most important, the Canadians had broken the vaunted Drocourt-Queant Line and forded the formidable Canal Du Nord. Now, by taking command of the high ground overlooking Cambrai, they had made the enemy's position there untenable. Its fall was merely a question of time.

But at this stage Currie had strong misgivings about just how much time that might entail, and at what cost. Over the last few days, enemy resistance had stiffened so strongly, the Germans were fighting, in the corps commander's own words, ''like a cornered rat.'' Some division and brigade commanders, who had begun to have self-doubts about their own leadership ability, were convinced that a victory at Cambrai could not be obtained until the turn of the year. But their pessimism was totally unfounded. Their perception was restricted entirely to their own sector of operations, and discoloured by a temporary failure to see their objectives reached as quickly as they had hoped. Overall, on the broad front, there was every cause for optimism. The Germans were hurting, badly, all down the line and for this the Canadians could take a large share of the credit.

Foch's offensive had forced the German High Command to shuffle troops from one trouble spot to another because they lacked the reserves to reinforce their positions. This could be attributed directly to the pressure brought to bear upon them by the Canadian Corps. Since August 8, at one time or another, the Germans had been forced to employ 47 divisions against the Canadians — a quarter of the entire German army. This large commitment to a single small sector had to be made at the expense of other larger local fronts. This allowed Foch to pick his assault points at his own time and choosing, and keep the enemy constantly off base. On September 26, the First United States Army demonstrated the value of the intense, concentrated American combat training when, in its first major battle, it thwarted a German withdrawal in the St Mihiel Salient.

More good news. On September 26, General John "Black Jack" Pershing's American forces joined with the French Fourth Army to strike between Reims and Verdun. Next day the First British Army crossed the Canal du Nord south of the Canadian sector while the Third Army converged on the Canal de Saint-Quentin. On September 28, the Second British Army and the Belgians recaptured Passchendaele. The final break came on the 29th when the Fourth Army, spearheaded by the Australian Corps, smashed through the Hindenburg Line at Saint-Quentin.

Those weren't Germany's only headaches. The fatherland was starting to crumble in disarray, its allies falling by the wayside. In Palestine, the British had torn the Turkish army to shreds and in Salonika, they had defeated the Bulgarians so badly and thoroughly that they dropped right out of the war. At home, a starving German population was growing restless, looking upon the army with scorn, and in some cases heaping abuse upon it.

On the day the British crashed through the Hindenburg Line, after learning that nothing had been done to open peace feelers through the neutral powers as ordered by the Kaiser earlier in the month, Erich Ludendorff met with Field Marshal Paul von Hindenburg. Ludendorff implored the chief commander of the Central Powers, to put pressure on the government at once. No sooner asked than executed. In a stern note to the cabinet, Hindenburg wrote: "the only right course is to give up the fight."

On October 5, a proposal was drawn up and submitted, through the U.S. embassy in Switzerland, to U.S. President Woodrow Wilson. The Germans considered him the most pliable of the Allied leaders. The document agreed to Wilson's Fourteen Points, which he considered essential to concluding a peace. But these were unacceptable to the British and French who insisted on unconditional surrender. The German peace proposal was turned down. Meanwhile the war would continue until total victory, the Canadians ever in the forefront.

After nearly a week's rest, in which its actions were limited to reconnaissance patrols, the Canadians Corps prepared for the final assault on Cambrai, short by one division. On October 7, Henry Burstall's First Division was temporarily attached to the British First Army's XXII Corps on the Canadians' left flank north of the River Sensee to speed things up. The XXII had been dragging its backside so badly it hadn't even reached the Drocourt-Queant Line in that sector. The remainder of the corps poised for operation "Peace Proposal," a two stage assault aimed at a quick conquest of the textile city.

The basic plan called for Archie Macdonell's Second Division to seize the Canal L'Escaut bridges, most of which were still intact, south-west of Cambrai. Once across, the Canadians would enter the city cutting it off from the north, while Frederick Loomis' Third Division followed up with a secondary attack later. As a precaution, to prevent an enemy withdrawal and provide cover, the British Third Army's XVII Corps would take the town of Awoingt on the high ground south-east of Cambrai.

Currie decided on a night operation to prevent heavy casualties that would most certainly befall the Second Division on the slopes approaching the canal. Stage one got started at 4:30 a.m. on October 8, but by nightfall the British were nowhere near their objective. When it became clear by 1:30 the following morning, his Zero Hour, that Awoingt would never be reached on time, with some trepidation, Currie decided to go ahead anyway and ordered the attack.

Currie need not have concerned himself. In the first place the Germans, those still around, were caught completely by surprise. In the second, there was no resistance at all; the enemy was in the process of evacuating the city, while putting it to the torch. The only opposition, if it could be called that, came from a party of Germans who tried to stop Captain Norman Mitchell, an engineer with the Fourth Central Ontario Battalion, from defusing demolition charges on one of the Escaut bridges. Mitchell promptly killed two of his attackers and took the other 12 prisoner. He thus became the only Canadian engineer to win the Victoria Cross during World War I.

By 8:30 that morning the city was completely secured, leaving the British 11th and the Canadian Second Divisions free to consolidate gains in the country to the north. This was completed by October 11, by which time they had reached the Sensee River. The Canadian Corps now traded places with the British XXII to the north.

Since the beginning of the Arras-Cambrai Campaign on August 26, the Canadians had advanced 23 miles through the heart and backbone of the German defence system. Over that six week period, they had suffered 30,000 casualties but, as the aggressor with their enormous use of artillery, had probably inflicted an even greater number on the enemy (who never released casualty lists). More than 19,000 Germans had been taken prisoner and 370 enemy guns and 2,000 machine-guns had been captured. This was a monumental achievement and there was yet more Canadian glory to come during this "War to end all Wars."

PART 4 — THE FINAL 32 DAYS
OCTOBER 11 to NOVEMBER 11

For the first few days in their fresh surroundings facing north along the Canal de la Sensee, the Canadians stood pat, content to "test the waters" each morning by firing off an artillery salvo in hopes of measuring the enemy's presence. At this stage, Currie was in no rush to attempt to ford the canal in force which, in its flooded state, presented a prodigious undertaking. The hiatus was a welcome one to the exhausted and depleted troops. In any case, from German prisoners and reconnaissance forays across the waterway, it was learned that civilians were being evacuated from the towns and villages, bridges, roads and railways were being prepared for demolition and supplies were being removed or destroyed. Frequent fires and explosions behind enemy lines were observed. In fact, on October 8 Ludendorff had ordered a general withdrawal, fighting rearguard actions only enroute, to Germany's final bastion, the Hermann Line, which ran from the Scarpe River in Flanders to the north, through Valenciennes in the Canadians' sector, and to the Oise River in the south. Ludendorff knew full well that this defence line could not hold out for long. It was still under construction, incomplete and disconnected, with wide gaps everywhere. Besides, the forces at his disposal were fast dwindling; he had already been forced to disband

22 divisions due to lack of reinforcements. News on the home front was just as discouraging. Widespread food riots had broken out and to make matters even worse the country found itself in the grip of the deadly influenza epidemic that was to kill 21 million people worldwide in 1918-19.

On the morning of October 17, when the customary retaliation to the Canadian barrage failed to materialize, it was soon discovered that the enemy was retiring from the Sensee under a heavy blanket of fog and mist. Patrols were quickly dispatched across the canal to lay cork footbridges and pave the way for a crossing in force. Hard on their heels came Archie Macdonell's First Division and David Watson's Fourth. The chase to Valenciennes was on! Accompanying Currie in the pursuit was Captain Windsor, formally the Prince of Wales, the future King Edward VIII, who had joined Currie's staff several days earlier.

The advance was not without difficulties. The Germans had stripped the countryside of all farm produce, cattle, pigs and poultry, leaving the civilian population without food. This proved a formidable assignment for the Canadian Army Service Corps which had to bring up extra supplies by horse transport. By the time the Canadians reached Valenciennes, the CASC had fed 70,000 extra people.

The enemy had also left a trail of devastation in its wake: demolished bridges, cratered roads and torn up railway lines. Wet weather, rain and fog added to the chaos. To keep casualties to a minimum, Currie issued strict orders that every effort should be made to avoid contact with the enemy. In the case of strong positions, the defences should be carefully reconnoitered and probed before engaging in combat.

The advance proved a strange new experience for the Canadians. While they were compelled to struggle through, over or around obstacles created by German sabotage, they moved ahead quickly and steadily without being shot at. They could hear the explosions as the enemy blew up bridges and other communications ahead of them but there was an almost eerie absence of gunfire. Perhaps the most unusual sensation of all, and certainly the most moving, was the welcome they received from the French population who greeted them as liberators. Bands struck up as they entered the towns and villages, 40 of which they had already freed, while the civilians cheered, bedecked them with flowers, and offered them coffee, soup, wine and champagne.

As the Canadians neared Valenciennes, this relaxed, easygoing progress and the festive, friendly atmosphere abruptly changed. On October 21 they ran into roadblocks covered by machine-guns, and experienced long-range shelling. Over the next two days opposition increased steadily as the Third and Fourth Divisions cleared the west bank of the Canal de L'Escaut. On both flanks, the British again failed to keep pace with the Canadian advance. On the right, the XXII Corps was halted at the Ecallia River while on the left, the VIII Corps also got bogged down. Currie decided to delay an attack on Valenciennes until both flanks caught up. It was a tactically judicious move. Valenciennes would be no pushover. It formed the key point in the Hermann Line. The Canal de L'Escaut barred the approach from both west and north and the Germans had dug trenches on the west bank. They had also opened the sluice gates to flood the low-lying ground. The only dry approach was from the south and in its way stood Mont Houy. Of the five German divisions defending Valenciennes, three of them were concentrated on the 150 foot high mountain.

First Army commander, Sir Henry Horne, ordered the 51st Division of the XXII Corps to take Mount Houy on October 28. Two days later Frederick Loomis' Fourth Division was to attack the southern outskirts of Valenciennes and advance to the high ground to the east, effectively outflanking the city. This would allow the remainder of the Canadian Corps to cross the Escaut and drive on towards Mons.

Currie had no confidence in the plan and even less in the XXII Corps, which had failed to capture the mountain on two previous occasions. He doubted very strongly that they would succeed a third time. And in that event, he knew it would be up to the Canadians to take it.

Currie's prognostications proved correct. The element of surprise had been lost when the Germans captured two cyclists carrying plans for the attack. However, the 51st did succeed in taking possession of the mountain but only up to a point. By noon the Germans had recaptured it, driving the British back down the southern slopes.

A bitter exchange now ensued between Horne's headquarters staff and Currie as to the procedure and timing for the Canadian Corps to take over from the 51st Division. Obviously, the Mont Houy defeat had upset the schedule. But General Headquarters wanted to stick with the original timing; that is immediately. Currie insisted, and got, a 24 hour postponement to prepare properly for a fresh attack on the mountain. Critical to this were arrangements by Andy McNaughton's counter-artillery batteries to bring up 303 guns of all calibres to support the assault.

GHQ stepped in again with two provisos. The first was that to avoid civilian loss of life, there was to be no shelling of the Valenciennes suburbs, where the Germans had purposely left thousands of civilians for just such a safeguard. Secondly, there was to be a strict conservation of ammunition. Currie chose to ignore both stipulations.

Supported by an artillery barrage throughout, which expended 2,140 tons of shells — equal to the amount exploded by both sides during the entire South African War — the Canadians' attack began at 5:15 a.m. on Friday, November 1. By eight o'clock that morning, the mountain was in Canadian hands. Results were impressive: 1,800 Germans were captured, another 2,600 killed. Canadian casualties were 400, 80 of them fatal. Four battalions from the Fourth Division's 10th Brigade took part: the 44th New Brunswick and the 47th Western Ontario spearheaded the assault, while the 46th South Saskatchewan leapfrogged them and charged ahead; the 50th Calgary was charged with mopping up. The 47th easily reached the southern outskirts of Valenciennes, while the 44th occupied the village of Aulnoy to the north-east of Mont Houy, where it took 800 Germans prisoner and captured three 77-millimetre field guns, at a loss of 89 casualties.

By midday, the Germans were so engrossed and overwhelmed by the attack on Mont Houy that the 38th Ottawa Battalion and the 72nd Seaforth Highlanders of Canada of the 12th Brigade were able to cross the 60-foot wide Canal de L'Escaut and enter the south-west and north ends of Valenciennes respectively. The 72nd infantrymen paddled their way across the canal in rafts and collapsible boats covered by a field gun brought right up to the west embankment. This was supported by riflemen and machine-gunners firing from upper story windows of nearby houses, who drove out the defending gunners on the opposite bank. By early afternoon the Highlanders had captured the city's railway station and yards, while engineers built bridges across the canal.

During the afternoon, the Germans mounted a series of counter-attacks which were repeatedly repulsed by the artillery. In the end, the day's fighting had proved to be too much for the Germans. That night they not only abandoned Valenciennes but the entire Hermann Line as well. It was the beginning of the end and the Canadian Corps' last major battle. It was also the last encounter during the war in which a Canadian earned the Victoria Cross for an action Currie described as a "superhuman deed."

It had been a busy afternoon for Sergeant Hugh Cairns of the 46th Battalion. When a German machine-gun opened fire on his platoon, he coolly picked up a Lewis gun, killed five of the enemy and captured the gun. Later, he repeated the performance against another machine-gun, this time killing 12 Germans and capturing 18 others. Wounded in the shoulder, he led his men forward once more, this time against a field gun as well as several machine-guns, accounting for a dozen of the enemy killed and 50 taken prisoner. Then with three others he reconnoitered the hamlet of Marly. Breaking down a barn door, he led the party into a courtyard where they forced 60 Germans to lay down their arms. However, an officer approached Cairns and shot him in the stomach. Bleeding profusely, and in excruciating pain, Cairns levelled his Lewis gun at the German and killed him. This created a donnybrook, with the Germans and Canadians blasting away at each other, but the latter soon had the situation under control. However, Cairns was so badly wounded he collapsed from loss of blood and had to be evacuated using the broken door as a stretcher. Next day he died in hospital.

From the North Sea to Verdun in the south, the German army was falling back in disorder. Ludendorff had been fired and the army now lacked leadership. The navy had openly mutinied. At home the country was on the verge of rebellion. Rioters in the streets called for the Kaiser's head. Roving bands of deserters and criminals bent on destruction burned and looted. The German communists were putting in their own two marks worth, fomenting uprisings in the main centres. Law and order was on the verge of collapse. Everywhere, everything, it seemed, was falling apart. On October 24, the Italians had inflicted a telling defeat on the Austrians and, two days after the Canadian victory at Valenciennes, Austria-Hungary surrendered to join Bulgaria and Turkey, who had thrown in the towel on September 29 and 30 respectively.

Whether aware of the overall picture in whole or in part, Sir Douglas Haig scheduled a final offensive against the Germans for November 3, but for all the wrong reasons. They were personal. After the victory at the Hindenburg Line, he had received congratulatory telegrams from King George, as well as from British parliamentarians and politicians from all over the empire. Prime Minister Lloyd George, whose vendetta with his field commander continued unabated, was the last to congratulate Haig and it was half-baked, half-hearted and somewhat snide. Haig was understandably both upset and annoyed. Almost vengefully, in a sort of "I'll show you" gesture, he decided upon a final decisive attack by his First, Third and Fourth divisions. If unwittingly, he was in a sense acknowledging Lloyd George's charge that: ''Haig does not care how many men he loses.''

The assault was postponed until November 4, and when it took place, it was more like an obstacle chase than a bona fide battle. The fight had gone out of the Germans. Resistance was spotty and spasmodic. As soon as the shelling — the specialty of the Canadian Corps — started, the enemy would retreat in the face of it. But the Germans continued their practice of leaving the ground they gave up in a shambles through demolition and dynamiting. The Canadians engaged in only sporadic skirmishes during that last week of the war. One took place on November 5 when two battalions of Victor Oldum's 11th Brigade crossed the River Aunelle from France into Belgium. At 2:30 that afternoon, held down by machine-gun fire, the first attempt by the 75th Mississauga and the 87th Canadian Grenadier Guards, failed. At six o'clock they tried again, this time successfully; by wading through the waist-deep water, they secured a bridgehead on the far embankment. Next morning the 102nd Central Ontario Battalion joined them and proceeded ahead to capture the village of Marchipont and establish a toehold across the River Honelle.

On November 10, when two battalions of John Clark's 7th Brigade, the Royal Canadian Regiment and the 42nd Royal Highlanders of Canada reached Mons — the site of the first major battle between the Germans and the British in 1914 — they ran into spirited resistance from German machine-gun fire. It came as a distinct surprise. They had expected that the Germans would have abandoned the town just as they had done with all the other communities the Canadians had captured over the past ten days. Captain William Grafftey from the 42nd, manoeuvred his unit into a position where it surrounded two of the enemy machine-gun nests. He then worked his way around three more strongpoints. For this action, he was awarded a bar to his Military Cross, to become the last Canadian to be decorated in the Great War.

Clark concluded that an attack would be necessary beginning at dawn. But after darkness fell, several companies of the two battalions worked their way into the town from the north, west and south in a pincer movement to reconnoitre the situation. There were no Germans to be found. Following the day's fighting, the enemy had simply slipped away. By two o'clock in the morning of November 11, both battalions were in Mons without a shot having been fired. It now became a question of which one would reach the centre of town first.

Lieutenant Martin King of the RCR won the race and by daybreak Mons was in Canadian hands. At seven o'clock news was received at Canadian Corps Headquarters that an armistice had been signed, to be put into effect at 11:00 a.m.

Canada's valiant "100 Days" had come to an end. During the period between August 8 and November 11, the corps had seen its hardest fighting of the war: 45,830 Canadians had been killed, wounded or went missing — a fifth of the total losses of 212,638 for the entire war. But on the credit side, during those one hundred days, the Canadians took 31,357 German prisoners and captured 623 cannon, 2,482 machine-guns and 362 trench mortars. They had also liberated 500 square miles of enemy held territory, including 228 cities, towns and villages.

At precisely 11 o'clock on the bright morning of November 11, 1918, the guns that had thundered across the Western Front for the past four years fell silent. The war to end all wars was over. Peace at last — at least for another 20 years.

PART 5 — AFTERMATH & CONSEQUENCE

On December 13, 1918, to the tune of "The Maple Leaf Forever," as part of the British Army of Occupation, troops of the Canadian Corps marched across the bridge over the Rhine into Germany at Bonn. It was raining but nothing could dampen their spirits. Midway across the span, their proud commander, Sir Arthur Currie, took the salute. Finally, in February 1919, the last of the Canadian occupation troops left the Rhineland and by May every division was home in Canada.

The Canadian Corps had established a reputation unsurpassed in the Allied armies. Following the Somme its record was one of unbroken victory. In Currie's own words:

> In no battle did the corps ever fail to take its objective; nor did it lose an inch of ground, once that ground was consolidated, and in the 51 months that it has been in the field the Canadian Corps has never lost a single gun. I think one cannot be accused of immodesty in claiming that the record is somewhat unique in the history of the world's campaigns.

The Great War was a milestone in the development of Canada as a nation. In 1914 the country had entered the conflict as a colony, a mere adjunct of Great Britain. Not for long. By 1918 she had forged ahead into full nationhood. Beginning the war with a single division under a British general, an independent corps had grown into the finest, most efficient fighting force on the continent.

For a nation of only eight million people, Canada's war effort had been truly remarkable. A total of 619,836 men and women served in the Canadian forces, of whom 66,655 lost their lives and another 172,950 were wounded. One out of every ten Canadians who fought the war never returned.

The country's notable war record earned the nation the right to a separate signature on the peace treaty as well as a seat at the League of Nations. At heavy cost, Canada's nationhood status had been established for all time.

✦ **12** ✦

UNREPAID SACRIFICE

Reference map "Hong Kong."

They never stood a chance — and those responsible for their being there knew it. Like sacrificial lambs being led to the slaughter, they were deliberately fed to the wolves, figuratively and physically, by their own political and military leaders. Of the 1,975 Canadians who fought in the uneven 18-day battle for Hong Kong against the Japanese late in December 1941, 290 were killed and 493 were wounded, while another 267 died as prisoners under the most shocking, barbarous and medieval conditions imaginable. The entire experience scarred the 1,418 survivors for life. But, while the Canadian government (in 1988) saw fit to apologize to the British Columbian Japanese community and compensate it for the wartime internment of Japanese Canadians as a safeguard against possible sabotage and fifth column activity, even today — over half a century later — an ungrateful nation still refuses to increase the meager compensation that those Hong Kong veterans still living, receive as former prisoners of war. That in itself is as disgraceful as the circumstances surrounding the decision to send those improperly trained — many had only been in the army for 16 weeks — and ill-equipped — they were without motor transport — volunteers into a totally impossible no-win situation in the first place.

Originally, Hong Kong, which had been ceded to Great Britain in 1842 following the Opium War, was established as a strategic location for trade with southern China. In 1860, a 360-mile tract directly to the north on the mainland was leased from the Chinese government for 99 years and became known as the New Territories. Hong Kong soon developed into the main base for the China Station of the Royal Navy. But by 1940 it had become merely a military outpost against the possible threat of war with Japan, with a garrison of 12,000 made up of four battalions and a local volunteer defence unit. The defence on the mainland consisted of a partially built line of fortifications and pillboxes, known as the Gin Drinkers Line, named after the bay on its left flank. The island of Hong Kong itself was fortified with coastal guns supported with 72 pillboxes, minefields, and barbed wire entanglements against the possibility of an invasion from the sea.

After the fall of France and Italy's entry into the war in June, 1940, Britain was forced to stretch her naval forces to control the Mediterranean. This left the Pacific without a British fleet and Hong Kong and Singapore defenceless against naval attack. Hong Kong's naval defence consisted of the First World War destroyer HMS Thracier, (which, in the first week of December 1941, was undergoing repairs), eight motor torpedo boats limited to machine-guns and depth charges, four river gunboats and a number of minelayers and patrol vessels.

The air defence was even more pathetic. In fact defence was a misnomer. The five aircraft at the tiny Kai Tak Airfield, on the mainland to the west of Kowloon, were officially listed as a training flight. It consisted of three Vickers Vildebeestes torpedo bombers used for towing target drogues and two Supermarine Walrus amphibians.

Before the arrival of the Canadians, the fate of Hong Kong rested with four infantry battalions, two British and two Indian. The 2nd Battalion, Royal Scots had been in the colony the longest, having been transferred from India in 1936. The other British unit, the 1st Battalion, Middlesex Regiment, had been posted to Hong Kong the following year and had been converted to a machine-gun battalion. The two Indian regiments were the 5th Battalion, 7th Rajput Regiment and the 2nd Battalion, 14th Punjab Regiment. All four units had highly reputable service records and backgrounds but the "soft" life of years in a far-flung colony had impaired some of their efficiency. The Indians also suffered because many of their veteran officers and men who had been transferred, were replaced by raw, partially trained, recruits.

Additionally there was the Hong Kong Volunteer Defence Corps composed of British residents, European nationals and Chinese, which trained part-time and made up four artillery batteries and seven infantry companies.

The fixed coastal defences on the south side of the island, primarily designed to counter an attack from the sea, were formidable, consisting of eight 9.2-inch, 15 6-inch, two 4.7-inch, and four 4-inch guns. On the north side, the guns facing across the harbour and the 450-yard Lye Mun Passage to resist an invasion from the mainland were as formidable, but hopelesly ineffective. The ammunition supplied to its 9.2-inch guns was armour piercing, fine against a battleship. But what was needed against attacking troops were shrapnel shells that would explode on impact when striking the ground or the water.

The mobile artillery was abysmal, made up of four obsolete 60-pounder guns, and 12 6-inch, eight 4.5-inch, eight 3.7-inch mortars, and limited to 25 rounds per man. The anti-aircraft batteries were in even shorter supply.

To the north of Hong Kong, the Japanese forces had been gaining in strength for some time, as had their preparations for the capture of the island. In 1938 troops from the rising sun landed at Bias Bay taking possession of the entire coast of China as well as Canton which placed them only 20 miles north of Kowloon and Hong Kong. When in June 1939 they acquired the island of Hainan, the isolation of the British colony was complete. By the end of October 1941, the Japanese had amassed squadrons of heavy bombers and more than 30,000 troops in the Canton area. Then on November 6, 1941 the Japanese Imperial General Headquarters ordered its commander-in-chief, in China, to prepare plans for the capture of Hong Kong with all arrangements and preparations to be ready by the end of the month.

The attack was entrusted to Lieutenant General Sano Tadayoshi's 38th Division of the 23rd Army. The plan was simple and straightforward. First, all naval and air defences would be knocked out by 40 single engine Kawasaki Ki 32 bombers from the 23rd Army's light bomber regiment (to be joined later by an 18-plane heavy bomber regiment). That accomplished, three infantry battalions would cross the border, breach the Gin Drinkers Line and complete the occupation of the mainland. Next step would be to establish a beachhead on the island's north shore and proceed to enlarge their hold from there.

The three infantry battalions, the 228th under Colonel Teimichi Doi, the 229th under Colonel Tanaka and the 230th under Colonel Toshishige Shoji, which made up the Sano Force named after the divisional commander, would be supported by a Light Armoured Car Unit with ten cars, the 38th Mountain Artillery Regiment with three battalions, the 38th Engineering Regiment and the 38th Transport Regiment along with signal, ordnance, veterinary and medical units plus two field hospitals. Also attached to the division were two Independent Mountain Artillery regiments, the 10th and 20th, two Independent Anti-Tank Gun battalions, the 2nd and 5th, the 21st Mortar Battalion, the 20th Independent Engineering Regiment, three transport regiments, plus three companies of another, and two river crossing companies. Supporting the division's own artillery and attached to it would be the entire artillery of the 23rd Army, which included a siege unit with a regiment of 150-mm howitzers and two independent battalions with 9.4-inch howitzers.

Clearly Sano Force represented a force to be reckoned with. But even had his intelligence been aware of the calibre of this battle seasoned, superbly coordinated, in-depth assault body, it would probably not have changed Major General Charles Maltby's low opinion of the Japanese soldier. The general officer commanding, Hong Kong dismissed reports of Japanese strength, as well as their successes against the Chinese, as exaggerated. He truly believed that Asians were an inferior race, mentally, militarily and physically. Their optical make-up, he often repeated to his staff, made it almost impossible for them to fight or fly at night.

Nevertheless Maltby, who had taken command of the garrison in July 1941, went about the preparation of its defences methodically and meticulously. Geographically it presented difficulties — both to the attackers and to the defenders. The New Territories on the mainland formed a 360-square mile peninsula, 15 miles deep from Kowloon to the Chinese border in the north. Most of it was mountainous and only sparsely populated. Hong Kong Island was compressed into 32 square miles, eight miles across and four miles deep and in places was densely populated. On the south, seaward side, a series of inlets indented the coastline. Most of the island was mountainous with deep valleys called gaps.

Before he knew the colony was to be reinforced with two Canadian battalions, Maltby planned to place the Punjab regiment at the Gin Drinkers Line to fight a rearguard action and buy some time. It wouldn't last long. Completion of that defence had been abandoned some time earlier. The main stand would be on the island. But what Maltby feared most was an invasion from the sea. In fact, the Japanese had no such intention. They probably knew that the south coast

would be well fortified and no thought was given to such an undertaking. It would be much easier to tackle it overland and across the
harbour.

When Maltby learned that the Canadian battalions were scheduled
to arrive in late November, he promptly altered his defence plans. He
now decided to detach three of his six battalions to the mainland for
a rearguard action. It certainly made better sense than trying to defend
it with one battalion. But to attempt to hold an incomplete fortification
spread out over a distance of 11 miles with little more than 5,000
men and the equipment he had available, was to badly underestimate
Japanese strength and quality. As early as 1937, a previous garrison
commander, General Arthur Bartholomew, believed that at least a
division would be needed and at the same time questioned the feas-
ibility of making a stand against a mass attack at all. This was more
consistent with earlier logic and thinking that might have prevented
the Canadians from being sent to their doom at Hong Kong. In 1938,
British policy finally settled on the fact that the colony, which it
regarded as an outpost (i.e.: its only function to delay an enemy
attack), should be limited to the four battalions already there. In
October 1940 the chiefs of staff committee on the Far East reported:

Hong Kong is not a vital interest and the garrison could not long
withstand Japanese attack. Even if we had a strong fleet it is
doubtful whether Hong Kong could be held now that the Japanese are firmly established on the mainland of China, and we
could not use it as an advance naval base.

However, that December, after a visit to Hong Kong, Air Chief
Marshal Sir Robert Brooke-Popham, the new commander-in-chief of
the far east, proposed increasing the garrison to six battalions by
releasing two from Malaya. Prime Minister Winston Churchill killed
the bid:

This is all wrong. If Japan goes to war with us there is not the
slightest chance of holding Hong Kong or relieving it. It is most
unwise to increase the loss we shall suffer there. Instead of
increasing the garrison it ought to be reduced to a symbolical
scale. Any trouble arising there must be dealt with at the peace
conference after the war. We must avoid frittering away our
resources on untenable positions. Japan will think long before
declaring war on the British Empire, and whether there are two

or six battalions will make no difference to her choice. I wish we had fewer troops there, but to move any would be noticeable and dangerous.

This in no way ended the ill-advised and ill-conceived crusade to reinforce the Pacific outpost, however. By inference it began to re-emerge early in the new year — not in Britain, but in Canada. A possible precursor of what the future might hold could perhaps be read into a note Prime Minister Mackenzie King recorded in his diary in February 1941 when he stated: ''possible first move would be Japanese demand for the surrender of Hong Kong.'' Another probable omen of what lay in store might have been seen in the discussion at a meeting of the Canadian Cabinet's War Committee on May 13 of Canada's participation in World War II to date. The Canadian Army had yet to fire a shot in anger, morale among troops stationed in England was low, and public interest in the conflict was dwindling. At a later meeting, contrary to the prime minister's feelings, the committee issued a statement in which it was affirmed that war with Japan was unlikely.

Although it could be said that all this laid the groundwork for the reinforcement of Hong Kong in which Canadians were to be sacrificed in such a hideously ignominious role, it was not until August that it came under serious consideration.

At that time, Canadian-born Major General Alan Grasett visited Ottawa on his way home to England after having served as general officer commanding, Hong Kong, since 1938. There, in the Canadian capital he met with Chief of the Canadian Staff, Major General Harry Crerar, a former classmate at the Royal Military College. Among the topics discussed were the Hong Kong defences. Crerar recalled that the discussion revolved around the fact that the ''addition of two or more battalions...would render the garrison strong enough to withstand for an extensive period of siege an attack by such forces as the Japanese could bring to bear against it.'' There is, however, no record of any indication of agreement or commitment on Crerar's part.

But on September 3 at a meeting at the War Office in London with the Chiefs of Staff, Grasett briefed them on the Hong Kong situation and submitted a proposal in writing that the garrison be immediately increased by two battalions and that Canada might be willing to supply the troops.

After some deliberation, the chiefs of staff recommended to the British prime minister that the garrison be reinforced with the recommended two battalions. On September 15, in a reversal of his previous stand on the issue, Churchill assented with the proviso that: "It is a question of timing...a further decision should be taken before the battalions actually sail."

Four days later a telegram through the Dominions Office was wired to the Canadian government via the Department of External Affairs stamped MOST SECRET, in which it stated:

> His Majesty's Government in Canada will be aware of the difficulties we are at present experiencing in providing the forces which the situation in various parts of the world demands, despite the very great assistance which is being furnished by the Dominions. *We should therefore be most grateful if the Canadian Government would consider whether one or two Canadian battalions could be provided for this purpose* [emphasis in original].

The Canadian Cabinet War Committee wasted no time in complying with the request. With perhaps a twinge of conscience, it satisfied itself that this was an opportunity to fulfill its duty. After all, the Australians, the New Zealanders and the South Africans had been fighting in various theatres. It would be derelict to refuse. Besides, such a show of strength might act as a deterrent to Japanese aggression. It does not seem to have occurred to anyone concerned that the seasoned Japanese army was not about to have its plans for conquest upset by the addition of less than 2,000 troops to an isolated outpost. In fact, the committee had sealed the fate of 1,975 Canadians by delivering them into a situation where there was virtually no hope of survival and certainly no chance of relief or evacuation. Even the most naive, amateur theoretician would have had to be aware of this. Certainly it was apparent to the British War Office, which spelled it out clearly in a bulletin dated November 6: "Our policy regarding the defence of Hong Kong remains unchanged: It must be regarded as an outpost and held as long as possible."

By that time, the Winnipeg Grenadiers and the Royal Rifles of Canada comprising C Force were sailing to Hong Kong. Both fell into the Class C category of the 26 battalions: "due either to recent employment or insufficient training, are not recommended by DMT [Directorate of Military Training] to be available for operational consideration at the present time." So why were they chosen? There were many reasons, none of which stand up in the glare of subsequent knowledge and events.

Brigade commanders of Class A and B categories were reluctant to break up their forces by assigning their battalions. Both the units selected had seen overseas service, in Newfoundland and Jamaica respectively, where their duties, the Chief of the General Staff, General Crerar, satisfied himself "were not in many respects unlike the task which awaits the units to be sent to Hong Kong."

The selection also had political over- and undertones. Crerar was quick to point out that it represented both Eastern and Western Canada. And while the Royal Rifles was nominally English-speaking, its men were drawn from an area French-speaking in character, and many of them were Canadians of French-Canadian descent.

All that aside, the bare fact of the matter was that neither unit was properly trained for the role into which they were being cast — or any operational role, for that matter. Their overseas service had amounted to guard duty and during its entire Jamaican tour the Winnipeg Grenadiers had not fired a single shot. What little weapons training they did receive was hampered by widespread sickness.

By contrast, the Royal Rifles' stay in Newfoundland allowed plenty of time for training. When the harbour froze over, guard duties were reduced by a half. This enabled the unit to carry out rifle and Lewis gun practice.

This was all very fundamental, however. As with every battalion in Canada, there was no opportunity to train with mortars, hand grenades, submachine-guns and signal sets because such equipment only became available in Canada at the end of 1941.

When C Force, under the command of Brigadier John K. Lawson, set sail from Vancouver on the evening of October 27, with its full complement of 98 officers and 1,877 other ranks it should have been the best equipped Canadian detachment to be sent overseas. That it was not was due to a great deal of bureaucratic bumbling and buck-passing. While the force was well supplied with clothing, ammunition and weapons, its allotted mechanical transport, universal carriers, trucks and water tanks was not aboard the *Awatea* when she sailed. All 212 vehicles were loaded onto another vessel, *Don Jose*, which did not leave Vancouver until November 4. It finally arrived in Manila on December 12, five days after war with Japan started and, as a result, never reached Hong Kong. On November 16, escorted by two British warships, *Awatea* steamed into Hong Kong harbour and tied up at Holt's wharf in Kowloon as the two Vildebeestes torpedo bombers and three Walrus amphibians droned overhead in welcome.

Coincidentally, a few weeks earlier, the British had decided to add some muscle in the Pacific by dispatching two of their battleships, HMS *Prince of Wales* and HMS *Repulse*. But this was about the only encouraging aspect to the Asian scene. A Canadian businessman returning from a trip to Japan, interviewed by Canadian Military Intelligence, painted a gloomy picture. Japan was preparing for war at any time. Her navy would employ a fresh element of surprise. But she had no intention of attacking Hong Kong from the sea. That would take place from China. And, he emphasized, "no troops should have been landed. Rather...we should evacuate."

With the arrival of the Canadians, of whom he had initially formed a low opinion, Charles Maltby, the General Officer Commanding, Hong Kong, altered his defence plans. He divided his forces in two: an Island Brigade and a Mainland Brigade. Brigadier Lawson was entrusted with the Island Brigade which consisted of the Middlesex Regiment manning the 72 pillboxes and other fixed fortifications, and his two Canadian battalions assigned to defend against a landing from the south. On the mainland the 2nd Royal Scots and the Punjabs and Rajputs were to hold the Gin Drinkers Line under the command of Brigadier Cedric Wallis.

Once the Canadians had settled in — the Royal Rifles in Nanking Barracks, the Winnipeg Grenadiers in Han Kow Barracks, both in Kowloon on the mainland — the battalions began training, mostly bayonet drills and route marches over the rugged terrain. The British were flabbergasted at the lack of training of their reinforcements. The Canadians in turn were aghast at the state of the defences, particularly the pitiable air force of five obsolete planes. None of this helped to allay the sense of mistrust that quickly developed between the British and Canadians. However, despite that state of affairs, the Canadians began to settle into their new surroundings quite comfortably.

Rumours ran rife throughout the colony, as early as November 19, that the Japanese had already declared war. But if these proved false there was little doubt of Japanese intentions as far as the British and United States governments were concerned. There was also clear evidence of rampant fifth column activity in Hong Kong, particularly in Victoria, the capital. Worst of all for the defenders, perhaps, was Maltby's woeful intelligence organization's underestimation of Japanese strength. They actually believed, and Maltby, given his poor regard for the Japanese soldier, accepted it, that the Nipponese forces numbered a mere 5,000 in the Canton area and that reports that the figure was nearer to 30,000 were pure exaggeration. In fact, Maltby told the Canadians that "the Japanese...judging by their defence preparations around Canton appear distinctly nervous of being attacked." This might explain his obsession with fearing an attack from the sea. But it sheds no light whatsoever, on the fact that all practice tactical manoeuvres were geared to defending a mainland assault.

In fact, at one point the Japanese had considered cancelling their plans. On the night of December 1, a transport plane bound for Canton crashed in Chinese-held territory. Among those aboard was Major Tomozuki Sugisaka, a courier carrying the secret orders for Operation Z, the simultaneous attacks on Hong Kong, Manila, Pearl Harbor, Malaya, Guam, Wake, and the South Seas.

This incident created pandemonium and panic at Army General Staff headquarters in Tokyo. Had Sugisaka had time to destroy the document? Had it been burnt up in the crash? Or was it on its way to Chiang Kai-shek who would naturally relay it to Franklin Roosevelt? Next morning, a reconnaissance pilot reported Chinese swarming around the crashed transport, 50 miles north-east of Canton. Should the operation be cancelled?

It would appear that the Chinese failed to discover any evidence in the wreckage. That afternoon Emperor Hirohito sanctioned December 8 as X-Day for the attacks. The fate of Hong Kong and those of two Canadian battalions had been sealed with the stroke of an imperial pen.

All the same, over the next four or five days, despite tight security on their part, intelligence filtered into Maltby's headquarters that the Japanese were massing on the Chinese border. Though he still believed that reports of their strength were exaggerated, on Saturday December 6, he issued a warning that war was imminent. Next morning all units were put on alert and took up battle stations. The two Canadian battalions ferried across the harbour from Kowloon to the island and took up their defence positions on the south coast. At the same time the Middlesex Regiment moved into the 72 pillboxes dotted around the island, while the volunteer group's role was to protect key installations. Brigadier Lawson and his staff moved into his Island Brigade Headquarters in the Nei Chong Gap located at the heart of the island's road network while Maltby and his staff moved into the Fortress Headquarters, a well-protected underground installation in Victoria.

On the mainland, the Royal Scots, the Punjabs and the Rajputs were in position on the Gin Drinkers Line while ten miles to the north, a company of Punjabs along with demolition teams to cut roads, railways lines and bridges, under Major George Grey, occupied a position just behind the Chinese border.

On Monday December 8, at 4:45 a.m., the British received a signal from the Japanese that war was imminent. This as far as can be ascertained was at Hirohito's request. It is known that he had issued similar instructions that the Americans were to be warned about the attack on Pearl Harbour but these were not obeyed. The war on Hong Kong as planned and predicted, began with an air raid on Kai Tak Airfield. All but one of the five aircraft on the field was destroyed. The Canadian barracks were also bombed and straffed but they had been empty for nearly 24 hours. However the Mainland Brigade HQ suffered severe damage and had to be moved north of Kowloon.

On the ground, the three Sano Force Japanese infantry regiments, from west to east, the 229th, the 228th and the 230th, steamrollered across the frontier, forcing the forward Punjab troops back to the Gin Drinkers Line. By next afternoon, the Japanese had reached the line, surprised at the little resistance they had encountered. When they did meet any, they simply sent their men around it. Their original intention had been to reconnoitre the line and prepare an attack within a week or so. Colonel Doi of the 228th began probing the defences around 3:00 p.m. The key, as he quickly learned, was the Shing Mun Redoubt on high ground that overlooked the Jubilee Reservoir and the mainland approaches to Kowloon. It was well fortified with pill-boxes adjoining fire trenches and underground tunnels. But all that could be spared to hold it was a single platoon of Royal Scots.

That night, at 11 o'clock Doi sent in his troops, preceded by a bombardment of hand grenades. It was no contest. By 1:00 a.m. next morning, the redoubt was in Japanese hands. The defeat, which he blamed entirely on the Royal Scots' overconfidence and unreadiness, sent Maltby into a rage. He might, instead, have reconsidered his assessment of the Japanese soldier's inability to fight at night due to poor eyesight. But eyesight or no, the Gin Drinkers Line defences were so sparsely stretched, Doi could have punched a hole in it pretty well anywhere he wanted.

Maltby promptly ordered a company of the Winnipeg Grenadiers to Kowloon to bolster the two Royal Scots and Rajput reserve companies. Meanwhile, he withdrew the Royal Scots from their present position in the line to try to establish a new defence line on the left running from Golden Hill to the coast. This was accomplished between dusk and midnight on December 10, with some difficulty but without, thankfully, any enemy interference. It was a short-lived respite, however. Early next morning, Colonel Shoji's 230th Regiment attacked in force, three well supported battalions against a single understrength one. It ended in a rout with the Royal Scots losing both the Golden and Black Hills. With two quick jabs, the Japanese had successfully crumbled the left flank of the British mainland defences. This placed the Punjabs in the centre in a precarious position, since the road to Kowloon ran parallel to the Gin Drinkers Line for some distance.

By the same token, it also put both the Punjabs and Rajputs, who were being heavily engaged on the right of the line by Colonel Tanaka's 229th Regiment, in jeopardy. With the left flank exposed, they were in danger of having any escape route cutoff. If nothing else, Maltby was decisive. At midday on Thursday December 11, he issued orders for the evacuation of the mainland. That afternoon, the company of the Winnipeg Grenadiers sent over from the island the day before rushed in to fill the gap between the unbreached portion of the line and the Royal Scots. The Grenadiers thus became the first Canadian Army unit to come under fire in World War II.

The evacuation took place that night, the Royal Scots and the Grenadiers crossing over via Kowloon. To the west, the Rajputs and Punjabs broke off engagements with the enemy and headed south for Devil's Peak. The plan was to evacuate the Punjabs while the Rajputs formed a defence line. This was a key position that dominated the Lye Mun Passage to the island, which would afford the enemy an excellent artillery and observation post. On December 12, the Rajputs put up a spirited defence against a Japanese assault, repelling the attack with the help of artillery and mortar support from the island. The Japanese, suffering heavily, withdrew, allowing the remainder of the Punjabs to be evacuated. Next day, Maltby changed his mind about holding the line at Devil's Peak and decided to abandon the mainland altogether.

The Japanese had not expected to win the mainland so handily and in such a hurry — only five days. They were so far ahead of schedule they had to pause to reorganize. The casualties of only 400 had been remarkably light, given the task at hand and the success so quickly achieved. British garrison losses, 46 killed, 65 missing 93 wounded, and the speed with which the enemy had overrun the mainland left the Canadians, not to mention the islanders themselves, with the impression that not much effort had been made to resist the Japanese onslaught.

Stunned by the rapidity of the defeat on the mainland, Maltby now had to reorganize his forces to defend the island. That there had been no game plan seems incredible, and, even though the Japanese were obviously massing and preparing — the island was already under enemy artillery bombardment — for a cross-channel attack from the mainland, Maltby was still obsessed by the notion that the assault would come from the sea. That being the case, the obvious solution was to centralize all the forces then dispatch them to any threatened point. But in Hong Kong because of the poor roads, lack of transport and complete enemy air superiority this was clearly impossible. So, instead of concentrating his forces at the most likely point of attack, along the north shore, he decided to point his defences in all directions, spreading his forces loosely all around the island, encompassing the 72 pillboxes. The Middlesex Regiment and the two Canadian battalions occupied the defences on the south coast. The two Indian regiments manned positions on the north coast. The Royal Scots, which had been badly mauled on the Gin Drinkers Line, were held in reserve for a temporary rest at Fortress HQ.

For practical purposes, the garrison was split into two brigades, East and West. The dividing line was just east of the north-south road at the foot of the east side of Violet Hill, running north from Repulse Bay through Wong Nei Chong Gap to the channel coast. The East Brigade was commanded by former Mainland Brigade commander, Brigadier C. Wallis, and included the Canadian Royal Rifles, and Rajputs. Brigadier Lawson commanded the West Brigade, which was made up of the Winnipeg Grenadiers, Punjabs and Royal Scots. The Middlesex Regiment came under Fortress HQ. The various volunteer and artillery units were under the commander of the brigade in whatever area they were positioned. Wallis made his HQ at Tai Tam Gap, the headquarters of the Royal Rifles, while Lawson continued to occupy his HQ at Wong Nei Chong Gap. Unfortunately this reformation separated the two Canadian C Force battalions. This did not sit well with the senior commanders and was to have repercussions once the fighting on the island started.

If Maltby still held any further illusions that the Japanese invasion would come from the sea, they should have been sharply dispelled on December 13, when a Japanese truce party under a white flag crossed the harbour from Kowloon with a demand from Lieutenant General Takshi Sakai, commander of the 23rd Army, for the surrender of the island with the threat of powerful aerial and artillery bombardment in the event of failure to comply. It was, of course, rejected. Now Hong Kong came under a severe siege of shelling and bombing made all the more tangible thanks to espionage; the Japanese knew from their fifth column agents the exact location of the British fixed defences.

Counter-artillery fire against the enemy was largely impotent due to the mobility of the Japanese guns; the enemy simply moved them out of the line of fire. Also, the armour piercing ammunition for the heavy British guns was totally ineffective. By contrast, the Japanese bombardment had a telling effect immediately. Amongst the civilian population in overcrowded Victoria, it created havoc. Chinese fleeing the city for the comparative safety of the south choked the roads. Civilians employed in defence work failed to report. Military transport drivers deserted.

During the three days following the surrender ultimatum, several of the coastal defence guns were knocked out and some of the pill-boxes suffered a similar fate. The Royal Rifles, occupying an area from Repulse Bay in the south to Lye Mun in the north, were among the battalions hardest hit. All company positions, as well as the HQ at Tai Tam Gap, came under increasingly heavy shelling, during which water, electrical and telephone services were constantly disrupted.

By December 16, Japanese heavy bombers became available and intense bombing got under way, which put half the British pillboxes out of action. Fifth columnists appeared to work hand-in-hand with the bombing and shelling. On December 17, the Canadian Service Corps stationed at Deep Water Bay reported that in addition to 20 vehicles destroyed by enemy artillery, another 12 had been immobilized by sabotage.

On that same day, the Japanese delivered another surrender ultimatum. As in the first instance, it was refused. But there was little doubt that this latest demand was an ''or else'' signal that a rejection would mean imminent invasion. For some time, it had been observed that small water craft had been accumulating in Kowloon Bay. On December 18, the Japanese had concentrated most of their shelling and bombing on the north shore. Oil storage tanks had been set on fire at North Point. Yet, in the face of all this, Maltby made no attempt to reposition his forces to meet an attack that would obviously be coming from the mainland. The Middlesex Regiment and the two Canadian battalions remained in place on the south shore.

The unit most exposed to enemy fire was the Rajput Regiment on the eastern section of the north shore, a three-mile section of the coastline defended by only 700 infantryman. It was here that the Japanese 229th Regiment landed between 8:30 and 9:00 p.m. in the evening of December 18, in collapsible powered assault craft, oar propelled assault craft and impressed civilian boats. By 11:00, the Rajput defence had collapsed with the Indian troops in rout. This was the last time that regiment took part in the fight for Hong Kong.

The next infantry that Tanaka's battalions encountered was Major Walter Bishop's C Company of the Royal Rifles at Lye Mun. The night was dark and there was some rain. This, combined with the smoke from the burning oil storage tanks, added to the confusion that followed. This was not helped by a mix-up in orders — a relief company never arrived — and jumbled communications between the field and East Brigade HQ. But around midnight, the situation had sorted itself out and Bishop's company confronted the Japanese 229th' s 2nd Battalion heading south towards Sai Wan and Tai Tam Gap. This was the first resistance the Japanese had encountered since landing and it forced them to abandon plans to advance south for the Shek Peninsula and thrust instead towards the western slope of Mount Parker toward Repulse and Deep Water bays.

C Company finally withdrew to a new position between Lye Mun and Tai Tam Gap where they were issued ammunition and food. By this time Mount Parker was being held by a single Canadian platoon and two sections from another. A party of 20 from A Company, led by Lieutenant C.A. Blaver, was sent out as replacements. Then at 3:00 a.m. on the morning of December 19, Captain Clarke from the HQ Company, with D Company's 16th Platoon proceeded to Mount Parker to take command and reorganize the defences. Blaver's party did not reach the mountain until 7:30, by which time the crest was in Japanese hands.

Although he could see that the enemy numbered well over 100, Blaver decided to try his luck and attack with his troop of 20. However, the Japanese clobbered the Canadians with machine-gun fire and rolled hand grenades down the slope towards them. After losing ten of his men, Blaver gave up. Watching from a ridge 500 feet below the crest, Clarke, who had arrived on the scene, estimated that two extra platoons would be needed to wrest the mountain from the Japanese. He called Brigade HQ for reinforcements which duly arrived. Luckily the attack was cancelled. By this time the entire Japanese 2nd Battalion had reached the Mount Parker area. To try and assault it with three platoons would have been suicidal.

Surveying the situation, Wallis decided to withdraw the Royal Rifles, all that was left of his brigade with the demise of the Rajputs, south near Tai Tam Bay. This was accomplished by nightfall, at times under enemy fire. The first day's fighting for the East Brigade had been a disaster except for a gallant stand by C Company and a brave but foolhardy attempt to attack Mount Parker. The Royal Rifles had suffered 109 casualties.

At the same time, to the west the Japanese 230th and 228th regiments had landed at North Point and Braemer Point. They had quickly overcome the Rajput defence and then proceeded inland, skirting around Braemer Hill, then advancing towards Jardine's Lookout overlooking Wong Nei Chong Gap. The 230th's 3rd Battalion intended to occupy the Gap while the 2nd Battalion overran the Lookout where two platoons of Volunteers occupied pillboxes.

Lawson reacted by ordering three Winnipeg Grenadier columns forward to meet the advance. One positioned itself at a road junction to the north. A second, under Lieutenant G.A. Birkett, went forward to Jardine's Lookout and a third, under Lieutenant French, went ahead to Mount Butler. But it was a wasted effort, a fiasco — a platoon against a battalion.

By the time Birkett's platoon reached Mount Butler, just before dawn, it was already occupied by the Japanese. As he pulled his men back, the enemy attacked and Birkett was killed while covering the withdrawal with a Bren gun. Some of the survivors of the platoon managed to reach a few of the Volunteer unit's pillboxes on the south-east slope, where they held out into the afternoon. At the Lookout, French encountered a similar situation and was forced to withdraw; he was killed while covering the retreat.

In the meantime Lawson brought up A Company from Little Hong Kong Village and ordered its commander, Major A.B. Gresham, to clear Jardine's Lookout as well as Mount Butler. There is no record of what occurred at the Lookout but, led by the company sergeant major, Johnny Osborne, the group seized Mount Butler at bayonet point and held on for three hours. However, in the face of overwhelming enemy superiority, the company was eventually forced to withdraw. That afternoon, the unit found itself completely surrounded, within hand grenade throwing range of the enemy. When the Japanese began lobbying the missiles at the Grenadiers, Osborne began picking them up and hurling them back, until one landed where he couldn't retrieve it in time. Osborne deliberately sacrificed himself by jumping on top of it. The action, for which he received the Victoria Cross, killed him instantly. There were no survivors from the Mount Butler battle; the entire company was wiped out, either killed or taken prisoners.

Lawson was beside himself. All this fighting had left the Wong Nei Chong Gap, where he had established Brigade Headquarters, and upon which the 3rd Battalion of Colonel Shoji's 230th Regiment was now advancing, in jeopardy. All that stood in the way of the Japanese were two platoons from D Company of the Grenadiers. When those went under Lawson would be left with only D Company Headquarters, Brigade Headquarters and, for what it was worth, the headquarters of West Group of the Fortress Artillery. However, they were reinforced by Lieutenant T.A. Blackwell and 20 Grenadiers, detached from the Headquarters Company at Belcher's Bay, extremely well armed with Bren and Thompson machine-guns.

Several attempts were made to lift, what by then amounted to a siege, by the Royal Scots and three naval platoons from HMS *Thracian*. None succeeded. By ten o'clock in the morning of December 19, Lawson knew the situation was hopeless. Out of ammunition, Brigade HQ could no longer hold out. Contact was made with Fortress Headquarters informing them that the Brigade HQ was evacuating to Black Link. After destroying the records and the telephone, the staff vacated the premises. But as he emerged from the shelter, Lawson was gunned down by Japanese bullets and killed.

When he realized that Lawson was probably dead, Maltby personally took charge and ordered a coordinated full-scale counter-attack by the West Brigade to halt the Japanese, clear the Gap, and link the two brigades. Ambitious to say the least, not to mention totally unrealistic. The plan called for the Punjabs to attack towards the North Point Power Station still held by the Volunteers. The Royal Scots were assigned to attack south to clear Jardine's Lookout and the Wong Nei Chong Gap. One company would simply circle around Mount Nicholson, south-west of Jardine's Lookout, while the other two struck for the Gap. The Winnipeg Grenadiers were ordered to counter-attack at the Gap, clear the area, and proceed on to seize Mount Parker, east of Mount Butler. Just like that!

Well, it didn't quite work out that way. In the first place, it is unclear whether the Punjabs ever received their orders; in any case, the Power Station fell to the enemy late in the afternoon. Then, at Mount Butler, the Royal Scots came under such heavy fire, they had to disperse and wait until darkness fell to continue their advance. The best that the Grenadiers Headquarters Company could do was to scrape together 40 men for their part in the counter-attack due to their heavy losses, of which doubtless Maltby's staff was unaware. Major E. Hodkinson dispatched Lieutenant L.B. Corrigan to cover his flank from Mount Nicholson. Fighting its way to the top, it arrived with only five unwounded men, then continued down the slope above the Gap and engaged the enemy until midnight when they ran out of ammunition.

Meanwhile, Hodgkinson and the remainder of the company rounded the mountain along the Black Link Road, where they ran into 500 Japanese enjoying their lunch. Not for long! As soon as the Winnipeggers opened fire, the enemy fled in disarray, leaving behind a host of casualties. The company then pushed ahead to a junction in the main road where they were to have rendezvoused with the Royal Scots at 5:00 p.m. The party now split up, with Hodkinson taking four men to clear the Gap from the north and reoccupy the evacuated Brigade Headquarters, while Lieutenant Campbell cleared the Gap from the south-west and west. Here they made contact with the Grenadiers' D Company HQ still holding out with 27 men, 20 of whom were wounded.

Hodkinson's Company, now reduced to 36 men, was ordered to capture the police station and proceed on towards Mount Parker. They never made it that far. Charging up the slope, the Grenadiers were met by 40 Japanese who riddled them with machine-gun fire and bombarded them with hand grenades. In the battle, Hodkinson was seriously wounded and many of his men killed or taken prisoner. Several more attempts were made to secure the position by detachments from both the Punjabs and the Royal Scots, but they all failed.

During the 36 hours since the Japanese invasion began, the West Brigade had certainly fared a lot better than its eastern counterpart. But, all the same, its headquarters had been annihilated and its commander killed. The Royal Scots had been reduced to a fraction of its full strength and one company of the Winnipeg Grenadiers had been decimated, while two others were virtually wiped out. The saving grace was that it still had two ''fresh'' battalions, the Middlesex and the Punjabs, which had yet to meet the full force of the Japanese invaders.

The dizzying speed with which the Japanese had devoured a quarter of the island left them panting. They needed to catch their breath and regroup before embarking on the next phase of the invasion plan

— a drive west. Next day, December 20, while Doi's 228th and Shoji's 230th regiments gathered their forces together, as part of his share of the spoils Tanaka drove his 229th Regiment south to Repulse Bay in readiness for his part in the westward plunge. By 8 o'clock that morning, this had effectively split the British East and West brigades in two. Both commanders, Brigadier Cedric Wallis, and the newly appointed head of the Western Brigade, British regular officer, Colonel H.B. Rose, were determined to link up. But their half-hearted, shilly-shallying, uncoordinated efforts got them nowhere. From Wallis's standpoint the most direct route was westward through the Gauge Basin south of Mount Parker to the Wong Nei Chong Gap where D Company of the Winnipeg Grenadiers was quartered. But Tanaka's regiment had already pushed back the Volunteers in that area, sealing it off. Wallis decided instead to move up the coast road through Repulse Bay, then swing north towards the Gap.

A Company of the Royal Rifles succeeded in reaching the Repulse Bay Hotel, clearing the Japanese from around it and was given with orders to hold it at all costs and to protect the women and children living there (not to mention a score of Middlesex, Volunteers and naval personnel). Wallis next sent D Company north to the Wong Nei Chong Gap via the east side of Violet Hill. It seems incredible. He disregarded the fact that if the Japanese had advanced as far as Repulse Bay, they would certainly have occupied the country north of it. As it turned out, the Royal Rifles ran into such stiff resistance that they were forced to withdraw. Leaving their ammunition behind them, they returned to Stanley View by 11:00 a.m. completely exhausted.

That afternoon, B Company fell victim to Wallis's recurring indecisiveness. At 4:30 p.m., having advanced through Repulse Bay, then along the road past Eucliffe Castle, it received orders to fall back to Sugarloaf Mountain. It had reached Stone Hill, when at 5:30, orders were given to advance again on Repulse Bay. Half an hour later, it was told to return to Sugarloaf. By the time it reached the mountain, it was raining and one platoon was missing.

The Royal Rifles HQ Company was also ordered into the Repulse Bay region where it came under enemy artillery fire between the bay and Stone Hill. At 10:30, it was ordered to halt at the outskirts which was being swept by small arms fire, forcing the men to take cover. There they stayed until 5:00 p.m. when orders arrived to retire to Palm Villa.

After the vicious fighting of December 19, the day had passed relatively quietly for the Eastern Brigade, though any hope of joining up with its western counterpart was becoming increasingly remote.

Colonel Rose, whom Maltby finally got around to appointing as commander of the West Brigade shortly after noon, even though Lawson, his predecessor, had been killed the morning before, had inherited an almost intolerable situation. His forces were spread all over the place, barely hanging on in most cases. At 10:00 a.m., B Company of the Winnipeg Grenadiers had been brought up to attack the Wong Nei Chong Gap area jointly with the Royal Scots. But inexplicably, the latter never showed up. In fact by nightfall they had retired from the eastern slopes of Mount Nicholson.

The Grenadiers split into two to circle the mountain from opposite directions, spend the night, and attack at dawn. But in the meantime, as fog descended and it began to rain, Colonel Doi decided on a gamble to try and capture the Gap in the dark. With his 1st Battalion, in the absence of the Royal Scots, he at first encountered no opposition. Then suddenly he ran smack bang into the Grenadiers. A fierce fight broke out in which the Winnipeggers lost 23 men and finally retired to the Middle Gap. By day's end, both brigades remained split apart — for good. But next day, December 21, they were as determined as ever to break out and continued to take an offensive stance. This now became increasingly difficult. By this time the Japanese had been able to bring up their divisional artillery to support their operations with relentless firepower. They had also begun bringing their reserves over from the mainland.

D Company HQ of the Winnipeg Grenadiers still tenaciously hung on to the Wong Nei Chong Gap, while at dawn B Company attacked Colonel Doi's 228th Regiment's 1st Battalion from both sides of Mount Nicholson and over the crest. In the savage counter-attack that ensued, both sides lost heavily. All the Grenadiers' officers and NCOs and 29 men became casualties. Doi's losses amounted to 40 percent of his 400-man force. Nevertheless, the Grenadiers had suffered a setback and there was now no longer any hope of recapturing Mount Nicholson. A new defence line was set up on Mount Cameron, the next hill to the west.

In the south, the East Brigade made an attempt to link up with the Royal Rifles and a Volunteer company driving north to Tai Tum Tak, it then planned to turn west and down a road leading to the Wong Nei Chong Gap via the Gauge Basin. The only possible excuse for choosing such a route was that it probably had never been tried before.

Tactically, everything mitigated against it. From Mount Butler and Jardine's Lookout, the Japanese could rain down rifle and machine-gun fire, as well as hand grenades. Add to that artillery fire, and the situation rapidly becomes "mission impossible."

Only 15 minutes after starting out, the party ran into stiff resistance from both sides. The Royal Rifles despatched flanking guards to flush out Notting and Bridge and Red hills. But the fire became so intense that more and more men had to be despatched until the entire advance guard was involved. Even D Company, the main guard, was compelled to join in the fracas. By 1:00 p.m., the firing had stopped and they moved steadily ahead. Shortly afterwards, the Royal Rifles took out an enemy machine-gun post. Then at five o'clock, the Japanese attacked with armoured cars, which the Royal Rifles forced back with relentless fire from all sides. By the time the force reached the Gauge Basin an hour later, they received orders to fall back to the Stanley area. Nothing was accomplished but a lot of fighting, marching, fighting, marching. At least Wallis had the grace to say in his report that the Royal Rifles had made "a great effort."

That same afternoon at Repulse Bay, A Company of the Royal Rifles was holding its own against Japanese fire from the hills above. Then much to the annoyance of Wallis, the garrison commander Maltby, on the strength of telephoned advice from residents in the hotel (the Japanese had not cut the lines, finding it more advantageous to eavesdrop) ordered Major C.R. Templer of the Royal Artillery to proceed to the bay and take command of operations there. Templer marshalled together two Royal Rifles platoons, two Volunteer machine-gun crews and two trucks and arrived at the hotel by 3 o'clock. He then loaded A Company into the two trucks and headed north towards the Gap through the Ridge as darkness fell, intending to attack the police station. But Templer soon realized that the Japanese had occupied the Gap in some depth and withdrew his party to the other side of the Ridge. Two platoons inadvertently moved into an area occupied by two of Colonel Tanaka's battalions and were ambushed, suffering severe casualties.

This marked the last day that the defenders could take any further offensive action; there was no further hope of linking up the two brigades. From then on the Japanese seized and maintained the initiative, applying such pressure that the British and Canadians were restricted to a defensive posture.

Early next morning, December 22, the Wong Nei Chong Gap finally fell to the Japanese after a valiant three-day stand by D Company of the Winnipeg Grenadiers. By 7:00 a.m., with their ammunition spent, the gallant little garrison surrendered, among them 37 wounded. Those unable to walk into captivity were brutally bayoneted to death by their captors.

To the west, the new defence line on Mount Cameron, defended by 100 Grenadiers and 30 Royal Engineers, held out all day against heavy enemy shelling and mortar fire until 8:30 p.m. that evening, when Colonel Doi's 228th Regiment attacked. After a tough fight, the Japanese broke through and the defenders were forced to retire to Wan Chai Gap. This placed Major Bailie's C Company, covering the naval base at Aberdeen on Bennet's Hill to the south-west, in an untenable position and the company was compelled to retire to Pok Fu Lam which it reached at dawn the following day.

At noon, to the south-east, what was left of Wallis' battered and exhausted brigade now faced four Japanese battalions which laid down a heavy mortar barrage augmented by machine-gun and rifle fire on the Royal Rifles positions on Stanley Mound and Sugarloaf Mountain. At 6:00 p.m. the firing eased off allowing two platoons to withdraw to Stone Hill. At nine o'clock when the firing began again in full force, the Japanese attacked with a bayonet charge and B Company retreated to the south slope of Stanley Mound. This left the Japanese free to overrun Sugarloaf and Notting Hill, capturing two Middlesex machine-guns and another machine-gun at Palm Villa. But not for long.

Captain W.A.B. Royal dashed foward under fire and commandeered the Palm Villa gun which he turned on the enemy. Simultaneously, Sergeants M.T. Goodenough and Roberts and Corporal Sannes recaptured the other two guns. Sannes was killed and Goodenough was wounded but still managed to keep his gun firing while Roberts ran forward through a mortar barrage to rescue Major W.A. Bishop who had been wounded. Bishop called for volunteers to take back the Sugarloaf. Three parties were formed which recaptured it by nightfall.

At Repulse Bay the defenders moved forward to the Ridge where they were held down by enemy infantry supported by mortar and machine-gun fire. Although the situation was fast degenerating the stand taken there by the Royal Rifles was tying down Colonel Tanaka's 2nd and 3rd battalions, preventing them from attacking west as planned. The Japanese took over the Repulse Bay Hotel the following day, but Tanaka's 3rd Battalion had suffered so heavily against the

Royal Rifles A Company that it took no further part in the battle for Hong Kong.

Wallis refused to lie down. He wanted to fight back. Next day, December 23, he set as his objective the recapture of Stanley Mound, a task to which he assigned B Company of the Royal Rifles. For once, the troops enjoyed the benefit of covering artillery shelling. But their own machine-guns set the grass on the slope on fire hindering their advance. The Japanese were quick to turn the situation to their own advantage, raining down volley after volley of their own fire on the attackers. That was that. Stanley Mound remained in enemy hands.

The East Brigade had been pushed into a corner. Its defence lines formed up directly in front of the necks of the Stanley Peninsula, between Stanley View and Stanley Village, on the right and the small adjoining Chung Hum Kok peninsula on the left. Wallis knew his forces, which faced the Japanese to the rear of the Stone Hill-Sugar-loaf-Palm Villa area, could not hold out much longer. The Royal Rifles' strength had dwindled down to 350 men, all of whom were thoroughly exhausted, practically falling asleep on their feet.

The West Brigade now prepared for a last ditch stand, also forming up its defence positions running from south to north as follows: Royal Navy personnel occupying a line from Aberdeen to the south slopes of Bennet's Hill; The Winnipeg Grenadiers holding Bennet's Hill itself and north to the south-west slopes of Mount Cameron; the Royal Scots positioned on the west slopes of Mount Cameron; B Company of the Rajputs and assorted Punjabs taking up station between Mount Cameron and Leigh Hill; Z Company of the Middlesex holding Leighton Hill. In addition, another company of Middlesex was assigned to Little Hong Kong forward of the southern section of the line to protect the Ordinance Depot there, while two Volunteer and two Punjab companies were held in reserve behind the line.

During the day, the Japanese kept up a steady pressure of bombing and shelling all along the line. There were several attacks, more of a probing nature than anything else, in which the Rajputs were forced to withdraw and Z Company of the Middlesex had to give up a little ground, but the Leighton Hill position held firm; a later enemy assault was repulsed. For both British brigades, it was now a matter of wait and see. Nothing more could be done.

In the east, Japanese artillery fire continued all night long. Meanwhile, Colonel Tanaka's 2nd Battalion had started moving west to join in the assault there, while his 3rd Battalion remained at Repulse

Bay. His 1st Battalion, together with Shoji's 230th Regiment, kept the heat on Wallis's battered force along the Stanley line.

By Christmas Eve 1941, the wear and tear on the Royal Rifles had begun to tell. The men had been without rest for five days and nights and were collapsing from exhaustion. They, and the Volunteer Battalion which had fought alongside them, bitterly resented the fact that they had borne the brunt of the fighting and that the two Middlesex companies had never been near the front line.

Colonel W.J. Home, the Canadian Rifles' commanding officer, insisted that his men be relieved. Wallis, in consultation with Maltby, reluctantly agreed and by 11:00 p.m. that night, troops of the Middlesex took over the Canadians' positions on the Stanley Peninsula part of the line. However, B Company at the neck of the Chung Hum Kok Peninsula was not so fortunate. Replacements could not reach them because the Japanese had occupied the main stretch between the two headlands, leaving them isolated.

In the West Brigade sector, the Japanese maintained a persistent bombardment on all sections of the line from the air and by artillery. The defenders now knew that this was a softening up, a prelude to the final assault. To the men of Z Company of the Middlesex it appeared to have already started. That afternoon, attacked on three sides, they were forced to give up Leighton Hill or be annihilated. As it was, they lost 25 percent of their men during the withdrawal.

With the loss of the high ground, the rest of brigade limited itself to patrols. Then at 10:00 that Christmas Eve, a message from the southern sector seemed to sound the death knell. It reported that Doi's and Shoji's regiments had begun advancing north from the Mount Nicholson and Mount Cameron area toward the race course at the eastern tip of Victoria. Meanwhile, to the south of the island, the 2nd Battalion of Colonel Tanaka's 299th Regiment, moving west from Repulse Bay, occupied Brick Hill. Then, bypassing Little Hong Kong, where the Ordinance Depot was located, it pushed north to link up with Doi's 228thh and Shoji's 230th regiments, south of Mount Cameron. All three regiments, six battalions strong, were in place for the kill. Tanaka reached Bennet's Hill where he launched an attack against the Winnipeg Grenadiers around midnight. But the defenders drove the Japanese back with heavy losses; although one Grenadier platoon was pushed off Little Bennet's Hill, Major Bailie immediately began organizing a counter-attack to recapture it. However, events rapidly began to overtake the fighting.

At Fortress Headquarters in Victoria Maltby knew that time was running out. Only two companies of Punjabs were left to defend the HQ conclave which included Government House, the Royal Navy Yard and the Military Hospital. The rest of the brigade was in the front line fighting. But how long could it be expected to hold out? What shook Maltby and those about him the most was their exposure for the first time to the relentless Japanese artillery and mortar fire and aerial bombardment that Christmas morning. The enemy had also begun to demonstrate the kind of brutality that lay in store for the vanquished. Shortly after six o'clock, 200 Japanese broke into an emergency hospital at St Stephen's College and started to bayonet the wounded in their beds. Two doctors who tried to stop them were shot, then bayoneted repeatedly. Before the massacre ended, 56 patients had been stabbed to death. Three British nurses were murdered and their bodies mutilated. Four Chinese nurses were raped repeatedly.

Meanwhile at 9:00 a.m., two civilians under a white flag delivered a Japanese demand to surrender, with the promise of a three-hour truce while the ultimatum was under consideration. The immediate effect was to kill Bailie's plans to recapture Little Bennet's Hill.

The Hong Kong garrison was hardly in a position to refuse the surrender demand. The front line was stretched thin, the men outnumbered and exhausted. Only six mobile artillery guns were left, with a mere 160 rounds of ammunition per gun remaining. Most of the reservoirs were in enemy hands. And acute water shortage appeared imminent. But, preserving stiff upper lip pride and aplomb, the ultimatum was rejected. Within three hours, the slender defences had fallen apart. The Japanese simply overwhelmed them. They overran Parish Hill on the eastern outskirts of the city placing the HQ in danger. At 3:15 p.m., Maltby advised the governor of the island that further resistance was futile. He then advised his commanding officers to lay down their arms and capitulate to the nearest Japanese officer, and hoisted the white flag.

Shortly afterwards, Lieutenant-Colonel R.G. Lamb was despatched by car flying a white flag to the East Brigade sector to advise Wallis of the surrender. But, because the order was not in writing, Wallis refused to accept it. He did agree to a ceasefire, however, while Lamb returned to Fortress HQ for formal instructions; these reached Wallis at 12:45 a.m. December 26 — Boxing Day. To the end, Wallis had been determined to hold, no matter how many Canadian lives it cost. At 2:30 a.m. Christmas morning, the Middlesex and Volunteer defenders, who had replaced the Royal Rifles the night before, came under heavy enemy attack. Desperate, Wallis ordered the Royal Rifles back into the battle with instructions to counter-attack. It failed for lack of artillery support and cost the battalion another 122 casualties, to absolutely no avail.

During the 18-day struggle for the island, the Canadians had ac-quitted themselves nobly. Improperly trained, unfamiliar with the terrain, lacking transport and fighting vehicles, and hampered by the early loss of their two most senior commanders, they had still carried out most of the fighting. The Royal Rifles alone made more counter-attacks at the company level or above, than all four of the British and Indian battalions combined. Furthermore, their record in battle was heroic and exemplary despite the vacillating, incompetent leadership of the British command.

The battle over, a far more severe ordeal lay ahead for the Cana-dians as they were taken into captivity — slavery would be a more accurate term. As prisoners, they were subjected to the most barbaric conditions. Most were shipped to Japan to work in the mines at bayonet point. More than 200 died of disease, such as beriberi, epi-demics, starvation. Others were executed or tortured to death. Most of the survivors never fully recovered from this horrific experience.

Irresponsibility goes hand in hand with this tragedy when review-ing the official British history which admitted that the battle of Hong Kong represented a "lamentable waste of manpower." Even before it had ended, the Dominions Office advised External Affairs that: "The capture of Hong Kong would gain them some strategical ad-vantages but would not materially alter the strategical situation of China Sea as a whole."

In 1942 the Ontario Conservative leader, George Drew, charged that the Canadian Hong Kong mission was mismanaged and ill-prepared. A subsequent Royal Commission Study by Chief Justice Sir Lyman Duff proved to be nothing more than a cover-up, a white-wash that found "no dereliction on the part of the government or military advisers."

Many years later, Prime Minister Jean Chretien would say: "No troops ever fought more bravely or with greater skill against more hopeless odds." Isn't it about time his government addressed the question of proper compensation for the war veterans he glorified so eloquently?

✤ 13 ✤

THE NINE BLOODIEST HOURS

Reference map "The Dieppe Operation."

In his novel *The Paladin*, Brian Garfield's central character, a teenage intelligence agent answerable only to Winston Churchill, is instructed to turn traitor to reveal to German Foreign Minister, Joachim von Ribbentrop — a schoolmate of his father's — plans for a British raid at Dieppe on the French coast in the summer of 1942. By tipping off the enemy, the prime minister is deliberately intent on tempting fate and courting disaster to impress upon the impatient Americans and beleaguered Russians, the futility of a premature "Second Front Now!"

That is fiction. But how close is it, or was it, to the truth? In their brilliant narrative, *Dieppe: Tragedy to Triumph*, Shelagh Whitaker and her husband Brigadier General Denis Whitaker, relate that on August 20, the day after the raid, the latter told Lord Louis Mountbatten that before evacuating the beach, he had interrogated a German prisoner who facetiously boasted: "We have been waiting for you for a week!" Mountbatten, who had charge of the assault, haughtily refused to believe him. "I want constructive comments," he snapped, "not excuses!"

Excuses? Look at who was talking! Excuse: the lack of aerial and naval bombardment. Excuse: poor navigation that set troops down on the beaches late — in daylight instead of darkness and in many cases in the wrong place — eliminating the element of surprise. Excuse: faulty intelligence that underestimated German defence strength by three quarters (even the identity of the German division occupying Dieppe was wrong). Excuse: lack of judgement in not calling off the assault when the attack force collided with a German convoy in which the exchange of gunfire warned the defenders, instantly placing the garrison on the alert.

Oh yes, despite Mountbatten's snide denial, the Germans had certainly been awaiting an attack and were well prepared and ready to cope with it. The Canadian commander of the military operation, Major General Hamilton ''Ham'' Roberts and the planners, had been led to believe that Dieppe was defended by a single battalion of the 110th Division with headquarters at Arque-la-Bataille, four miles south-east of the port itself. In fact, the 110th had never been any-where near Dieppe. It was fighting on the Russian Front where it had been all along. Dieppe was defended by three battalions of the 302nd Division headquartered at Envermeu and commanded by Major General Conrad Haase, who in addition to 2,500 front line troops, could call on the corps and army reserve battalions. Also, one of the Wehrmacht's crack tank units, the 10th Panzer Division based at Amiens, was a mere four hours away. To bolster defences against a possible sustained British assault, Hitler had recently transferred three battle hardened infantry divisions from the Russian Front, along with a parachute division, to northern France.

Most significantly, Field Marshal Gerd von Rundstedt, whom Hitler considered his most capable general, had been appointed commander-in-chief west over the 30 divisions stretched out from Holland to Spain. Oh yes, Lord Louis, the Germans had been waiting alright, ready and waiting. There were two chief reasons for this state of alert. Ever since the fall of France in June 1940, the British had been carrying out commando raids on the enemy coast to keep the Germans off balance. Though small and limited, they had been highly successful. At Bruneval in Normandy, a radar station had been captured. At Vaagso in Norway, shipping had been disrupted. By far the most incisive was a raid on the port of St Nazaire in Brittany in March 1942, where the dry docks had been blown up. To the German High Command, these raids had been seen as an omen, a prelude to a probable attack on a much broader scale. The other reason for Hitler's concern was that he took very seriously the pressure being applied to the British by their allies, the Americans and Russians, insisting on a Second Front Now! And well he might have; that was the basic, underlying reason for the raid on Dieppe in the first place.

"Jubilee," as the Dieppe operation came to be coded, was the bastardized offspring of "Rutter" and "Sledgehammer." These in turn were the direct outgrowth of early Anglo-American negotiations. The first semblance of unity was the American agreement to place the war in Europe against Germany ahead of the war in the Pacific against Japan. This resulted in "Operation Bolero," the pouring of Americans into Great Britain in readiness for "Round-Up," an invasion of the continent in 1943 entailing 48 American and 18 British divisions supported by 5,800 aircraft on a front between Le Havre and Boulogne.

But the Americans, to use one of Churchill's pet expressions, also wanted "Action, this day!" This was not entirely impetuosity on the part of their military chiefs. Franklin Roosevelt, facing fall congressional elections, had to consider public opinion, which was being strongly influenced by communist propaganda, not only in the United States but in Great Britain as well. The Russians could well justify this measure on the basis that they were carrying the load. In the first six months since the Germans invaded in June 1941, three million of their countrymen had been killed. Facing 206 German divisions, compared to the seven opposing the British in Africa, they wanted a Second Front Now, to draw off at least 40 of those divisions from the Eastern Front.

Soviet Foreign Minister Vyacheslav Molotov went so far as to suggest that it would be impossible for Russia to hold out for longer than a year without Anglo-American help, and in that event, the Allies would go down to defeat also. In the face of all this, the Americans proposed to the British in April that "Operation Sledgehammer" be launched later in 1942. It was to be an invasion of the continent in which the Allies would establish a bridgehead employing ten British and two American divisions. At the same time the Americans encouraged the British to continue their commando raids.

At this time Churchill assured Roosevelt that the two countries were in full accord, though this could not have been further from the truth. Below this superficial surface of agreement lay a fundamental difference in strategic thinking. While the British basically agreed that Europe would have to be invaded to take the heat off Russia, they disagreed about the timing. To do so prematurely would imperil Britain's meagre military resources, a blow from which it might never recover. The British believed that occupied France should not be attacked until German strength had been considerably weakened and Allied military equipment and manpower in Britain considerably

222 THE NINE BLOODIEST HOURS

strengthened. They believed that the only way to beat Hitler was to encircle him with a ring of bases from which they could attack the continent. In other words, they wanted to weaken the enemy while building up Allied strength. In this context, the British were adamant in vetoing "Sledgehammer." The compromise was "Rutter," an amphibious assault on the port of Dieppe, supported by aerial bombing and naval artillery. It was to provide Canada with the bloodiest nine hours in her military history, a day in which the Canadian Army lost more men as prisoners of war than they did during all the rest of the European campaign.

In that short period of time, the Canadian Army was to have all the action — and then some — for which it had been clamoring so loudly and strongly over the two and a half years since its arrival in England in 1939. But behind the choice of Canada as the invading force — its troops, though inexperienced, were considered among the best trained in the world — also lay strong political over- and undertones.

Prime Minister William Lyon Mackenzie King wanted to avoid conscription, both for the sake of preserving national unity and also for fear of losing votes, particularly in French Canada. However, his minister of national defence, Colonel James Layton Ralston, with the help of the English-speaking media, was finally able to persuade him that the measure was absolutely necessary if the army was to be brought up to proper strength. In June 1940, King invoked the National Resources Mobilization Act. To smooth anti-conscriptionists, a proviso guaranteed that the conscripts would only be employed at home. But the issue did not end there. Ralston and English Canada were far from placated.

To settle the affair, King launched a national plebiscite to determine whether the populace approved of releasing the government from its pledge not to send the "Zombies," as the conscripts were scathingly tagged, overseas. Outside Quebec, a resounding 64 percent were in favour, however, in that province, 76 percent were against. King neatly sidestepped the dilemma by guaranteeing that conscripts would be sent overseas only "if necessary." All this had done little to gain Canada international military stature, though her role as "the aerodrome of democracy," home of the British Commonwealth Air Training Scheme, was universally admired.

Overseas, the behaviour of Lieutenant General Andrew McNaughton, the much-lauded artillery expert of The Great War, now in charge of the Canadian troops in England, did nothing to champion Canada's military prestige internationally either. In fact, his arrogant, chauvinistic insistence on his army remaining strictly Canadian, independent in command and nature, had begun to irritate his British colleagues, particularly General Sir Alan Brooke, chief of the Imperial general staff, who had served under him in World War I. McNaughton was just as vigorously opposed to conscription as Mackenzie King and this naturally put him at loggerheads with Ralston.

But by this time, changes were afoot that would ensure the Canadian Army's second engagement with the enemy in World War II. Under pressure from the media, the public and even the Department of External Affairs, who wanted the army in action as soon as possible, Mackenzie King relaxed an early restriction allowing McNaughton to wield the forces under his command in Great Britain at his own discretion, without need of Cabinet approval, as had previously been the case. In January 1942 McNaughton returned from England for a three month visit to Canada and the United States. Lieutenant General Harold Crerar, chief of the general staff, took over command of the Canadian Second Division overseas and proceeded to lobby for its participation in any future British operation. Unlike McNaughton he was received with enthusiasm and his persistence soon paid off. On April 30, Lieutenant General Bernard Law Montgomery, Commander South-Eastern Army (SECO), formally approached McNaughton, by this time back in England. The stage was now set.

Put simply, "Rutter" was a hedge against "Sledgehammer." As Philip Ziegler, Mountbatten's biographer, noted: "the minimum we could get away with." In other words, it was a deliberate sop to the Americans, and the Russians, in lieu of an instant Second Front. The port of Dieppe had originally been selected, among a dozen other venues for small "butcher and ball" commando raids.

The site of a radar station which had been targeted for an attack, it was ideally suited for a raid of the scope originally planned: a compact force of 500 commando trained men for a hit and run foray, nothing more. Darkness, so essential for an operation of that kind, would have provided that necessary element of surprise.

"Rutter" was a horse of another colour, one that would entail ten times as many men — 5,000! Then and there, experience and mobility went out the window. Responsibility fell to Commander, Combined Operations, Lord Louis Mountbatten, who presented his plan to the chiefs of staff for their approval.

Essentially Dieppe was chosen as an ''invasion'' port because it was in range of the Royal Air Force fighter fields in the south of England and it could be reached by water — a distance of 67 miles — under cover of darkness to achieve surprise. Airborne troops would attack the extreme flanks and destroy the coastal batteries there. Landings would be made at Puys to the east and Pourville to the west, to support a frontal attack on Dieppe itself. The assault was to be preceded by heavy aerial bombardment, backed by naval artillery.

At the beginning of May, the formula was accepted by the chiefs of staff and by McNaughton and Crerar. The Canadian Second Division fell under the command of Major General Hamilton Roberts, a curious appointment in a way. Roberts was a veteran artilleryman from World War I, but his knowledge of infantry warfare was limited. And it was that expertise that was needed for the Dieppe raid, where artillery was sorely lacking. His force comprised the 4th Infantry Brigade, commanded by Brigadier Sherwood Lett, and included the Royal Regiment of Canada, the Royal Hamilton Light Infantry and the Essex Scottish Regiment; the 6th Light Infantry Brigade under Brigadier William Southam, made of Les Fusiliers Mont Royal, the Queen's Own Cameron Highlanders, and the South Saskatchewan Regiment; the 14th Canadian Army Tank Regiment (the Calgary Regiment); a unit of the 1st Army Tank Brigade; light anti-aircraft and field artillery detachments (the Toronto Scottish MG, the Black Watch of Canada and Royal Canadian Artillery); over 300 Royal Canadian Engineers and many administrative units. In other words, six battalions of infantry with engineers, along with a regiment of 60 Churchill tanks.

A total of 237 ships, including eight destroyers, would support the assault. Sixty squadrons of fighters would provide cover for the flotilla and the landings, while 150 high-level bombers and four squadrons of low-level bombers would flatten the town immediately prior to the assault. The raid, which was to seize the town and vicinity and re-embark, would be of two-tide duration — about 15 hours. All neat and tidy.

On paper the logistics made for a tight, smooth operation from which much might be learned for a major invasion later on. It was also hoped to lure the Luftwaffe into a major air battle and to force the Germans to take some of the weight off the eastern front. But what figures and statistics, theories and ambitions fail to take into account is the topography and defences, not to mention reality. It has already been shown that faulty intelligence had given a false impression of enemy strength in the area. And what aerial reconnaissance could not reveal was the armament and gun defences. The steep cliffs commanding the approaches to the beaches were riddled with caves in which guns were concealed along with countless other gun emplacements — a veritable curtain of fire. Furthermore, along the beaches themselves the sea walls had been reinforced and laced with barbed wire. And for some reason or another, no one had studied the nature of the beaches themselves, which were steeply graded with large slippery rocks. The raid was scheduled for sometime after mid-June. In the meanwhile there would be "dummy runs," practice operations on the Isle of Wight.

Across the Atlantic, the Americans were not yet aware that to all intents, "Sledgehammer" had been torpedoed in favour of "Rutter." But Roosevelt must have had some inkling of what lay in store, when on May 27, after a visit to London by Molotov on his way to Washington, he received a signal from Churchill suggesting that the Allies land in North Africa instead of Europe. But, four days later, under pressure from the Soviet foreign minister, the United States president advised the British prime minister that he had sent Stalin a cable pledging that the Allies would stage a Second Front in 1942. To his horrified chiefs of staff, Roosevelt insisted it was better to lie to the Russians than send them home without hope of support.

It was a signal for Action Stations! Within a week, Churchill was in Washington where the whole issue of a Second Front Now! had to be thrashed out once and for all. But the British prime minister now held a card, that if played at the propitious moment could be used to satisfy all concerned: that ace in the hole was "Rutter."

On the Isle of Wight, to which the Canadians moved in the last week of May, all of the population not gainfully employed was evacuated and the area was sealed off, there was no access except for key military personnel. The khaki clad 5,000 Canadians had no conception that they were being drilled for an operation. To them, it was just one more training exercise. A unique sight for the islanders was the appearance of tanks. They had never seen one before. Another new experience was amphibious landings, which had never before been attempted. Various methods were tested for making the vehicles capable of moving through as much as eight feet of water. Ironically the Churchill tanks were offloaded on the firm white sand at Osborne Beach — Queen Victoria's old bathing ground. The beach at Dieppe was composed of chunks of chert stones, boulders and rocks which damaged the tank track links and the 20 degree slope meant that the tanks tended to dig themselves in. All the testing and practice would be for naught. The tanks and their crews might just as well have been left behind.

Other training included cliff scaling, scaffold climbing, crawling through culverts, shooting from the hip and street fighting. It was rugged and demanding, but for the most part the men enjoyed it. There was something competitive about it all and it fostered teamwork and comradeship.

Finally, with the assault date set for June 21, weather permitting, on the evening of June 11, all personnel were loaded aboard the landing craft and mother ships for ''Exercise Yukon.'' Though the rank and file did not know it, this was to be the last full-scale rehearsal before the actual raid itself. It boded disaster. The sea was so rough the men became seasick. For the most part, navigation by the naval pilots steering the landing craft, was way off course. The South Saskatchewan Regiment found itself landed three-quarters of a mile from its intended destination. The same was true of the Queen's Own Cameron Highlanders of Canada. The tanks of the Calgary Regiment put down an hour late; some never landed at all, while others got lost. The Royal Regiment of Canada arrived an incredible two miles west of its assigned beach. In general there were so many errors, so much confusion, that Montgomery ordered further training and practice with a second rehearsal scheduled for June 21. That postponed the raid itself until sometime in July.

The second practice exercise, which did not take place until June 23, was only slightly more successful but still highly unsatisfactory. Rear Admiral Harry Baillie-Grohman, the naval force commander of the operation, began to have serious doubts about staging ''Rutter'' at all. He knew that a delay of even 15 minutes in getting the troops ashore on the beaches of Dieppe could court catastrophe. But Montgomery assured all concerned that all the problems were being overcome and would be worked out. He now set the assault date for June 24, but bad weather postponed it until the night of July 2, when the Canadians boarded the landing craft to sail for Dieppe.

However, due to the weather, for the next five days the Canadians languished in the boats impatient to get on with the job, confident that they could pull it off. Everything had been planned to a tee. First the paratroopers would be dropped three hours ahead of H Hour to take out the coastal batteries to the east and west. Heavy bombers would flatten the town. Half an hour before the main assault, two flanking battalions would land in the darkness, seize the beaches, scramble up the cliffs and neutralize the enemy guns on the east and west headlands overlooking the main beach. Minutes before the main frontal assault, medium bombers and fighter bombers would knock out the remaining artillery and gun posts. Meanwhile, under heavy naval gun support, tanks would lead the way into the town itself. The Germans were going to be completely taken by surprise. A piece of cake!

Oh yeah? On June 5, Mountbatten announced at a planning meeting that Churchill had cancelled the heavy bombing of Dieppe. Reasons remain obscure, though excuses abounded: that a high-level bombing attack at night could not guarantee accuracy; that casualties to French civilians would be unacceptable; that the rubble caused in the streets would make them impassable to the tanks.

And as if that wasn't enough, naval support was to be limited to eight Hunt-class destroyers, only four of which would directly support the landings, with light four-inch guns covering a front six miles wide. The Admiralty refused to risk the possibility of an air or submarine attack on a capital ship in the confines of the English Channel. So: no battleship or even a cruiser, period. Baillie-Grohman, for one, was appalled.

Weather had forestalled the raid again and a deadline was now laid down for July 8, the last date on which the tide would be favourable for the enterprise. If, by that time, the weather had not improved, the force was to be disbanded and the operation remounted at a later date. Then shortly after six o'clock on the morning of July 7, a German Focke-Wulf 190 leading three other fighter-bombers at low level, suddenly spotted the assault fleet anchored at the Isle of Wight and attacked with bombs and cannons. The "tip and run" did little damage but the raiding force had been discovered. Of necessity, "Rutter" was cancelled.

By this time, Churchill had returned from the United States, having promised Roosevelt and Stalin the "super-raid" the British Chiefs of Staff had now been forced to cancel. Under these circumstances, the Americans pressed for a renewal of "Sledgehammer." This the British could not agree to, but what could they offer instead? It was impossible to design a "Rutter" replacement for a raid that summer so they were left with only one alternative: resurrect the Dieppe raid. General George Marshall, Roosevelt's chief of staff, had acknowledged that this would satisfy both the president and Stalin.

Operation Jubilee, as the Dieppe assault came to be recoded, presented its share of problems. Time was at a premium. The same troops would have to be employed. There would be no further training or rehearsals. The men would have to be assembled at the very last minute and assigned to assault craft and mother ships dispersed at various ports instead of the Isle of Wight. In the interests of security, their weapons would not be distributed until they had embarked. Everything was last minute. Not even their escape kits would be issued until they were aboard. And in addition to lack of bombing and weak naval support, there was another change. Commandos would take out the coastal batteries instead of paratroopers, due to the weather standards the airborne needed to perform their tasks. That meant landing the infiltrators by sea, a key factor in the debacle that lay ahead.

Meanwhile, Montgomery, who had been so enthusiastic over "Rutter," now had strong doubts about its successor and recommended that it be cancelled altogether. Probably the reason for his about-face was the knowledge that the German 10th Panzer Division, with its powerful Mark III and Mark IV Tiger tanks, lay in wait at Amiens. In any case, he was removed from all further responsibilities for the operation.

At the same time Baillie-Grohman was relieved of his duties as naval force commander for his outspoken objections to the lack of proper support, and replaced by Captain John Hughes-Hallett.

On August 4, the battalion commanders were informed that the Dieppe raid was being remounted, the date set, weather willing, for two weeks later. There was an important change made before the ships sailed. With the knowledge that the German 10th Panzer Division could be brought up to the coast within four hours, the plan was shortened from a two-tide to a single-tide operation. That would reduce the time ashore to approximately seven and a half hours.

Ironically, Churchill and a chosen few, including British Lieutenant General Sir Bernard Paget, Commander-in-Chief, Home Forces, who was ultimately responsible for Jubilee, were privy to German dispositions through the Enigma decoding device. They knew that potential enemy strength in the Dieppe area was formidable but they could not share this information with their colleagues and certainly not with their underlings, for fear of revealing their secret advantage to the enemy. Understandably, there was a lot more at stake in conducting a war than a single limited coastal raid. In any case, one glaring fact stands out. They knew very well that the Canadians would be heavily outnumbered. This, General "Ham" Roberts and his officers and men, did not know. They were being thrown into battle, confident that they had the upper hand. In Roberts' own words to his troops: "Don't worry, men, it will be a piece of cake!" It is also clear in retrospect that regardless of the shortcomings and omissions, the plan to proceed with the "super-raid" was to go ahead at all costs for political reasons. In the minds of Churchill, Roosevelt, and Stalin, those reasons far outweighed the probable massacre of Canadian manpower. For their own ends the sacrifice would be worth every last drop of blood spilled.

On August 18, last minute photographic reconnaissance flights took place to reveal any new positions or movement. Nothing had changed. That afternoon the assault force of 6,000 men began embarking. It comprised 4,961 troops from the Second Canadian Infantry Division, 1,057 British commandoes and 50 United States Rangers. By nine o'clock that evening, all 237 vessels, manned by 3,000 Royal Navy personnel, sailing from Gosport, Southampton, Portsmouth, Newhaven, and Shoreham, had cleared their ports. The night was bright, calm, and clear with a high moon as the ships began to converge to take up stations behind 16 minesweepers, to lead them through a minefield in mid-channel At two o'clock next morning, August 19, the armada had cleared the minefield. An hour later the troop carriers started transferring the men into the landing craft.

An hour and a half earlier, the Beachy Head radar station on the Sussex coast had picked up echoes that a German naval convoy was heading from Boulogne to Dieppe. That placed it on a collision course with the Jubilee fleet. A signal went off to Hughes-Hallett in the command ship HMS *Calpe*. At a quarter to three, two other south coast radar stations picked up the enemy convoy's echoes and again it was reported to Hughes-Hallett. Neither signal was acknowledged. It was later established that *Calpe* had received both signals but it was never discovered why Hughes-Hallett chose to ignore them. That he apparently chose to do so had dire consequences for the Dieppe operation.

At precisely 47 minutes past three, the section of the flotilla carrying No 3 Commando in wooden R-boats, which was to destroy the six-gun coastal battery at Berneval east of Puys known as "Goebbels," was intercepted by the German convoy consisting of a tanker and six speedy E-boats. A star shell lit up the sky and the commandoes were raked by 44-mm Bofors fire. Both sides suffered heavily. Six of the defenceless R-boats were sunk and the steam gunboat carrying their commanding officer was hit and disabled. Worse still, the sound and sights of gunfire had given the show away and alerted the defenders.

Major Peter Young, the second in command, took charge. With a single boatload of 18 men, he headed for Yellow Beach and disembarked. His first task was to scale the 100-foot high cliff fortified with barbed wire. It took 20 minutes to reach the top. From there they could see that five other R-boats were landing on the beach. While they waited to rendezvous with them, the Germans opened up with machine-gun fire. The commandos returned it with their own mortar fire. Young had intended to position his men in the village church, but this now proved impossible, so he moved them to the south which placed them just to the rear of the gun battery. There they came under such heavy hidden fire that they were forced to move again.

A corn field to the west presented the best possible spot from which to attack "Goebbels" so Young positioned his men there on the theory that "a field of growing corn will stop a bullet." It may have been conjecture, but for the next 30 minutes, while they kept up a steady stream of fire on the gun battery, not one man was hit. Then suddenly the Germans opened up with their heavy naval guns. It was a wasted effort — they could not be depressed enough to do the commandos any harm. Young and his men kept up their rain of fire on the Germans for another hour and a half. By that time, fearful that tanks would soon appear, they discreetly withdrew to the beaches. Though they had not destroyed "Goebbels," they had kept the battery distracted from firing on the fleet for more than two hours.

When the other party of five boats of commandos landed shortly after five o'clock, they had no idea of the whereabouts of Young and his men. But following orders, they set about trying to reach the gun battery. The first problem they faced was barbed wire blocking the gully they intended to climb. So dense it could not be blasted with Bangalore torpedoes, they had to cut their way through. Then, as they made their ascent to the top, the air suddenly exploded with machine-gun fire. However, with dogged determination, they fought their way to the top, then moved inland. But finally they ran into such stubborn resistance and suffered such heavy casualties that, with most of their ammunition spent, shortly after ten o'clock, they were forced to surrender.

Not far away, at Puys, where the Royal Regiment of Canada was to land at Blue Beach, scale the cliffs to reach the headland, and neutralize the guns dominating the main beach, the Germans had also gone on full alert with every gun manned. For both Yellow and Blue beaches, the surprise element, so crucial to the entire Jubilee venture, had already been lost.

But this was not yet quite the case on the right flank. As they drew within a mile of Orange Beach at Varengeville, where they were to take out the "Hess" coastal battery, Lieutenant Colonel Lord Lovat and his No 4 Commando, could hear the distant sounds of gunfire to the east and glimpse the sight of tracers. But although the harbour lighthouse, on the Pointe D'Ailly, suddenly doused its lights and a shower of star shells burst above, the alarm had yet to be sounded.

Three miles offshore, the convoy split into two columns, which would land on either side of the Pointe D'Ailly, at Orange Beaches 1 and 2. C Troop would put down at Vasterival on the left, just below Varengeville, while on the right, the rest of the force would land near Quiberville. The objective, the "Hess" battery, some 1,000 yards from Orange 1, was heavily defended by ack-ack guns and machine-guns, two of which were protected by pillboxes, all enclosed by barbed wire. To the east two steep gullies led into a wood 300 yards from the battery. And on the south side of the defences, there was another woodland.

The plan was simple. C Troop would attack the batteries from the front while the rest of the force would attack from the rear. At 6:30 a.m., cannon firing Hurricane fighters would strafe the gun sites and ten minutes later the commandos would begin their assault. C Troop would retire to establish a bridgehead from which the force could withdraw.

The landings took place at 4:45 a.m., right on schedule without a shot being fired. However, the exits from both beaches had been heavily blocked with barbed wire. There was no choice but to risk alerting the defenders by blasting through with Bangalore torpedoes. Fortuitously, at that very moment, Hurricane fighters hit the lighthouse with their cannons, drowning out the sound of the explosions. The commandoes were soon off the beaches and quickly moving inland.

C Troop, led by Derek Mills-Roberts, advanced through the woods to the west, within sight of the "Hess" battery, the enemy apparently unaware of their presence. There the commandos set up their two-inch mortar and established an observation post. At 5:40 a.m., with rifles, Bren guns and anti-tank rifles, they succeeded in knocking out three machine-guns defending the northern approach. At 6:07, with their mortar, which was now correctly positioned, they blew up several ammunition dumps.

Utter confusion resulted in the enemy camp as ammunition exploded and fires broke out. All the while the commandoes kept up a relentless rain of small arms fire and mortar bombs. Then out of the sky the Hurricanes dived on the battery and defences at low-level, raking them with their cannons. At 6:30 a.m., right on time, Lovat's forces, which had landed on Marguerite Beach west of the Phare D'Ailly, signalled with rockets their readiness to attack. Time for C Troop to retire. Mills-Roberts established a bridgehead at the cliff top in anticipation of an enemy counter-attack, but none developed. In fact, during the entire operation, the unit lost only one man killed and two wounded. The remainder of No 4 Commando was not so fortunate. To begin with, the enemy had been alerted and they ran into resistance from the start.

A Troop lost four men trying to get through the heavy barbed wire. But once that had been accomplished, using steel ladders, they reached the top of the cliff where they blasted the Germans out of their pillboxes. To the west, B and F troops ran into heavy mortar shelling and machine-gun fire while struggling through the barbed wire at the mouth of the River Saane, taking eight casualties. Five minutes later, however, they were off on the double along the east bank of the river towards the woodland south of the battery. There they split up, F Troop heading for the north side of the wood, B Troop to the south side. From there they could hear the explosions set off by C Troop.

Before advancing to their start lines over open ground, from which they would attack their objectives, the first step was to blow holes in the barbed wire protecting the battery perimeter. While edging through an orchard, B Troop encountered an enemy machine-gun which they quickly overcame. From there, shielded by smoke, they leaped forward to their jumping-off position in front of their objective, a building to the right of the battery. Advancing down a road under cover of smoke, F Troop ran into stiff enemy resistance in which the troop leader was killed, a section officer mortally wounded and the sergeant major seriously injured. Captain Pat Porteous, though wounded himself, took charge. Fighting every inch of the way, they reached their assembly point in a ditch opposite the gun emplacement.

As soon as the cannon firing Hurricanes had finished their attack, which German fighters had failed to prevent, C Troop laid down a smokescreen to blind the enemy gunners. In came the commandos, F Troop on the guns, B Troop tackling the building. In a few minutes they had created chaos. Then the demolition teams took over destroying everything in sight, guns, houses, stores.

No 4 Commando left behind a scene of flaming, smoking, smouldering devastation and wreckage in what marked the single successful action of the Jubilee operation. The withdrawal from Vastervel was smooth and without incident. By eight o'clock that morning, the force was on its way home with four German prisoners, having lost 12 dead and a score wounded.

While the commando raids were in progress, the assault craft, carrying the 5,000 men of the Canadian Second Infantry Brigade, were fast approaching the beaches in between. To the east on the left, the Royal Regiment of Canada was to land on Blue Beach at Puys, destroy the "Rommel" battery behind it and attack the east headland from the rear. On the right flank to the east, were the South Saskatchewan Regiment and the Queen's Own Cameron Highlanders of Canada. It was their job to capture the fortified enemy positions at Les Quatre Vents Farm and attack the west headland from the rear. Both of these operations called for the troops to land in darkness. In the centre, assigned the objective of a frontal attack on Dieppe itself, were the Essex Scottish Regiment to land on Red Beach to the east, and the Royal Hamilton Light Infantry to disembark on White Beach to the west. Both regiments were to be supported by the tanks of the Calgary Regiment. In reserve were Les Fusiliers Mont Royal.

At five minutes to five, the advance party of the South Saskatchewan Regiment landed in darkness, on time and unopposed. But when they blew holes in the wire with Bangalore torpedoes, they alerted the Germans who responded with light small arms fire. This was nothing to worry about, and the regiment was soon off the beach, over the sea wall and into the village of Pourville, which it quickly captured.

It had been planned to land two companies on the east side of the River Scie, one to advance along the high ground and capture the radar station on the edge of the cliff, the other to take Les Quatre Vents Farm. But due to a navigational error, the companies assigned to take the radar station, had been landed on the west side and now faced the prospect of having to cross, under fire, a wide, exposed bridge 200 feet long, before they could begin their assault on the headlands. It was murder. The Germans were quick to take advantage of the situation by bringing up machine-guns and mortars as well as artillery. The first men to try and get across were cut to ribbons. The situation called for leadership of the highest order. The regimental commanding officer, Lieutenant Colonel Cecil Merritt, calmly strode up the road, revolver dangling from his hip, took his helmet off and asked what the trouble was. It was impossible to get across, he was told. Merritt ran ahead, then halfway across the bridge turned and waved his men forward with his helmet, shouting, "Follow me. We're going across. There's nothing to stop us!" Four times he led his men over the crossing under deadly enemy fire.

For this deed Merritt was awarded the Victoria Cross, but for all the valour, little was accomplished. To all intents the battle was over for the South Sasks. The advance on the radar station was stopped cold. Even with reinforcements from the Queen's Own Cameron Highlanders of Canada, no headway could be made against the Quatre Vents. In fact, the Camerons had their own share of troubles. Due to a navigational error — another one! — they had landed an hour late and astride the River Scie, splitting them up. The ships had been greeted with heavy machine-gun and mortar fire. Among the casualties was the commanding officer, Lieutenant Colonel Alfred Gostling. Thereafter Major Andy Law quickly took command. Their assignment was to pass through the South Sasks and capture and destroy the aerodrome at St Aubin. But with the Quatre Vents still in German hands, and the Pourville bridge under vicious fire, Law decided to detour those three companies on the west side of the river, along the west bank, cross the bridge at Petit Appeville and rendezvous with the Calgary tanks at Bois des Vertues.

Marching along the Pourville-Bas Hautot road, they came under fire from Quatre Vents forcing them to take shelter in the woods. At a junction, two companies turned left towards Petit Appeville, while the other went right to secure the high ground. But with time running out, Law decided to abandon the attack on the airfield.

By this time the Germans were constantly strengthening their positions so that the Camerons came under continual mortar, machine-gun, and artillery fire. Knowing that nothing further could be accomplished, Law ordered a withdrawal and, at that very moment, instructions arrived from the South Sasks to return to Pourville where evacuation would begin at 10:00. By the time they reached the village, the evacuation had been delayed an hour. The South Sasks had been driven from the high ground and now the Camerons launched a counter-attack. But it was hopeless; they were repulsed and driven back into the village. By the time the landing craft appeared, the Germans controlled the high ground on either side of the beach so that the evacuation took place under continuous fire as well as a Stuka dive-bombing attack. By noon the vessels were packed to capacity with the living and wounded. Two vessels returned at 12:30 to evacuate those fighting a rearguard action but were driven off. The 200 Canadians defending Pourville fought to the last bullet before they were captured.

The landing on Blue Beach at Puys on the left flank, where the Royal Regiment of Canada (along with a company of the Black Watch) was to destroy the Rommel gun and attack the east headland, was an even greater failure. From the time they transferred to the landing craft the role of Royals seemed doomed to disaster. Once again navigational ineptitude played the leading part. To begin with, their landing craft caught the tail-end of the convoy fight, too close for comfort. Then the navy pilot lost their chief gunboat which cost the flotilla a precious 30 minutes to find, guaranteeing a late arrival — in daylight — on the beach. To make up for lost time, the pilot then accelerated the lead boats. This imbecilic decision left the slower ones behind. With the flotilla thus dispersed, the navigator then made an ever more idiotic decision: to double the length of his run and allow the slower craft to catch up, he aimed the lead boats at the port before turning east for Puys. This conveniently and effectively signalled the presence of the assault force to the port defenders who turned on their searchlights and opened fire.

By the time the flotilla reached the 200-yard-wide Blue Beach seven minutes after five o'clock, it was light — no surprise, no chance. In a matter of minutes, the first wave was cut to ribbons. Ross Munro, the Toronto *Globe and Mail* war correspondent described it:

The men in our boat crouched low. The ramp went down and the first infantrymen poured out. They plunged into about two feet of water and machine-gun bullets laced into them. Bodies piled up on the ramp. Some men staggered to the beach.

I was near the stern and to one side. Looking out the open bow, I saw 60 or 70 bodies, men cut down before they could fire a shot. A dozen Canadians were running along the beach toward the 12-foot high sea wall, 100 yards long. Some fired as they ran. Some had no helmets. Some were wounded, their uniforms torn and bloody. One by one they were hit and rolled down the slope to the sea.

I don't know how long we nosed down on that beach. It may have been five minutes. It may have been 20. It was brutal and terrible and you were shocked almost to insensibility to see the piles of dead and feel the hopelessness. One lad crouched six feet from me. He made several attempts to rush down the ramp but each time a hail of fire had driven him back. He had been wounded in the arm but was determined to try again. He lunged forward, and a streak of tracer slashed through his stomach. I'll never forget his anguished cry as he collapsed on the bloody deck: "Christ, we gotta beat 'em, we gotta beat 'em." He was dead in minutes.

I could see sandbagged German positions and a large house on the cliff. Most of the German machine-gun fire was coming from the fortified house and it wrought havoc. They were firing at us point-blank. There was a smaller house on the right and the Germans were there too.

The men from our boat ran into terrible German fire and I doubt that any ever reached the stone wall. Mortar bombs were smashing on the slope to take those not hit by machine-gun bullets that streaked across the tiny beach. Now the Germans turned their anti-aircraft guns on us. The bottom of the boat was covered with soldiers. An officer was hit in the head and sprawled over my legs. A naval rating had a gash in his throat and was dying. A few who weren't casualties stood up and fired back at the Germans, even when they knew the attack was a lost cause.

Orders were to land troops, then pull back to sea. It was useless to remain a sitting target. Everyone who had tried to leave the boat had been cut down. Our naval officer ordered the craft off the beach. Ponderously we swung around. Through an opening in the stern I got my last look at the grimmest beach of the Dieppe raid. It was khaki with the bodies of Canadian boys.

We limped a few hundred yards to sea in the brilliant sunshine. Of the 80 we had taken in, 20 were left and more than half of them were wounded. Nobody had counted on casualties like this....

Some men did make it to the beach where they huddled on the stones and pebbles. Others reached the sea wall where they managed to climb up and blow a hole in the wire with Bangalore torpedoes. Covered by the fire from their comrades on the beach, they struggled through the gaps to try and reach the houses that had been enfilading the beach with machine-gun and mortar fire. They were killed before they reached them.

The second wave, which included the commanding officer, Lieutenant Colonel Doug Catto, coming in under heavy fire, faced a beach strewn with slain bodies. Leading a small party, Catto and his men attacked the two houses, killed the occupants and destroyed the guns. But, retiring to the beach, they came under such intense fire they had to hide in a wood. After several hours, they were discovered and taken prisoner.

The officer in charge of the Black Watch of Canada, following in behind the second wave, noticed that the heaviest fire was coming from the western end of the beach. He therefore directed the pilot to land his men there. Though they got off without casualties, they were trapped and eventually captured. At 6:30, a single landing craft tried to come in, but encountered such heavy fire it had to back off without unloading its cargo.

On the beach and crouched against the wall, the survivors of the 550-man Royal Battalion waited for ships to arrive to take them off, their fate unknown to General Roberts, aboard *Calpe* command ship, who had not been receiving wireless signals from the beach. In fact, he was under the impression the Royals had not even landed. But at 7:30 a signal was received from Blue Beach requesting to be taken off. However, Roberts and his staff were suspicious that this might be a German message designed to confuse them. Nevertheless a motor boat and several landing craft were dispatched to Puys. There they were met with such a powerful gun barrage only one craft, badly riddled with bullet and shell holes, managed to get through. However, overburdened with the weight of the desperate men who had rushed to get aboard, as it pulled away into deep water, it sank. A few of the survivors were picked up by the other vessels, the only ones to make it off Blue Beach.

The Royals left behind were finally forced to surrender. The murderous enemy fire — the German four-gun battery alone had fired off 550 shells in less than two hours — had cost the regiment 227 dead and 270 wounded of which 130 were taken prisoner. The inhumanity at Puys did not end there. The Germans, probably expecting a second landing, allowed only a few Canadians to return to the beach and rescue some of the wounded. But by mid-afternoon a 22 foot tide swamped the beach drowning many who might otherwise have recovered from their wounds.

In contrast to the navigational errors that had plagued the landings at Pourville and Puys, the landing craft carrying the assailants for Red and White Beaches at Dieppe, were right on the mark. On the left the Essex Scottish headed for Red Beach, near the harbour wall. On the right, the Royal Hamilton Light Infantry would land on White Beach, close to the west headland. With the RHLI were the Royal Canadian Engineers whose job was to break through the barbed wire entanglements. Behind these assault groups came the tank landing craft with the 60 Churchills manned by the Calgary Regiment which would land in nine successive waves. Farther out to sea were the floating reserves, Les Fusiliers Mont Royal and the Royal Marine A Commando. This flotilla was escorted by several gunboats and motor launches as well as eight destroyers in support. As Zero Hour neared — 5:20 a.m. — gun flashes and flares could be seen on the right and left as the Pourville and Puys landings got underway. It was an omen that the enemy would be alert, ready and waiting.

The scene ahead, facing this armada, was deceptively serene and tranquil. The sloping beach spread some 300 yards wide. Behind a four-foot high sea wall was a promenade and maritime boulevard, Boulevard Marachel Foch. Behind the boulevard were lawns and gardens 150 yards deep running the entire length of the beach. On the land side of the gardens lay the Boulevard Verdun parallel to the sea and lined with hotels and boarding houses. Slightly to the left were the two chimneys of a tobacco factory and on the right, under the west headland, the high-towered casino from which Dieppe derived the sobriquet, "The Poor Man's Monte Carlo." Intersecting the Boulevard Verdun, providing access to the town, were 14 streets from the Rue Synagogue on the right to the Quai de Hoble at the base of the harbour wall on the left.

Behind this peaceful façade lay a veritable fortress, a lot of it unknown to and unsuspected by the British. Royal Air Force aerial reconnaissance photographs and Intelligence established that concrete walls with gun positions had been built across the entrances of the 14 streets. The gardens were loaded with rifle pits and trenches. Artillery posts had been spotted along the promenade. Heavy wire entanglements had been laid along the entire length of the beach. The west headland boasted a number of machine-guns trained on the beach. Others were hidden in caves in the cliff wall. Field guns had been placed in the castle on the headland. The Germans had built several pillboxes next to the casino, where more machine-guns were concealed.

The hotels along the sea front housed artillery as well as machine-guns. At the East Hill, behind the jetties, atop which observation posts had been set up to command the beach, machine-guns had been installed in the caves in the sides of the cliffs. In addition there existed a heavy concentration of anti-aircraft guns in the area, many of which could be trained on the beach. The defenders were also well prepared for a tank landing. Nine undetected anti-tank guns had been positioned in the area, two of them in the casino. Two others were easily visible, one in a pillbox near the harbour wall, the other in a tank that had been cemented into the pier. Also, unknown to the British, the enemy had eight French 75-mm guns positioned on the two headlands to defend the beach. And on either side of Dieppe were four batteries of 10-cm field guns, making 16 guns in all.

At exactly ten minutes after five o'clock in the morning, the assault began with a barrage from the destroyers' four-inch guns, and cannon firing Hurricanes strafing the hotels lining the sea front. It was a pretty weak effort to support 2,000 men about to land on a fortress defended coastal port. In ten minutes it was all over and the ramps came down. What greeted the men flabbergasted and horrified them. They'd expected to see a town in ruins, a sea front demolished by bombing. But it was clearly visible through the smoke that had been laid down by Boston bombers to screen the landings, but which was fast disappearing, that the buildings were intact, not even the windows, bright and shining in the morning sunlight, were shattered.

As the men struggled onto the beach they were met with a hail of fire from all sides. Hundreds were gunned down, their comrades stumbling over the dead bodies. Others flopped onto their bellies to take what cover they could among the rocks and the pebbles. Some managed to make it as far as the barbed wire. It was sheer butchery. One company of the RHLI was almost completely wiped out in seconds. In those first few minutes the Battle for Dieppe was irretrievably lost. The Canadians had been pushed into a trap. Tank support? Forget it. They had not even arrived. Due to a navigational error, the three carriers carrying the first nine Churchills were 15 minutes late. When they did appear, German anti-tank fire stopped most of them in their tracks. Others floundered and became mired in the pebbly, stony beach surface.

Miraculously a few lumbered through, pulled themselves onto the promenade and headed down the Boulevard Foch, firing at enemy guns in the hotels and pillboxes. Nice try. But so what? They were unable to penetrate the town because of the concrete walls blocking the streets. Out in the open they were sitting ducks, and were ultimately forced to return to the beach where they were eventually brought to a standstill. They continued to answer enemy fire with their own, however. So far they had been immune to the French 75-mm's on the headlands, the only guns that could penetrate their armour. The tanks were still obscured by smoke, so that the crews found that if they stayed inside, they were relatively safe.

However, by the time the third wave of tanks was sent in — and this was to be the last tank landing, in the face of this final debacle the rest were sent home — the smoke had cleared and the 75-mm gunners took aim on the landing craft bringing them. In all 29 tanks made it onto the beach, 16 of which climbed the sea wall only, like their predecessors, to be frustrated by the concrete walls blocking the entrance to the town. Forced to return to the beach, they continued to fight it out there. So much for tank support. However, at least they did form an important part of the rearguard action when the time came to evacuate.

RHLI Captain Denis Whitaker's platoon was one of those lucky enough to get across the beach to the barbed wire protecting the sea wall. Two of his men, one of whom was killed, blew a hole in the wire. But it became abundantly clear that they would never make it over the wall without being mowed down. Men were being cut to shreds all around as it was. After laying down smoke cannisters, Whitaker led his men around the wall towards the casino, the entrance of which was blocked by wire. After clipping their way through it, they ran into the building, firing their Sten guns. The place was full of Germans, most of whom put up their hands while others scrambled to get away. At the east side of the lobby, looking out a window, the Canadians could see a line of slit trenches filled with enemy infantry. With the use of a Bren gun and an anti-tank rifle, they took the Germans by surprise and cleared up the position. They then jumped out the window and made their way across the trenches over the bodies of the dead Germans to a low wooden shelter. Once inside, mortar bombs began crashing all around them. The Canadians flung themselves down onto the concrete floor only to discover the place had been used as a latrine. There they had to lie face down in human excrement for 50 fetid minutes until the bombing let up.

To the east on Red Beach, the Essex Scottish had gotten through the two barbed wire defences but were pinned down huddled against the sea wall. In only 20 minutes after landing, they had already sustained losses of nearly 40 percent. But one group of 14 men, led by Company Sergeant Major Cornelius Stapleton, managed to assault the wall, dodge enemy fire across the heavily enfiladed promenade and gardens, and make their way behind the Boulevard Verdun where they barged into houses clearing them of their German occupants. Stapleton and his men got as far as the harbour where they encountered several German snipers. Then, with their ammunition gone and, realizing that no other Essex Scottish had gotten across the wall, they withdrew back to the beach. In fact, several other attempts had been made without success, and by this time, an hour after landing on the beach, the battalion's casualties had risen to 75 percent of its strength.

Ironically, and as it turned out, tragically, Whitaker's and Stapleton's derring do unintentionally set off a batch of garbled and misleading wireless signals that led the force commander, General Ham Roberts, to believe that the RHLI and the Essex Scottish were on the verge of capturing the town. In fact, by now he had lost control of the battle and was under the mistaken impression that it was only a matter of time before Dieppe would fall into Canadian hands. With that erroneous knowledge at hand, he decided to reinforce his "successes" by committing his floating reserves. Thus Les Fusiliers Mont Royal were ordered in to support the Essex Scottish, a blunder of the first magnitude.

Meanwhile at 6:30 a.m., unaware that he was an innocent party to this errant tactical strategy, as soon as the mortaring let up, Denis Whitaker, with great relief, decided to make a dash for it across the esplanade into town. Zigzagging, with bullets splattering all around him, he made it. Crouched by a low wall, he instantly became the target for a German machine-gunner. Bullets slammed into the wall in front of his head and stomach. He decided to get away while still in one piece. Running along a wall, he entered a building through a window where he pondered his next move.

Around seven o'clock, German observers on the west headland watched a flotilla of 26 landing craft suddenly steering towards shore. The gunners, who had been harassing the troops on the beaches, now shifted their aim out to sea. The intention of the FMRs had been to land on Red Beach and proceed inland to join up with the Essex Scottish who, they had been told, were already in the town. And, as if the Jubilee operation needed one more thing to go wrong, a strong current, caused by the ebbing tide, swept the flotilla west and with the beach obscured by smoke, the navigators had no idea where they were. As a result, nearly half the battalion ended up on a narrow strip of shingle cut off from the beach, west of the headland. Here they were exposed and trapped, at the mercy of the Germans who tore them to pieces by dropping hand grenades on the 300 hapless men.

The rest of the regiment which landed on White Beach was met with heavy fire from the headland and the houses behind the beach. But one small party, led by an adventurous Sergeant Pierre Dubuc, managed to make its way around the sea wall and enter the town via the Rue de Synagogue, opposite the casino, and turn east towards the docks. There the French Canadians killed several Germans manning a pair of barg   but they then ran into a larger enemy force which, after a stiff fight, took them prisoner and forced them to strip down to their underwear. However, with the help of several others, Dubuc throttled the sentry guarding them, then made off, scantily clad, through the town back to the beach.

At 17 minutes after eight o'clock, General Roberts compounded his earlier folly. In the mistaken belief that the RHLI had command of the situation, he ordered the Royal Marine A Commando to land on White Beach, join the Hamiltonians in the town, and capture the East Hill. As soon as the landing craft emerged from the cover of smoke, it was met with the most demonic, wicked fusillade of high explosive and machine-gun fire experienced that morning. Too late, their commanding officer, Lieutenant Colonel Joseph Picton-Phillips, gave the order to turn back. He and 66 of his marines perished.

That failure brought to a halt all further offensive effort. The Canadians had been beaten and were now ready to concede defeat. At nine o'clock, the force commander, Ham Roberts, gave the order to retreat: VANQUISH 1100 HOURS. Organization for the evacuation began under the most arduous conditions. Luftwaffe aircraft attacked the shipping and shelling from the shore became heavier. From the headlands, the Germans sprayed the beach unmercifully.

Denis Whitaker had figured it out for himself. By ten o'clock he realized that it would be pointless to proceed any further into town. Obviously, the CO, Bob Labatt, and most of the regiment had been pinned down on the beach unable to move, so he returned to the casino where some other members of the battalion were holding German prisoners. When they received the word to evacuate, they began to withdraw under cover of smoke. Only 217 RHLIs got back to England: 190 were killed, 109 wounded and 175 taken prisoner.

Meanwhile, to the east, many of the Essex Scottish moved back to the water's edge in readiness to re-embark. But there they became the targets of heavy shelling and dive-bombing, so volatile it prevented the landing craft from getting in to take them off. Of the 553 who had landed, 530 became casualties, 382 were taken prisoner; only 51 returned to England, half of them wounded.

By this time the entire Western European fighter strength had been thrown into the fray — 945 aircraft from Belgium, Denmark, France, Holland, and even Germany — just what the doctor ordered. But as usual with aerial combat, the results are blurry. Air-fighting statistics are rarely accurate. The best guesstimate is that the Germans lost 48 aircraft destroyed and 24 damaged, while 106 RAF planes were shot down. Of greater significance is the fact that the Germans were forced to maintain the greatest part of their fighter strength in the west from that point on, weakening the Mediterranean and Eastern Fronts. For the record, it is also worth noting that at Dieppe, 12 RCAF squadrons made a valiant account of themselves.

On the beach, as the hour for the evacuation neared, 6th Infantry Brigade Commander William Southam detailed his orderly to try and escape and to burn his papers then and there. Too bad he didn't take his own advice. In his briefcase were orders stating that any German captured was to be manacled to prevent him from escaping. When this fell into enemy hands, in retaliation, the 1,874 Canadians taken prisoner at Dieppe were shackled or tied with rope, for 409 days of the nearly three years they spent as prisoners of war in camps Oflag VIIIB at Eichsatt and Stalag VIIIC.

On reaching the beach following their foray and capture in town, Pierre Dubuc and his party, clad only in their underwear, assisted in carrying the wounded to the boats. Among them was the FMR's commanding officer, Lieutenant Colonel Dollard ''Joe'' Menard, by this time unconscious from five wounds. In total, the ill-fated regiment in their brief sojourn, had lost 119 killed.

On Red Beach, Padre John Foote, who had no business being there in the first place, and who had disobeyed orders to take part in the assault, likewise helped evacuate the wounded. Then, as the last boat pulled away, Foote decided that he could be of more theological value to his men in a prisoner of war camp than back in England. He climbed back out of the landing craft and joined his fellow Essex Scottish in surrender. That action and his subsequent efforts to build morale in the prison camps earned him the Victoria Cross, the only Canadian chaplain ever to be so honoured.

At 20 minutes past noon, the naval commander, Captain Hughes-Hallett signalled: NO FURTHER EVACUATION POSSIBLE, WITHDRAW. At one o'clock Ham Roberts added his own directive: VANCOUVER, ordering the fleet to return to England, leaving over 2,000 of his force in France at the mercy of the enemy. An hour later, the German artillery, after firing 7,458 rounds, fell silent. Jubilee was over, but far from forgotten. Of the 4,963 Canadians of the Second Infantry Division who had embarked on the venture, only 2,210 returned to Great Britain, many of them wounded. Among the 3,367 casualties, 907 lost their lives. Not since the bloodbath of the Somme had a Canadian unit suffered such terrible casualties. By contrast, enemy losses were 591 killed, wounded, and taken prisoner.

Was it worth it? The theory, so often put forth, that the lessons learned at Dieppe were responsible for the success achieved with the Normandy landings on D-Day is highly doubtful and, indeed, somewhat ridiculous. It doesn't need a military genius to finger the weaknesses of this "trial" Dieppe invasion: lack of aerial bombardment, artillery, and proper naval support to name just a few. All these became integral parts of the triumphant invasions of North Africa, Sicily, and Italy at Messina and Salerno. Isn't it a fair assumption that these latter experiences contributed at least as much, and possibly a lot more, than did *Jubilee*, to the success of "Overlord" on June 6, 1944? Perhaps — and it's a big perhaps, because a rank war games amateur could easily reach the same conclusion — Dieppe illustrated that the capture of a port would so destroy it that it would be of no use to the invader until it was rebuilt. Hence the development of the prefabricated Mulberry Harbour which was towed across the channel to support the Allied invasion of Europe.

Winston Churchill later wrote: "My general impression of 'Jubilee' is that the results justified the heavy cost." But, hold it. Wily old Winnie's carefully veiled vindication must be taken in a political rather than a military context. Churchill was always a master of literary manoeuvre in combining the two areas to make his point. In fairness, from a strategic standpoint his point of view bears scrutiny. Churchill had persuaded the Americans to embark on "Torch" — the joint landings in North Africa — a strategic move that paved the way for an assault on the soft Axis underbelly. Tobruk had fallen and Rommel was on the rampage towards Alexandria, threatening to cut off the Middle East oil lines. It was essential to land forces at the Desert Fox's back door to threaten him from both sides. This commitment by the Americans also ensured that they would not have sufficient forces in England to undertake an invasion of Europe in 1942 and, most probably, not in the following year either. In the interim, Dieppe would keep everybody, even Uncle Joe, happy. Only days before the raid on Dieppe, Churchill had convinced Stalin that the enterprise would make Torch possible by diverting German attention to the West Wall, away from the Mediterranean. The Soviet premier, though he continued to carp on the need for a Second Front Now! enthusiastically embraced the scenario on the basis that it would commit the Americans to something — anything. Politically, then, if not militarily, Dieppe had "justified the cost," even, tragically, for the Canadian Army.

Despite horrendous losses and an admitted defeat, the raid had instilled in the Canadian soldier a vital fresh sense of pride, one of unmitigated self-confidence. As a fighting force, Canadians had lived up to the example of their ancestors and predecessors and were more anxious than ever to come to grips with the enemy again at the first opportunity.

On September 3, 1944, following the victorious Battle of Normandy, the Second Canadian Division briefly returned to Dieppe where they staged a march past in tribute to their fallen comrades. The French populace, who had turned their backs on the German funeral parade on the day following the raid on their port, dutifully, and solemnly bowed their heads as the Canadians marched by.

What did it — does it — all mean? Denis Whitaker, who earned the Distinguished Service Order at Dieppe, surely deserves the last word. He has written:

> What it comes down to, for me, is that Dieppe was a tragedy but not a failure. It was a strategic success. Canadians are inclined to downgrade or dismiss their achievements. This is one reason that the unity of our country is at stake.
>
> The men at Dieppe fought heroically under impossible odds. Their efforts should never be denigrated. They contributed a great deal towards the ultimate victory. All Canadians can be proud of that.

❦ **14** ❦

THE DEATH FRENZY

Everything before this was a nursery tale.
Major General Christopher Vokes
Commander First Canadian Division

The first big street-fighting battle.
Winston Churchill
British Prime Minister

The Canadians became, among the Allied soldiers the acknowledged masters of house-to-house fighting.
Robert Wallace
American Historian

Reference map "Ortona, Italy."

The July 10 to August 18, 1943 conquest of Sicily by the Allies, in which the First Canadian Infantry Division took part, resulted in the fall of Mussolini and the subsequent invasion of Italy on September 3. By the beginning of December, the Canadians, as part of the British 8th Army, were south of the Moro River on the east with orders to strike north to relieve pressure on the Americans driving north from Naples towards Rome.

Their objective now became the picturesque medieval port of Ortona, perched on a ledge overlooking the Adriatic. The northern section, known as the Old Town, consisted of confined streets with buildings connected by common walls, designed around a broken-down fortress, that overlooked the artificial harbour formed by a pair of stone breakwaters. Two huge towers dominated the town, the fortress itself and, 200 metres inland, the cathedral of San Tommaso where St Thomas, the 12th apostle, is buried. The newer section to the south was laid out in rectangular blocks but here too the streets were narrow and cramped.

The peacetime population had been about 10,000 but most of the male citizens had either been conscripted by the Germans as slave labour or had fled to the hills. In some ways they were fortunate; they were spared the dangers of being walled up in a stronghold under relentless attack. The entrance to Ortona from the south was via Route 16 which became the Corso Vittorio Emanuele, the main street leading to the town square, the Piazza Municipale. Unlike most of the places on the route of the Eighth Army in its march north, Ortona had been spared aerial and naval bombardment. The British wanted to use it as a port as well as an administration and rest centre.

In fact, by the time the bitter eight day struggle for the German stronghold ended — the fiercest battle the Canadians fought in all their time in Italy, which CBC's Matthew Halton described as the ''death frenzy'' — this once peaceful little coastal community had been reduced to a skeletal heap of ashes and rubble, a complete shambles.

From every standpoint, structurally and topographically, Ortona was ideal for the German purpose: to use a built-up area as a strongpoint for the first time in the Mediterranean. Defending it was the crack 1st Parachute Division. Before the Canadians had even reached the approaches, the Germans had begun the systematic destruction of the town in preparation for the attack. They had wrecked the harbour, blocking it with sunken vessels and breaching the moles. Houses had been deliberately demolished to provide rubble to block the side streets and confine the attackers to the Corso Vittorio Emanuele. Machine-guns, anti-tank guns, and mortars had been strategically positioned at every corner and around the Piazza Municipale to turn the town square into a killing ground.

Ironically, neither side had anticipated, or, even wanted a fight for Ortona. Its military value was dubious to say the least. But three things combined to dictate events. Hitler had insisted that the Gaeta-Ortona line be held no matter what. Major General Christopher Vokes, commander of the First Canadian Infantry Division, bent on cracking the line and advancing to the Arielli River before winter weather set in, sensed that it would be difficult, costly, and perhaps impossible to bypass Ortona. He therefore decided to take it by storm.

General Fieldmarschall Albrecht "Smiling Albert" Kesselring, German Commander-in-Chief South-west, had misgivings from the start. But the day after the battle got underway, the Associated Press referred to the struggle as a "miniature Stalingrad." That was an image the Germans could not afford to ignore. "We did not want to defend Ortona decisively," Kesselring said later, "but the English made it [seem] as important as Rome."

The battle began at noon on Monday, December 20. The Loyal Edmonton Regiment, supported by Sherman tanks of the Three Rivers Regiment, a steady artillery barrage, and shielded by a smoke-screen on their inland flank, advanced along Route 16 the mainroad leading into town. Just before darkness fell, they encountered sporadic, light enemy fire. Lieutenant Colonel Jim Jefferson, the battalion commander, ordered his men to dig in rather than risk a night battle. This gave the 90th Anti-Tank Battalion time to move into position as support. Next day the advance continued and by nightfall the regiment had reached a point a quarter of a mile from the heavily defended Piazza Municipale. There had been no enemy resistance and that cast an eerie sensation on the troops of the battalion whose strength, badly depleted by earlier battles, had been reduced to 60 men to a company.

Next morning, December 22, pre-dawn patrols reported that the Corso Vittorio Emanuele was clear of roadblocks for at least 300 yards. Major Jim Stone, one of the company commanders, then devised a daring plan. The Sherman tanks in low gear with sirens screaming and guns blazing rattled down the main street taking the startled, and badly frightened, Germans by surprise. All went well for about 100 yards, then the lead tank suddenly clanked to a stop. Stone was furious. Climbing up on the vehicle he demanded to know why the driver had come to a halt. The cautious tank commander admitted he had been afraid of the danger of mines.

In the initial astonishment and impact, the impetus had been lost. The tank column stalled and a firefight erupted. Nevertheless, despite this setback, the Edmontonians fought their way through to the Piazza Municipale by dusk. With the tanks immobilized by a roadblock, Jim Stone led his company into the town square where they were immediately pinned down by five machine-guns at the entrance, three of them in one of the surrounding buildings. Private Colin Rattray and two others rushed the house. While his comrades cleared the ground floor, Rattray ran up the stairs two at a time to the top floor, where he single-handedly captured five of the German paratroopers and their three machine-guns. Meanwhile, Stone directed the destruction of another machine-gun and an anti-tank gun with the use of hand grenades.

Although the Loyal Edmontons, in a rare display of innovation and daring, had made remarkable progress, it was obvious that a single, understrength regiment was not enough to take the town. After all, the Canadians were up against two battalions of German paratroopers. A company of the Seaforth Highlanders of Canada had already been sent in to cover the left flank, and next day, December 23, the rest of the regiment joined in the fighting along with scouts and snipers from the Princess Patricia's Canadian Light Infantry. Jim Jefferson and Major Syd Thomson of the Seaforths carved up the battlefield between them, the Edmontons on the right, the Seaforths on the left, with the Corso Vittorio Emanuele the dividing line. It was a house-to-house fight all the way, so that over and above the battalion objectives were company and even platoon objectives, the latter consisting of assaults on two or three houses at a time.

The Loyal Edmontons' Captain Bill Longhurst developed a form of house-to-house combat that earned the Canadians their reputation as masters of that style of fighting. Because it was suicidal to venture onto the streets, the troops worked themselves between houses through courtyards and balconies. Using an explosive or a pick and shovel, they would break through the walls of the upper floor of an adjoining building. Then, stair by stair, room by room, they would clear the house before "mouseholing" into the next one.

In the confines of the narrow streets and the roadblocks thrown up by the enemy, the difficulties with the tanks were never really overcome. But they proved invaluable nonetheless, singly or in small numbers as assault guns and pillboxes. They were also used for bringing up ammunition and mortars as well as carrying the wounded from the battlefield under fire. Under the circumstances and given the conditions in which they had to fight, it seems incredible that only three of the Three Rivers Regiment's Shermans were lost.

The close-in fighting prevented the normal type of artillery support except when specific targets could be accurately pinpointed by the infantry. For the most part the gunners had to content themselves with harassing enemy movement along the coast road north of the town.

But where firepower was concerned, the Canadian soldier once again demonstrated his ability for innovation and readiness to adapt to the conditions in which he found himself. For example, the Type 36 hand grenade was an ideal firearm for bowling down hallways;

the 2-inch mortar perfect for firing through windows; the 4.2-inch mortar and the PIAT—portable infantry anti-tank gun—highly suitable for street fighting. Also devastatingly effective were the infantry's 6-pound anti-tank guns and the 17-pounders of the Anti-Tank Battery. These were able to penetrate areas the tanks could not reach and also had the capability of firing from sharper angles.

In the midst of this bitter house-to-house, hand-to-hand fighting, Ortona would seem an unlikely place in which to celebrate Christmas. Most Canadians managed to steal away from the fighting long enough to wolf down a Yuletide meal behind a wall or a shed before going back into the fray. The Seaforths were luckier. They were served a sit-down dinner in style complete with tablecloths and chinaware in the battered Church of Santa Maria di Constantinopoli. The regimental cooks outdid themselves with a feast of soup, roast pork and applesauce, cauliflower, mashed potatoes and gravy, then Christmas pudding and mince pie topped by a bottle or two of beer. As one company after another came in for the sittings they were greeted by the battalion padre Roy Durnford who announced cheerfully: "Well at last I've got you all in church." In the distance the sound of machine-gun fire and bursting shells seemed incongruous with the merry chatter and laughter. How many realized that for some it would be their last meal?

The bitter struggle for Ortona, which the Ottawa *Evening Citizen* described as the "hardest of any wherein the Canadians have taken part in this war," reached a zenith on Boxing Day, December 26. That morning the Loyal Edmontons' Lieutenant Edward Allen and his 23-man platoon had taken possession of a house that had been booby trapped. The explosion appeared to have killed everyone, but while the dead were being carried away, someone heard screams from the rubble. A frantic rescue ensued. The confined space allowed only two men to claw away the rubble of bricks and mortar which was passed hand-to-hand, along to a chain of helpers. By the time they pulled out Lance Corporal Roy Boyd, he had been buried alive for three days. "It's like coming back from the dead," he told his rescuers.

The Loyals soon got their revenge, as the CBC's Matthew Halton broadcast to his listeners back home in Canada:

[O]ne officer, the Regimental Interpreter, crawled alone to a window on this building to hear the Germans talking. He heard an officer upbraiding his men for having let the Canadians get to the top floor. Then the Canadian crept away and found some of his engineers. In half an hour the engineers had placed high explosives under the building. And after the Canadians on the top floor had been warned to get out, the building was blown up and 48 or 50 Germans in it were killed or crushed.

On that same day, Major Douglas Harkness of the Edmontons had what he later described as his closest brush of the war. The future cabinet minister was in the process of bringing up rations to his embattled anti-tank gunners when a German 88 shell landed at his feet and exploded. Harkness was knocked back head over heels, but although badly shaken was able to crawl away and stagger into the battalion's headquarters where he was given a stiff drink. His escape from death was some sort of a miracle. Had he been standing an inch to one side or the other, shrapnel would have shredded him to pieces. He had been in the small arc of the shell explosion's weak or blind side.

By eight o'clock on the morning of Tuesday, December 28, a strange silence had fallen over Ortona. During the night, the Germans had pulled out. The town lay shattered, in ruins, the grotesque smell of death everywhere. Before leaving, in one last defiant pagan act of desecration, the enemy had destroyed and gutted the ancient San Tommaso cathedral. To harry the victors, they had left countless mines and booby traps concealed everywhere. It would be some time before it was be safe for the civilians to return.

For the Canadians, it had been a costly conquest. The Loyal Edmonton Regiment had lost 172 and the Seaforth Highlanders of Canada 103 killed and wounded. For the survivors, it had been a trying experience. A quarter of those reporting sick — 484 — had come down with sheer exhaustion and scarred nerves. As some consolation, there were awards for bravery: five Distinguished Order decorations, including one to Syd Thomson of the Seaforths, and three Military Crosses, and seven Military Medals. German losses remain unknown but the Canadians recovered the bodies of 100 paratroopers.

Chris Vokes, the Canadian commander, proclaimed: ''We have given the 1st German Para Division a mauling it will long remember,'' and all Canada stood up and cheered. A year and a half after Dieppe, the news of the fall of Ortona took a lot of the sting out of that earlier catastrophe. On the day of the victory, the *Toronto Star* was blazoned with the red banner headline: Canada Bayonets Win Ortona. The Montreal *Gazette* more mildly, but just as proudly, said:

"Ortona will always rank and be remembered definitely as a Canadian show."

Just as aptly, if somewhat provincially smug, the Edmontons and Seaforths painted and posted a sign at the entrance to the town that read:

THIS IS ORTONA
A WEST CANADIAN TOWN

✤ 15 ✤

THE NORMANDY CONQUEST

Reference map "The Battlefields of Normandy."

Full cycle! On April 9, 1940, the "Phony War" came to an end when the German Werhmacht attacked Norway in what was the first air-sea-land invasion in the history of warfare. Four years and two months later, almost exactly to the day, the Allies had brought the technique to a high state of the art when, on D-Day, June 6, 1944, they landed troops in France along the Calvados coast of Normandy in the Baie de le Seine. And in this, the greatest invasion the world has ever seen, Canada and Canadians played a heroic and integral part.

Of the five army divisions to hit the beaches shortly after dawn, that morning, two were American, two British and one Canadian — the 3rd Canadian Infantry Division supported by the 2nd Canadian Armoured Brigade. From the air, the 1st Canadian Parachute Division was dropped east of the Orne River on the left flank, while heavy bombers of the 6 Group of the Royal Canadian Air Force were the first to plaster the coastal defences in the all-night bombardment of the assault areas. During the day 16 RCAF fighter squadrons from 83 Group of the Royal Air Force Second Tactical Air Force swept the skies over and beyond the bridgehead and attacked ground targets. At sea, 115 ships of the Royal Canadian Navy formed part of the 4,126-vessel Allied fleet providing escort, minesweeping and artillery support, and landing tanks and troops.

Operation Overlord, as the invasion came to be coded, had been a long time in the making. It can be said that it had its genesis on the night of June 23, 1940, after the French officially surrendered to the Germans at Compiegne, when 100 British soldiers were landed by high-speed RAF launches on the dunes of Boulogne and the sands of Le Touquet in France. The damage they inflicted was negligible but it was the gesture that counted, one of defiance and a herald of what lay in store.

More tangibly, in July 1941, shortly after the Germans attacked Russia, the Inter Services Training and Development Centre, then the experts on amphibious warfare, drew up a plan (on the assumption that America would become an armed ally) which estimated that 15 armoured and 20 infantry divisions would be required to launch an invasion of north-west Europe. It drew attention to the fact that such a force would have to be supplied from England and to the need for a tremendous amount of shipping.

With the Japanese attack on Pearl Harbor on December 7, 1941, and the United States declaration of war on Germany, the probability of an Allied invasion of Europe took on new meaning. In the spring of 1942, the US Army produced an invasion plan that called for 48 divisions supported by 5,800 combat aircraft. Seven thousand landing craft would have to be built and reinforcements would be required at the rate of 100,000 men a week. Everything was to be ready by April 1943. In fact, by that time there were less than 200,000 American troops in Great Britain. At the Washington Conference in May, it was agreed that the invasion of Europe, now known as Overlord, would have to wait until May 1, 1944.

Earlier, at the Casablanca Conference in January, Winston Churchill, Franklin Roosevelt, and the combined joint chiefs of staff decided that plans for the invasion should get underway immediately. In March Lieutenant General Sir Frederick Morgan was appointed chief of staff to the supreme Allied commander (or COSSAC) with headquarters at Norfolk House in London.

Morgan was given three goals. The first was to prepare a diversionary raid on the Pas de Calais. The second was a sudden cross-Channel assault to relieve the Russians, and finally, the full-scale invasion itself — Overlord.

The key to the latter was where it would take place. The most obvious choice was the Pas de Calais. It was by far the shortest route. Limited fighter range ruled out Norway, the Bay of Biscay, and even Antwerp. To support an invasion army, a port would be needed, and Le Havre or Normandy's Cherbourg both filled the bill nicely. And compared to the Pas de Calais, Normandy's defences were sparse, thinly strung out. American and British opinions differed and often the two were at complete loggerheads.

Agreement on the venue and Anglo-American harmony on the issue, came with the intervention of the head of Combined Operations, Lord Louis Mountbatten. As a member of the British chiefs of staff, he wielded great weight. He had also been studying intensely the problems of landing in France. His commando raids had yielded first-hand experience of the strength and weaknesses of enemy coastal defences. His headquarters was confident that a landing could be successfully achieved and that artificial harbours (Mulberries) and pipelines under the sea (Pluto) could supply an army ashore.

Mountbatten arranged for a conference of senior officers, code named Rattle, to review all aspects of the invasion scheme. On June 28, 1943 at Largs in Scotland, it met in the comparatively holiday atmosphere of the Highlands away from the gloomy offices of London. It worked; it cleared the air. At the end of the two-day seminar, there was total unanimity between the Americans and British over Overlord for the very first time. Even the landing venue had been agreed upon: somewhere between the Contentin Peninsula and Dieppe in the Baie de la Seine. From then on COSSAC's efforts would be concentrated solely on Overlord without any diversionary landings.

To the British chiefs of staff, Mountbatten outlined the type of support that would be needed to launch the invasion. The area to be assaulted would have to be subjected to the strongest, most intense bombardment possible from the air and the sea. Special rocket firing barges and close support naval craft were essential.

In August, COSSAC unveiled the invasion plan to Churchill, Roosevelt, and the combined joint chiefs of staff at the Quebec Conference. The COSSAC study visualized an assault on Normandy by three seaborne and two airborne divisions, with two more divisions for immediate follow-up. After securing the beachheads along a 35 mile front between Caen and Carentan, the Anglo-American force was to concentrate on the capture of Cherbourg. Meanwhile, as agreed at Largs, the troops would be supplied by the prefabricated Mulberry harbour and the underwater Pluto pipeline. The plan called for landing 18 divisions in the first two weeks.

Morgan pointed out that from now on, the RAF and USAF would concentrate on reducing substantially the Luftwaffe fighter force. He also warned that the landings could only be successful if the Allies were faced with no more than 12 enemy reserve divisions — three on D-Day and nine by D-Day plus eight. Churchill wanted the Allied strength to be increased by 25 percent and also insisted that a landing be made on the Contentin Peninsula nearer to Cherbourg than the other landings along the Normandy coast.

Now the teams began to take shape on both sides of the channel. On December 7, on his way home from the Cairo Conference, Roosevelt appointed General Dwight Eisenhower supreme commander-in-chief Allied forces of liberation. Air Chief Marshal Sir Arthur Tedder became his deputy. General Sir Bernard Montgomery took over as commander-in-chief British army of Liberation, while Air Chief Marshal Sir Trafford Leigh Mallory was made Allied air commander-in-chief. The appointment of Allied naval commander-in-chief went to Admiral Sir Bertram Ramsey. Headquarters was a tent township located at Bushey Park on the outskirts of London.

By contrast, Field Marshal Gerd von Rundstedt, German commander-in-chief west, made his headquarters in Paris at the luxurious Chateau St Germain-en-Laye overlooking the Seine River. His responsibilities were formidable, well nigh impossible, as well as impractical. He had 3,000 miles of coastline to defend — from the Italian to the German frontier — and only 60 divisions, a lot of them cast-offs from the Russian campaign or low-grade units, with which to accomplish it.

As early as 1941 Hitler had given instructions for the construction of a new Atlantic Wall, the westward bastion of his *Festung Europa*. Begun the following year, it extended along the channel coast from the Pas de Calais to the Bay of Biscay. It was a mammoth task and even with the feverish, strenuous efforts of the German industry's Totd Organization, the result was an uneven chain of defences full of gaps, with the main concentrations focussed on the more obvious landing places such as Cap Gris Nez, the mouth of the Seine, Brest, and Lorient.

The Allies had picked the right place for a landing. The defences in Normandy were far weaker than those in the Pas de Calais and there were two and a half times as many troops employed in the north. Between Boulogne and Calais, the Germans had 132 guns, 93 of them protected by concrete emplacements. In Normandy there were only 37 guns, 27 installed in emplacements. And there were plenty of problems with them. For one thing the Germans had to contend with 28 different calibres and few of the weapons were equipped with proper rangefinding equipment. In many cases the concrete installations limited the range of fire, making it particularly difficult to sight on a moving sea target.

Actually the most troublesome defences installed by the Germans, other than the minefields, were the underwater obstacles designed to rip through the bottoms of the landing craft and tanks.

Von Rundstedt had no faith in the Atlantic Wall anyway. He considered it a façade, a myth, a waste of time and energy, that could easily be overcome by a determined assault which would be bound to find a breakthrough somewhere. He was totally disillusioned then, to make matters worse, in December 1943, Hitler appointed Field Marshal Erwin Rommel inspector of fortifications, from Norway to the Spanish border, an assignment bound to create dissension. When he arrived in France, Von Rundstedt made Rommel commander-in-chief Army Group B, placing him in charge of the sector from the Dutch-German border to the Loire River. The southern sector he entrusted to Field Marshal Johannes von Blaskowitz as commander-in-chief Army Group G.

Von Rundstedt planned to concentrate his forces at the most vulnerable points — the Pas de Calais, the mouths of the Somme and Seine Rivers, at Cherbourg, and at Brest. This ran contrary to Rommel's thinking. He believed in striking at the enemy the moment he got ashore. Better to have one Panzer division in place at the point of attack than to have three divisions three days later when it would be too late.

The Desert Fox had fallen victim to the strength of allied air power which had crushed his Afrika Korps. He concluded that the only way to stop the invaders from establishing a toehold was to have the Panzers — their Tiger and Panther tanks were far superior to anything the Allies possessed — deployed along the wide beaches of Normandy, where he was sure they would land, instead of at the well-fortified ports. The Panzers would then be ready to act at a moment's notice without having to run the gauntlet of American and British straffing and bombing, getting into place.

However, his strategy depended entirely on relocating the ten Panzers divisions, the only formidable reserves the Germans had in the west. Of the 58 divisions in the west, more than half were in coastal defence and training divisions, strung along the coast with most of the concentration in the Pas de Calais. Of the 24 field divisions, only ten were armoured, three of which were allocated to the southern sector. If he was unable to persuade Von Rundstedt and Geyr von Sheppenburg, general in command of Armoured Forces in the west, (who had a Panzer division at Antwerp) to relocate the Panzers, Rommel knew the battle was lost before it began.

But Von Rundstedt was adamant. He refused to commit the Panzers, claiming that the Allies might strike anywhere, particularly across the Straits of Dover, the shortest route to the German border to cut off the armies in France. This issue stirred up such a hornet's nest that Hitler sent his Inspector General of Panzers, General Heinz Guderian, to France to smooth things over. Guderian took Von Rundstedt's side, convinced that the Panzers should be held in reserve, not committed to any one place. Hitler, however, agreed with Rommel. He was becoming increasingly convinced that the Allies would land in Normandy. OKW — Oberkommando der Wehrmacht — German High Command Deputy Chief of Operations, General Walther Warlimont, stated that: "Hitler was the first to come to the conclusion that Normandy was the most probable spot...."

Der Führer settled on a compromise. Four of the Panzer divisions would be placed under his direct control, not to be moved without permission from the OKW. With that directive, then and there the fate of the Germans in Normandy was sealed.

Though the Allies had no inkling of this inner conflict, the enemy coastal defences from the Belgian frontier to Brest were not strangers to them. For two years they had come under penetrating aerial reconnaissance surveillance. In addition, midget submarines and motor launches probed and sounded out the beaches. And the French underground and Allied agents provided a plethora of information from stolen documents to clandestine photographs and troop dispositions. Everything — tides, geography, weather — underwent meticulous and scrupulous study and appraisal. Nothing was left to chance.

While the 1st Canadian Parachute Battalion and the 3rd Canadian Infantry Division underwent training and exercises in preparation for the invasion itself, airmen of the 6th Bomber Group RCAF and 16 RCAF squadrons of the 2nd Tactical Air Force were heavily engaged in paving the way for the assault by striking at targets all over occupied Europe. Chief among them were rail transportation centres and marshalling yards which RAF Bomber Command attacked at night. By D-Day, 80 centres had been smashed. Day and night, fighters and fighter-bombers of the tactical air forces struck at bridges, rolling stock, and transport of all kinds, along with tanks, ammunition dumps, headquarters, and military camps. During April and May the Allied air forces flew over 200,000 sorties and dropped 195,400 tons of bombs.

As the days wore on, and the first week of June approached, the heavy bombers began to concentrate on the coastal defences. Medium bomber attacks on radar stations were so effective that on the eve of the invasion, only 18 out of 92 were functional. All during this period bombers and fighter dive-bombers were alternately busy attacking No-Balls targets — the V-1 flying bomb launching sites in northern France.

The air forces also played a large part in the deception making the Germans believe the invasion would take place in the Pas de Calais by making it the principal target of the coastal bombing. In addition, fighters and fighter-bombers returning from forays would indicate over their radio transmitters that they were going down to land near Dover. Then at deck level they would fly west to return to their bases due north across the Channel from the Baie de la Seine. To complete the fraud, a bogus army pantomimed troop movements in Kent and Essex along with installations of wooden guns and tanks and dummy landing craft in the Thames Estuary. Enemy aircraft were deliberately allowed to fly over south-east England to photograph the phoney build-up to ensure that they completely accepted the hoax.

Four Tribal Class destroyers of the Royal Canadian Navy (RCN) also played an important role in the prelude to Overlord as part of the Royal Navy's 10th Destroyer Flotilla. They made regular offensive night sweeps against German shipping and coastal installations from Ostend in Belgium to the Bay of Biscay.

Only eight days in June promised a favourable combination of tide and dawn light for the landings. On May 8 Eisenhower had set the fifth of June as the date for D-Day. During the final days of May and the first days of June, American, British, and Canadian troops were ferried from their compounds to their assigned ships and landing craft. By Saturday, June 4, they were on the move to the rallying point south of the Isle of Wight. Then the weather began to deteriorate. The forecasts called for increasingly heavy seas and low cloud and poor visibility over the beaches. At 4:15 next morning, Eisenhower had no choice but to postpone the invasion for 24 hours and the ships were ordered back to the embarkation points.

That night the meteorologists broke the news that the weather was about to improve and should stay clear for 48 hours. Cloud conditions would allow heavy bombing on Monday night. The wind would die down but the sea would remain choppy and rough. At 11:30 on Sunday night, Eisenhower called a meeting of the SHAEF (Supreme Headquarters Allied Expeditionary Force) commanders at Southwick

House, the nerve centre near Portsmouth, to come to a decision. Tuesday, June 6, would be the last day in which the dawn/tide combination would be suitable for another two weeks. The consensus of opinion was that the operation should proceed. Next morning, with the weather report still favourable, Eisenhower gave the signal to go ahead. That afternoon the ships slipped their berths and began converging on the Isle of Wight towards the rendezvous point aptly named "Piccadilly Circus."

The basic strategy for Overlord called for landings on five designated beaches. Lieutenant General Omar Bradley's First United States Army would land at "Utah" at the eastern foot of the Contentin Peninsula and at "Omaha" between Pointe le Percee and Pont en Bessin on the west side of the Normandy beaches. To the east, Lieutenant General Miles Dempsey's Second British Army would land on, from left to right, "Sword" between the Orne River to the east and Lion, "Juno" between Courseulles-sur-Mer to the east and St Aubin-sur-Mer, and "Gold" between Arromanches on the right and La Riviere.

Overnight 20,000 airborne troops would be dropped on the right and left flanks. The US 82nd and 101st Airborne Divisions were to blanket themselves all over the neck of the Contentin Peninsula and, with the help of the French Resistance cutting telephone lines, create confusion in support of the landing on Utah Beach. The British 6th Airborne Division, of which the 1st Canada Parachute Battalion was a part, would be dropped to the east of Caen to seize the Orne bridges and support the Sword Beach landing.

As part of the British Second Army, the 3rd Canadian Infantry Division, commanded by Major General Rod Keller, would land on the four-mile wide Juno Beach with the British divisions on either side attacking Sword and Gold beaches. For assault purposes Juno was split into two segments. "Mike" on the right was the more open of the two and also the shortest, a half mile wide at low tide. It faced the hamlet of Vaux and the village of Graye-sur-Mer, a quarter of a mile inland. Backed by sand dunes ten feet high, the beach offered several outlets for vehicles. The 7th Brigade would use two battalions, the Royal Winnipeg Rifles (with a company of Canadian Scottish) to storm the beach defences and seize Vaux, part of Courseulles on "Nan" Beach, and Graye-sur-Mer, while the Regina Rifle Regiment cleared the eastern part of Corseulles. Thereafter the rest of the Canadian Scottish would come in ready for the next phase.

"Nan" Beach on the right, had the longer frontage and included the small shipping port of Courseulles-sur-Mer, the village of Bernieres-sur-Mer, and the western outskirts of the town of St Aubin-sur-Mer. The Queen's Own Rifles of the 8th Brigade would clear the beaches and take Bernieres while the North Shore (New Brunswick Regiment) moved on St Aubin. After that, the reserve battalion, Le Regiment de la Chaudiere, was to land, pass through the QOR's and attack enemy battery positions near Beny-sur-Mer, and advance to the village of Basly.

The 9th Brigade, in reserve, comprised of the North Nova Scotia Highlanders, the Highland Light Infantry of Canada, and the Stormont, Dundas and Glengarry Highlanders would land on whatever beach was firmly held in readiness for the move inland — the second phase of the landings. Their final objective for the day was to cut the road between the communication centres of Caen on the east and Bayeux to the west, and capture Carpiquet airfield beyond. Facing the Canadians would be the 716th German Infantry Division and, in reserve, the 21st Panzer Division.

Getting 50,000 troops to the beaches and supporting the landings was the purpose of Operation Neptune, the naval aspect of Overlord, and in this the RCN played many key roles. Probably the most exacting, not to mention nail-biting, was that of minesweeping. Sixteen Bangor-class minesweepers were assigned to an operation known as the Oropesa Sweep. Ten of them made up the 31st Canadian Minesweeping Flotilla. The other six were allotted to three different RN flotillas.

Their job, along with the 100 other Allied vessels in the same category, was to slash paths through the German minefields for the ten columns making up the 5,300 ships and landing craft of the assault armada — the largest naval invasion force ever assembled. On the evening of June 5, steaming five miles ahead of the fleet into the Baie de la Seine, the minesweepers began cutting into the eight-mile deep mine belt 40 miles north of the assault beaches.

Once they had sliced the alleyways through that defence barrier, which they carefully marked by dropping signal buoys along the routes, they had to clear new channels to an area seven miles offshore where the troop transports and bombarding battle wagons would drop anchor. Then, finally the flotillas had to clear the area inwards as close as possible to the beaches for the landing craft.

The RCN also participated in escort work, guarding Tribal destroyers, motor torpedo boats, and 11 frigates which were assigned to two RN escort groups.

Canada's naval contribution in the attack force itself numbered 19 corvettes, 30 landing craft, two troop ships, and two bombardment destroyers. The landing craft made up three flotillas. The 260th Canadian Flotilla consisted of seven craft carrying 250 Canadian and 1,050 British troops all attached to the 3rd Canadian Infantry Division. Also of the same divisions were 1,946 Canadian and 148 British men making up twelve craft of the 262nd Canadian Flotilla. Seven other LCT's of the 264th Canadian Flotilla carried 1,126 troops of the British Northumbrian Division.

While the invasion fleet was steaming south, the 1st Canadian Parachute Battalion had succeeded in destroying several bridges spanning the Orne River. C Company, which landed in the most easterly part of the drop zone near Varville, blew up a bridge over the Divette River then moved back to Mesnil, a village at a key road junction east of the Orne. The Canadian paratroopers had to beat off several enemy attacks while waiting to link up with the British in the area of the Benouville-Ranville bridges once the 3rd Infantry Division had secured Sword Beach.

At 17 minutes after six on the Tuesday morning of June 6, the Canadian troop carriers, *Prince David* and *Prince Henry* (former luxury liners converted into armed merchant cruisers) began lowering the landing ships into the water. As the little vessels began the rough hour-long run into the beaches, the RCN's bombarding destroyers *Algonquin* and *Sioux* opened fire simultaneously with 76 other Allied warships. *Sioux*'s target was two buildings near St Aubin housing 75-mm guns. Within two minutes they were silenced.

The DD (Duplex Drive) amphibious tanks, with collapsible canvas bulwarks, which were to have gone in ahead were delayed by the rough seas. To *Algonquin* and *Sioux* now fell the task of clearing the beaches with their fire. Then just before touchdown their guns fell silent.

H Hour for landing on Juno had been set back by ten minutes to 7:35 a.m. to allow the incoming tide to cover the rocky shales that had been detected by aerial reconnaissance, and a further ten minutes to 7:45 for the attacks on the flanks. But the shales turned out to be seaweed. That misinterpretation had cost the demolition teams valuable time for clearing the way through the obstacles. Courseulles was particularly well protected. On either side of the Seulles River, heavy concrete emplacements housed 88-mm guns and machine-gun nests. A high concrete wall had to be bridged or blasted before either infantry or tanks could get off the beach. On the eastern flank, the Germans had sown some 14,000 mines.

The aerial bombing and naval bombardment had thrown up so much debris that it made targeting difficult and many enemy guns remained intact. The tide was fast rising due to the delay in the landings and some of the landing craft were being swept against the obstacles. But most fared better.

On Mike Beach, the Canadian Scottish was on a stretch of open sand where the naval guns had destroyed all obstacles. They immediately pushed inland towards Graye. To their left, the Royal Winnipeg Rifles came under such heavy enemy fire that only one officer and 25 men of one company made it off the beach. On the eastern flank, at the north-west corner of Courseulles, the Regina Rifles encountered stiff enemy resistance at the four-foot concrete wall studded with 88-mm guns and machine-guns as well as small arms fire from a concrete trench. Nevertheless, they managed to sweep around the fortress in a flanking movement and, with the help of the tanks, which by this time had landed, they broke through the defences. When a German machine-gun crew made a dash with their weapons for some slit trenches behind a seawall, Lieutenant Bill Grayson, armed only with a Colt automatic pistol, forced the enemy gunners to surrender. Later in the morning he led three others from the safety of a group of houses into an enemy pillbox, and took ten more prisoners. Next, with only five of his men, he cleared out a tunnel along the bank of the Seulles River during which the Reginas killed a number of Germans and took 25 prisoners.

On Nan Beach to the left, the Queen's Own Rifles landed directly in front of the German strong point at Bernieres. Major Charlie Dalton' s company had already suffered heavy casualties in the landing craft from exploding mines. Once ashore they came under such intense enemy fire that 65 men were wiped out in minutes and Dalton himself was wounded in the head. Despite his injury, Dalton led his men across the sand and succeeded in knocking out one of the German pillboxes. In spite of heavy resistance, the entire German fortification was soon overcome. As a result of Dalton's aggressive leadership, successive companies behind his own landed on the beach without a single casualty.

His brother, Major Elliot Dalton meanwhile, led his company in such a fierce attack that German resistance was instantly overcome.

He then advanced with his unit through Bernieres where the company scattered the enemy defenders, driving them into the fields beyond the town. As in the case of his brother, his dauntlessness allowed the companies coming in behind his own, to land on the beach without a shot being fired at them. On the eastern flank at St Aubin, tanks of the Fort Garry Horse were prevented from leaving the beach by the seawall. Three of them forced an exit through a minefield where they were met with the fire from a German 50-mm gun which pummeled them into flames. Men of the North Shore Regiment busied themselves with silencing the enemy gun and the advance inland proceeded. During the attack on the beach Private Bob Adair found himself to be the only one left from his entire medical company. Although the battalion was under heavy enemy fire, Adair rendered first aid to the injured. When he had finished treating the wounded on the beach, although he had been warned that the Germans had placed booby traps all over the place, he continued to search for those in need of care until his medical supplies ran out.

By mid-morning the reserve battalions went in. Le Regiment de la Chaudiere had landed at Bernieres behind the Queen's Own Rifles, passed through them and soon ran into some temporary difficulties. Two miles inland, three German 88-mm guns held them up. A call went out for help, and Les Chaudieres signalled the Canadian Destroyer *Algonquin* to come to their aid. The crew couldn't see the guns so they had to rely on reports from Captain Tom Bond, the battalion forward observation officer ashore, to direct their fire. It was right on. Several broadsides from *Algonquin* soon put the 88s out of business and Les Chaudieres continued their advance towards Beny-sur-Mer. On two occasions Bond positioned himself well ahead of the leading company of the regiment and, despite heavy enemy fire, remained at his observation post until the objectives had been reached. Near Le Hamel he was actually shelled out of his observation post.

Approximately 14,000 Canadians had been put ashore on D-Day; they suffered 1,074 casualties, 359 fatal, which was much lighter than expected. By nightfall the 3rd Infantry Brigade was well established although it had fallen short of its objectives. The 7th Brigade had reached Ste-Croix-sur-Mer and Banville and was close to Cruelly. The 8th got as far as Beny-sur-Mer on the main road to Caen, the home of William the Conqueror, and the chief administration centre of Normandy as well as the main rail, road, and canal junction in the vicinity of the beaches, which Montgomery had wanted to conquer that day. It would be another 33 days before he saw that objective realized. The 9th Brigade advanced as far as Villons-les-Buissons, less than four miles from Caen but at this point it was held up by fierce German machine-gun fire short of Carpiquet airfield, the division's farthest inland objective. All that day under an aerial umbrella of some 5,000 Allied aircraft not a single enemy aircraft penetrated the air cover long enough to interfere with the landings. Nor had the Canadians encountered any German armour. D-Day plus 1 would tell quite a different story.

On the eve of D-Day, June 5, Field Marshal Erwin Rommel had left his headquarters at the Chateau Roche Guyen for a vacation at his home in Ulm on the Danube, content that for the next week "the tides will not be suitable for landings," or so he told his naval adviser. In fact the Germans had been taken by surprise and faced the dilemma of what should be done with the Panzer divisions. Rundstedt still pondered whether the Normandy landings were a feint. With all the evidence at hand, as a result of the Allied "fraud," it seemed certain the real attack would come from the Pas de Calais. But, in any case it was vital to push the Allies back into the sea wherever they landed and that could only be achieved by moving the Panzers into Normandy without delay. But that required Hitler's permission and the Führer was sound asleep, having given orders that he was not to be briefed on the war situation until after he had finished his breakfast. When advised of Normandy landings, he at first dismissed the news as a trick, the Allies trying to mislead him. Later, that afternoon, he agreed to release the reserves for an attack on the bridgehead. But by then it was too late; they would not reach the invasion area until the next morning. On their way south, the Panzers were so harassed from the air, they labelled the road from Vire to Beny-Bocage the *Jabo Rennstrecke* — the fighter-bomber racecourse. Hitler, however, would not agree to move the 15th Army to Normandy. The bridgehead would have to be annihilated by the troops already there.

The Canadians clashed with the 12th SS Panzer Division on the morning of June 7 at Authie, the first German counter-attack to defend Caen at all costs. The North Shore Regiment lost possession of the town and was badly mauled with 245 killed and wounded.

While that battle raged, the German Luftwaffe made its first and final attempt to interfere with the beaches in daylight. Shortly after 11:00 a.m., 12 Junkers 88 twin-engine bombers swooped down through the 1,000 foot five-tenths cloud — half clear — over Gold Beach. The leader crashed into a balloon cable and went up in smoke.

The rest, chased by an equal number of Spitfire IXs from 401 Squadron RCAF, jettisoned their bombs and tried to escape. The squadron commander, Lorne Cameron, accounted for two of the German bombers, while his pilots destroyed six others.

Next day, June 8th, the 25th Panzer Grenadiers, commanded by the ardent Nazi Kurt Meyer, and made up of fanatical 18- and 19-year-old Hitler Youth, attacked the Royal Winnipeg Rifles in Putot-en-Bessin, about five miles from Authie, and inflicted such heavy casualties that the battalion was forced to withdraw with no choice but to leave some of its men, many of them wounded, behind. The prisoners were taken by the Germans to the Abbaye d'Ardenne where the Hitler *Jugend* beat them, lined them up against a courtyard wall, and shot them in cold blood. Two more of the Winnipeggers were murdered a few days later. Their bodies were buried, but were later discovered by the Canadians. After the war, Meyer was tried for war crimes and sentenced to death. However it was commuted to life imprisonment, and he was subsequently released.

On the night of June 8, the 7th Brigade commander, Brigadier Harry ''Red'' Foster ordered the Canadian Scottish to counter-attack and Putot was retaken. Now the Panzers attacked the Regina Rifles at Norrey-en-Bessin and after a heated battle that lasted all night and into the next morning, the Canadians drove the Germans back, destroying five of their Panther tanks. The 25th Panzer had suffered a severe defeat.

On June 11 the Canadians again encountered Kurt Meyer, who by this time commanded the 12th SS Panzer Division, when the 6th Canadian Armoured Regiment and the Queen's Own Rifles made an attempt to capture Cheux through Le Mensil-Patry. It was there that, three days before, Captain Peter Griffin of the 1st Canadian Parachute Division, with 75 of his men, had led an assault on a group of farm buildings occupied by the German 857th and 858th Grenadier Regiments and well defended with machine-guns. Attacking through an orchard, the paratroopers captured a farm house and took many of the enemy prisoner.

The battle that took place on the 11th became known to the Canadians as the ''Charge of the Light Brigade.'' As the 6th Armoured and the QORs approached the village, the Germans brought down a rain of mortar and machine-gun fire on the infantry and the Tigers opened up with their 88-mm guns on the Sherman tanks. It was a disaster. The 6th Armoured's Shermans were slaughtered by the Tigers. Only two of them survived. Fifty-nine men were killed and

21 were wounded. The QORs lost 55 killed and 44 wounded. So much for Blitzkrieg tactics at this stage in the war, with too few men and too few tanks. After that abysmal failure at Le Mesnil, the 3rd Canadian Infantry Division was for all intents withdrawn from the fighting for the next three weeks. Up until this time, during the first six days of the invasion, Canadian casualties totalled 1,107 killed and 1,814 wounded. While the Americans were able to drive across the Contentin Peninsula and capture the port of Cherbourg by June 27, the battle on the British-Canadian front settled into a war of attrition. It was some compensation that the Allies at least enjoyed complete air superiority.

On July 4 the Canadians were once more placed on a fully operational level and on that date Operation Charnwood, to capture Carpiquet and the airfield south of the town, got underway. The 8th Brigade, spearheaded by the Winnipeg Rifles, and supported by the tanks of the Fort Garry Horse, and the AVRE (Assault Vehicles, Royal Engineers) of the 79th British Armoured Division, as well as RAF rocket firing Typhoons, along with the guns of the battleship HMS *Rodney*, swept in from the west to be greeted by a sustained and well directed machine-gun and mortar fire from the well entrenched SS defenders in concrete bunkers and hangars surrounding the control tower.

As so often proved to be the case, the massive preliminary barrage had achieved negligible results and done little real damage, so that the Germans were able to lay down a vicious crossfire that turned the airfield into a killing field. During the day's fighting, rifleman Carnet Sinclair of the Royal Winnipegs took over as stretcher-bearer for three of the battalion's companies. Working under the most hazardous conditions, he made five trips bandaging and evacuating the wounded. On one trek, although he was unarmed, four Germans actually surrendered to him.

From start to finish, the attack was poorly directed and executed. Major John Anderson remembered that his regiment, the North Shores, sustained more casualties that day than on any other during the entire war. The Canadians did succeed in capturing the town, however, but were unable to secure the southern part of the field even after a second attack. The divisional commander, Rod Keller, came in for strong criticism from his superiors for leaving his troops badly exposed during the assaults and for failing to recognize when to send in reinforcements. For the next five days, the Canadians held on grimly to the village and the northern part of the airfield until the fall of Caen which forced the Germans to give up Carpiquet.

By the night of July 9, Caen, a heap of rubble and buried bodies as a result of two raids by RAF Lancaster heavy bombers prior to the attack, was in British and Canadian hands. On July 8, to the north of the city, the 9th Canadian Infantry Brigade had captured Authie and Buron where Captain John Anderson spent the day rescuing wounded from the front line by driving his jeep into the face of savage enemy mortar fire, shelling, and machine-gun bullets, saving the lives of many men who would otherwise have died on the field.

Meanwhile, the 7th Brigade took the hamlets of Cussy and Ardenne. To the south-west, the 8th Brigade completed its occupation of Carpiquet. During the fighting for the Normandy capital, the Canadians lost 1,194 men, 334 of them killed. This was the first major defeat the Germans had suffered at the hands of the British and Canadians in Normandy. The time had now come to finish the job.

At this time, the restructuring of the Canadian Army in France had begun. On July 11, General Guy Simonds' 2nd Canadian Corps took over operational control of the 3rd Canadian Infantry Division from the British and also took command of the 2nd Canadian Infantry Division, commanded by Lieutenant General Charles Foulkes, which had begun arriving in Normandy along with the 2nd Canadian Armoured Division. General Harry Crerar, commander of the First Canadian Army, had already arrived in France and the 2nd Canadian Corps, as well as the 1st British Corps, would come under his control. Later the 1st Polish Armoured Division would become attached to the 2nd Corps.

Below Caen the country was open with a succession of low ridges rising to some 200 feet near Falaise 16 miles to the south. German anti-aircraft guns and mortars, which had accounted for 75 percent of all Allied casualties, controlled all movement in the area. The Verrieres Ridge was the key to these defences and was held by three German divisions.

On July 18, Simonds launched Operation Atlantic with the objective of securing the industrial suburbs of Caen — Vaucelles and Colombelles — and at the same time force a gap through the German armour. It began badly with the British 11th Armoured Division, on the left, running into the 1st SS Liebstrandarte Adolf Hitler Panzer Division, which destroyed 126 of its tanks and brought the advance to a dead stop. On the right, Keller's 3rd Canadian Infantry Division, following a massive bombing raid and heavily supported by artillery, succeeded in crossing the Orne River into Colombelles. The Queen's Own Rifles captured Diberville while the rest of the 8th Brigade moved south. By nightfall, 3rd Division troops were in command of Cormelles, east of the main highway leading to Falaise, and had occupied the eastern part of Vaucelles.

Next day the Black Watch Regiment from the 5th Brigade crossed the Orne and began advancing to the east side of Verrieres Ridge, the first of the series of low ridges between Caen and Falaise. On July 20, Simonds sent in the 6th Brigade spearheaded by the Essex Scottish, to attack the centre of the ridge. It began at three o'clock that afternoon, but a heavy downpour hampered manoeuvrability, put an end to air support, and made artillery ranging well nigh impossible. The Germans, however, turned the rain to their advantage and counter-attacked. Their tank fire and machine-guns routed the Canadians who shed their weapons and fled in disorder. Two companies of the Fusiliers Mont Royal were wiped out. Next morning the Black Watch counter-attacked with disastrous results. By then the Essex Scottish had lost more than 300 killed and wounded. Total 2nd Division casualties for Operation Atlantic reached 1,149 for which Simonds blamed Foulkes' ineptitude.

By this time, General Omar Bradley was ready to launch Operation Cobra to break out of the Normandy bridgehead west into Brittany and the Americans put the pressure on Montgomery to drive his forces south to bottle up the Germans on the Caen front. On July 25, two days after the headquarters of the Canadian Army became operational, a second attempt was made to capture Verrieres Ridge, code named Spring. The exercise called for the two Canadian infantry divisions to force a hole in the German defences through which the British armoured divisions could push ahead as far as possible toward the high ground around Bretteville-sur-Laize and Cintheaux.

The failure of Atlantic in broad daylight caused Simonds to begin his attack in darkness, employing "artificial moonlight" by using searchlights beamed against the cloud base. At 3:30 a.m. the North Shore Regiment, supported by the Fort Garry Horse tanks, attacked Tilly-la-Campagne, but by dawn they had only taken half the town. Most of the tanks had been destroyed and the North Shores were cut off. In the centre, the Royal Hamilton Light Infantry, commanded by Lieutenant Colonel John "Rocky" Rockingham, captured Verrieres village on the crest of the slope and held on desperately against German counter-attacks. The Royal Regiment of Canada, however, failed to reach its objective, Rocquanfort. On the right flank the

Calgary Highlanders reached the outskirts of May-sur-Orne but were driven back to their start line by determined German resistance. The Black Watch had as its objective the village of Fontenay-le-Marmion, but before it even reached the start line, both the commanding officer and the senior company commander had been killed. Reorganization required threw the advance way off schedule. At 9:30 a.m. the regiment, unaware that the Calgary Highlanders had been driven back, marched up the slope of the ridge and into a trap. Furious German tank, anti-tank, mortar, and machine-gun fire from all sides, cut them to pieces. That morning the Black Watch lost 123 men killed, 100 wounded, and 83 taken prisoner, the worst one-day loss in its history.

That same morning, Bradley's Operation Cobra swung into full gear with the United States First Army breaking out of the bridgehead at St Lo. The Germans now faced encirclement and should have withdrawn to the Seine River. But instead, Hitler ordered a counterattack — Operation Luttich. To try and stop the American spearheads pushing south and to isolate General George Patton's Third Army plunging into Brittany, the Germans moved west towards Mortain. In the face of this, Montgomery kept up the pressure on the Germans with thrusts south in the area of the Verrieres Ridge. Though these attacks rarely achieved their objectives they did keep the enemy tied down on the Caen front.

On August 8, the Germans launched Luttich, committing almost their entire armoured forces north of the Seine. Alerted by the Ultra code-intercepting device at Bletchley Park in England, the Americans were ready and waiting, and with the help of RAF Typhoons, dealt the Germans a mortal blow. The enemy advance had brought them further west to a position where they could now be surrounded. Two days later, Bradley ordered Patton to send the XV Corps of his Third Army east to Alencon then north to Argentan to link up with the Canadians whom Montgomery had decided to send south. This was a change from the original plan to encircle the Germans along the Seine. Now the blow would fall in the area of Falaise.

The 2nd Canadian Corps on his left flank was in the best position of any of Montgomery's units to attack towards Falaise, so the assignment to carry out Operation Totalize fell to Guy Simonds. The first phase began on the night of August 7 at 11:00 p.m. using "artificial moonlight" preceded by heavy air bombardment, directed by red and green flares fired by the artillery. The advance was initially made difficult by the dust churned up by the armoured personnel carriers and the tanks, but by daylight most objectives had been realized including the capture of Verrieres Ridge that had so often eluded the Canadians. They now paused to regroup, but in the meantime, Kurt Meyer brought up two battle groups from his 12th SS Panzer Division as well as a number of assault guns and Tiger tanks.

The first thing that went wrong with the second phase of Operation Totalize was the preliminary bombing by the US Eighth Air Force which scattered its loads on the 1st Polish Armoured Division and the 3rd Canadian Infantry Division. Rod Keller, the latter's commander, was wounded and replaced by Major General Dan Spry. The Sherman tanks of Major General George Kitching's 4th Canadian Armoured Brigade suffered fearfully from the well directed 88-mm gun fire from Meyer's Tigers. The British Columbia Regiment, led by Lieutenant Colonel Doug Worthington, with two companies of infantry from the Algonquin Regiment, got lost and ended up atop a hill they took to be their objective, Point 195, west of the Caen-Falaise road. Suddenly they found themselves surrounded and all hell broke loose. Hundreds were wounded and killed, including Worthington who lost his life. By nightfall the survivors made it back to the Polish lines. Totalize had gained a paltry seven miles — still a long way from Falaise or even the high ground.

By August 10, the build-up of German armour was still in the Mortain area to the west. Patton's XV Corps reached Le Mans, wheeled north and approached Argentan. However instead of entering the town, General Philippe LeClerc's 2nd French Division attached to the Americans, disobeyed orders and took a circuitous route, allowing the Germans time to reinforce the town. On learning this, Montgomery issued orders for Crerar to capture Falaise as soon as possible, which would make it exceedingly difficult for the Germans to withdraw to the east. However, Field Marshal Gunther von Kluge, who had replaced Von Rundstedt as commander-in-chief west, had already set in motion plans to retire to the Seine. Crerar assigned Simonds to head the attack and the 2nd Corps commander drew up a plan along the lines of Totalize — Operation Tractable. But this time the assault would be launched in daylight, its flanks protected by smoke fired from the artillery.

Then at the last minute Montgomery changed his mind, not for the last time by any means, and decided to allocate the task of capturing the town to the British Second Army. The Canadians were to take the high ground north and east of Falaise, then thrust south-east to Trun to the east. Kitching's 4th Armoured Division was assigned to attack on the left flank, the 3rd Infantry Division with the 2nd Armoured Brigade on the right. The assault date had been set for August 14, but it came as no surprise to the Germans. The day before, a Canadian officer lost his way and drove into the enemy lines. He was killed and his driver taken prisoner. Left in the jeep was a copy of Simonds' orders. Thus warned of the attack, the Germans began bringing up their artillery and anti-tanks weapons on the expected line of approach.

Low-flying medium bombers laid a carpet of bombs over the battlefield. Then the artillery fired off a shower of smoke bombs. The combination of the dust thrown up by the bomb bursts and the smokescreen made it almost impossible for the German gunners to see the attack. But having prepared themselves, and with their guns in position, they fired blindly as furiously as they could manage, inflicting heavy casualties and destroying and damaging a number of the vulnerable Sherman tanks. The infantry covered a lot of ground but by the end of the day, the objective had not been attained. It took until April 16 to take Point 195. On that same day, the South Saskatchewan Regiment, the Queen's Own Cameron Highlanders, and the Fusiliers Mont Royal of the 6th Brigade, supported by tanks of the Sherbrooke Fusiliers, captured Falaise. The Fusiliers Mont Royal overcame the very last resistance, a dozen fanatical SS grenadiers who fought to the end.

Montgomery now ordered the American XV Corps, which had come under his jurisdiction, to advance north. But it was too late to complete the encirclement of all the German forces, and thousands of them were fleeing through the ten-mile gap. To shrink it, Simonds ordered Kitching's 4th Armoured Brigade to thrust south to Trun while the 1st Polish Armoured Brigade made for Chambois. The 4th reached its objective on August 18, but the Poles did not reach Chambois until the next day, the date the first contact was made with the Americans. As thousands of Germans tried to flee through the narrow gap, Allied fighters and fighter-bombers had a field day, harassing them relentlessly and taking a horrendous toll of dead and wounded, as well as tanks, transport, and guns. The anti-aircraft fire was still deadly.

Flying from 126 Airfield at Beny-sur-Mer, Flying Officer Sandy "Duke" Halcrow of 401 Squadron RCAF was straffing the corridor when his Spitfire IX was hit by flack forcing him to bale out. He landed right in the middle of the gap. He was quickly made prisoner and led to a barn where several Germans had taken shelter from the straffing and bombing. Halcrow began to take some of his own medicine back. All day long the rattle of machine-gun and cannon fire and bursting rockets and bombs erupted around the building.

Late in the afternoon, an SS officer, who had been wounded in the foot, entered the barn to rest. He had been fighting all day and, although Halcrow could not understand German, he gathered that the officer was telling the others that the situation was hopeless. He then ordered one of the soldiers to write something on a piece of paper which he handed to Halcrow. It was in German but one of the men translated it as best he could. In effect the tables had been turned, the Germans in the barn had surrendered to Halcrow and were now his prisoners. Shit! Now what? None of those dumb briefings on how to conduct yourself when you got shot down, that he'd been subjected to by those ''desk flyers,'' had prepared him for anything like this. What, in God's name or anyone else's, was he expected to do?

Fortunately the SS officer now took charge, and spared him the embarrassment inflicted on him by his own inept, uninformed intelligence officers. Commandeering a transport, he waited until nightfall, then piled everyone into the truck and drove off in a westerly direction toward the Allied lines. They had gone no more than three miles when they reached a crossroads where a disabled tank was blocking the traffic in all directions. The SS officer made everyone get out and they continued on foot. It was dawn before they reached the lines and, to Halcrow's delight, a Canadian sergeant came forward, rifle at the ready, to take them all captive. But because Canadian pilots wore blue battledress similar to the German army blue, Halcrow was mistaken for a German and was about to be herded along with the rest. However, pointing to his CANADA shoulder patches he demanded: ''What's that? Scotch mist?'' whereupon the sergeant lowered his gun, grinned, and snapped off a pukka salute.

On August 21, after three days of bitter fighting at St Lambert-sur-Dives, the key escape route midway between Trun and Chambois, Major David Currie of the South Alberta Regiment and a squadron of 175 men, slammed the gate shut on the Falaise Gap. Supported by 16 tanks and armed with PIAT self-propelled anti-tank guns, as well as sundry other weapons, the Canadians arrived at the outskirts of the heavily defended village on the morning of August 18, where the lead tanks were damaged by enemy fire. The enemy put up such stubborn resistance that by late afternoon, Currie was the only officer who had not become a casualty, directing the evacuation of the crews from two disabled tanks.

That night, reinforcements arrived: two half companies from the Argylls and the Lincoln and Welland Regiment. Next morning, Currie organized an all out assault on the village and by noon he and his men had succeeded in seizing and consolidating a position halfway inside the village. For the next 36 hours, the Germans launched one counter-attack after another but in every case the assaults were repulsed. By this time, another squadron of the South Albertans had joined in the battle, together with the 15th Field Regiment, from a hill north of St Lambert where they could direct their fire down onto the stream of Germans crowding the road towards the village in the hope of escaping out the gap.

At dusk on August 20, the Germans tried to mount a final decisive assault to break their way out. It failed utterly, miserably. The attackers were routed before they could be deployed. Seven German tanks, 12 88-mm guns, and 40 vehicles were destroyed, 300 Germans killed, 500 wounded, and 2,100 taken prisoner. Currie promptly ordered an attack and completed the capture of the village, effectively blocking the Chambois-Trun escape route. The gap was now closed, shutting off all escape.

Throughout the three days and nights of almost continuous fighting, Currie had not only directed his men, but had participated in the fighting himself. An amazing man, on one occasion, he personally directed the fire of his command tank onto a German Tiger tank and knocked it out. During a subsequent attack, he used his rifle from his gun turret to kill enemy snipers. Another time, even though his unit's artillery fire was falling within 15 yards of his tank, he ordered it to continue because of its devastating effect on the Germans. Currie had no respite during the battle except for an hour's sleep. When relief finally arrived he was so exhausted he fell asleep on his feet and collapsed. For his gallantry and leadership under fire Currie was awarded the Victoria Cross, the only Canadian in the Battle of Normandy to receive the medal.

The Battle of Normandy, which had cost the Germans a whopping 400,000 men, 200,000 of them taken prisoner, was over. (In the final phase of the Falaise fighting, the Canadians alone had captured over 13,000 Germans.) The First Canadian Army was now assigned the task of clearing the coastal areas and opening the channel ports for vital supplies. By the end of September, the Channel coast had been cleared except for Dunkirk and the Canadians had put an end to the V-1 menace by overrunning the Flying Bomb launching sites in northern France.

On June 6, 1994, the Canadians returned to Normandy. They bore no arms this time, but 50 years had not dimmed their memories of battles won and comrades lost. At a ceremony in the immaculately attended Canadian military cemetery outside Beny-sur-Mer, on the 50th Anniversary of D-Day, Canadian veterans of the Normandy campaign from ''sea to briny sea'' bowed their heads in reverence to their comrades who never made it home. They remembered, as all Canadians must, as all Canadians should, that D-Day and the Battle of Normandy stand in our history as a hallmark, an emblem of our military heritage, one in which we can take take a fervent national pride. In Normandy, Canadians fought together province *avec* province, and were victorious in helping liberate Europe from the Nazi oppressor. Do not forget that. Let it stand as a lesson, a monument that, hopefully, will continue to help keep our nation unified, strong, great, and free.

✦ 16 ✦

THE MIRACLE OF THE WEST

Reference map "Antwerp."

It should never have happened. And it need not have. If the British 11th Armoured Division had been allowed to continue its lightning advance across France and Belgium into Antwerp on Tuesday, September 5, 1944, it would have cut off the remnants of the fleeing German 7th and 15th armies as well as the 5th Panzer Army, and the Battle of the Schelde, in which the Canadians suffered 6,730 casualties, would not have transpired. Although the British still had plenty of fuel left, their tanks were brought to a halt by an order to rest and refit for 48 hours with the lame explanation that the division had outrun its administrative resources.

Lieutenant General Guy Simonds, the energetic, innovative commander of the 2nd Canadian Corps, had pleaded with his immediate superior, General Harry Crerar, commander-in-chief of the 1st Canadian Army, to have Field Marshal Montgomery's order for the Canadians to clear the channel ports changed so that they could give full chase to heading off the escaping Germans instead. "I suggest sir," he wrote, "that 2nd Canadian Corps push up the coastal sector, behind the coastal forces simply masking the fortresses with light forces."

Through the Ultra decoding signals to which he was privy, Simonds knew that the enemy was trapped. Why not, he reasoned, channel all our energies into clearing the lengthy Antwerp approaches immediately and nab the German Army at the same time — two birds with one stone. He argued that:

> The coastal ports are not an offensive threat on our flanks. By making for Breskens and sweeping eastwards from there along the south bank of the Scheldt toward Antwerp, we could catch the German 15th Army and refugees from the 7th Army and the 5th Panzer Armies in a second pocket. To hook around the Scheldt first would delay the attacks on the Channel ports by only a few days; their capture would contribute nothing [to the supply shortages] at that juncture.

This view was an echo of Admiral Sir Bertrand Ramsay's concerns on the subject. The commander-in-chief of the Allied naval forces issued a directive to Supreme Headquarters Allied Expeditionary Forces and to Montgomery's 21st Army Group, predicting that the Germans would mine the Scheldt River to block the Allies from using the port unless the river was immediately broughy under Allied control. "If the enemy succeeds in these operations," he warned, "the time it will take to open the port cannot be estimated." In his diary he noted: "Antwerp is useless unless the Scheldt Estuary is cleared of the enemy."

That urging might well have persuaded Crerar to plead Simonds' case with Montgomery had it not been for a petty rift between the two. When the Canadian 2nd Division captured Dieppe on September 2, Crerar staged a seven-hour parade to honour the dead of the abortive raid on the port in August 1942. This respite delayed the division's advance and angered Montgomery. Crerar wasn't looking for more trouble and was not about to take issue with his superior over a proposed change in plans from attacking the Channel ports to cutting off the Germans at the Scheldt. In any case, Montgomery would probably have ignored Ramsay's warning and Simonds' recommendation. He had his mind set on a quick thrust into the Ruhr that would end the war before Christmas and had given the scheme top priority. But if the Allied hierarchy seemed incapable of appreciating the importance of clearing the port and danger of a German threat to Antwerp keeping it closed, Hitler sensed how essential it was to the Allies at this stage of the war. They had advanced farther and faster than they had foreseen and their supply lines had been stretched to the limit — all the way back to Normandy. Allied bombing before

D-Day had destroyed all French rail transport and most of the roads were in disrepair.

With 2,000,000 men on the continent, the appetite of General Dwight Eisenhower's Allied armies' 36 divisions was phenomenal. It required a daily supply of 25,000 tons — ammunition, fuel, food, medicines, and other essentials. As the second largest port in Europe, Antwerp, with its daily capacity of 60,000 tons, could easily handle all the Allied requirements — and it was close to the front, too — necessary for a swift and decisive victory before the end of 1944. Hitler was determined to deny them that opportunity. At the same time, he was planning a paralyzing blow; a drive through the Ardennes with Antwerp as the objective. All this would buy him time to shatter England with his new rocketry, the V-2.

Hitler ordered General Gustav von Zangen, commander of the 15th Army, to cross the Leopold Canal on the Belgian-Dutch border to the west of Antwerp, then make for the port of Breskens on the south side of the West Scheldt River. There, by rafts, barges, and merchant ships, the Germans crossed the waterway to Walcheren Island on the north shore then travelled east along the Beveland Isthmus through its narrow neck to Woensdrecht and Hoogerheide. Hitler then instructed General Gerd von Rundstedt, the reinstated commander-in-chief west following Von Kluge's recall, dismissal, and subsequent suicide, to bolster the defences at Walcheren as well as the north and south shores of the Scheldt. These positions, he emphasized, were to be held at all costs, defended to the death. Any man attempting to withdraw would be shot and any surrender would bring swift retaliations against his family by the Gestapo.

By September 6, the key fortress at Flushing on Walcheren Island was manned and the river was being heavily mined. Hitler feared the Allies would cross the Albert Canal east of Antwerp and drive north toward the Dutch market town of Berge op Zoom at the east end of the East Scheldt River threatening to cut off his retreating 15th Army heading in the direction of Woensdrecht. General Kurt Chill had been assigned the task of defending the canal, his meagre force supported by scattered German police, security troops, air force, and naval personnel, until the 15th Army could be regrouped and bolstered with fresh paratroopers.

To protect his army from a rearguard attack, Hitler reinforced the Leopold Canal with the 70th German Division commanded by Lieutenant General Wilhelm Daser.

What Hitler had achieved in less than three weeks was truly a "Miracle of the West." The Germans had once again illustrated their ability to recover from a heavy reverse. A beaten army had been completely rebuilt and its morale restored. In the 19 days it took to evacuate across the Scheldt, 86,100 troops had been rescued along with 616 guns, 6,200 horses and 6,000 vehicles. It was an incredible feat. Incredible too was the fact that, for three weeks after September 4, the British and Canadian armies had the escaping Germans trapped. Yet, not a single move was made — or allowed to be made — to drive the mere ten miles northward to Woensdrecht to intercept the enemy.

To add insult to injury, on September 9 Montgomery reinforced his order that the 1st Canadian Army concentrate on freeing the channel ports and forget about the Germans fleeing across the Scheldt. But at least two armoured divisions under Canadian command, the 4th Canadian and the 1st Polish, were "allowed" to take up the chase. A backhanded licence. The Breskens Pocket, as the area became known, was polder country — land reclaimed from the sea — and it made tanks useless. The Poles did manage to capture the port of Terneuzen, 12 miles east of Breskens. But it would be impossible for tanks to cross the Leopold Canal where all the bridges had been blown. And even if the armour did reach the north side it would be useless. The Germans had taken advantage of the polders to flood the countryside. Only infantry could make any headway and most of that was being wasted attacking the Channel ports.

And all the while the Germans were growing stronger. On September 3, Hitler had ordered Colonel General Kurt Student, who had developed the German airborne forces, to create the new 1st Parachute Army of 30,000 men, a further manifestation of his "Miracle of the West." This elite unit was made up of remnants of the Hermann Goering and SS regiments as well as the crack 6th Paratroop Regiment under the exceptional, and inspired, leadership of Lieutenant Colonel Friedrich Augustus von der Heydte, Germany's most experienced airborne commander. And just to allow the Germans some more time to hone their defensive skills and consolidate their positions, on September 13, there was further bad news for the Canadians. Eisenhower authorized the postponement of any further assault (*further* assault?) to free the approaches to Antwerp until the conclusion of Montgomery's airborne attack to break through the Rhine — Operation Market Garden.

In the Breskens Pocket, Simonds decided to use the battalions of the 4th Armoured Division's 10th Infantry Brigade: the Algonquin Regiment, the Lincoln and Welland Regiment, and the Argyll and Sutherland Highlanders of Canada. South of the Leopold Canal, on September 8, the Argylls, supported next day by the Lincolns and Wellands, made an attack across the Ghent Canal, five miles south of the Leopold, against the hamlet of Moerbrugge. They had been told that the area was weakly defended and that opposition would be negligible and were therefore stunned when greeted by ferocious fire and the counter-attacks that followed. By seven o'clock next morning, they had thankfully beaten off the last of the enemy assaults and the sappers had finally built two bridges for the tanks. During the two days of fighting, the Canadians had taken 250 German prisoners.

Three days later, in a late evening operation, the Algonquins crossed the Canal Deriviation de la Lys to establish a bridgehead at the village of Moerkerke from which to cross the Leopold Canal. Once again intelligence had badly underestimated enemy strength and the crossing was met with intense enemy fire. But by 11:00 a.m. all four companies were across the canal. However, German resistance proved so strong and steady and casualties so heavy that by noon the next day the regiment was ordered to retire. Algonquin losses amounted to 66 men taken prisoner, 58 killed, and 29 wounded, 42 percent of the entire battalion strength.

Simonds ordered that for the time being, no further attempts should be made to cross the Leopold Canal. Meanwhile operations were limited to clearing and patrolling the area south of the waterway.

Apart from limited forces at his disposal and poor intelligence reports, as well as overwhelming enemy strength, Simonds faced another problem: that of lack of combat trained reinforcements, a situation directly related to the conscription crisis in Canada in which conscripts were not obliged to fight overseas. (This was later amended but it was too late and too little to serve any useful purpose.) The result was that in most cases, men in other roles — clerks, chefs, maintenance, stores — had to be crash trained — or weren't trained at all — and went into battle having never even handled a weapon, let alone fired one.

Now, on September 15, two days before Market Garden began, and with all the Channel ports captured except Dunkirk, Montgomery ordered Crerar to move to the Scheldt Estuary on the double to free up the approaches to Antwerp. Then on September 26, with the collapse of Market Garden, he called on Crerar to protect the left flank of General Miles Dempsey's Second British Army which was poised to begin an attack on the Ruhr from the Nijmegan Salient. Having accomplished this by assigning the Canadians' 1st British Corps, Crerar flew to England to undergo medical tests for a severe case of anaemia.

Simonds now took over the 1st Canadian Army (Lieutenant General Christopher Foulkes temporarily replaced him as commander of the 2nd Canadian Corps) with full responsibility for planning and coordinating the Scheldt campaign, a fortunate and fortuitous set of circumstances. His formula involved four operations. The first was to clear the area north of Antwerp and close the South Beveland Isthmus. The second was to clear out the Breskens Pocket between the south bank of the Scheldt, the Leopold Canal, and the Canal de Deriviation de la Lys. The third operation was the reduction of the Beveland Peninsula. The final operation was the capture of Walcharen Island.

Cutting the South Beveland Isthmus and reducing the peninsula was the job of the South 2nd Canadian Infantry Division. Clearing the Breskens Pocket fell to the 3rd Canadian Infantry Division helped by the 52nd British (Lowlands) Division and the 4th Canadian Armoured Division. For the finale to the campaign, Simonds had decided that, due to the topography of Walcheren Island and the nature of its defences, the only way to tackle its capture was to "sink" it by aerial bombing.

Up until the Scheldt offensive began, the 5,000 men of the 4th Canadian Infantry Brigade, comprised of the Royal Highland Light Infantry, the Essex Scottish Regiment, and the Royal Regiment of Canada, were assigned the defence of the port of Antwerp; there was always the fear that the Germans might try to recapture it. On September 16, the RHLIs took over from a Welsh regiment in the Second British Army to guard the docks south of the village of Oorderen. The Essex Scottish overlooked the suburbs of Merxem and Eekeren where the Germans were heavily entrenched. The Royal Regiment took up a defensive position along the Albert Canal to the east. Further along the waterway, it was defended by the 5th Canadian Infantry Brigade: the Black Watch of Canada, the Calgary Highlanders, and Le Regiment de Maisonneuve.

In the dock area, the RHLI was constantly harassed by the Germans and skirmishes frequently broke out. The Allies strengthened their line at stations around the village of Wilmarsdonck which, along with Oorderen, Eekeren, and Merxem, still remained in enemy hands.

On September 23, the RHLIs, to prevent enemy infiltration, extended their line into the villages of Wilmarsdonck and Oorderen, encountering mortar and machine-gun fire, but there were only four casualties, none of them fatal. Now the floodgates, opened by the Germans during their retreat, were finally closed. But many of the low-lying lands around the captured villages were half-flooded and Oorderen was smouldering from fires. By this time the Germans had strongly established themselves on the railway tracks in the marshalling yards north of town and had entrenched themselves in freight cars.

The stage was now set for the initial phase of the Scheldt campaign. On the Antwerp front, the 2nd Canadian Infantry Division faced a force, commanded by Lieutenant General Kurt Chill, of 24 tanks and 25 batteries of 88-mm anti-aircraft guns defending a three mile front near Merxem, and being regularly infused with troops from the reconstituted 15th Army along with fresh, young paratroopers.

On September 26, the Calgary Highlanders of the 5th Brigade were ordered to form a bridgehead over a footbridge at the badly damaged lock gate at Wommelgehm, a few miles east of the Antwerp docks. Led by Sergeant Clarence Crockett, as a party of ten made their way forward they were challenged by a German sentry. Crockett killed him with his knife. Two enemy machine-guns then opened fire and Crockett silenced them with his PIAT. The Calgarians quickly established a foothold which the enemy attacked furiously in an effort to dislodge them. But, bolstered by reinforcements from the battalion, the position was soon secured and the engineers began building a bridge across the canal.

Meanwhile the 6th Brigade, made up of Les Fusiliers de Mont Royal, the Queen's Own Cameron Highlanders of Canada, and the South Saskatchewan Regiment, began an assault on the Antwerp-Turnout Canal, flowing north-east from the port.

Under cover of smoke, Les Fusiliers on the right and the South Sasks on the left, successfully crossed the Albert Canal and established a bridgehead at Lochtenberg where the Sasks were held down by a pair of German tanks. Two men crept forward, damaged one tank with a PIAT, and forced the other to withdraw. In the meantime Les Fusiliers were forced back across the waterway by 200 German infantry and 12 tanks. The Sasks were promptly ordered to withdraw. Divisional HQ now decided to make the crossing with both the 5th and 6th Brigades. The 6th was to create a diversion while the Calgary

Highlanders, the Regiment de Maisonneuve, and the Black Watch launched a fresh attack to the east.

On September 28, the diversionary crossing by the South Sasks was successful, enabling the Maisonneuves to form a bridgehead at the town of St Leonard. From there the Black Watch captured the town, then advanced toward Brecht where the Calgarians had established a base. Together they attacked the village, finally capturing it on October 1. The three day battle cost the Black Watch dearly, with 119 casualties sustained.

At three o'clock on the morning of October 2, the Royal Regiment of Canada of the 4th Brigade, supported by a Belgian Secret Army Battalion, sent two companies across the Albert Canal at Merxem. Later in the morning, the Essex Scottish entered the town from the west across the Groendaal Canal, taking 153 prisoners. By evening, all four companies were consolidated in the northern outskirts of the suburb. The force also occupied the power plant and other strategic buildings. Next day the Essex Scottish pushed through Eekeren then north to Starboeck near the Dutch border.

That same day, the objective of the South Sasks was the town of Lochtenberg which, with the help of rocket firing RAF Typhoons, they quickly captured. Now, having cleared both the Albert and Turnhout canals, the 6th Brigade, with the Sasks on the left and the Camerons on the right, advanced south-west to take the town of Braschaet in the Breda and the nearby military camp, which it accomplished the next day.

By October 4, all three brigades of the 2nd Canadian Infantry Division were poised along the Dutch border ready to drive north and cut off the South Beveland Peninsula at Woensdrecht and push the enemy off the peninsula into the North Sea.

Two days later, to the west, the 33rd Canadian Infantry Division's offensive to crush all German resistance in the Breskens Pocket, the South Schelde Fortress, got underway. By the end of September, the 1st Polish and 4th Canadian armoured divisions had forced the Germans back along the north side of the Leopold Canal which ran from Heyst in the west to the Braakman Inlet to the east. There, three regiments of General Knut Eberding's German 64th Infantry Division defended an area 20 miles long.

On October 6, the 7th Canadian Infantry Brigade launched an attack on the canal. The failure of the Algonquin crossing on September 12 in which the regiment lost 153 of its men, had taught the Canadians that any new attempt would need far more weight and much greater artillery support. This time there were three battalions instead of one. The Canadian Scottish Regiment on the east and the Regina Rifle Regiment in the west would spearhead the crossing toward the village of Strooiburg, four miles east of where the Algonquins had met their demise, and then link up. The third battalion, the Royal Winnipeg Regiment, would be held in reserve. And the fire support would be devastating.

Two hours before H-Hour — 5:30 a.m. — the start of the crossing, 327 field guns of the Royal Canadian Artillery commanded by Brigadier Bruce Matthews, senior gunnery officer of the 2nd Canadian Corps, rained down an unmerciful barrage on known enemy positions, the weight of which was equal to five times the normal artillery strength of an entire division.

Immediately prior to the start of the crossings, 27 Wasps — Bren gun carriers armed with flame-throwers, the brainchild of the Chemical Warfare Branch — swept the opposing dykes with deadly flames that ricocheted off the sloping embankments and bounced up and down into the slit trenches directly behind. The defences immediately confronting the assailants were completely eliminated. Most of the enemy were burned alive, others were terror-stricken. The Wasp attack had been so effective that the two leading companies of the Canadian Scottish crossed the canal without a single casualty. But the Germans, as usual, recovered quickly and directed mortar, machine-gun fire, and hand grenades against the attackers. However, only 50 minutes after the crossings had begun, the engineers had completed a kapok footbridge across the canal.

The Germans threw everything they had at the Canadian Scottish, Winnipeg Rifles, and the Reginas hanging desperately onto their small bridgehead, even fire from their heavy coastal guns at Flushing on Walcheren Island. The Canadians also suffered under the prevailing conditions: mud and constant rain.

However, at three o'clock on the morning of Sunday, October 9, an operation by the 9th Infantry Brigade led by Brigadier John "Rocky" Rockingham, was soon to ease the pressure on the beleaguered men of the 7th. A flotilla of 97 Buffalo LVTs (Landing Vehicle Track, amphibious carriers that could transport 30 infantrymen), brought north from Ghent to the Schelde, left the port of Terneuzen and began making its way across the mouth of the Braakman Plaat (inlet) under heavy artillery cover to land 2,000 men with their vehicles, equipment, and supplies at what Rockingham himself called "the back door" of the Breskens Pocket, on the south shore of the Scheldt. By mid-morning, all three battalions of the brigade, the Highland Light Infantry of Canada, the Stormont, Dundas and Glengarry Highlanders, and the North Nova Scotia Highlanders, had reached a point just east of the fishing village of Hoofdplaat.

The Germans had been taken completely by surprise. Although he now faced the Canadians on two fronts, General Knut Eberding was determined to drive them out of the Breskens Pocket. An equally determined Rocky Rockingham, was just as resolved to button up that pocket as quickly as possible.

It didn't take the Germans long to pull their defences together, as Eberding rushed over reinforcements from Walcheren Island. The battle soon developed into a platoon war over the dykes and polders with ground gains measured in yards, even feet. Casualties were high. Unlike Normandy, where mortars had taken the toll, the danger in the Scheldt was from small arms fire.

While the HLIs and the Novas were consolidating their position at the enemy's rear, Lieutenant Colonel Roger Rowley's Stormont, Dundas and Glengarrys were given the job, in his own words, of "kicking out in front." Operation Switchback called for the SD&Gs to breakout of the bridgehead , advance west along the coastal seawall and capture Hoofdplaat. After a bitter struggle, the village fell on October 8, but the victors found themselves surrounded. The Novas, who were to have advanced on the left flank, had been unable to do so. The SD&Gs had also outrun the range of their own field guns, so that they were without artillery support. But they were well within range of the heavy coastal guns at Flushing, and took a fearful battering for the next three days. Finally on October 11 the Novas arrived on the left flank. By that time the SD&Gs had lost 15 of their number killed and 46 wounded. Then on October 21, they were ordered to capture the well-defended port of Breskens to the west, the focal point of the pocket. A formidable assignment!

This flanking assault by the 9th Brigade had greatly eased the pressure on the 7th Brigade, fighting for its life on the north bank of the Leopold Canal, and by the middle of October the Strooiburg bridgehead had been considerably enlarged. Then, about the same time the 9th received orders to advance west along the south shore of the Scheldt, the 7th was relieved by the 175 Brigade of the British 52nd (Lowlands) Division.

In the meantime, the first German stronghold in Holland fell to the 2nd Canadian Infantry Division driving north of the Albert-Turnhout canals when, on October 7, the Royal Regiment of Canada captured

Ossendrecht. This formed a solid base of operations from which to launch an attack on the formidable Woensdrecht fortress, three miles to the north. It dominated the road and railway line running through the South Beveland Isthmus that linked Walcheren Island with the German supply depots and military centres to the east. Behind the town, a centuries old seven foot high dyke presented the only rise in an otherwise flat countryside. In it the Germans had embedded guns sighted on the fields below.

Standing in the way was the village of Hoogerheide, adjacent to Woensdrecht on the west, whose defences gave some premonition of the bitter fighting still to come. It took the 5th Brigade's Calgary Highlanders three days to capture the village. Now it fell to the Black Watch to seal off the isthmus.

It was Friday the thirteenth and that fateful day for the regiment began at 6:15 a.m. Once again intelligence had badly underestimated enemy strength. The Canadians were up against Von der Heydte's tough young paratroopers. Operation Angus called for a frontal attack in broad daylight against these superbly trained Germans. Enemy machine-gun fire pinned down the Black Watch so effectively at first, that the troops were unable to reach their start line. The supporting tanks proved useless, wallowing in the heavily flooded countryside and in thick fog. Two companies managed to thrust forward but were quickly driven back with heavy losses. Major William Ewing deplored the lack of cover as he led his men across an open beet field 1,200 yards long. In all, "Black Friday" cost the Black Watch 183 casualties, 56 of them fatal — nearly half its regimental strength — thanks to poor intelligence, planning, and lack of reconnaissance. And not an inch had been gained.

The Royal Hamilton Light Infantry's turn came next. With orders to silence the guns of Woensdrecht, Lieutenant Colonel Denis Whitaker, the regimental commander, was given 48 hours to produce a plan. He sent out reconnaissance parties to gather much needed intelligence. Whitaker planned on a night attack to achieve as much surprise as possible. Strong artillery support was mandatory. Whitaker organized a battery of 165 guns to pave the way. The start line was between Hoogerheide and Woensdrecht and the schedule called for the attack to begin at three o'clock in the morning of Monday, October 16.

Outnumbered by five to one, the RHLIs ran up against Van der Heydte's hard fighting paratroopers. After the first 18 hours, 91 casualties had been evacuated. Over the first two days in the battle for Woensdrecht, the battalion hung on tenuously to the small gains they managed to achieve. Finally on October 21, the regiment was relieved by the Queen's Own Cameron Highlanders of the 6th Brigade who, along with the South Saskatchewan Regiment and Les Fusiliers de Mont Royal, cleared the town. Now their job was to mop up the area north of the newly won position. While this took place, the Calgary Highlanders of the 5th Brigade cut the road and rail links between Bergen op Zoom and Walcheren Island. The neck of the South Beveland Isthmus was finally sealed shut. The next step for the 2nd Canadian Infantry Division was to advance to the Walcheren causeway and lay siege for the final capture of the island itself. In the pocket on the south shore of the Scheldt to the west, the Stormont, Dundas and Glengarry Highlanders, led by their commanding officer, Lieutenant Colonel Roger Rowley, after a bitter fight succeeded in capturing the port of Breskens by October 22.

Two days later, after being subjected to tremendous artillery and aerial bombardment, Fort Frederik Hendrik, one of Hitler's fortresses, surrendered to Lieutenant Colonel Don Forbes' North Nova Scotia Highlanders. There were only 50 survivors.

By this time the Germans were being simultaneously attacked from several different directions. North of the Leopold Canal, the Regina Rifles, the Royal Winnipeg Rifles, and the Canadian Scottish of the 7th Brigade were struggling to enlarge their bridgehead. The 8th Brigade composed of the Chaudieres, the North Shores, and the Queen's Own Rifles made an amphibious landing on the west shore of the Braakman Plaat and advanced south and west. On October 26 they had reached Oostburg, directly to the south of Fort Frederik Hendrik. Six days earlier the 7th Brigade began a drive west toward Cadzand from the Leopold Canal bridgehead to free the Breskens Pocket west of the fortress. By November 2, the 7th Brigade had reached all its objectives.

Meanwhile, moving along the coast, on October 31, the SDGs and the HLIs had established a bridgehead at Retranchement near the Dutch-Belgian border. Passing through them, the North Shores advanced toward Knocke, the last German outpost. There, on November 2, at two o'clock in the afternoon, Don Forbes accepted the surrender of the coastal resort from General Knut Eberding, the commander of the 64th German Infantry. In the process 200 members of Le Regiment de la Chaudiere, who had been held prisoner in a garage cellar, were freed from captivity.

The Battle of the Breskens Pocket was finished. The south shore of the Scheldt was now in Canadian hands. It had taken the 3rd Infantry Division a month, during which it had captured 12,000 Germans, to clear it. Their own casualties were 314 dead, 2,077 wounded and 321, missing in action. German casualty figures, typically, have never been released.

By comparison, it took less than a week for the 2nd Canadian Infantry Division to clear the South Beveland Peninsula in its drive towards Walcheren Island. Beginning at dawn on October 24, the Royal Regiment of the 4th Brigade, started slogging its way west through the mud and water of the polders and icy cold salt marshes, the first objective the Beveland Canal running north and south at the east end of the peninsula.

The Royal Hamilton Light Infantry came next — the peninsula was wide enough to permit a two battalion front advance. By October 26, the RHLIs had reached the canal to find that the Germans had blown all the bridges. Now the 6th Brigade took over from the soggy, begrimed 7th with the objective of crossing the wide waterway that night. Though they encountered some enemy fire which was quickly subdued by their artillery, the Queen's Own Camerons, Les Fusiliers, and the South Sasks made it to the other side quite comfortably.

During the previous afternoon two regiments, the 6th Cameronians and the Royal Scots Fusiliers of the British 52nd (Lowland) Division, had crossed the Scheldt from Terneuzen by Buffaloes to make an amphibious landing on the south shore of the peninsula. They had been assigned to link up with the 2nd Canadian Division and create a pincer movement that would strangle any German attempt to escape to Walcheren. The Scottish in the south and the Canadians in central South Beveland, wasted no time advancing westward. The Cameronians quickly captured Elewououtdsdijk, the Canadians, Goes, Nisse, Nieuwdorp, and Heinkenszand. These fell easily but the Germans were prepared to put up a stiff fight to defend their last stronghold on South Beveland, the east end of the Walcheren Causeway over the Sloe Channel separating South Beveland from the island. Well fortified with machine-guns and anti-tank artillery embedded in concrete emplacements, the Germans began digging in. However, on October 30, the Royal Regiment reached the redoubt where Captain Jack Stothers, leading his company in an assault along the muddy shoreline outside the dyke, got in behind the German positions, including the gun emplacements and, with surprisingly little opposition, took 200 prisoners.

The curtain now went up on the final act of the Scheldt battle. At the beginning of October, after dropping leaflets to warn the Dutch civilians to evacuate the residential areas, the Royal Air Force plastered the dykes with high explosive bombs flooding the island and making amphibious landings possible. Guy Simonds had planned a triple-pronged, almost simultaneous, series of attacks on Walcheren. Two British commando and infantry landings would take place, one at dawn on November 1 at the city of Flushing at the mouth of the Scheldt, the second, four hours later, at Westkapelle, the German strong point on the west coast of the island. The third was to be launched by the 5th Canadian Infantry Brigade across the Sloe Canal, and once a bridgehead had been established, the 52nd British (Lowlands) Division would pass through and strike inland.

That was soon shelved and an alternate plan chosen. On close examination it was discovered that there was water in the Sloe Channel only twice a day at high tide and only for short periods; the rest of the time, it was a bed of mud. That ruled out an amphibious operation. There was only one way to get across to the other side and that was over the dreaded, unprotected, Walcheren Causeway. The only land access to the island, it supported a road, a railway line, and a bicycle path — all of them wide open. On the island side, the Germans had built concrete emplacements with 88-mm, 20-mm, and machine-guns, and a dug in tank with its gun pointed to fire straight down the road. The Germans were preparing a warm reception for the attackers. The railway had been torn up. The road, path, and embankment had been laced with mines. Deep craters had been dug, one of them halfway across the causeway filled with water, blocking the road. Sheer suicide.

But on October 31, the battered Black Watch, its four companies down to 50 or 60 men, launched a daylight assault in pelting rain. Enemy artillery, mortars, and snipers positioned in the marshes on either side of the causeway, opened fire on the Canadians who had to wade through the crater midway across, in water up to their armpits. The tanks had come to a stop. By nightfall the battalion was withdrawn.

Then the Calgary Highlanders were ordered to mount an attack just before midnight and, once across, to fan out to the right, while Le Regiment de Maisonneuve swept to the left. These attacks had been planned with the idea that the brigade's role in this operation was only temporary, simply a means of establishing a jumping-off point for the British to take over for their drive inland.

In the fighting that ensued, Major Ross Ellis, who had taken over command of the Calgary Highlanders, later reported candidly: ''They kicked the hell out of us.'' By 9:33 a.m. the next morning, November 1, however, they had established a small bridgehead at the midway point where the crater blocked the causeway; they hung on grimly. The following morning at four o'clock, the Maisonneuves were sent in. At this point, an aura of ironic optimism seemed to have spread through brigade headquarters. The Maisonneuves would establish a bridgehead on Walcharen Island itself where, an hour later, they would be relieved by the 1st Battalion of the Glasgow Highlanders of the British 52nd Division. The battalion went across under cover of a creeping barrage. But when this lifted at 26 minutes after four, the French Canadian regiment was met with heavy shelling. In 20 minutes, one company lost five of its eight officers. However, it managed to reach the halfway point across the bridge where it relieved the Calgary Highlanders. Then, once through the crater, they found another one directly ahead of it. By dawn, one company of Maisonneuves had established themselves at the Walcheren end of the causeway although they were down to less than 40 men.

Later in the morning, the Glasgow Highlanders moved in to consolidate the position. By this time the assaults at Flushing and Westkapelle had landed British commandos and infantry. The Germans were now besieged on three sides. What remained was a foot-by-foot mopping up operation and it was a week before Middleburg, the capital of the island, fell and all further enemy resistance ceased. It took another three weeks to clear the Scheldt of mines and it was not until November 28 that the first convoy sailed into Antwerp led, appropriately, by a Canadian merchantman.

Freeing the port of Antwerp marked a turning point in ending the Second World War in Europe, which still had a little over five months to run. With the supply lines firmly established, the Allies could now advance to the Rhine, ford it, and drive into Germany. During that period, the First Canadian Army flushed out the Rhineland and liberated the Netherlands. All these successes were direct manifestations of the Canadian sacrifice in clearing the Scheldt.

During that period between October 1 and November 8, 41,043 Germans had been taken prisoner, but the Battle of the Scheldt had also cost the Canadian Army 12,873 casualties, half of them Canadians. Many of those might have been spared had it not been for the shameful conduct of Mackenzie King and his government over the conscription issue. During the Zombie Crisis, serving soldiers threw their rifles overboard in protest against being shipped overseas. While men were dying and being wounded, the prime minister was playing politics to cover his own backside. The heroism of the Scheldt will never be forgotten but neither will the stain left in its wake by the politicians.

✦ 17 ✦

OMEGA

Reference map "Korea."

Finale! Kap'yong represents the last significant battle in Canadian military history. It also marked the first major action for Canadian troops during the Korean War. The 2nd Battalion of the Princess Patricia's Canadian Light Infantry — in effect an advance guard of the 25th Canadian Infantry Brigade — was awarded the United States Presidential Distinguished Unit Citation for gallantry and heroism under fire.

By late December 1950, when the PPCLIs arrived in the Land of the Morning Calm, as its people call that Asian peninsula, the war had see-sawed back and forth dramatically ever since the North Koreans invaded the south by crossing the 38th Parallel on the morning of June 24, 1950. That triggered the first policing action by the United Nations but, almost immediately, the South Korean forces, bolstered by United States troops, became encircled in a perimeter around the port of Pusan. However on September 15, the Americans landed at Inchon, the inland port to Seoul, the South Korean capital, and began a drive north to the Chinese border. By October, the end of the war seemed imminent. However, at the end of the month, six Chinese armies, with approximately 180,000 troops, crossed the Yalu River and began pushing the United Nations' forces back across the 38th Parallel; they recaptured Seoul, and reached a line 40 miles south of the city. Then, at the beginning of 1951, the UN forces mounted a new drive north. That February the PPCLIs, under the command of

Lieutenant Colonel James Stone, joined the 27th Commonwealth Infantry Brigade which consisted of two British and one Australian battalions, supported by the artillery from a New Zealand field regiment.

Alongside the British Argylls Regiment, the Canadians began an advance north-west up a valley north of Sangsok toward the ultimate objective, the high ground north-west of Hoengsong. As the push progressed it became increasingly apparent that the Chinese were withdrawing all across the front. On March 15, Seoul was liberated by the 1st Republic of Korea (ROK) Division. The 24th US Infantry Division was driving toward the 38th Parallel west of the Kap'yong River, while the Commonwealth Brigade proceeded up the Chojong valley until it reached a designated hill, numbered 1036. Then the brigade was moved east to the valley of the Kap'yong River where, on April 8, it successfully attacked objectives north of the parallel.

This latest turn of events raised the question of what new direction the war should now take. General Douglas MacArthur, commander of the UN forces, argued for a complete military victory which would require additional troops and would also extend the conflict beyond the Manchurian border, thereby risking an all-out war with China.

Fortunately, cooler heads prevailed. The alternative favoured by the UN and the US was a stabilization of the military situation and a negotiated peace. On April 11, when MacArthur publicly criticized this viewpoint, US President Harry Truman fired him and replaced him with General Matthew Ridgeway.

The withdrawal of the Chinese to the high ground north of the Imjin River delta was deceptive and directly linked to the new political scenario. A North Korean directive revealed the communists' true intentions:

> The enemy is concentrating his entire resources in this offensive. We are presently withdrawing on all fronts. This is part of our strategy to lure US troops into our position. We will hit them, inflict maximum casualties, and withdraw. This is our strategy.

In other words, keep the maximum pressure on the enemy in the field to strengthen your hand at the bargaining table. For their offensive, the communists had replaced their weary troops with fresh battalions, a force of some 700,000 men against the UN's 418,000, 152,000 of which were South Koreans. On April 22, just before midnight, the attack by the Chinese and North Koreans began. The heaviest weight fell on the west and west-central sectors against the 1st US and 9th US Corps, both of which were ordered to withdraw. In the 9th US Corps sector, the hardest hit were two battalions of the 6th ROK Division which were in grave danger of being cut off and completely destroyed.

Luckily, the Commonwealth Brigade was able to provide the perfect escape route along which the ROKs could retreat. It lay in the valley of the Kap'yong River near the junction with the Pukhan River where the valley was 3,000 yards wide. To the north it narrowed and curved and was dominated by the surrounding hills. From these promontories the exits and entrances fell under the control of the 3rd Australian Regiment on Hill 504 on the right, the PPCLIs on Hill 677 to the left, and the 1st Middlesex Regiment south of the Patricias.

As the ROKs fled south in disorder, the Australians now came under attack. Throughout April 23, and during that night and all next day, they successfully beat off attack after attack. But, by 9:00 p.m. on April 24, the Chinese had penetrated as far as battalion headquarters. It now became obvious that the Australians could not hold out for another night and the order was given to withdraw.

This now left the PPCLIs, who covered the face of Hill 677, A Company on the Right, C Company in the centre and D Company on the left flank, exposed to enemy assault which began almost immediately. At 10:00 p.m. mortar bombs began falling on the Patricias' positions, then the most forward platoon of B Company, occupying a small salient, came under direct attack. However, the troops managed to extricate themselves, falling back to the main company position immediately east of tactical headquarters. From there it was possible to observe the Chinese build-up across the Kap'yong valley to the north and east of Naechon. During the fighting Private Wayne Mitchell, armed with a Bren gun, was largely responsible for repelling the enemy attacks on the platoon. Though wounded in the chest, he continued fighting after having his injury dressed, moving from fire trench to fire trench as the Chinese pressed foward toward the company headquarters. He was wounded again but kept on fighting until by morning he could hardly stay on his feet due to loss of blood. Mitchell was subsequently evacuated by helicopter.

While the attack on B Company took place, some 100 Chinese attempted to infiltrate tactical headquarters. However, in the gully to the rear of the position, the battalion's 81-mm mortars, along with 50-calibre machine-guns, opened up from a range of 200 yards, and sent the enemy scurrying back down the ravine, leaving behind 71 of their dead.

By two o'clock in the morning of April 25, every weapon in the battalion was firing on the Chinese. It now became obvious that the attack on B Company was simply a diversion. The real target was D Company with its exposed flank to the north and west which was now assailed on all sides. One platoon was overrun and another cut off. Captain John Mills, the company commander, who seemed to be everywhere, encouraging and rallying his men, called for supporting fire.

After two hours the enemy advance had been stopped but sporadic enemy attacks persisted and by dawn the battalion found itself surrounded and its supply route severed. With the ammunition reserves and emergency rations depleted, Jim Stone, the battalion commander, coolly requested an airdrop. This message had to go the rounds, all the way from Command HQ to Japan, but at 10:30 a.m. four C119 transports dropped fresh ammunition and supplies. Only four parachutes landed outside the drop zone. By two o'clock that afternoon, the supply route had been cleared and additional supplies began arriving by truck. Next day the PPCLI and the rest of the 27th Commonwealth Infantry Brigade was relieved by the 1st US Cavalry Division.

The Battle of Kap'yong had been a fine example of dogged determination and bravery on the part of the Patricias and also one of outstanding leadership on the part of the battalion commander. Against overwhelming odds, the Canadians had inflicted heavy casualties on the enemy with light losses of their own: only ten killed and 23 wounded.

It had also shown how vulnerable the Chinese were against resolute resistance and properly deployed defences. The enemy telegraphed every single one of their attacks with machine-gun tracers to provide direction, and blowing bugles as signals to form up. This gave the Canadian company and platoon commanders plenty of warning and adequate time in which to bring down accurate artillery, mortar, and machine-gun fire. Before attacking, the Chinese did not properly reconnoitre the PPCLI's positions. Nor was the mortar and machine-gun fire accurately directed. On the other hand, the Patricias showed great resourcefulness in taking advantage of their loftier positions against the attackers by rolling hand grenades down the hills. Also the use of rockets in an anti-personnel role proved devastating. What it came down to is that the communists' army, like their regime, lacked initiative. If they had persisted in the intensity and frequency of their attacks, there is a little doubt that the PPCLI would have been overrun. As it turned out, by May 1 the Chinese offensive had been brought to a standstill.

The PPCLI stand led the way for the Canadian participation in Korea. Over the next two years and two months, 26,791 Canadians served, 516 of whom gave their lives. The country's contribution, along with the other 15 UN members who joined forces to resist communist aggression, was exceeded only by that of the United States and Great Britain.

The 25th Canadian Infantry Brigade, consisted of: The Royal Canadian Regiment, the Royal 22nd Regiment, C Squadron of the Lord Strathcona's Horse, the 2nd Field Regiment, the Royal Canadian Horse Artillery, the 57th Canadian Independent Field Squadron, the Royal Canadian Engineers, the 25th Canadian Transport Company, the Royal Canadian Army Service Corps, and the No 25 Field Ambulance, and Royal Canadian Army Medical Corps. Under the command of Major General John "Rocky" Rockingham, it arrived in Korea in late May 1951, and was attached to the 28th Commonwealth Brigade which in turn came under the command of the 25th US Infantry Division. Soon after the Canadian brigade's arrival, it was rejoined by the PPCLI whom it had preceded.

In July the brigade was transferred to the newly formed 1st Commonwealth Division which came under the operational control of the 1st US Corps and held a sector of the Kansas Line extending 10,000 metres westward from the Imjim-Hantan junction. Canadians remained in the thick of the fighting in both the defensive and offensive actions that took place while peace talks teetered back and forth over the next two years. The Korean Peace Agreement was finally signed at Panmunjom on July 27, 1953.

The Korean War marked a turning point in Canadian military foreign policy and thinking. By participating in the UN action it had established a precedent. In subsequent international crises there was no longer a question of standing on the sidelines, while politicians wrangled over the issue. In 1950, isolationist policy had been abandoned. As a member of the UN, Canada was committed.

The last two years of the war had been fought by professional Canadian soldiers, unlike previous conflicts — the Boer War, World Wars I & II — in which the armies (and air force and navy) had been made up of "citizen soldiers." By 1955, for the first time in her history, Canada had a professional expeditionary force. The Canadian soldier, seaman, or airman, had become a thorough professional.

When the Korean War ended, 7,000 of these professional soldiers were left behind to keep the peace during the uneasy two-year truce that followed. This was the start of a military involvement in world affairs that has seen Canadian troops deployed around the world in truce teams, peace commissions, and emergency forces. This new chapter in Canadian military history is, in a sense, a direct outgrowth of Kap'yong. That great Canadian battle and all others going back to the Plains of Abraham forged a nation without peer in heroism and sacrifice.

BIBLIOGRAPHY

Balmuir, Victor Suthren. **Defend and Hold: The Battle of the Chateauguay**. Ottawa, 1986.

Bercuson, David Jay. **Maple Leaf Against the Axis: Canada's Second World War**. Toronto: Stoddart Publishing Co. Ltd., 1995.

Berton, Pierre, and Scott R. Cameron. **The Capture of Detroit**. Toronto: McClelland and Stewart, 1991.

Berton, Pierre, and Scott R. Cameron. **The Death of Isaac Brock**. Toronto: McClelland and Stewart, 1991.

Berton, Pierre. **Historic Headlines: A Century of Canadian News Dramas**. Toronto: McClelland and Stewart, 1967.

Berton, Pierre. **Vimy**. Toronto: McClelland and Stewart, 1986.

Bishop, Arthur. **Courage At Sea**. Toronto: McGraw-Hill Ryerson Ltd., 1995.

Bishop, Arthur. **Courage on the Battlefield**. Toronto: McGraw-Hill Ryerson Ltd., 1993.

Bishop, Arthur. **Our Bravest and Our Best: The Stories of Canada's Victoria Cross Winners**. Toronto: McGraw-Hill Ryerson Ltd., 1995.

Boissonnault, Real. **Jacques Cartier: Explorer and Navigator**. Ottawa: Environment Canada Parks, 1987.

Canadians at War 1939/45, The. Commemorative Edition. Montreal: The Reader's Digest Association (Canada), 1995.

Copp, Terry. **A Canadian's Guide to the Battlefields of Normandy**. Waterloo: The Canadian Battle of Normandy Foundation, Wilfrid Laurier University, 1994.

Copp, Terry. **No Price Too High: Canadians and the Second World War**. Toronto: McGraw-Hill Ryerson Ltd., 1995.

Dancocks, Daniel G. **The D-Day Dodgers: The Canadians in Italy, 1943-1945**. Toronto: McClelland and Stewart, 1991.

Dancocks, Daniel G. **Legacy of Valour: The Canadians at Passchendaele**. Edmonton: Hurtig Publishers, 1986.

Dancocks, Daniel G. **Spearhead to Victory: Canada and the Great War**. Edmonton: Hurtig Publishers, 1987.

Dancocks, Daniel G. **Welcome to Flanders Fields: The First Great Canadian Battle of the Great War, Ypres, 1915**. Toronto: McClelland and Stewart, 1988.

Durnford, Hugh, and Peter Madely. **Great Canadian Adventures**. Montreal: The Reader's Digest Association (Canada) Ltd., 1976.

Encyclopedia Canadiana. Toronto: Grolier of Canada, 1968.

Fryer, Mary Beacock. **Battlefields of Canada**. Toronto: Dundurn Press, 1986.

Garfield, Brian. **The Paladin: A Novel Based on Fact**. New York: Simon and Schuster, 1979.

Judd, Denis. **The Boer War**. London: Hart-Davis, MacGibbon, 1977.

Kitching, George. **Mud and Green Fields: the Memoirs of Major-General George Kitching**. St Catherines: Vanwell Publishing Ltd., 1993.

Macksey, Kenneth. **The Shadow of Vimy Ridge**. Toronto: Ryerson Press, 1965.

Maguire, Eric, and Jonathen Cape. **Dieppe, August 19**. London, 1963.

Marrin, Albert. 1812, **The War Nobody Won**. Toronto: McClelland and Stewart, 1985.

McWilliams, James L., and R.J. Steel. **Gas! The Battle for Ypres, 1915**. St Catharines: Vanwell Publishing Limited, 1985.

Miller, Carmen. **Painting the Map Red**. Montreal: Queen's McGill Press, 1992.

Nasmith, Col. George G. **Canada's Sons and Great Britain in the World War**. Toronto: Thomas Allen, 1919.

Pakenham, Thomas. **The Boer War**. London: Weiderfeld and Nicolson, 1979.

Paterson, Thomas William. **Canadian Battles & Massacres: 300 Years of Warfare and Atrocities on Canadian Soil**. Langley: Stagecoach, 1977.

Rohmer, Richard. **Patton's Gap: An Account of the Battle of Normandy, 1944**. Toronto: General Publishing Co., 1981.

Stacey, Charles Peter. **Quebec 1759: the Siege and the Battle**. Toronto: Macmillan of Canada, 1959, 1984.

Summers, Jack, et al., **Military Uniforms in Canada, 1665-1970**. Ottawa: National Museum of Man, 1981.

Swettenham, John. **D-Day**. Ottawa: The National Museums of Canada, 1970.

Swettenham, John. **To Sieze the Victory: The Canadian Corps in World War I**. Toronto: Ryerson Press, 1965.

Tute, Warrent, et al. **D-Day**. London: Sidgwick, 1974.

Vincent, Carl. **No Reason Why**. Stittsville: Canada's Wings, 1981.

Vokes, Chris with John Philip Maclean. **Vokes: My Story**. Ottawa: Gallery Books, 1985.

Warren, Philip. **Passchendaele: The Story Behind the Tragic Victory of 1917**. London: Sidgwick & Jackson, 1987.

Whitaker, Shelagh, and W. Denis. **Dieppe: Tragedy to Triumph**. Toronto: McGraw-Hill Ryerson, Ltd., 1992.

Whitaker, Shelagh, and W. Denis. **Tug of War: The Canadian Victory That Opened Antwerp**. Toronto: Stoddart Publishing, 1984.

Wohler, J. Patrick. **Charles de Salaberry, Soldier of the Empire, Defender of Quebec**. Toronto: Dundurn Press, 1984.

Wood, Herbert Fairlie. **Strange Battlefield: the operations in Korea and their effects on the defence policy of Canada**. Ottawa: Queen's Printer, 1966.

Zaslow, Morris. **The Defended Border**. Toronto: Macmillan Company of Canada Ltd., 1964.

INDEX